RSVP

RSVP

MARIE FRANCE VAN DAMME

Photographs by Herbert Ypma

233 photographs, 124 in colour

Thames & Hudson

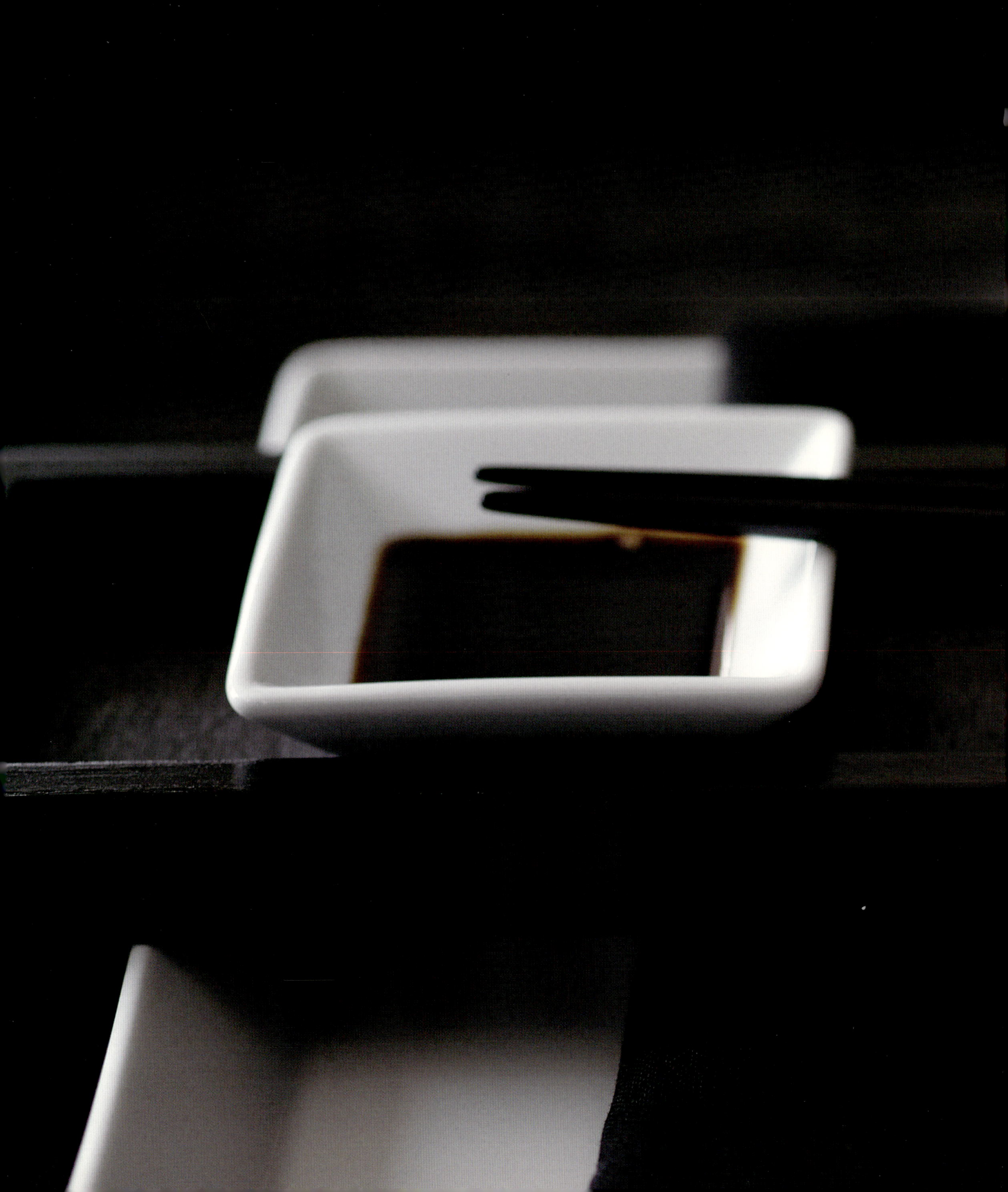

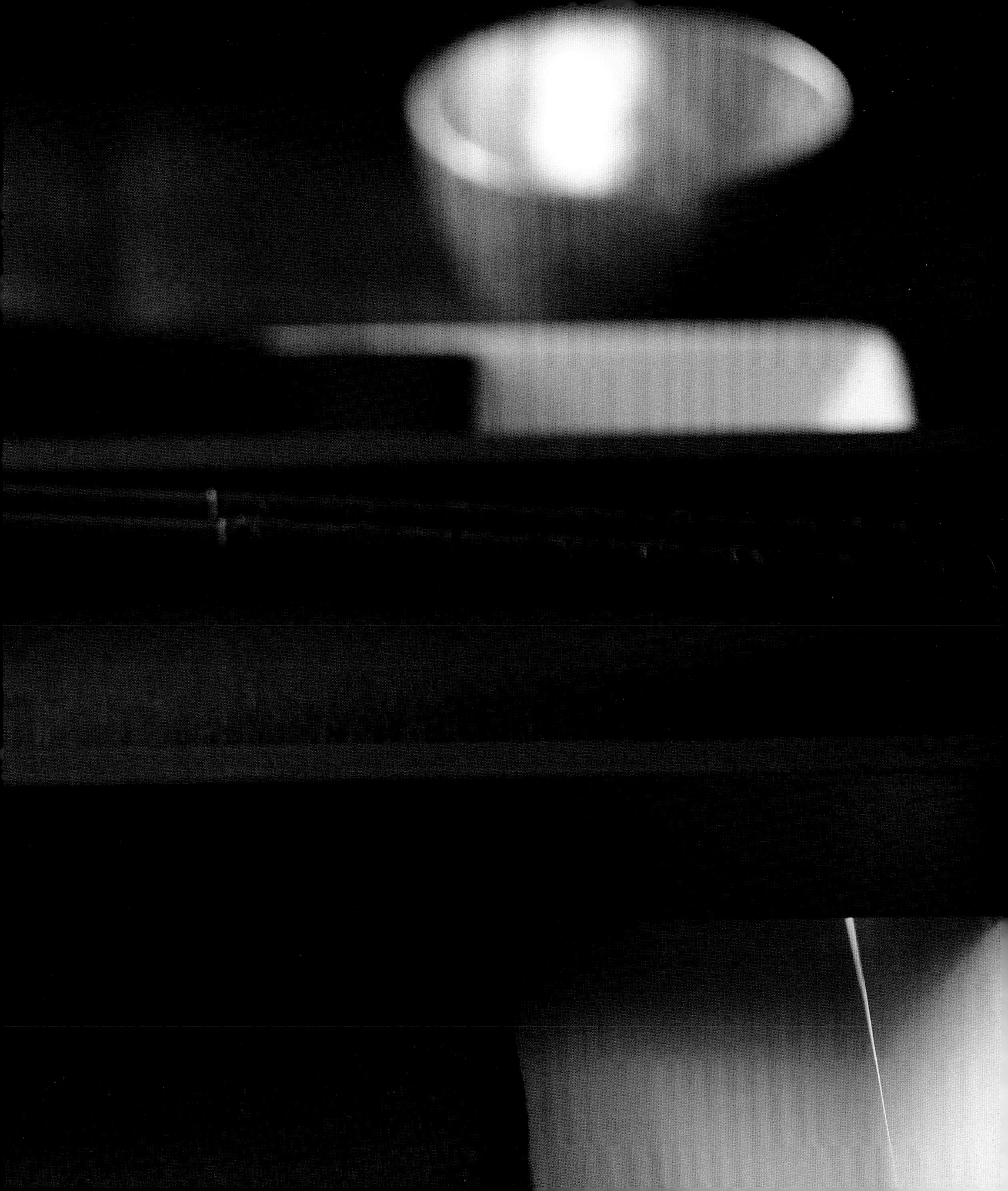

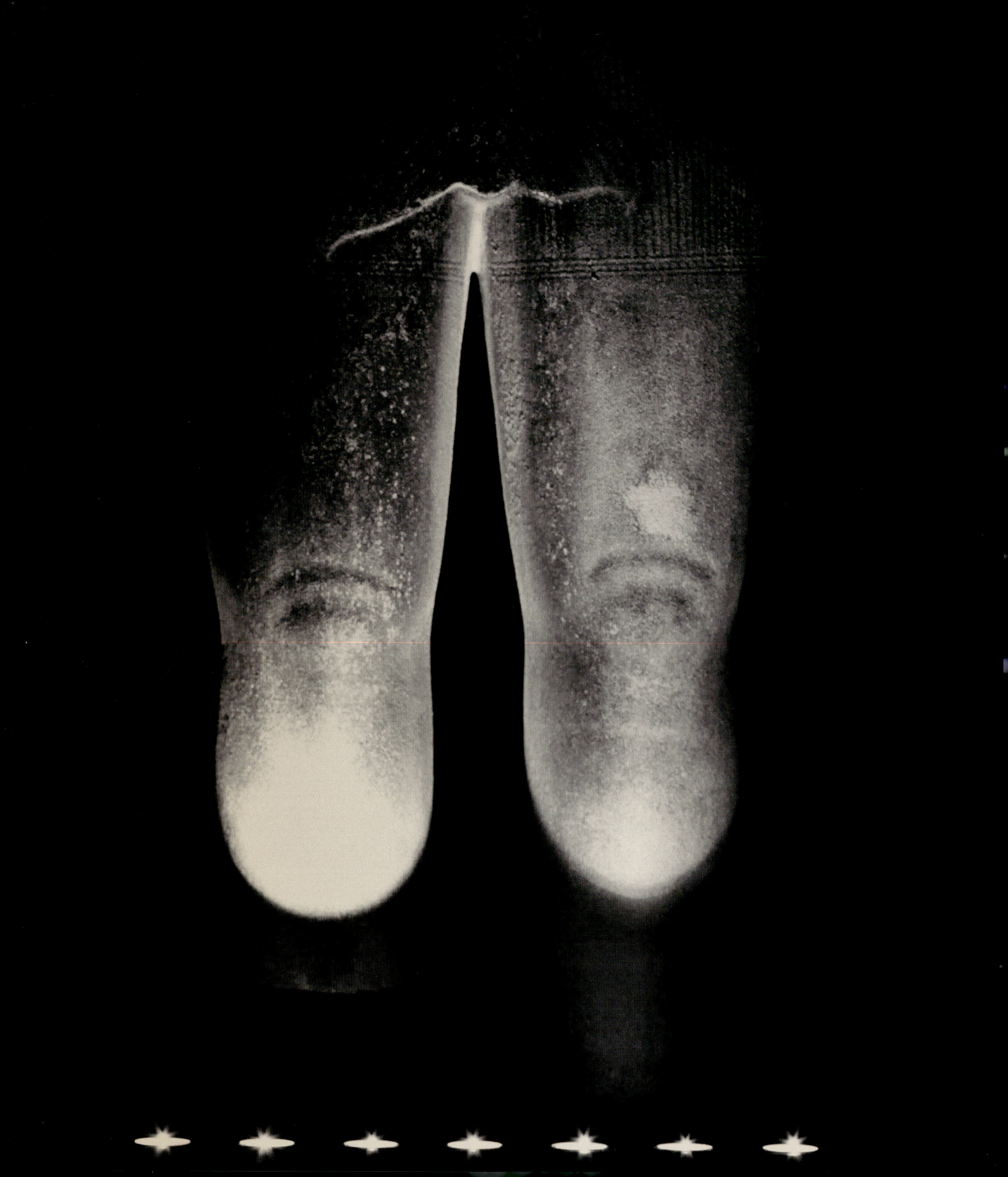

CONTENTS

FOREWORD
11

INTRODUCTION
15

1
FLOWERS
16

2
THE TABLE
54

3
FOOD
110

4
CANDLES
136

5
ART
166

6
ESSENTIALS
186

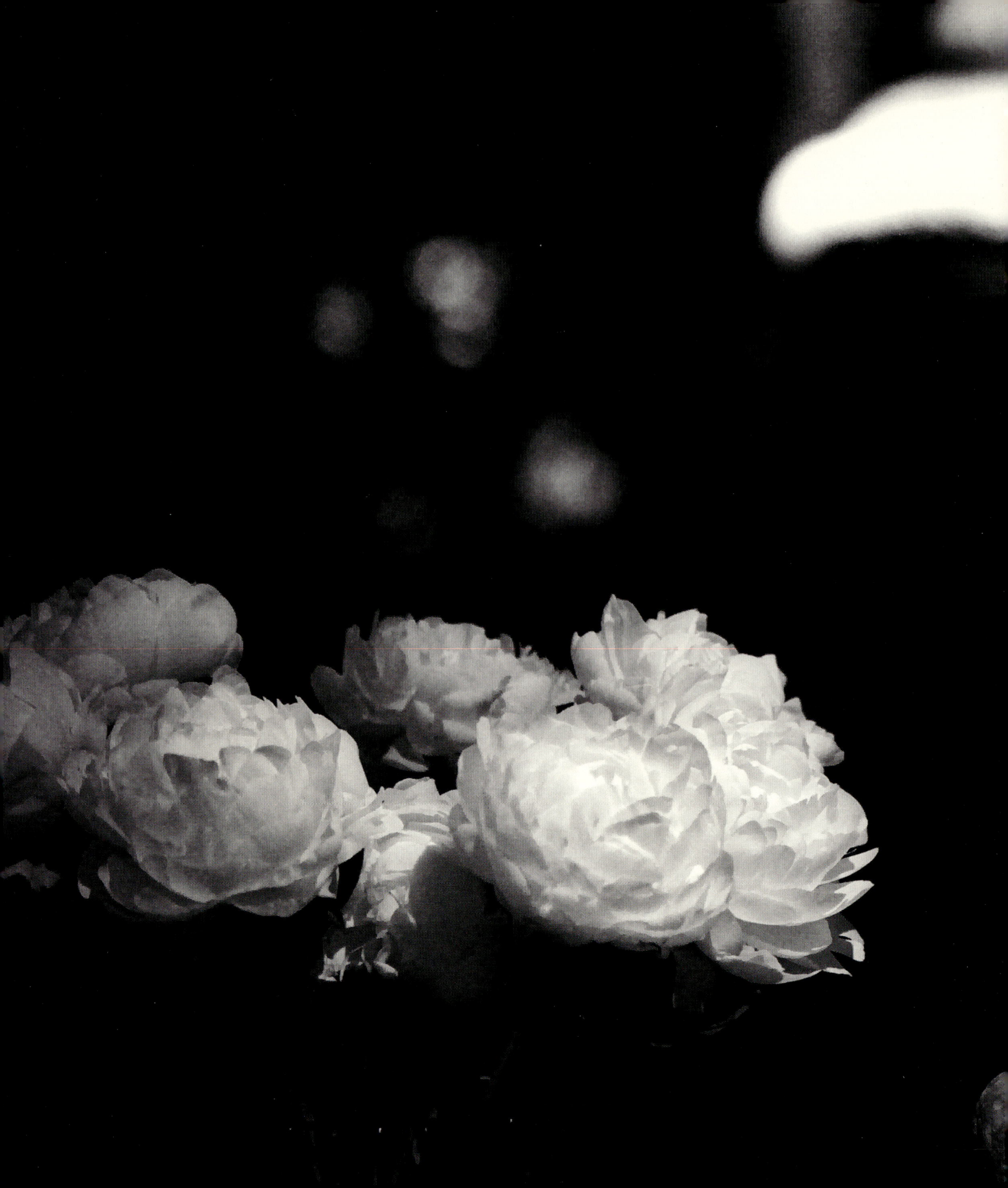

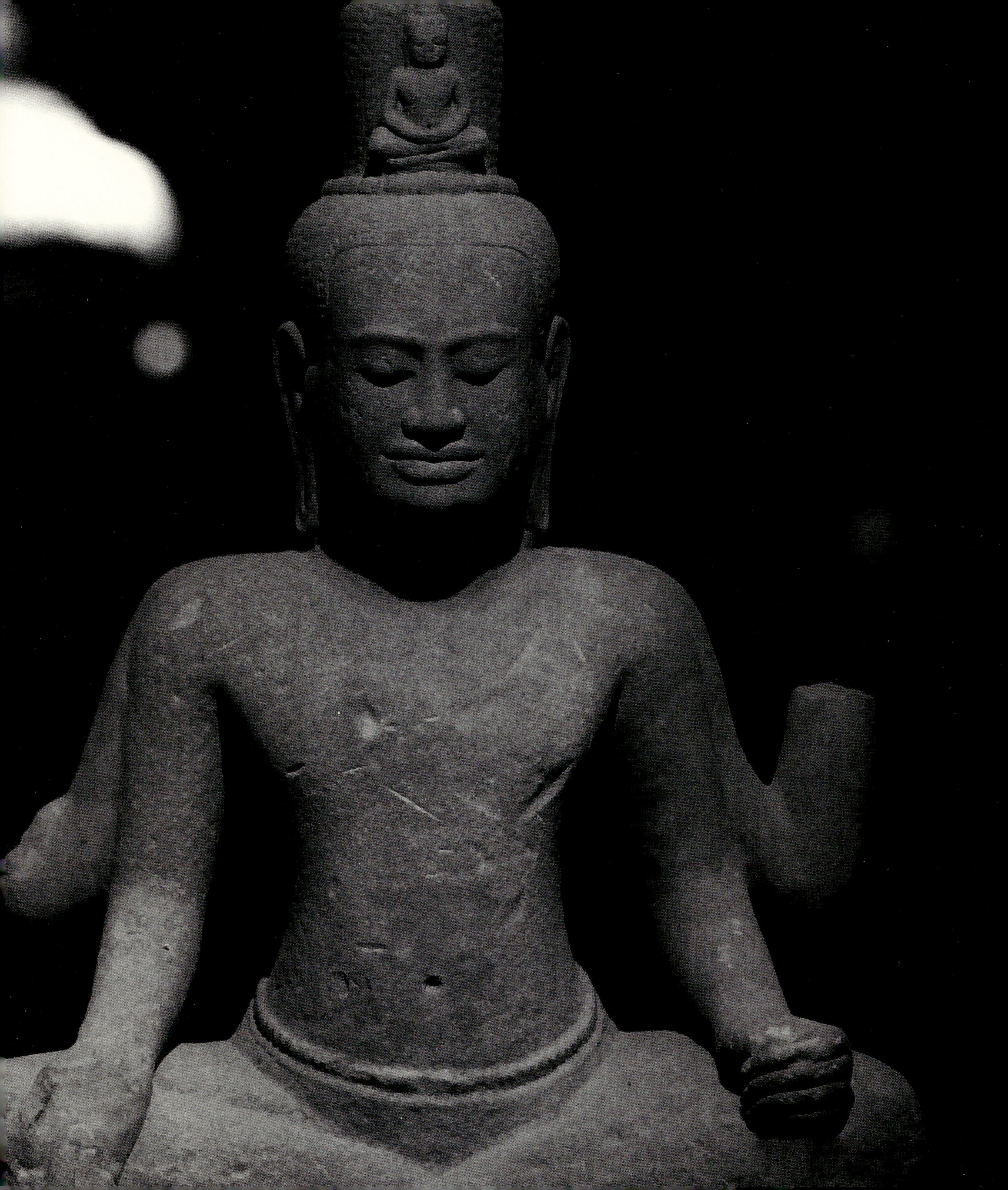

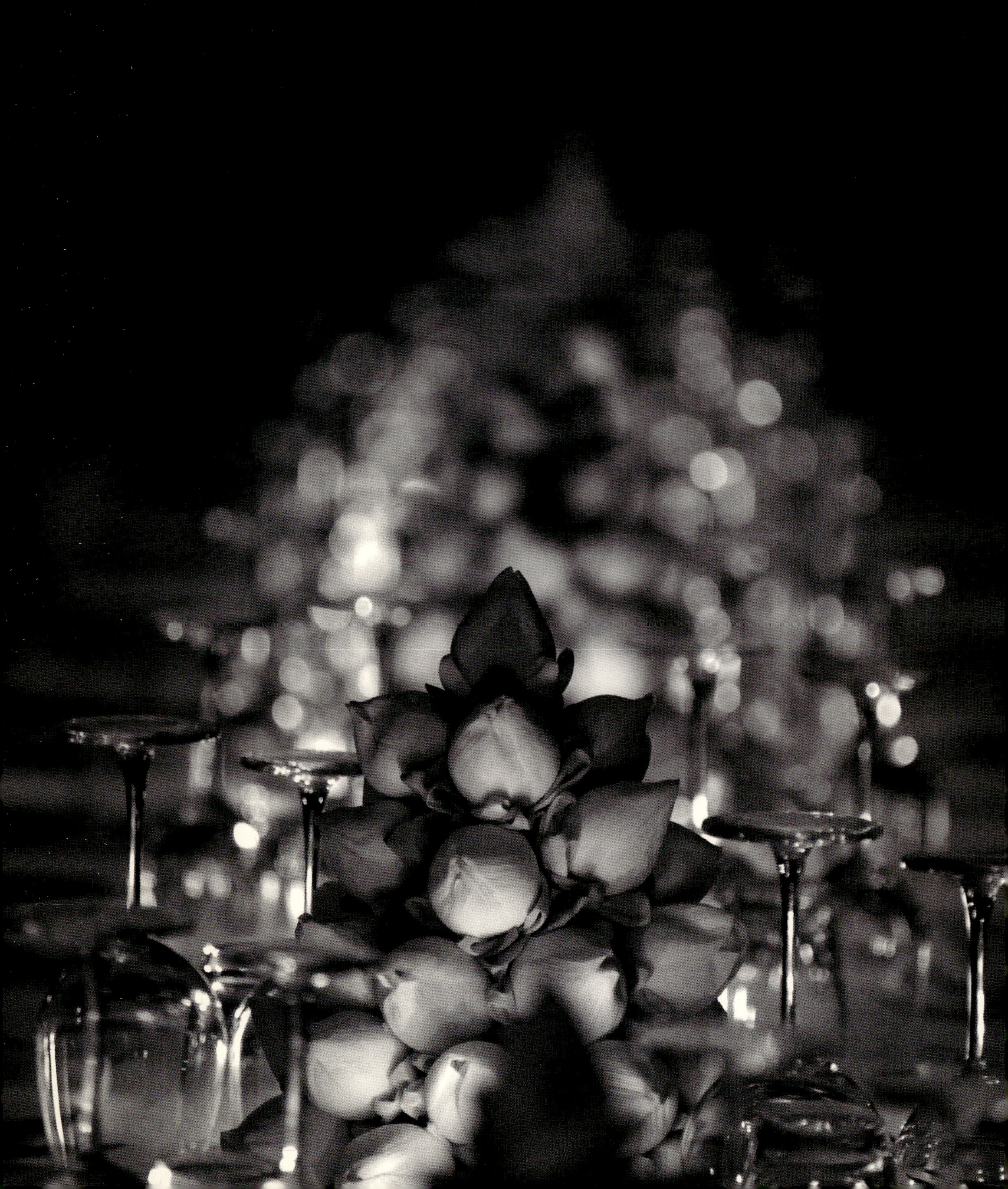

FOREWORD

The 'Zen attitude', 'understated elegance', 'Asian fusion', 'relaxed chic': these are all fashionable concepts that accord with the spirit of our times, yet they demand a subtle aesthetic and spiritual balance that is extremely difficult to achieve. The one home in which I always find them is that of fashion designer Marie France Van Damme in Hong Kong. To me, Marie France represents the perfect 21st-century hostess. Every detail of her dinner parties reflects her desire to create a casual and unpretentious atmosphere that is at the same time beautiful and voluptuous. So beautiful, in fact, that it could almost go unnoticed, and it is this apparent effortlessness that makes her style of hospitality so effective.

Perhaps the impetus for Marie France in developing this special talent was the memory of her childhood in Montreal, where time and time again she saw her mother organize dinner parties and then become too nervous to enjoy them because her preparations were so complicated. If the flowers were not delivered on time, or a guest arrived late, the party was deemed a disaster. The hostess would run incessantly from table to kitchen, so no one could enjoy her company. What had been intended as a pleasant and cosy evening would often turn into a nightmare for the whole family, and sometimes even for the guests.

In contrast, when Marie France and her husband Alex receive their family and friends, everything is arranged in a way that allows both of them to partake fully in the evening. They keep their preparations simple, making it impossible for anything major to go wrong at the last minute, yet the exquisite presentation of the table and dishes leaves an enduring impression on everyone.

Throughout the various chapters of this book, a number of useful principles are described, stunningly illustrated by the great photographer Herbert Ypma. The common thread can be summed up in one word: simplicity – the driving force in achieving this level of sophistication. Rather than large, busy table bouquets, for instance, a simple display of a single type of flower is enough – and far more elegant. Marie France is also a genius in using monochromatic colour schemes to ensure visual harmony. Her menus, which feature healthy, natural ingredients, are not overly ambitious and are therefore easily adapted to any number of guests. Although her dishes can come from IKEA or Stanley Market, careful presentation of the food transforms them into elegant tableware. She is an imaginative shopper who gathers unexpected objects from all over the world: large jade buttons become knife- or baguette-holders; a *huang wali* (Chinese paintbrush-holder) is turned into a vase. And inevitably, in the world of Marie France, there are candles everywhere, both indoors and out.

These ideas are applicable to any occasion, from a conventional sit-down dinner at home to a barbecue on a deserted beach. Even in an improvised last-minute meal, takeaway food can be nicely presented on attractive dishes, rather than simply left in its plastic containers. Indeed, the presentation of the food itself is another key element in achieving elegant simplicity. There is no need to go to great expense and serve foie gras or caviar to make a meal special and festive. Marie France prefers common – but always fresh – ingredients. A simple tomato will be sliced thinly and displayed in a bowl with a few sprigs of coriander, which are not chopped but left whole on the side. Strawberries are sliced into quarters and arranged in a pretty pattern in a frosted cup. Even cherries can be served whole and unstemmed, but here, again, they will piled in a modern, attractive dish, still wet and fresh, with a touch of mint.

Throughout these pages, the influence of Asia is evident. Like Marie France's approach to hospitality, Asian aesthetics emphasize paring down, returning to the basics and finding the right balance, while inserting beauty into every aspect of a meal or gathering. Yet these principles are universal and can be applied easily in any location, culture or society, from Hong Kong to London – even on a boat. In the end, it is all about having a pleasant and relaxing evening, not only as a guest, but also as a host or hostess. This is what will turn any reception into a memorable occasion.

François Curiel
President of Christie's, Asia

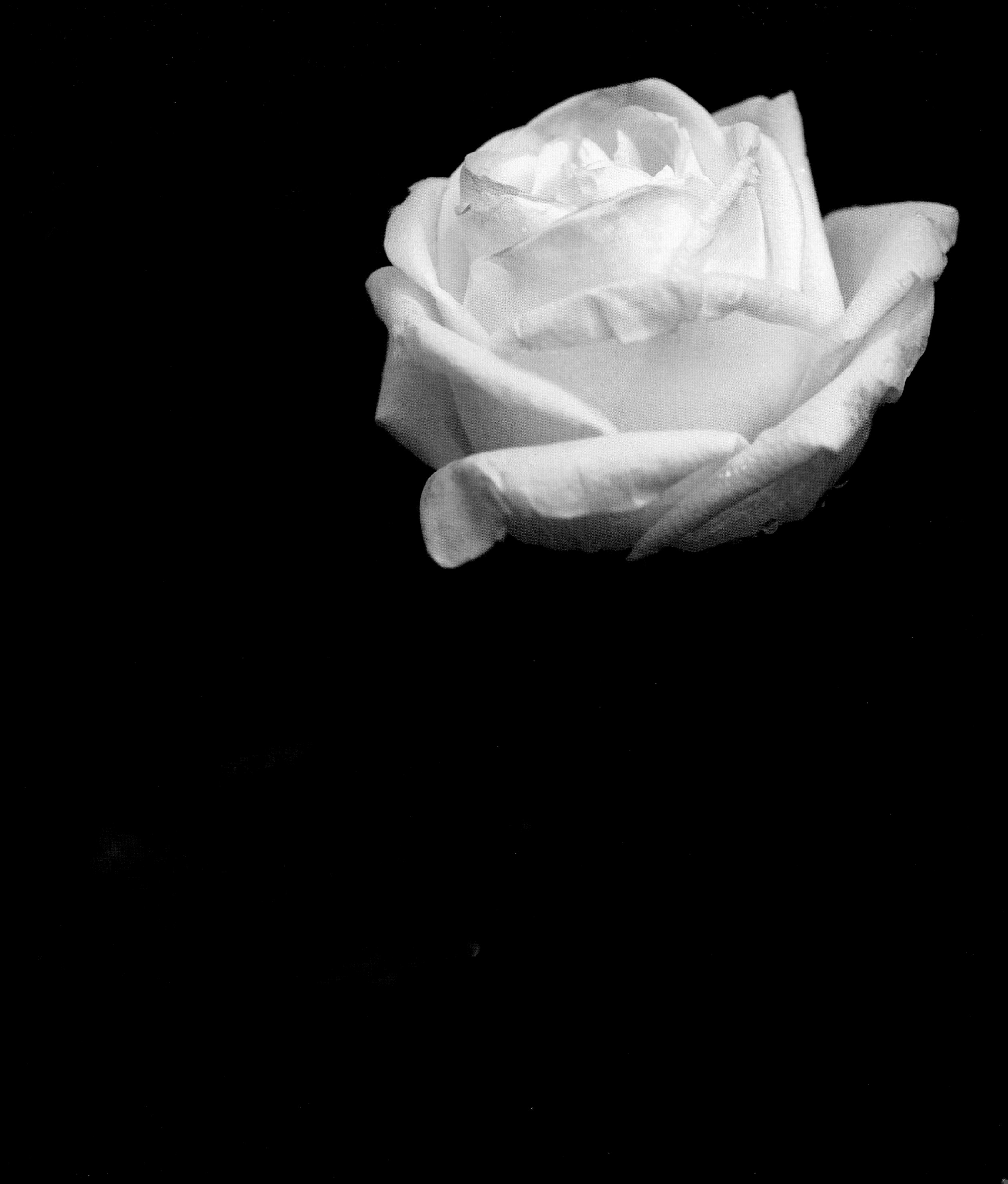

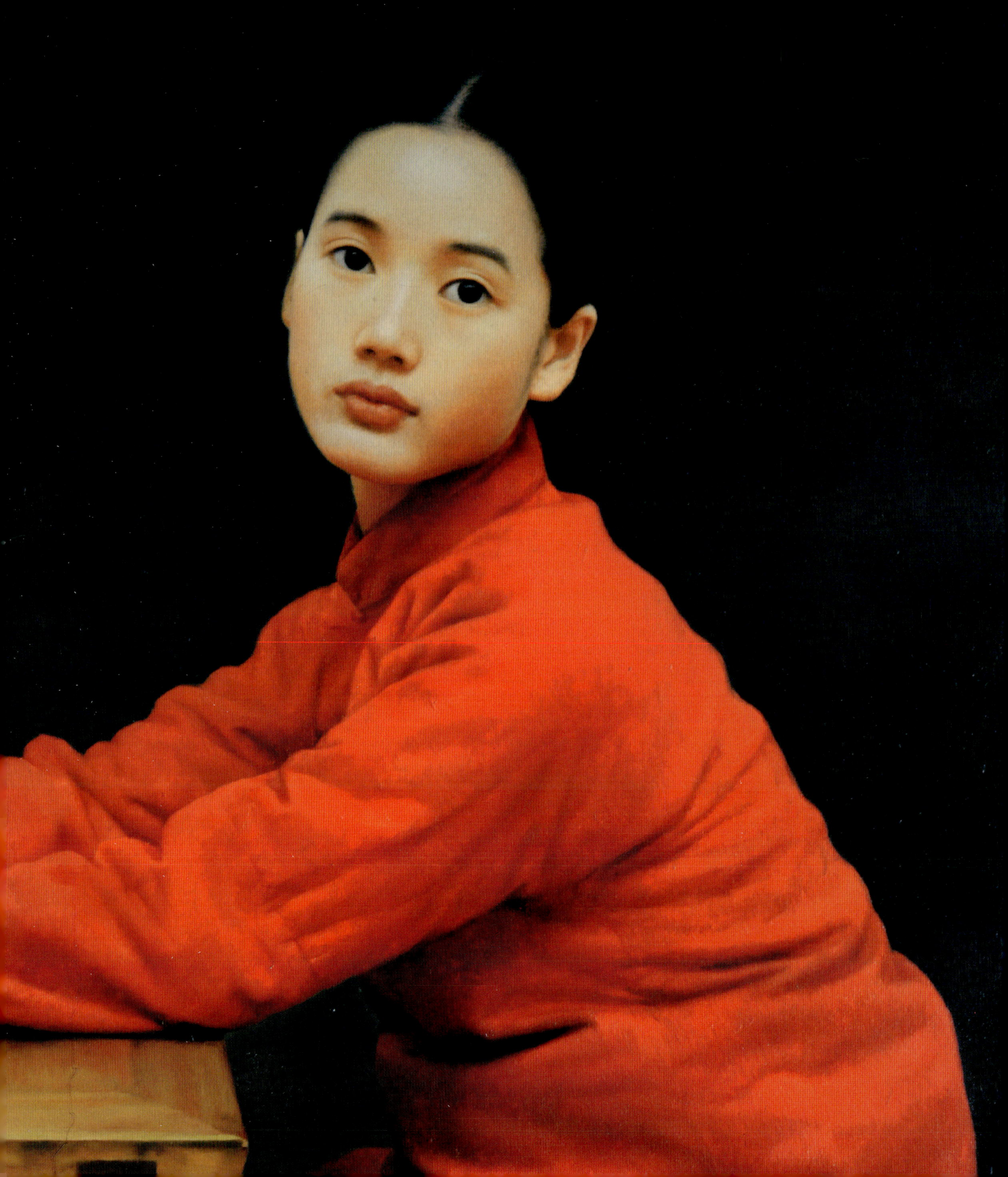

INTRODUCTION

Music, atmosphere, subtle lighting: these are the elements I respond to as a dinner guest.

A wonderful ambience does not have to be reserved for special occasions. I grew up in Montreal with downstairs neighbours who were, for me, the epitome of perfect hospitality. In the summer they would set a beautiful table on their tiny balcony, complete with candles and flowers, where they would have the most romantic dinners – just the two of them. That, to me, was successful entertaining.

Even on a larger scale, stylish entertaining is not difficult or expensive. There are only a few simple guidelines to follow and the object of this book is to spell them out in the most clear and vivid way. Over the past year, together with the photographer Herbert Ypma, we have chronicled a variety of occasions for entertaining, including my mother-in-law's eightieth birthday, my husband's birthday dinner, and other family celebrations – formal, informal and everything in-between.

Family is key, and memories make us who we are, so every opportunity to get together with family and friends should be made memorable, even the simplest occasions. Sunday-morning breakfast is an institution in my family and we always look forward to it and make it special. Part of the appeal of a celebrity chef like Jamie Oliver is that he takes you into his home and shows you how he cooks for his family. For many of us, this is when we are at our best as hosts, because we are completely relaxed and the focus is on the people we love. This book is about extending that sense of freedom and simplicity to all the parties in our lives.

Successful entertaining is accessible to everyone. You don't need to know how to cook – not even a little bit. You don't need expensive vases, family silver or fancy china – just flowers, food, candles and a table. With a little bit of effort and imagination – and a few very simple rules – even the most ordinary evening can become a memory to treasure forever.

Marie France Van Damme

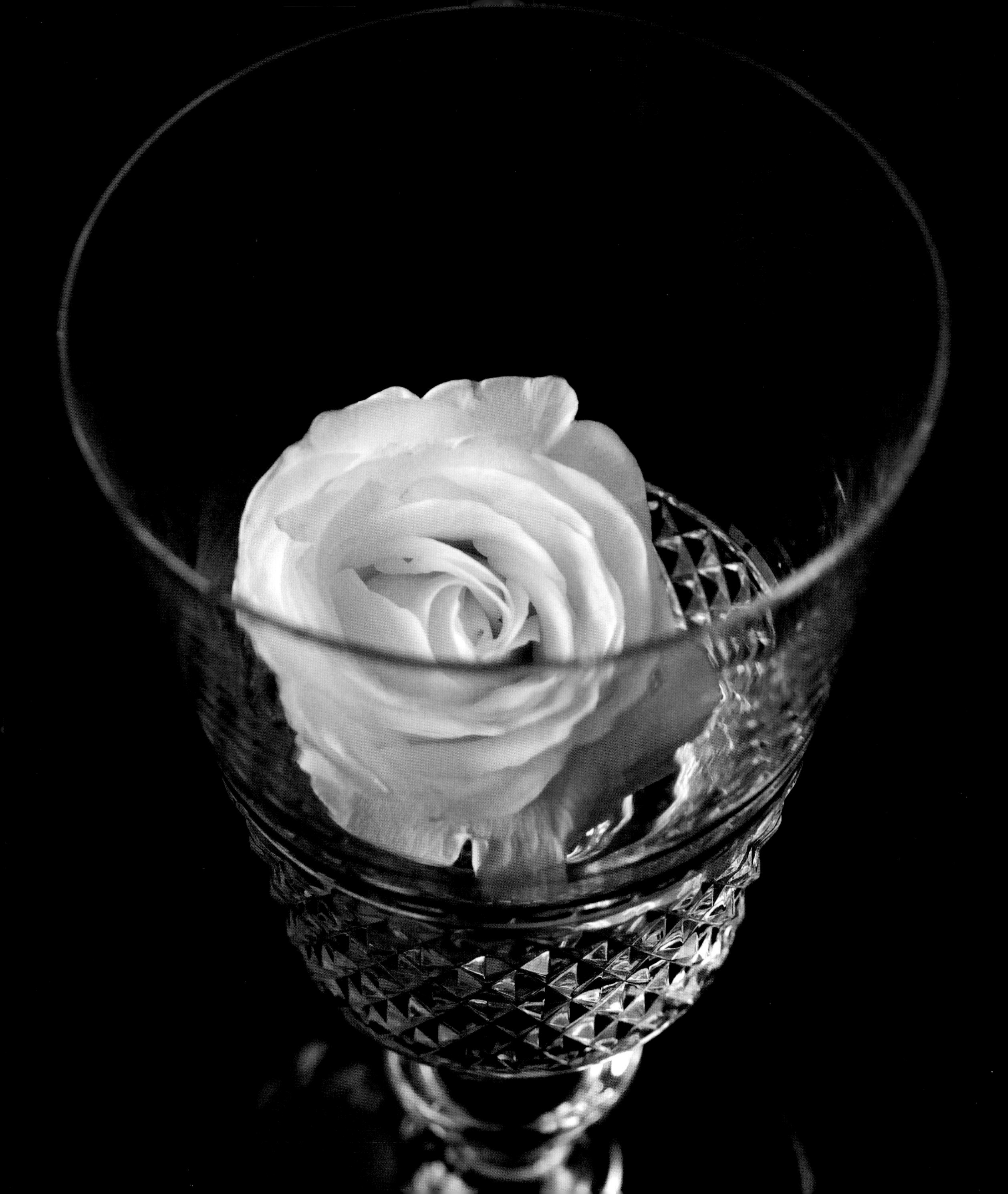

1
FLOWERS

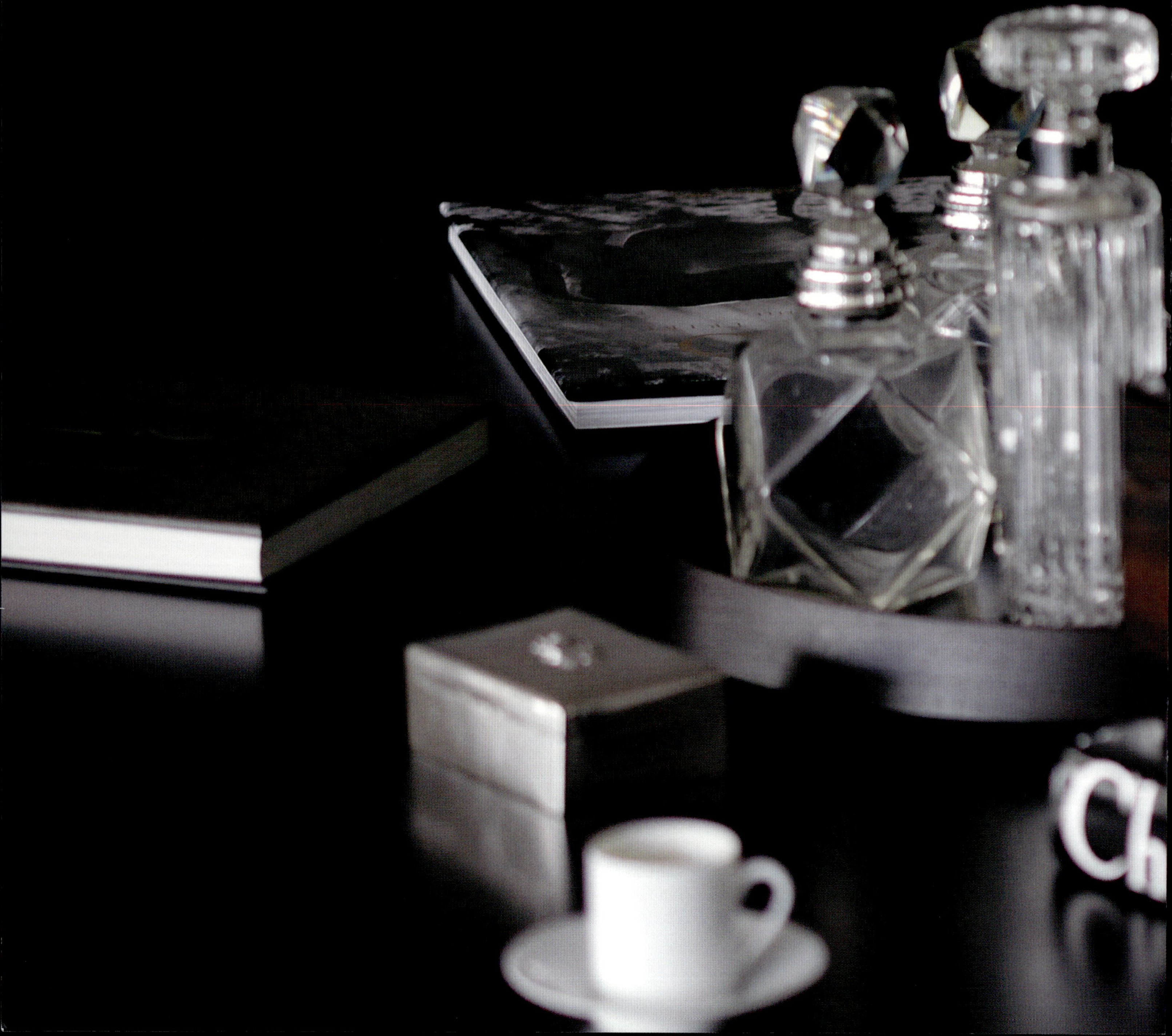
Ch

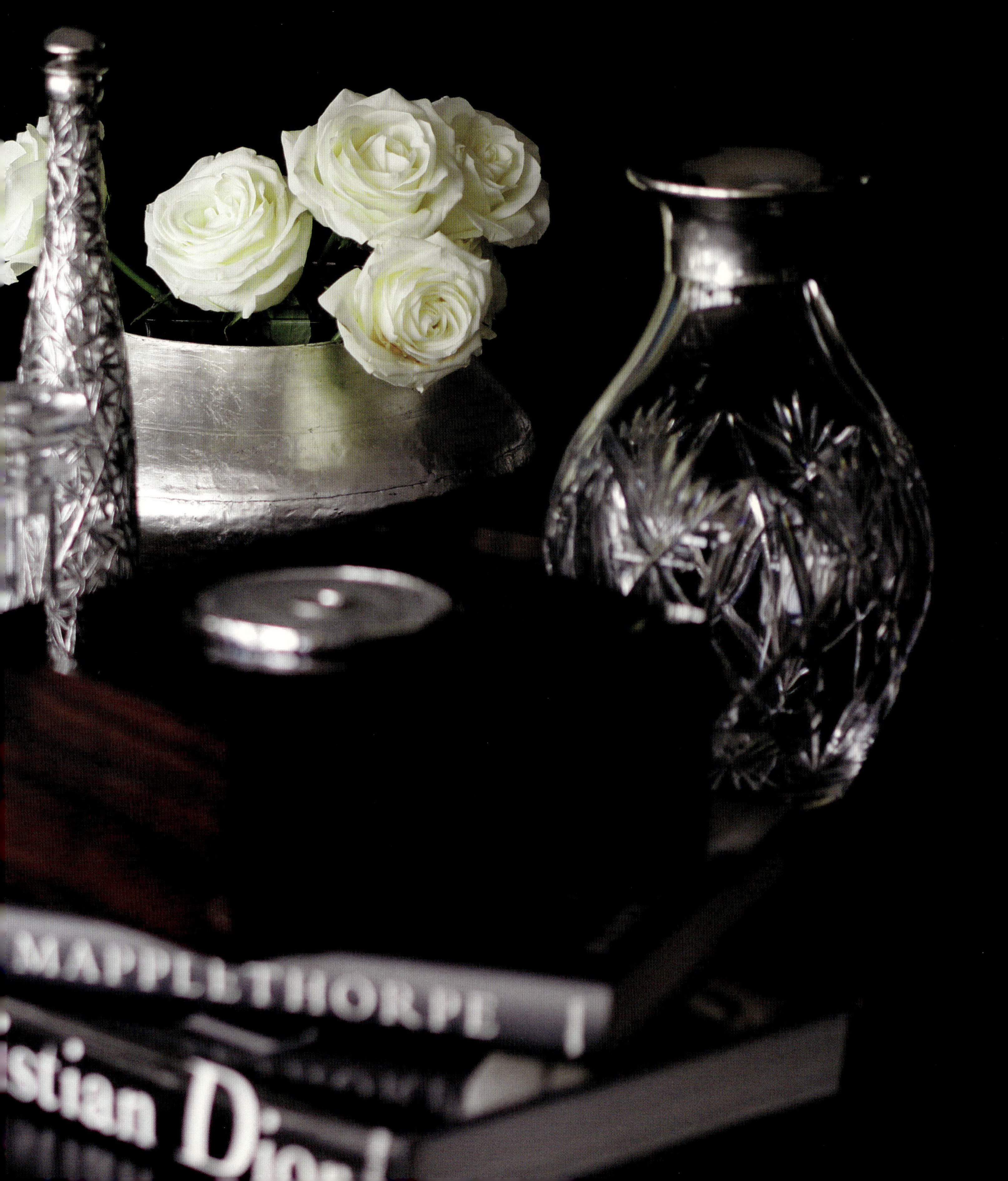
MAPPLETHORPE
stian Dior

Flowers create a sense of occasion.
They are a statement from you that says your guests are special.

But more is definitely not better. Bouquets that dominate the table and obscure your vision are annoying, and flowers need a certain amount of simplicity to be effective. A single rose, orchid or peony can be much more noticeable and dramatic than a massive arrangement straight from the florist. In fact, you don't need a florist. Big bunches of flowers usually cost big money – yet six white roses in simple glasses arranged in a line down the middle of the table are far more sophisticated.

Using flowers with great effect is simple, and requires nothing more than a little bit of restraint.

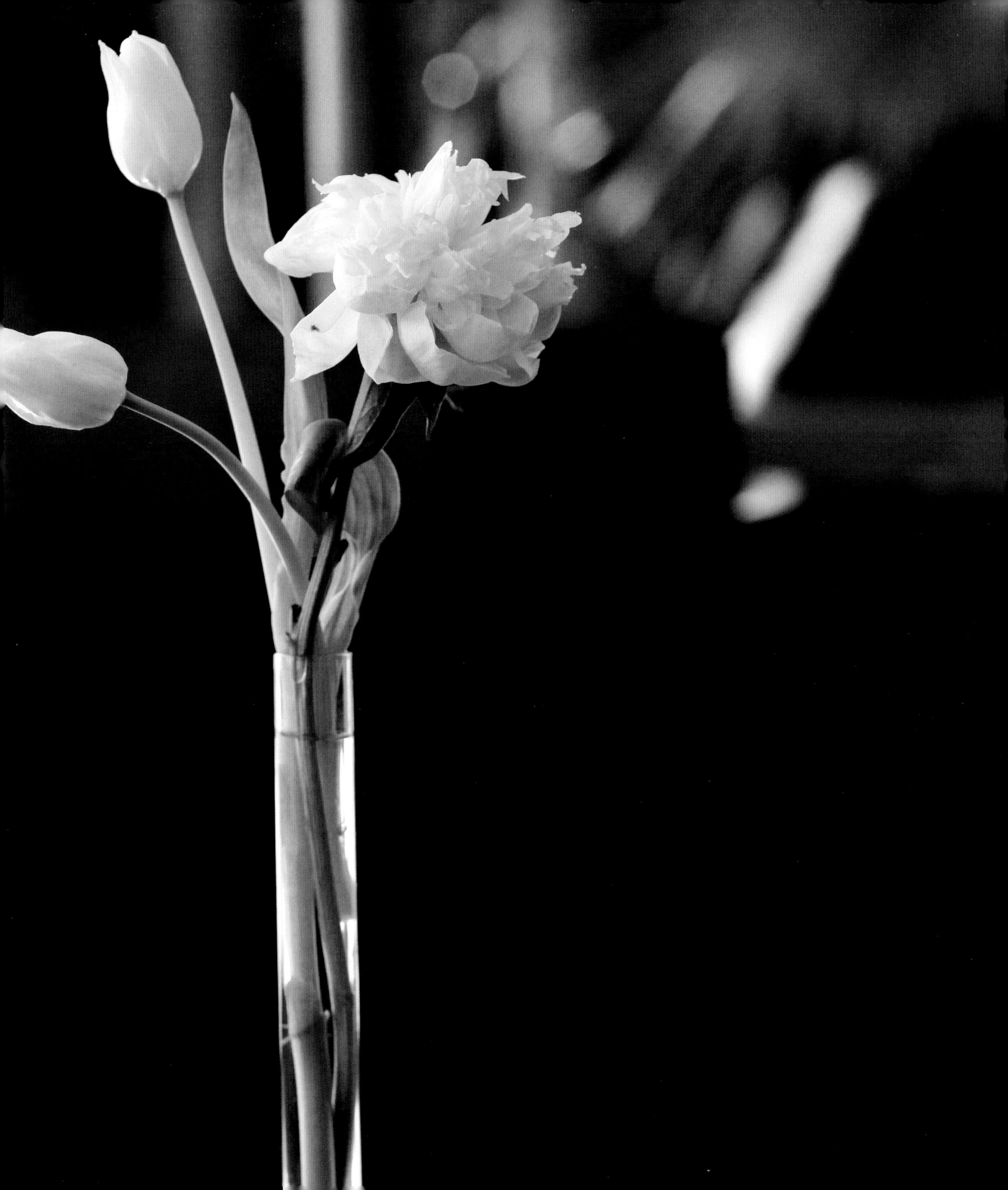

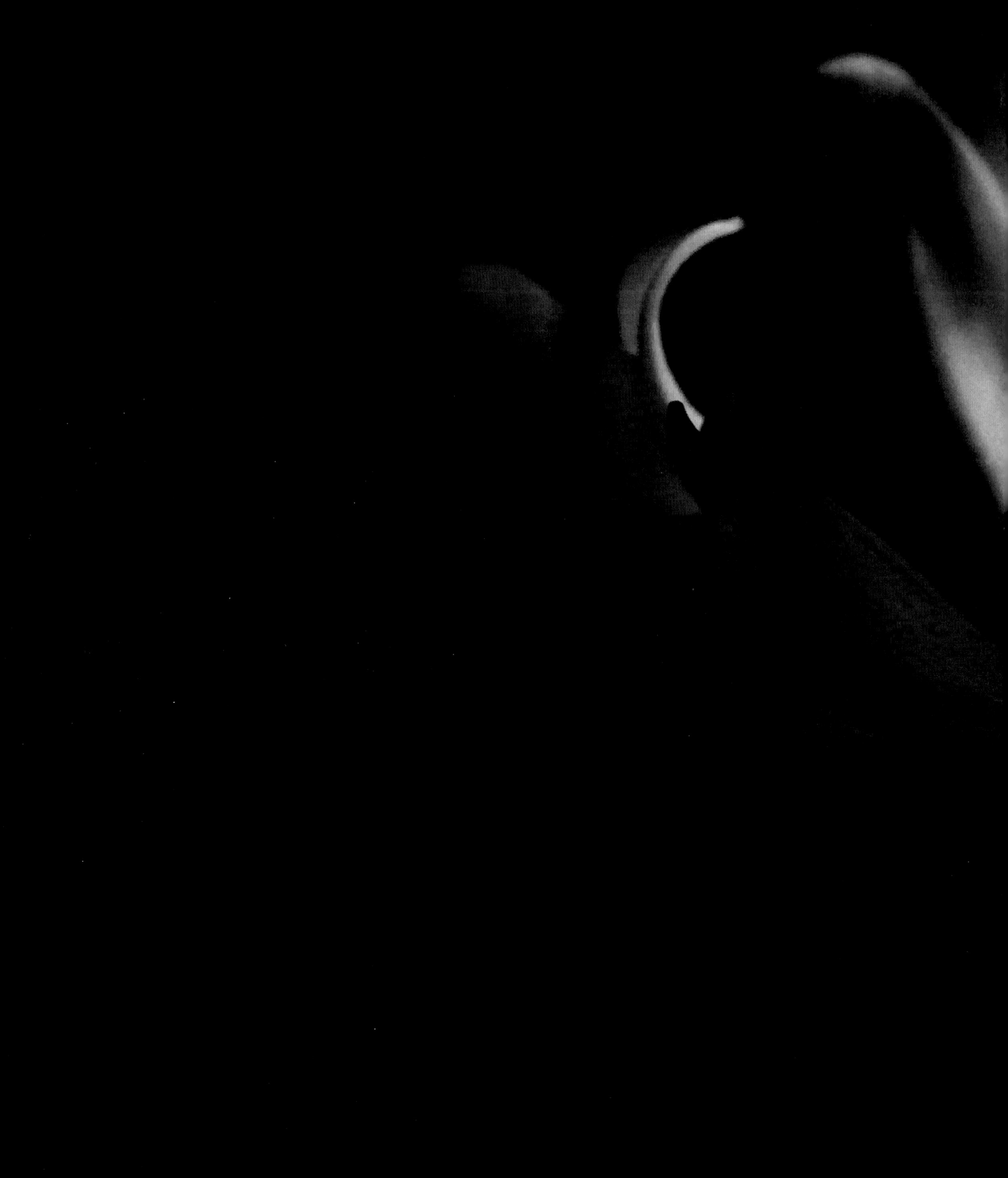

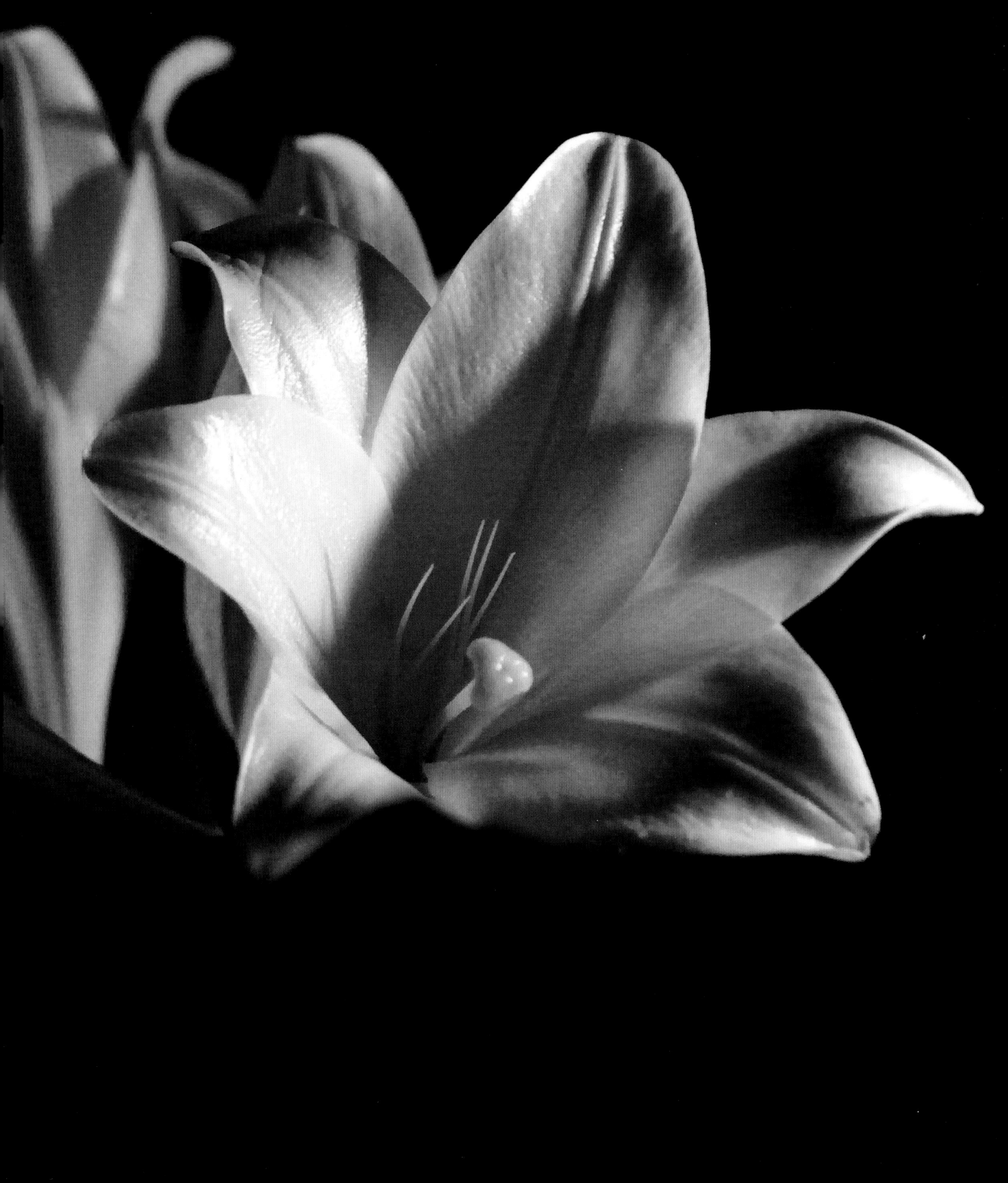

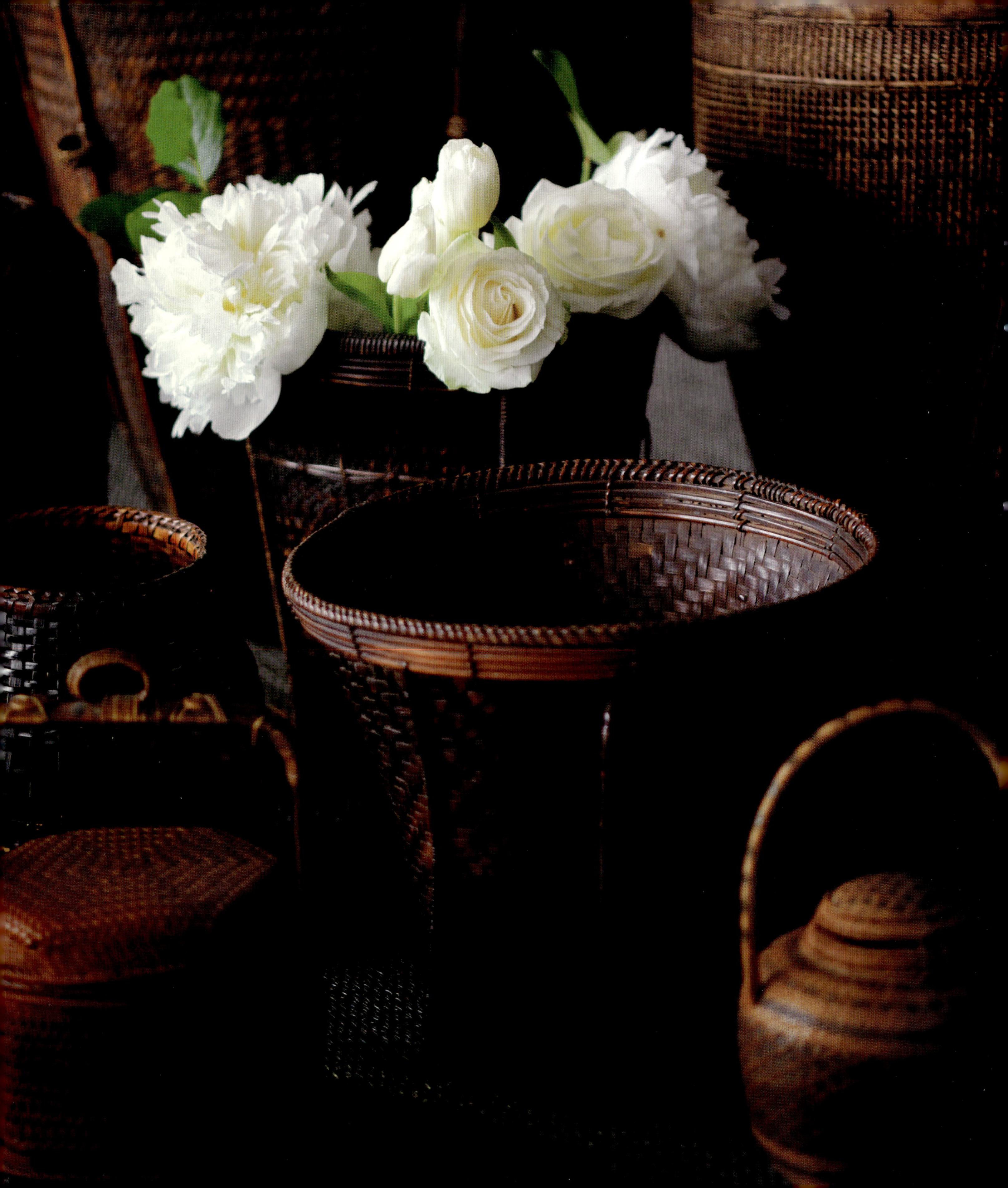

THE BEST VASES WERE NEVER
INTENDED TO BE VASES.

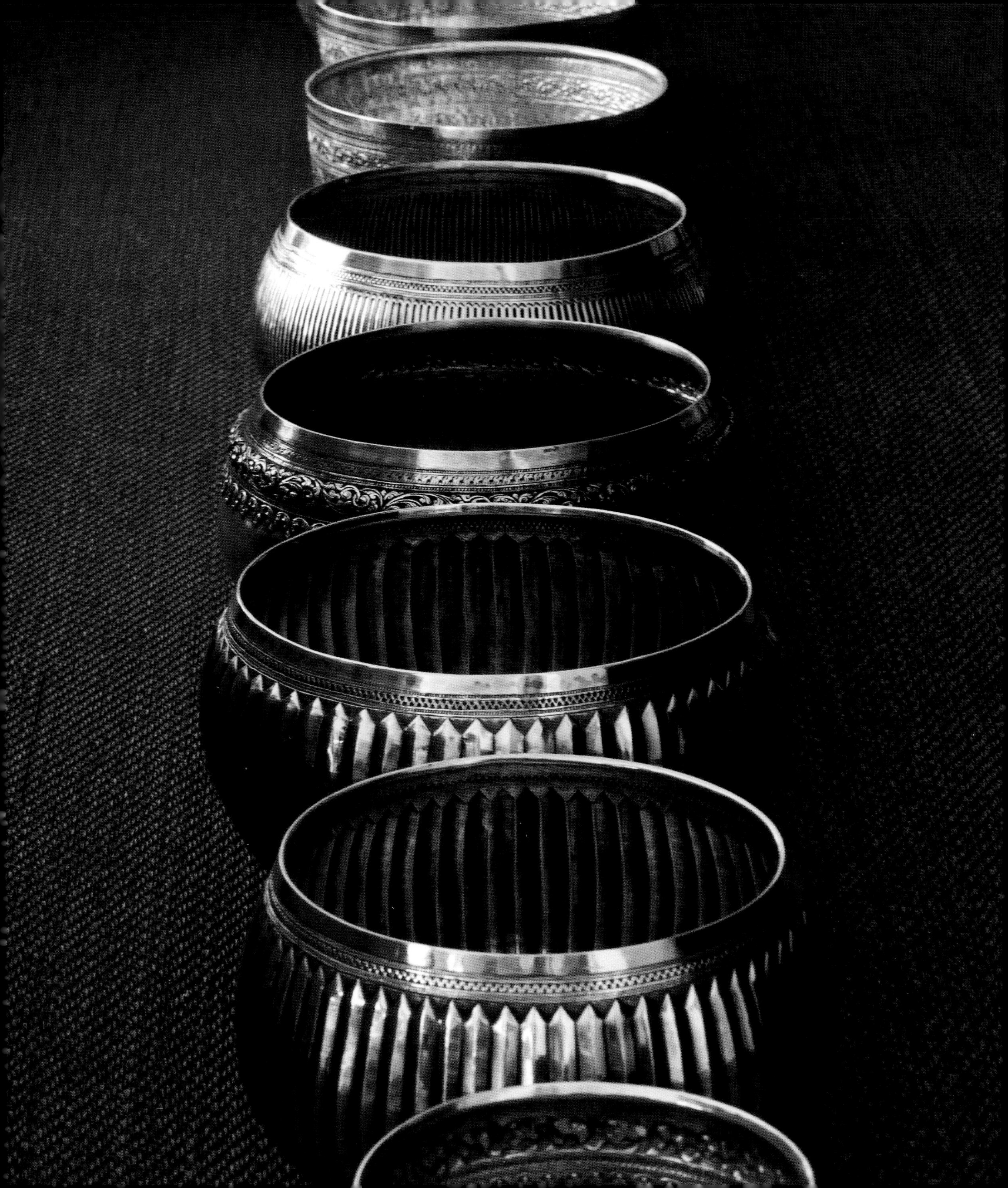

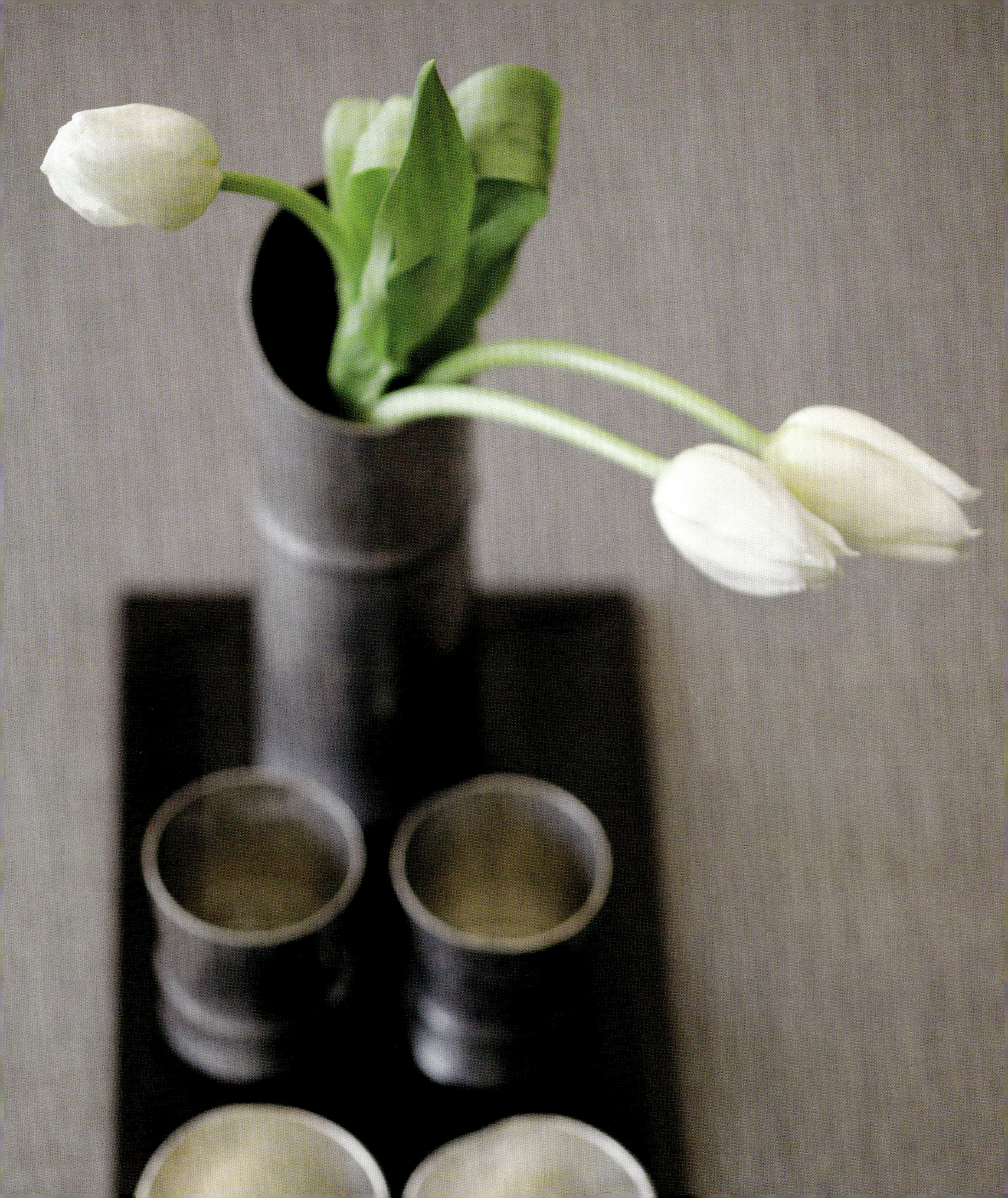

BOWLS, BOTTLES, URNS AND BASKETS...

FLOWERS

...EVEN OLD CLAY JUGS CAN MAKE GREAT VASES.

毛楚雄烈士遗像

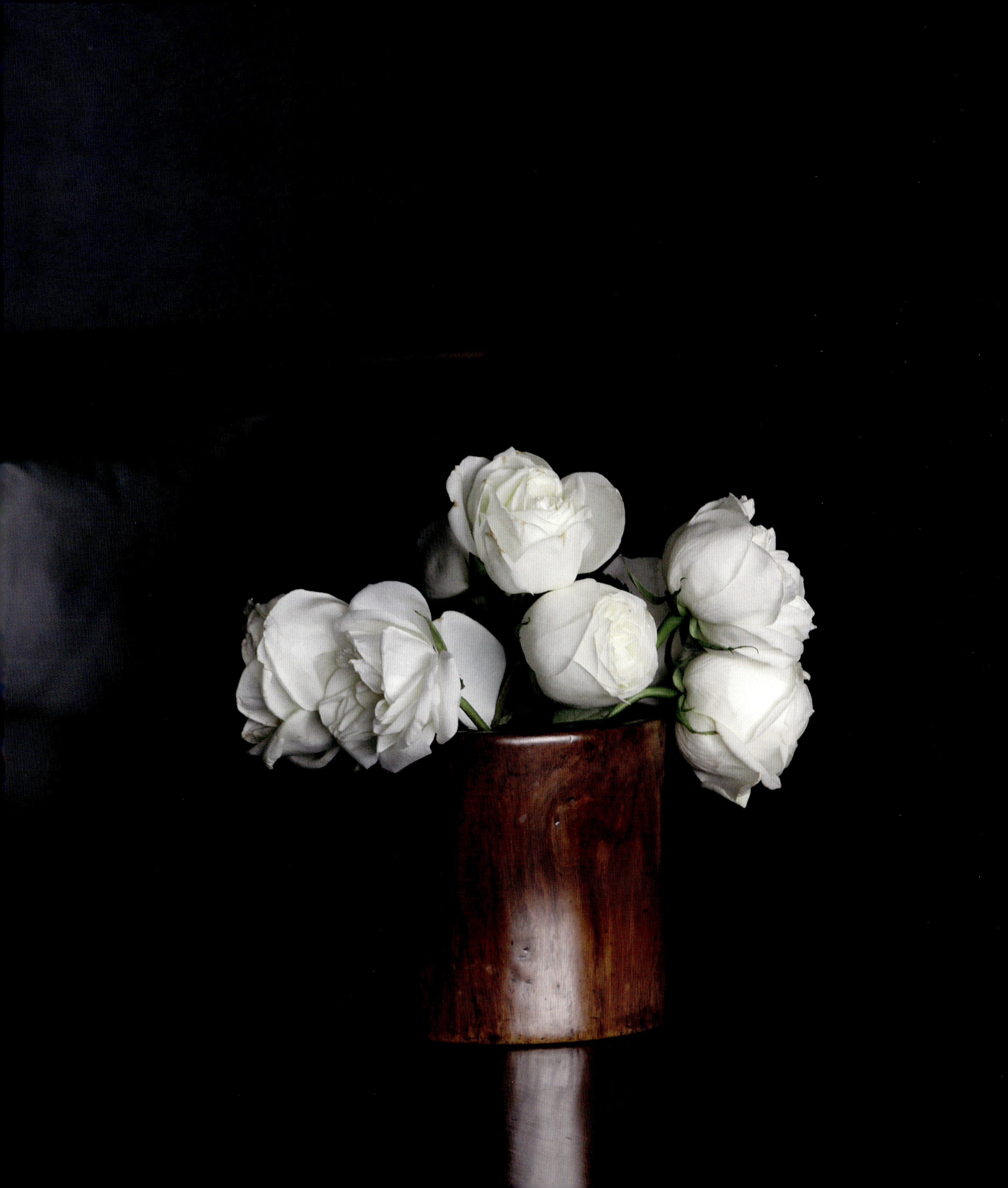

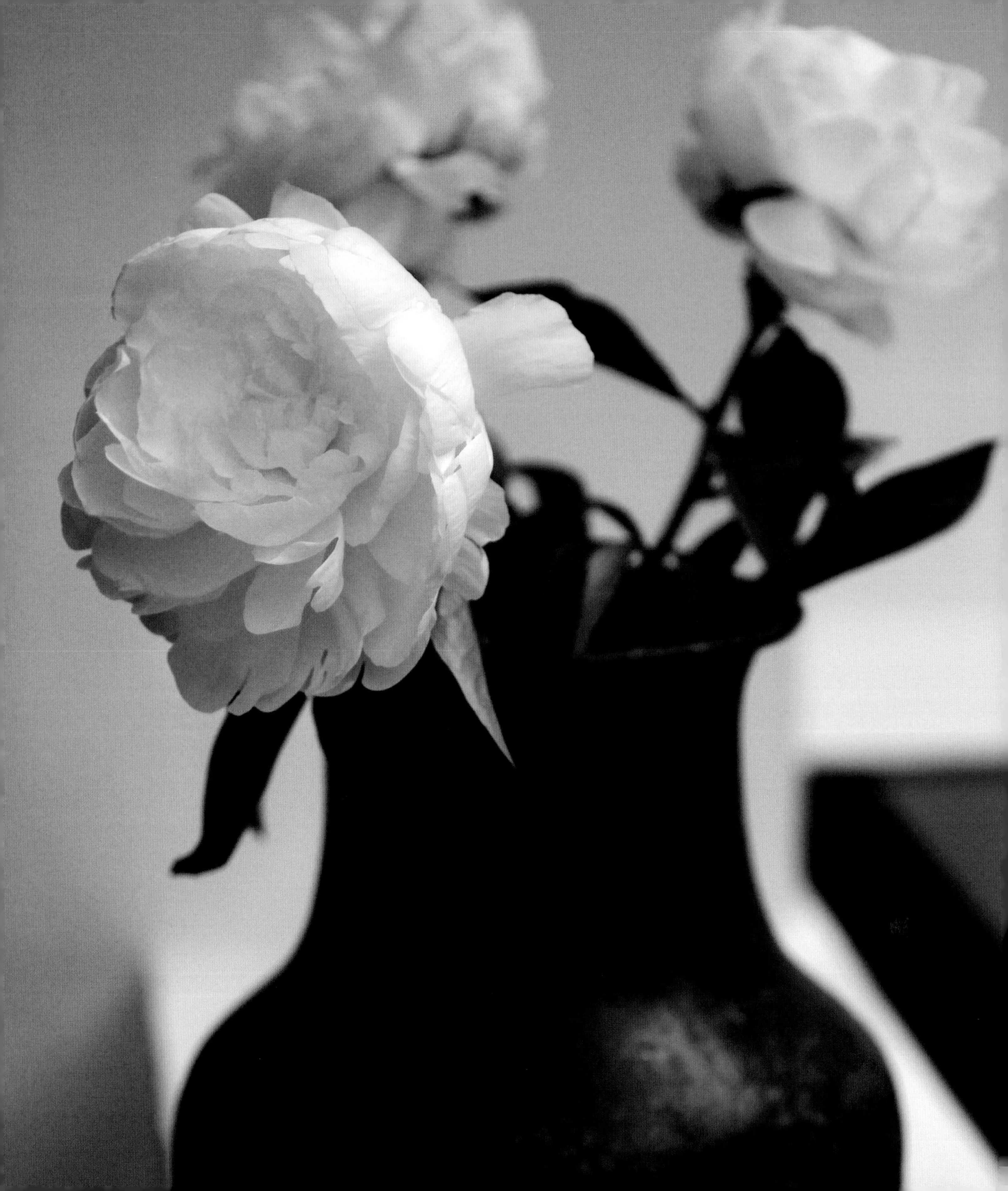

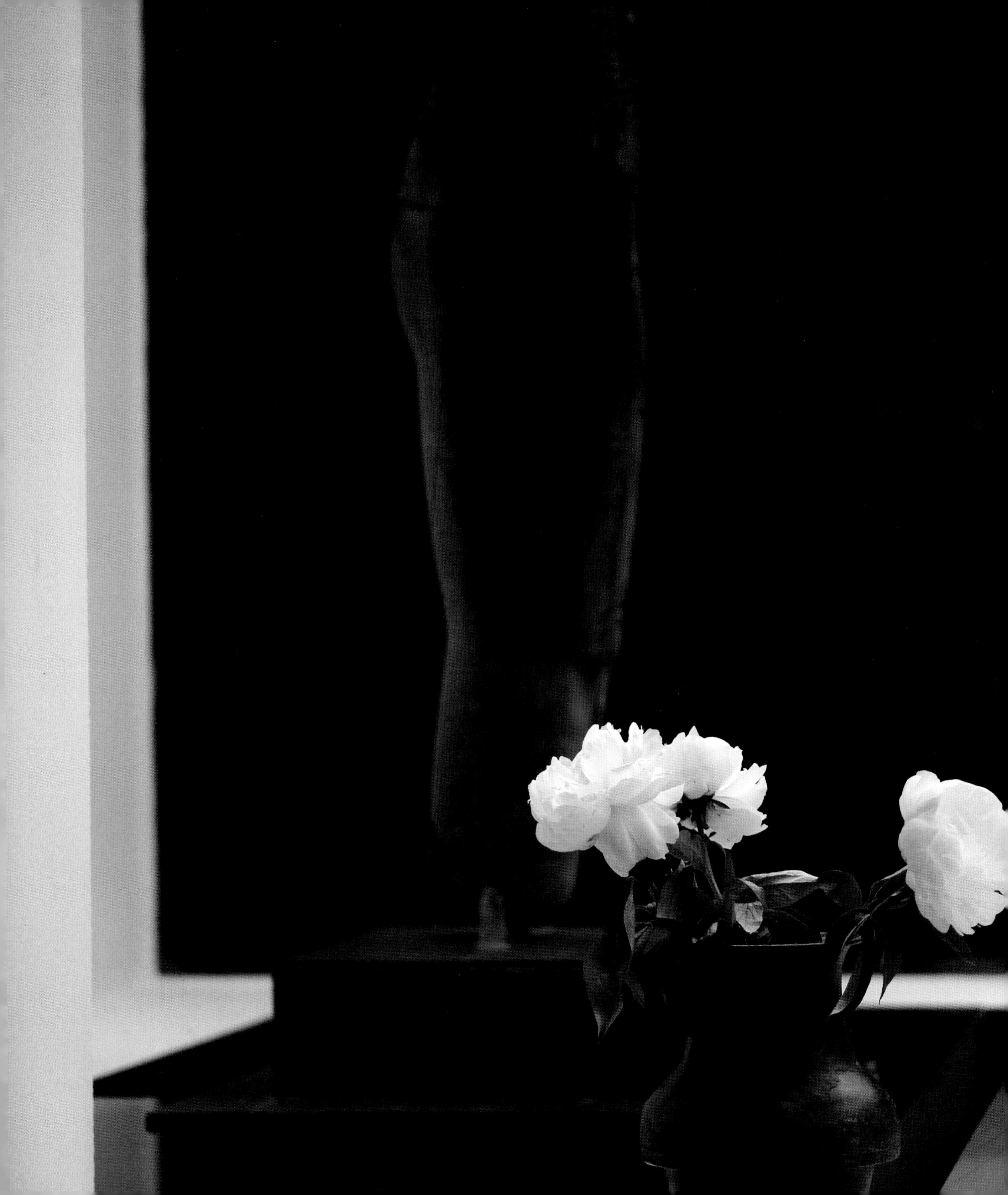

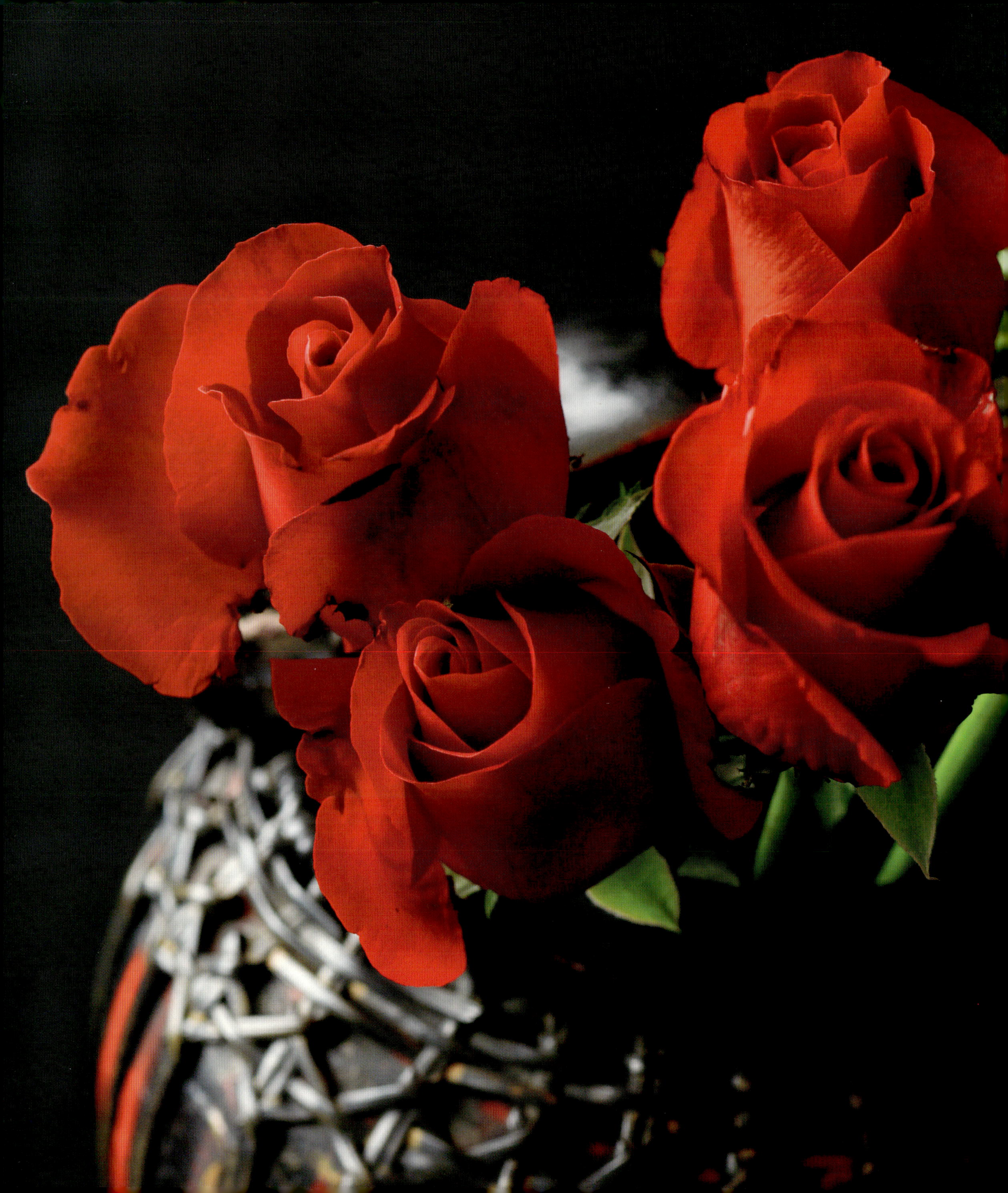

UNLESS YOU ARRANGE
FLOWERS FOR A LIVING
(YOU'RE A FLORIST OR A STYLIST)
STICK TO ONE COLOUR.

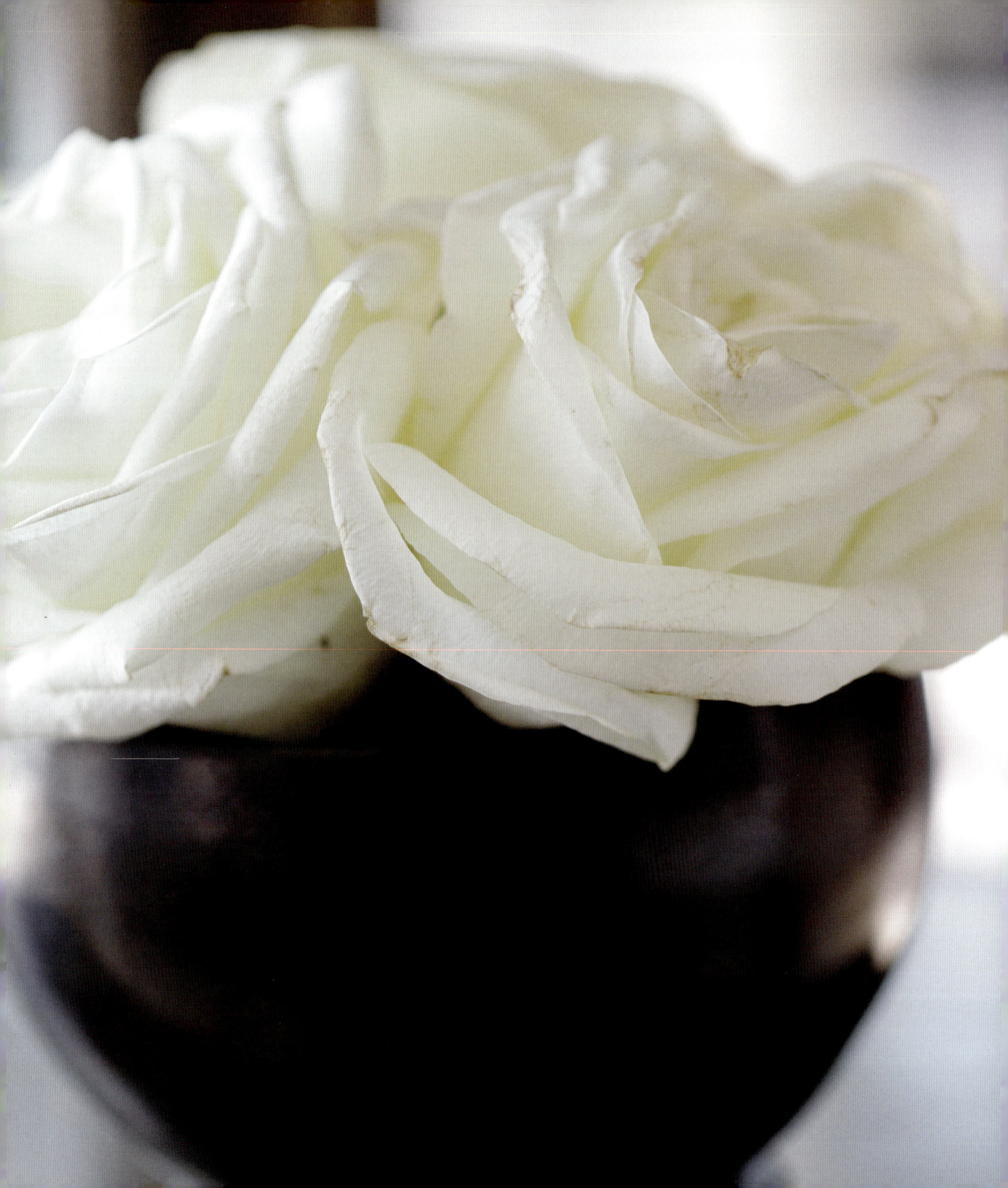

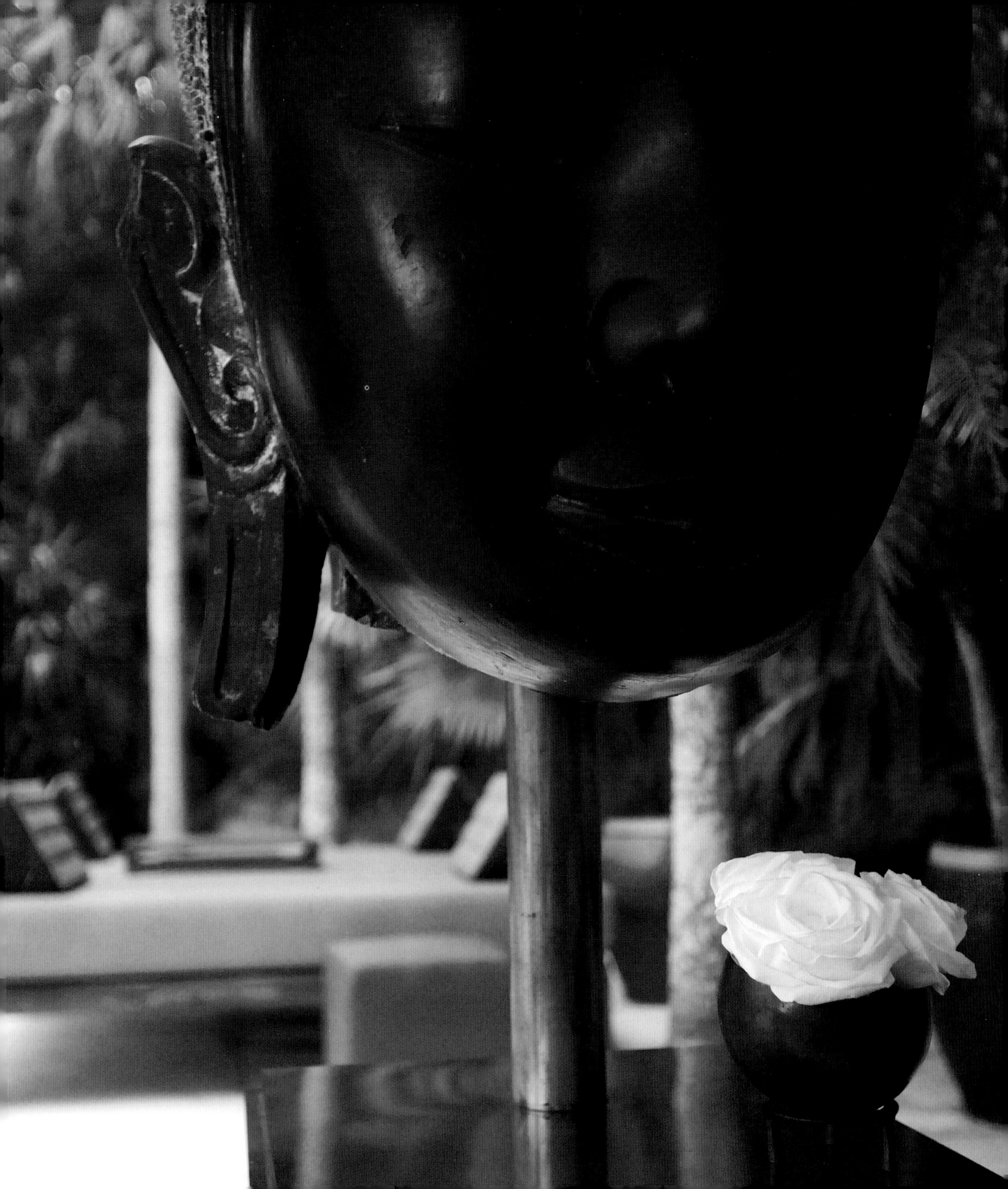

ODD NUMBERS WORK BEST.
EVEN A SINGLE, SOLITARY FLOWER
CAN HAVE GREAT IMPACT.

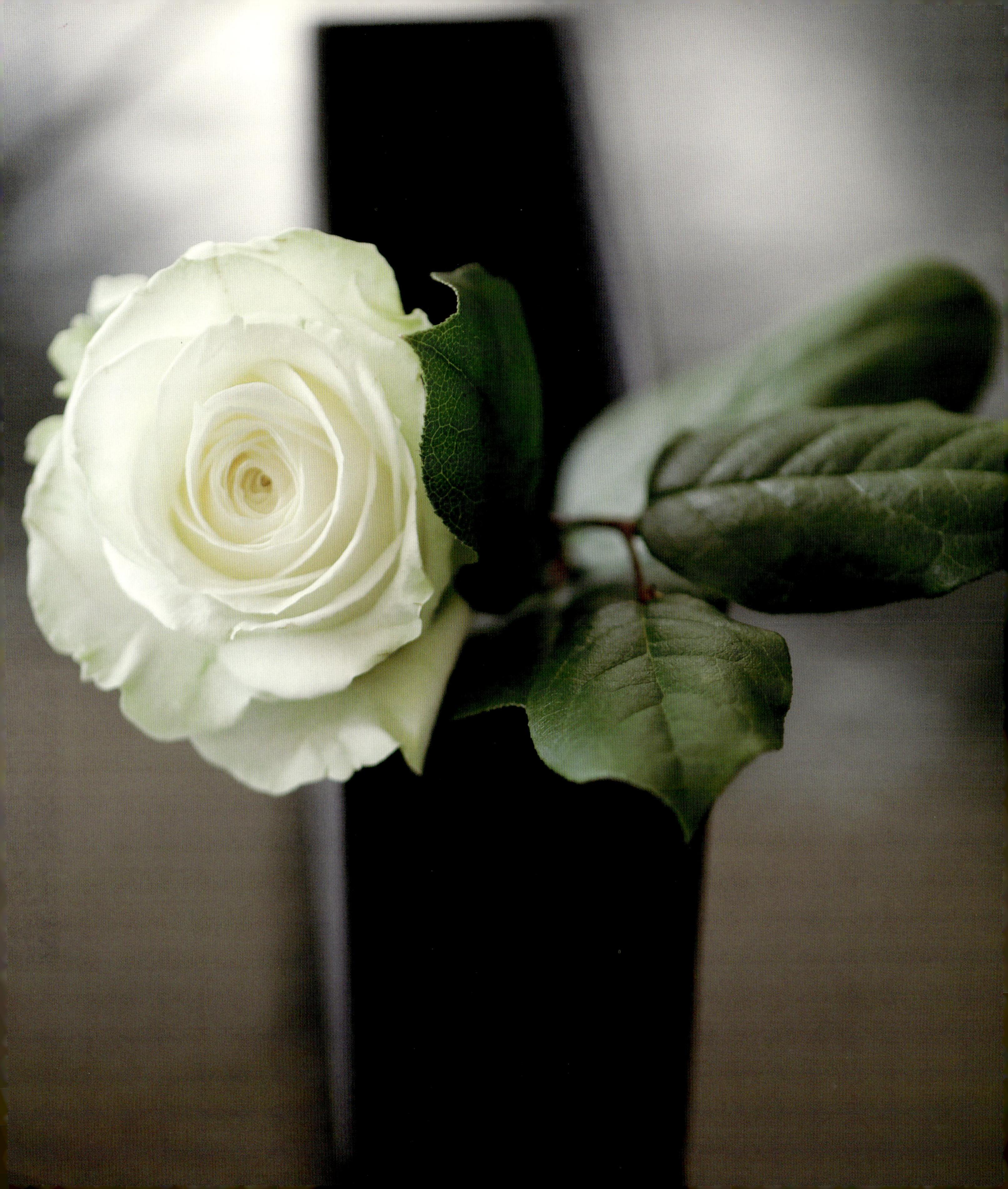

TRAYS ARE ESSENTIAL TO ENTERTAINING.
THEY CAN DO MORE THAN JUST HOLD DRINKS.

FLOWERS

EVERYTHING LOOKS BETTER ON A TRAY –
EVEN A VASE OF FLOWERS.

FLOWERS

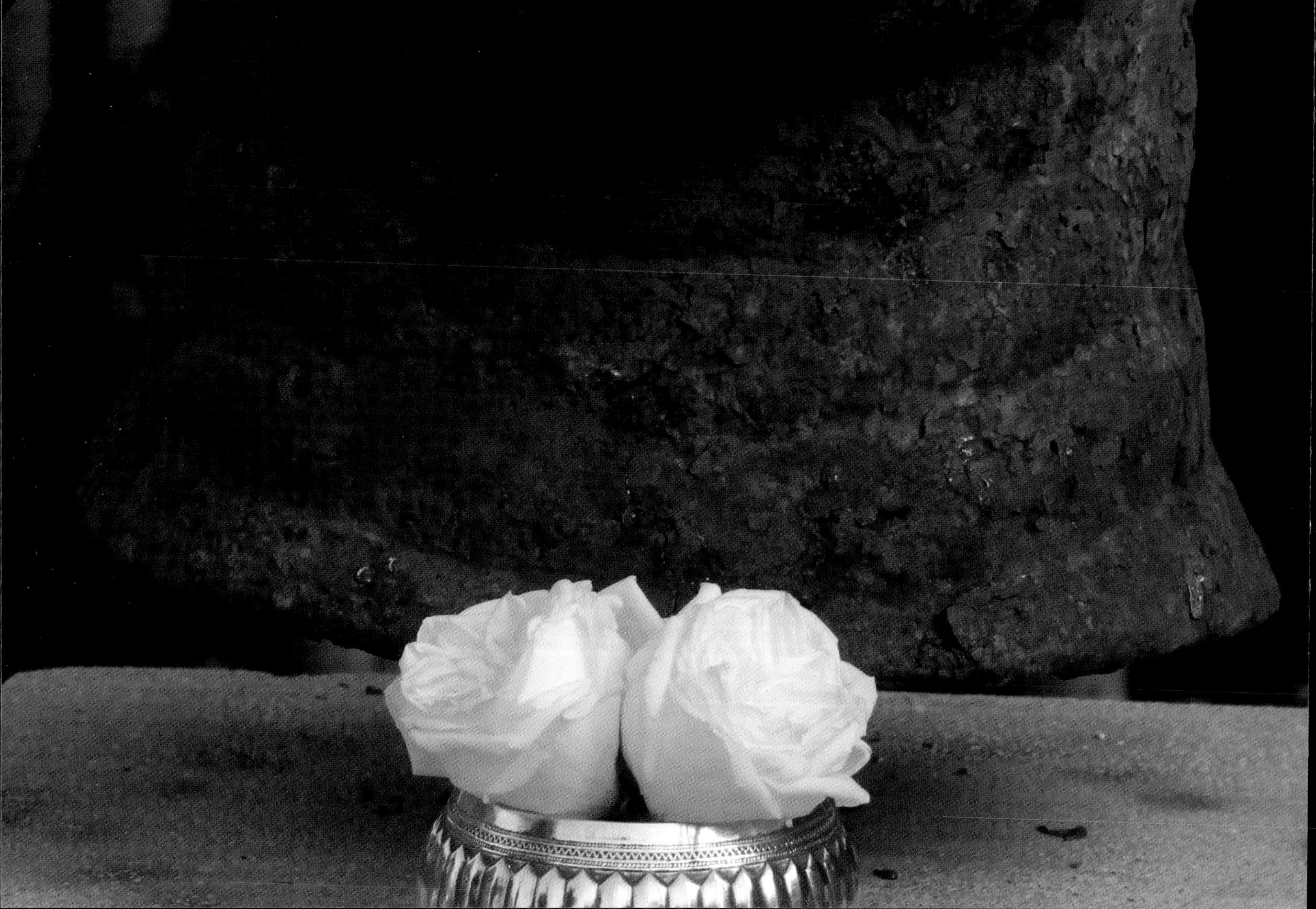

ART AND FLOWERS
HAVE BEEN TOGETHER
SINCE THE INVENTION
OF RELIGION.

FLOWERS IN PRACTICE: MY HUSBAND'S BIRTHDAY

My husband prefers entertaining at home to going out, so it was logical that I would celebrate his birthday by organizing a party for him at our house in Hong Kong. It was the end of November, and although it doesn't get too cold at that time of year, it can rain, so a tent was organized just in case. The 'tent' turned out to be more of a sculpted tarpaulin, which had the unexpected benefit of functioning as a reflective surface for the lighting on the table.

Black linen was chosen for the table covering and a local Japanese restaurant provided the sushi. The combination of tea lights, sparkling wine glasses, black chopsticks, the simple black lacquer trays on which the sushi was served and the odd spot of candlelight bouncing off the tarp created pure magic. The plain white roses in their silver bowls seemed to absorb light from all the shining surfaces and candles, and glowed like soft lanterns.

My husband and I prefer to keep our parties light and fun, so the dress code was informal. Since we are always up for something weird and unpredictable, we were happy to let one of our guests, Jean Claude Van Damme, arrive with a film crew in tow to record my husband's party for his reality television series.

I'm a firm believer in enjoying my own parties. Although I worked all day to get everything ready, the minute guests started arriving I concentrated only on enjoying the evening. Which is how it should be.

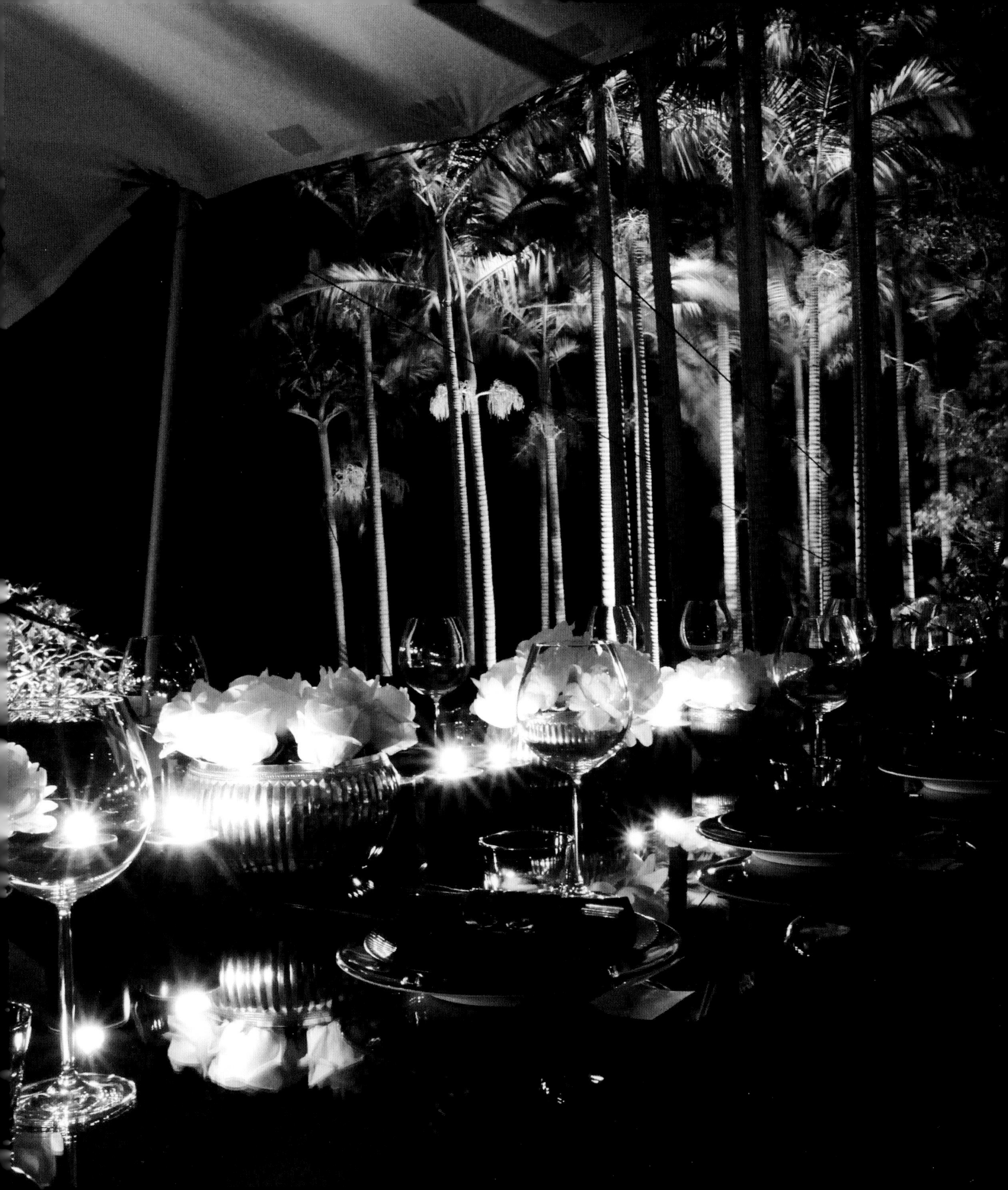

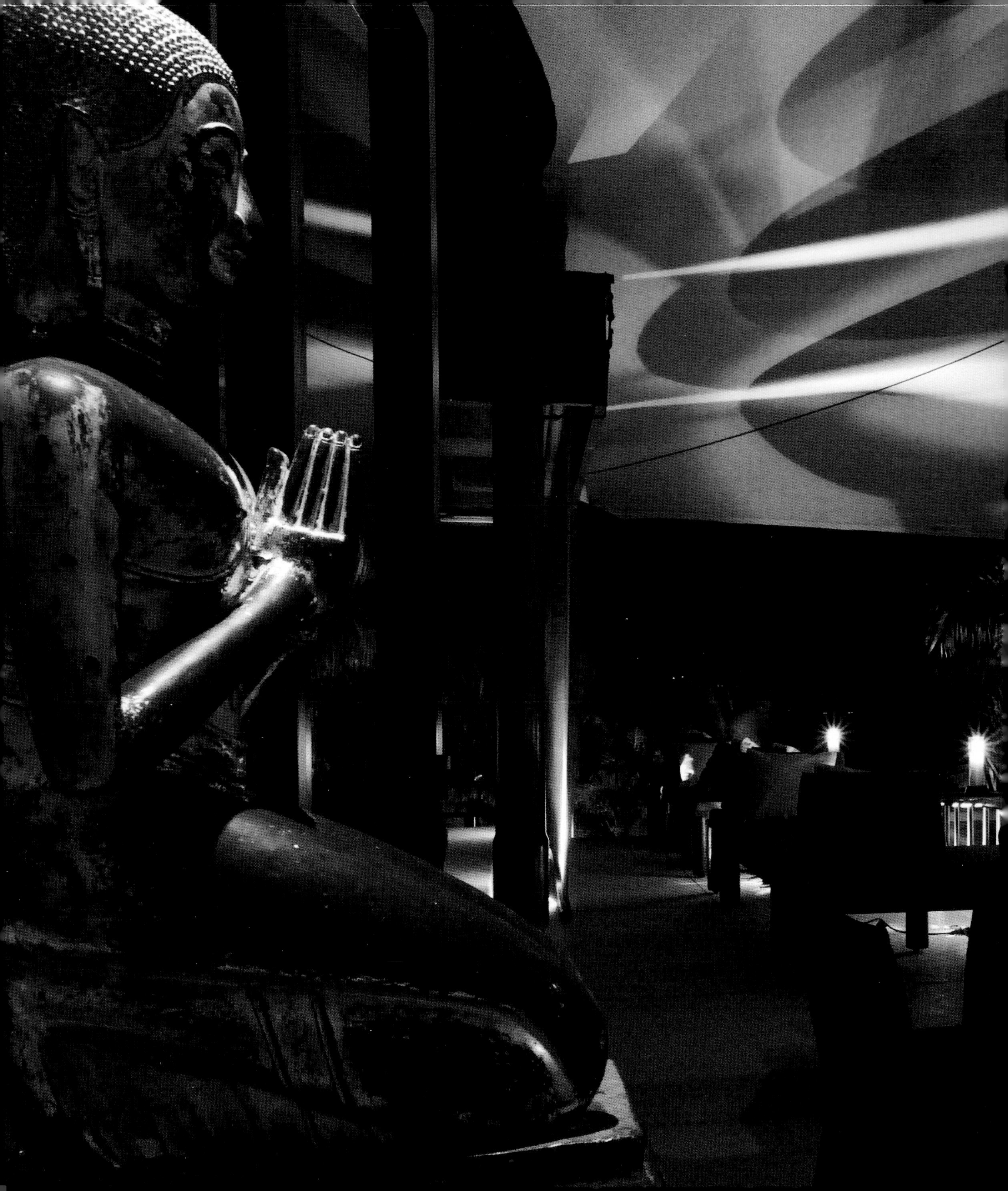

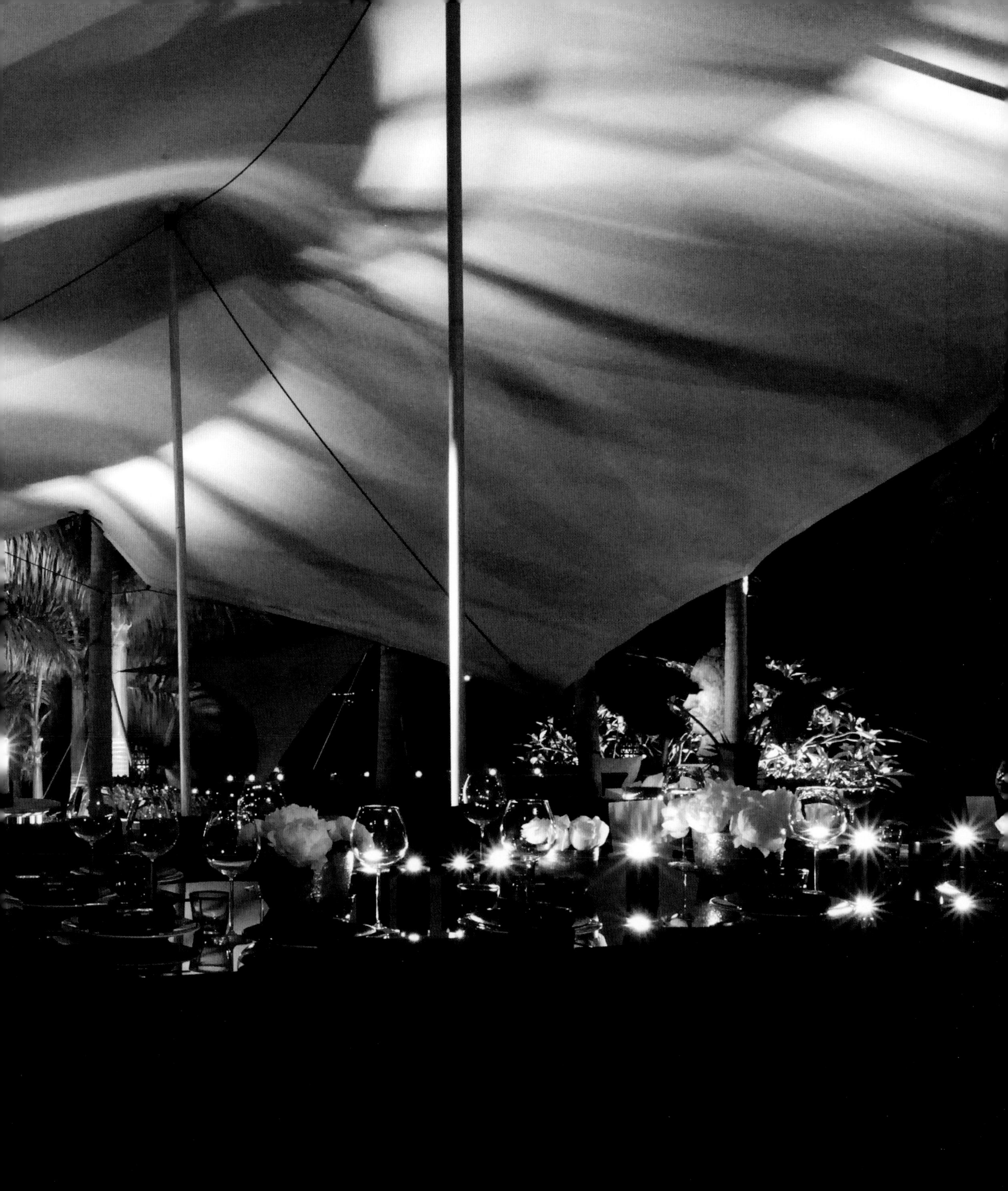

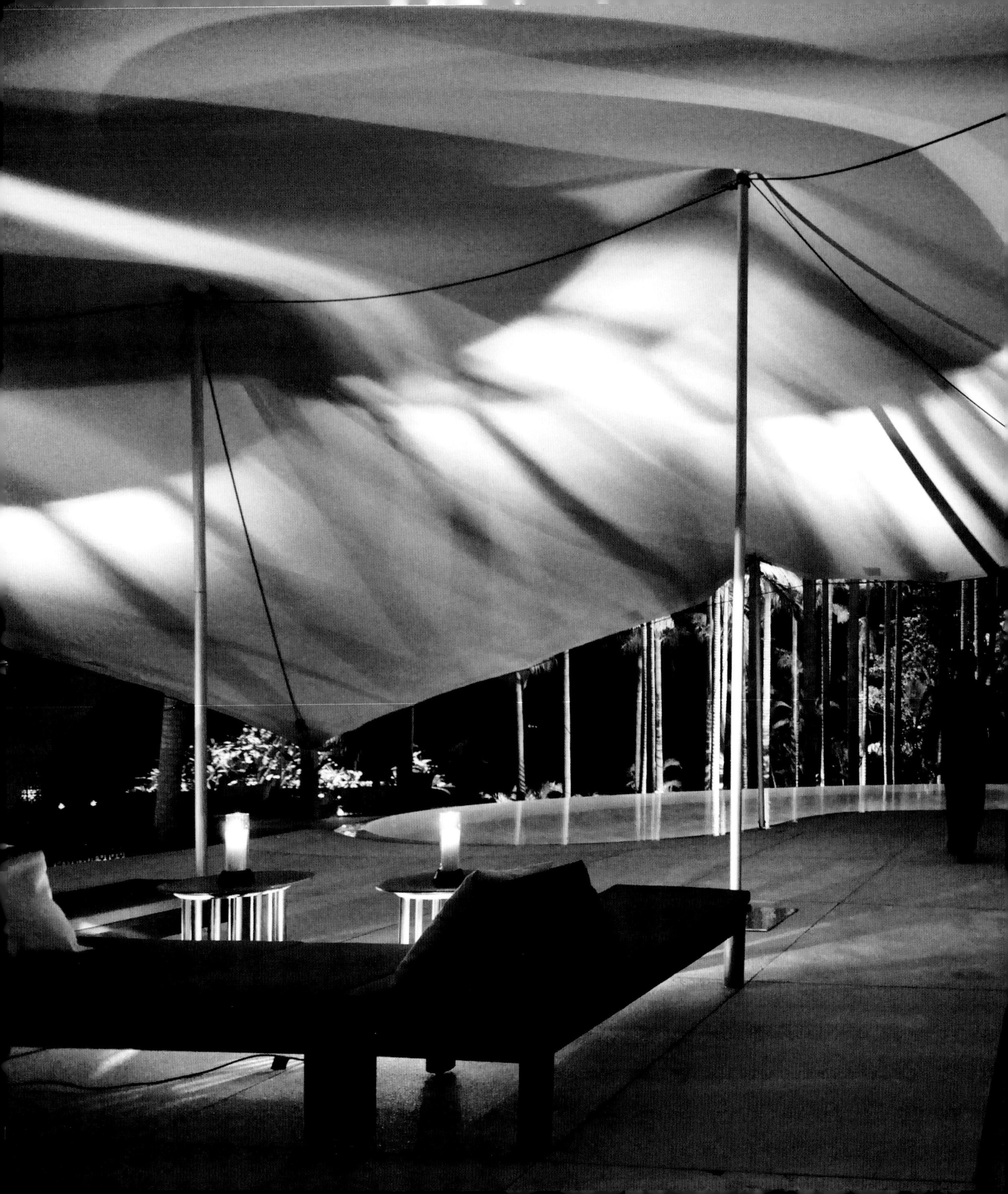

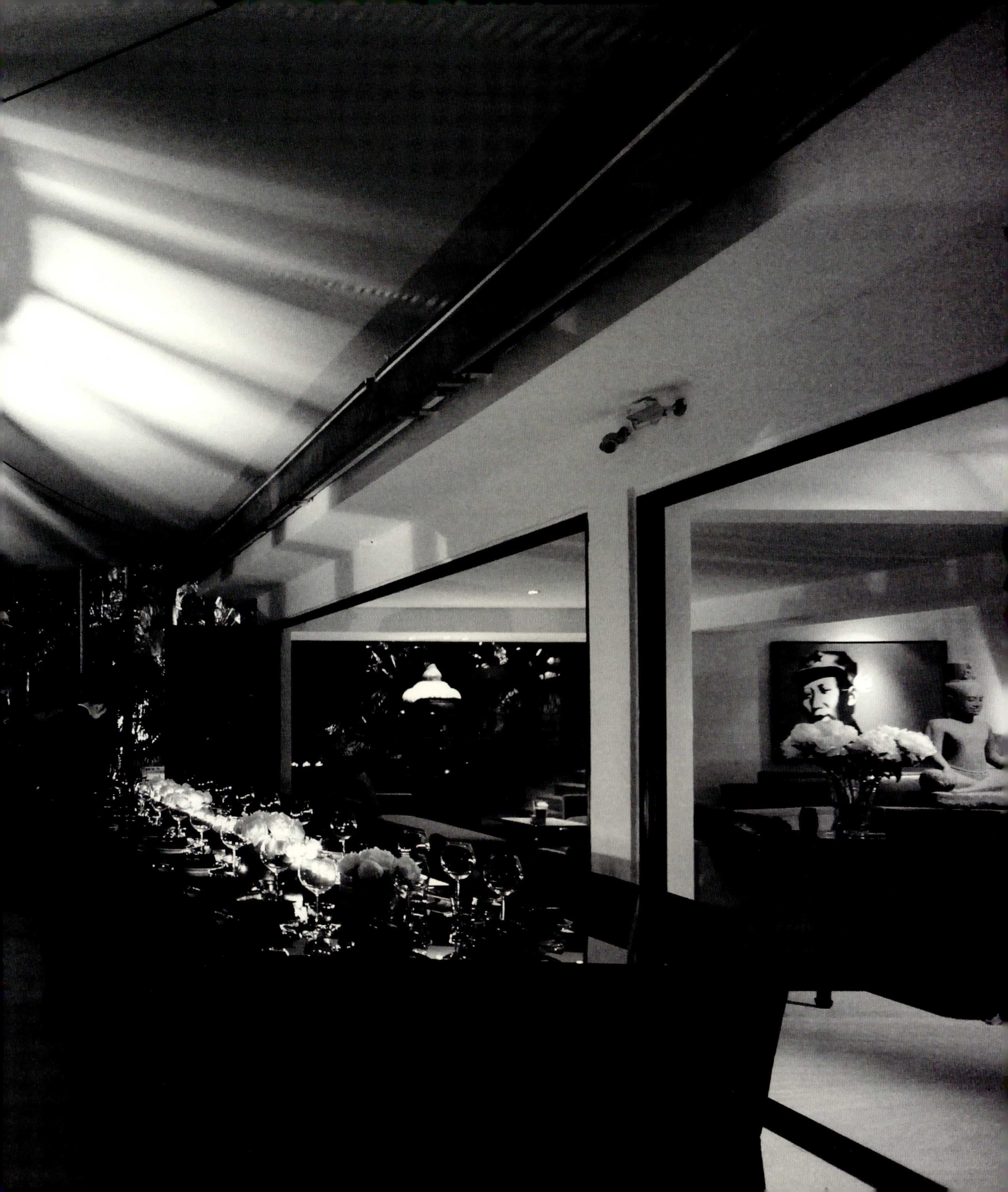

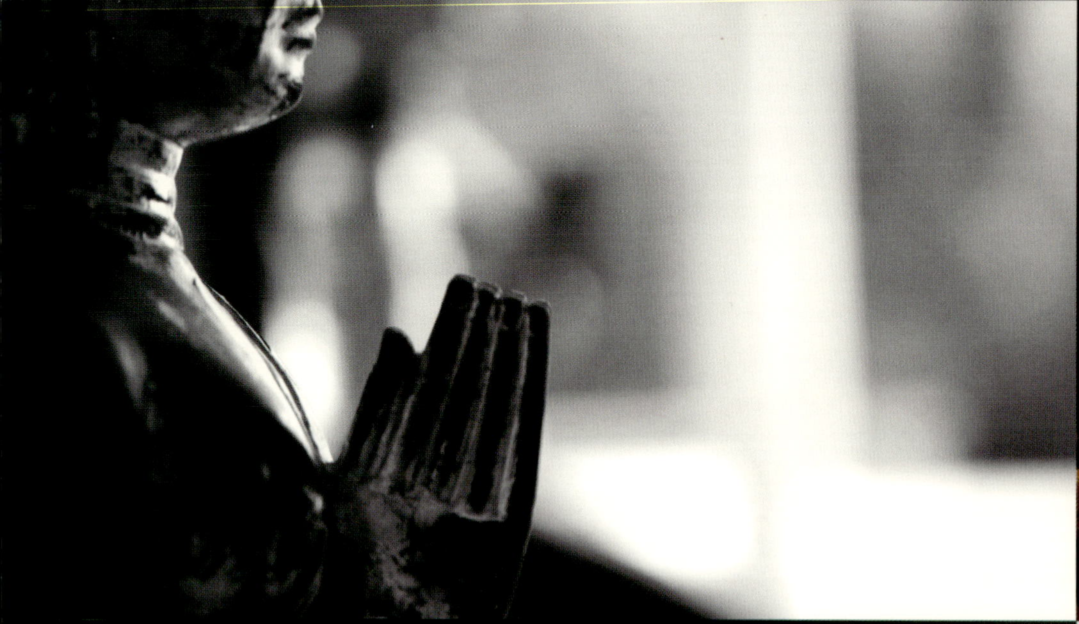

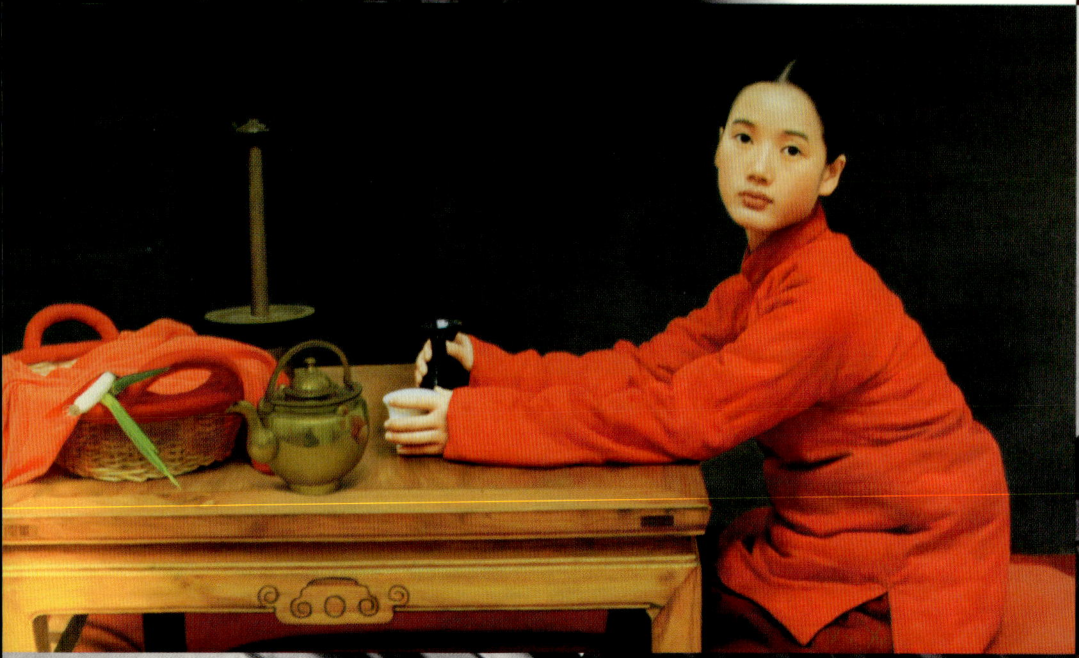
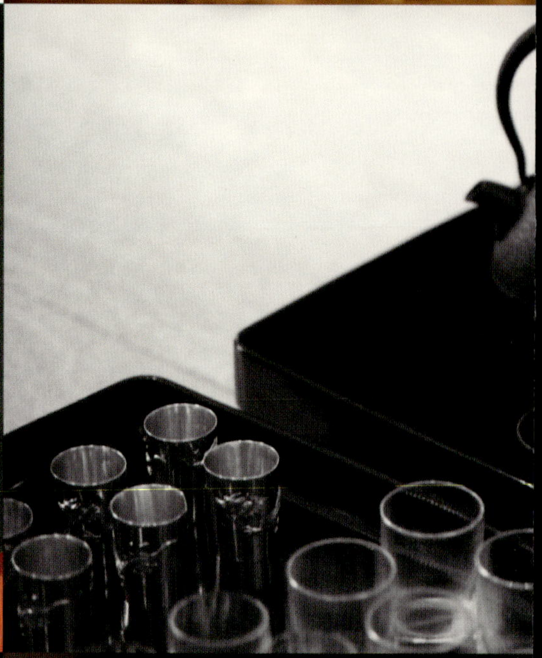
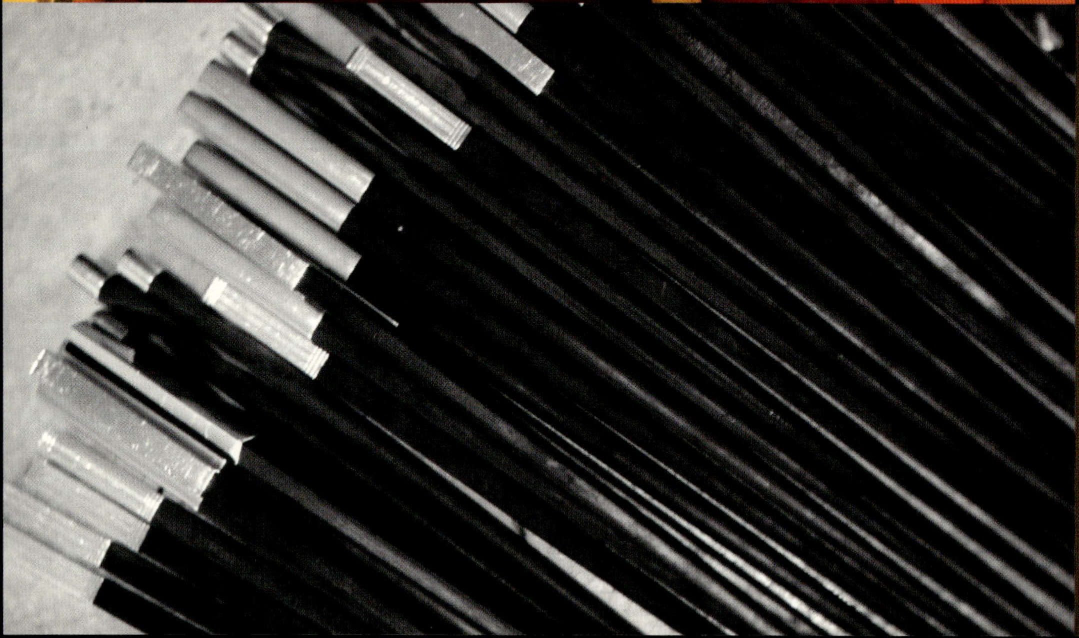

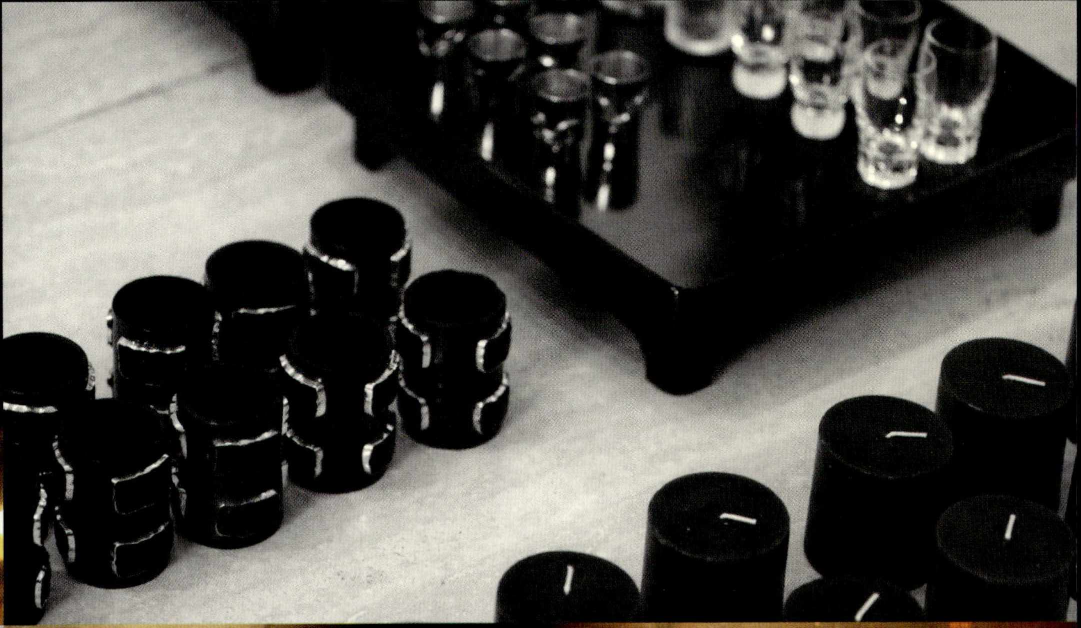
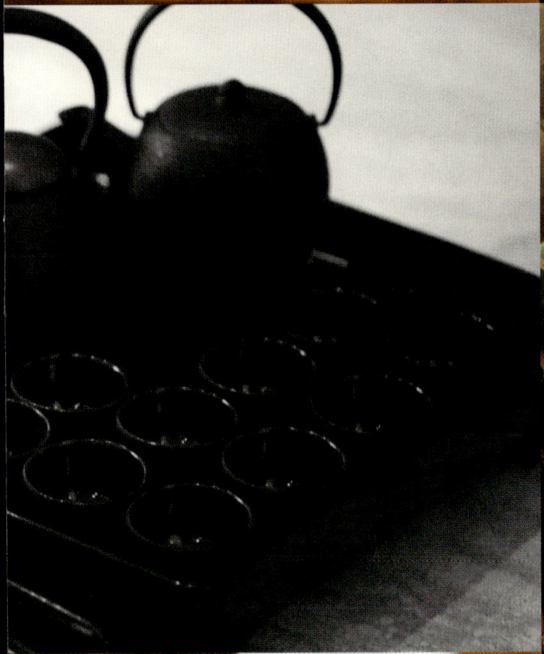
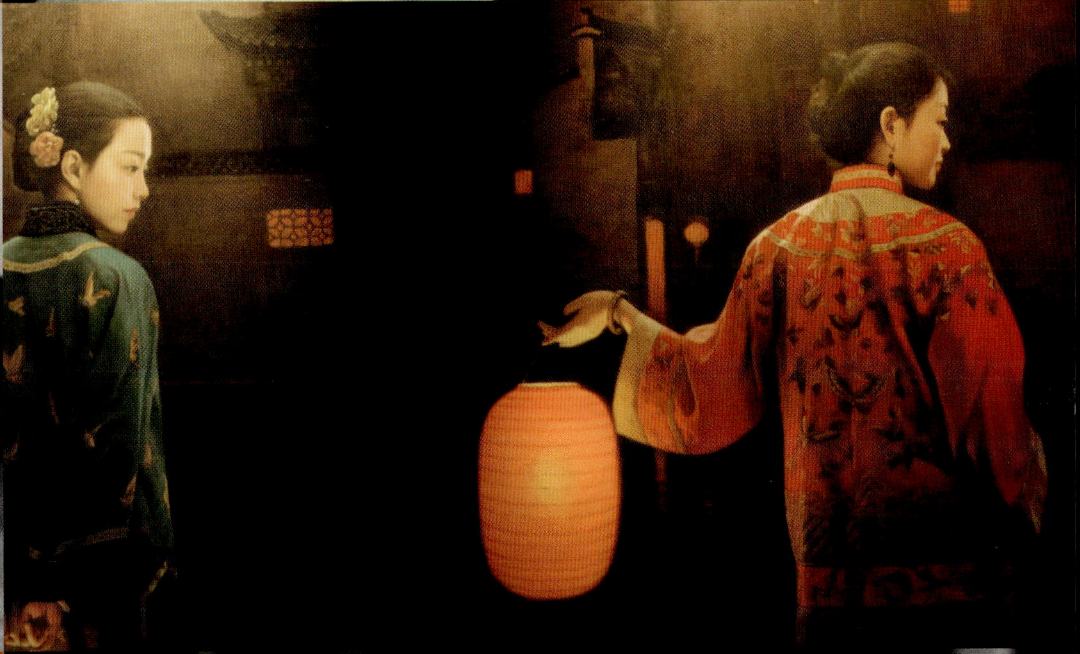
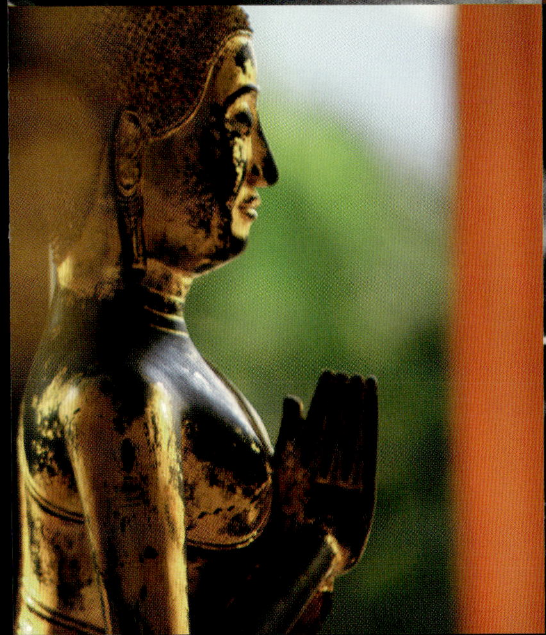
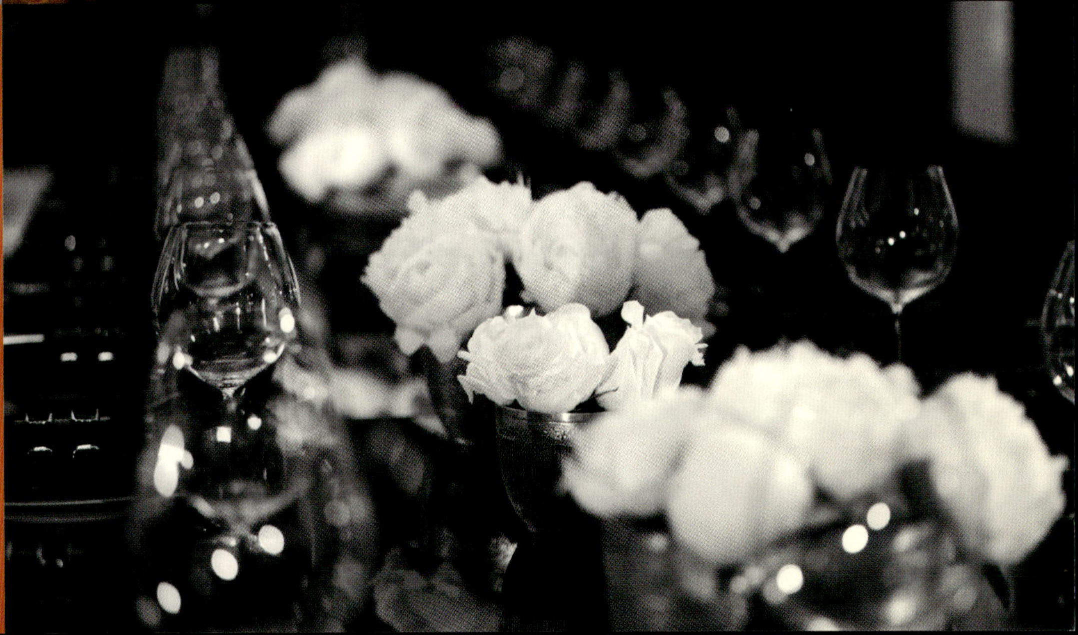

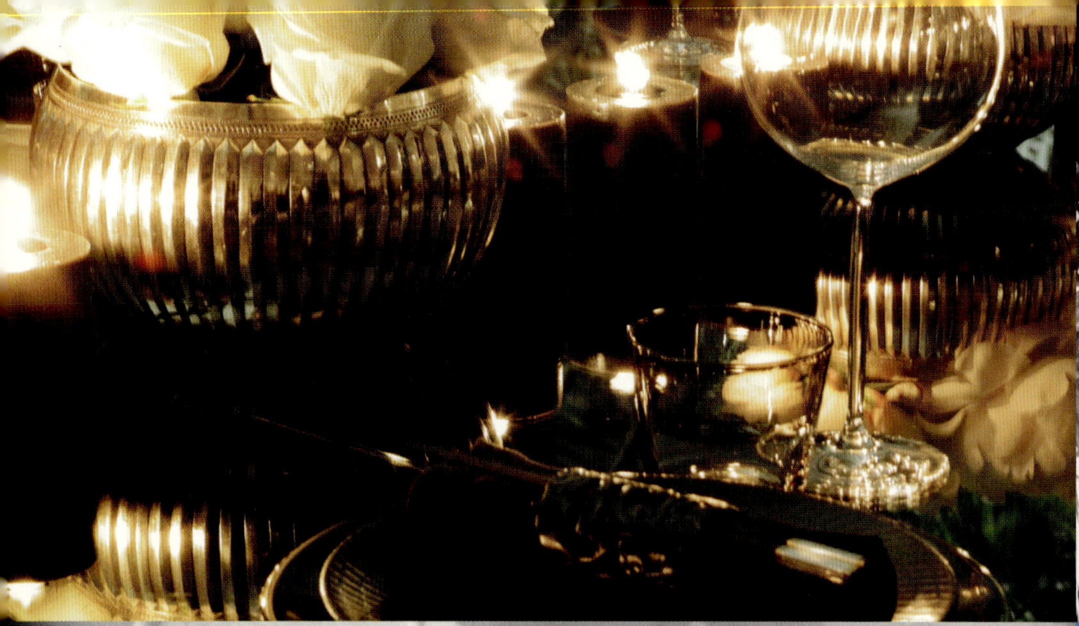
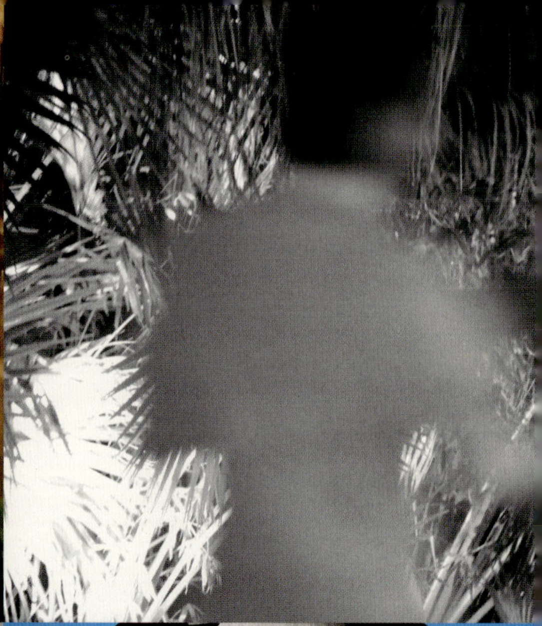
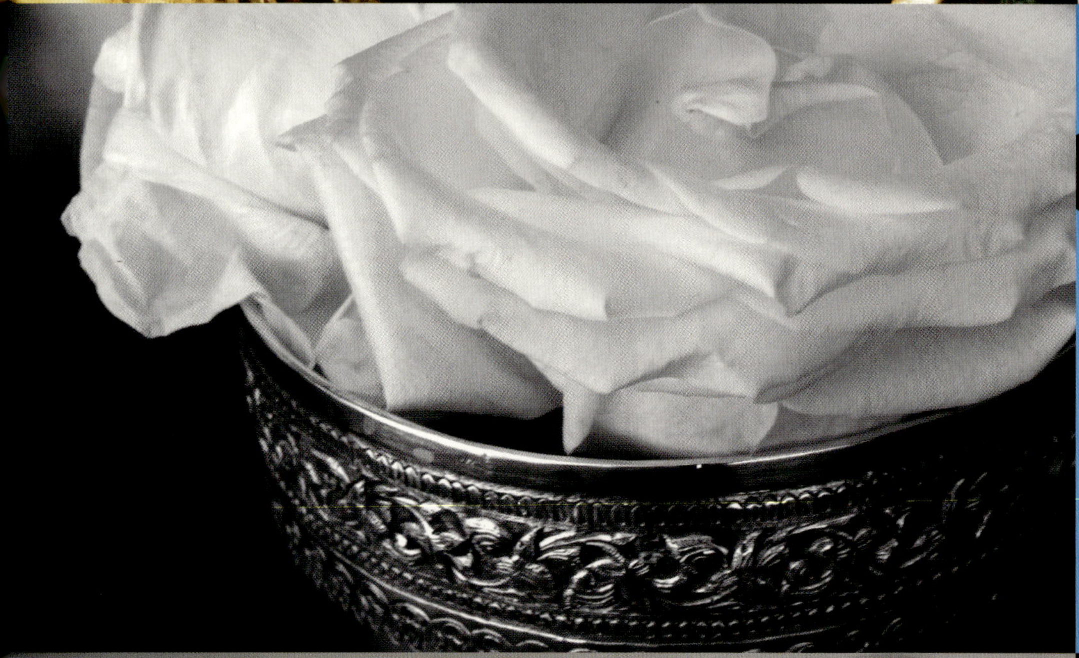
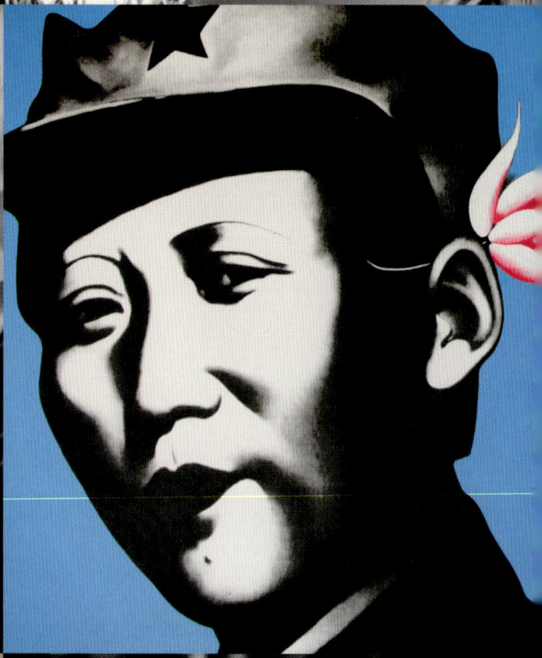
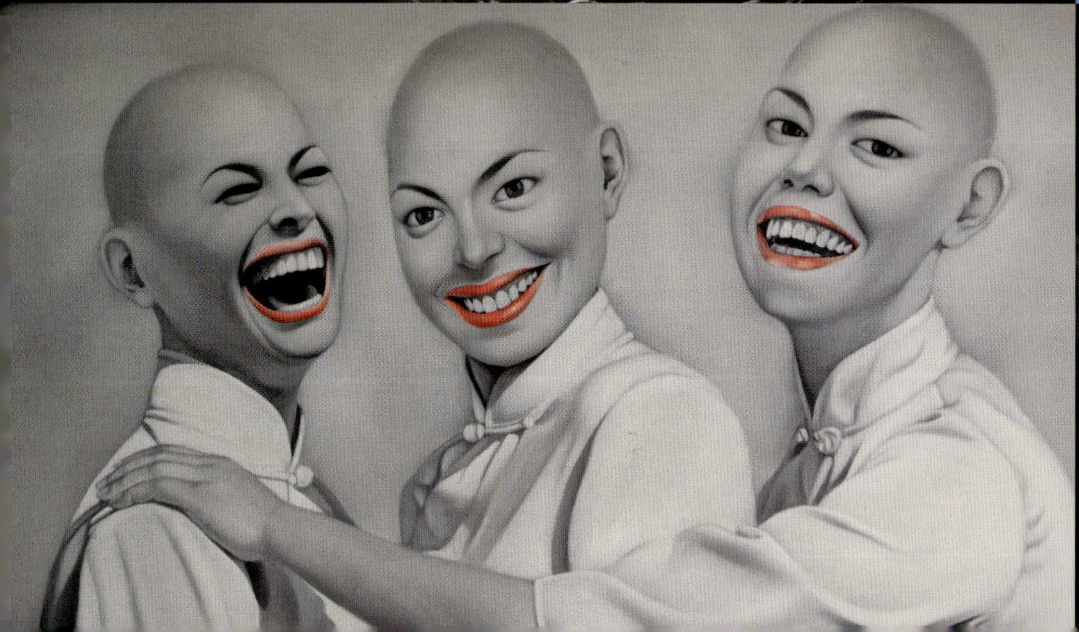
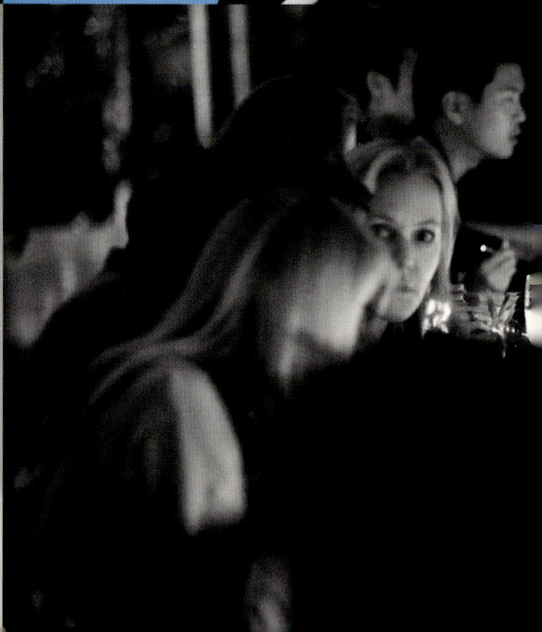

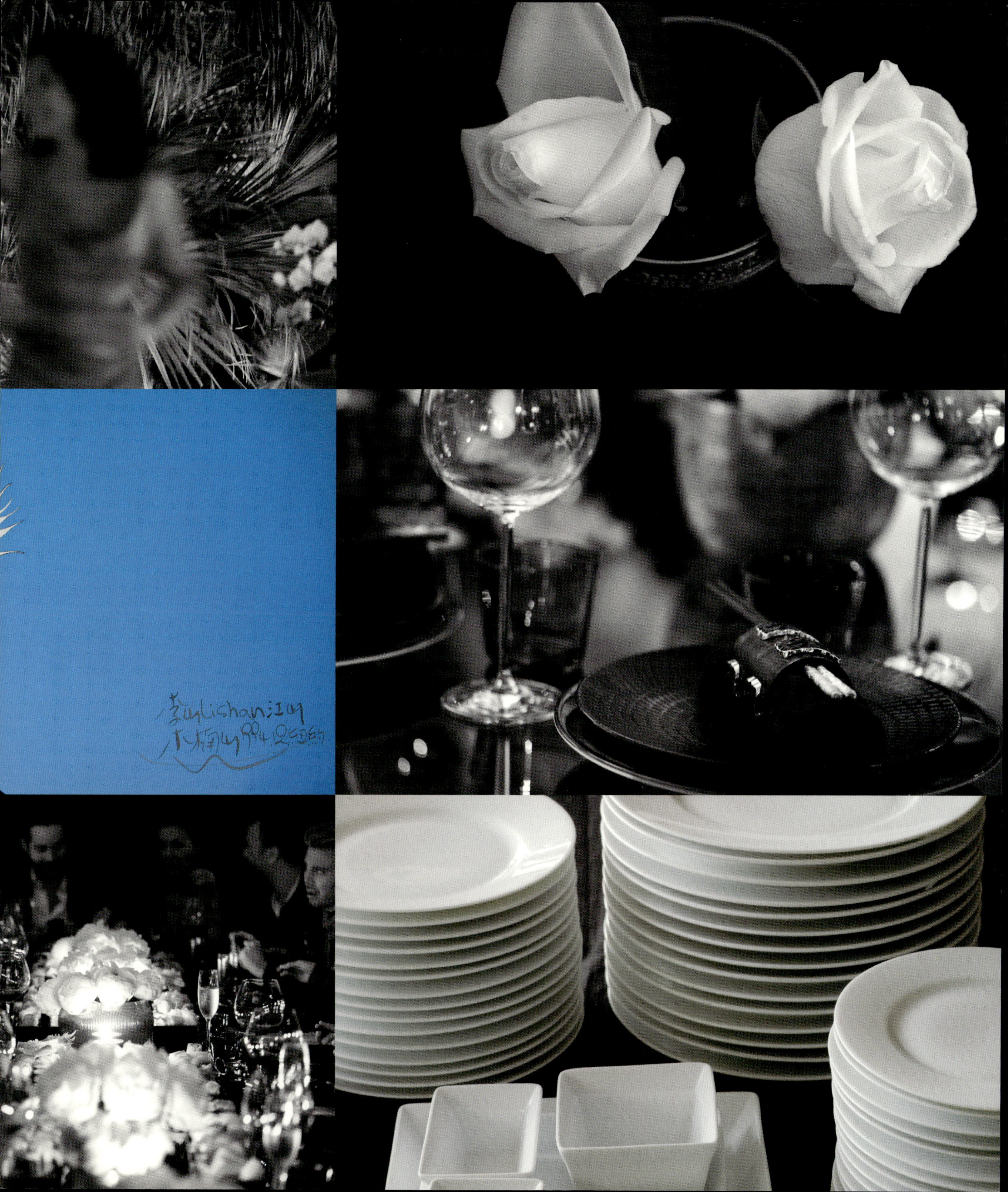

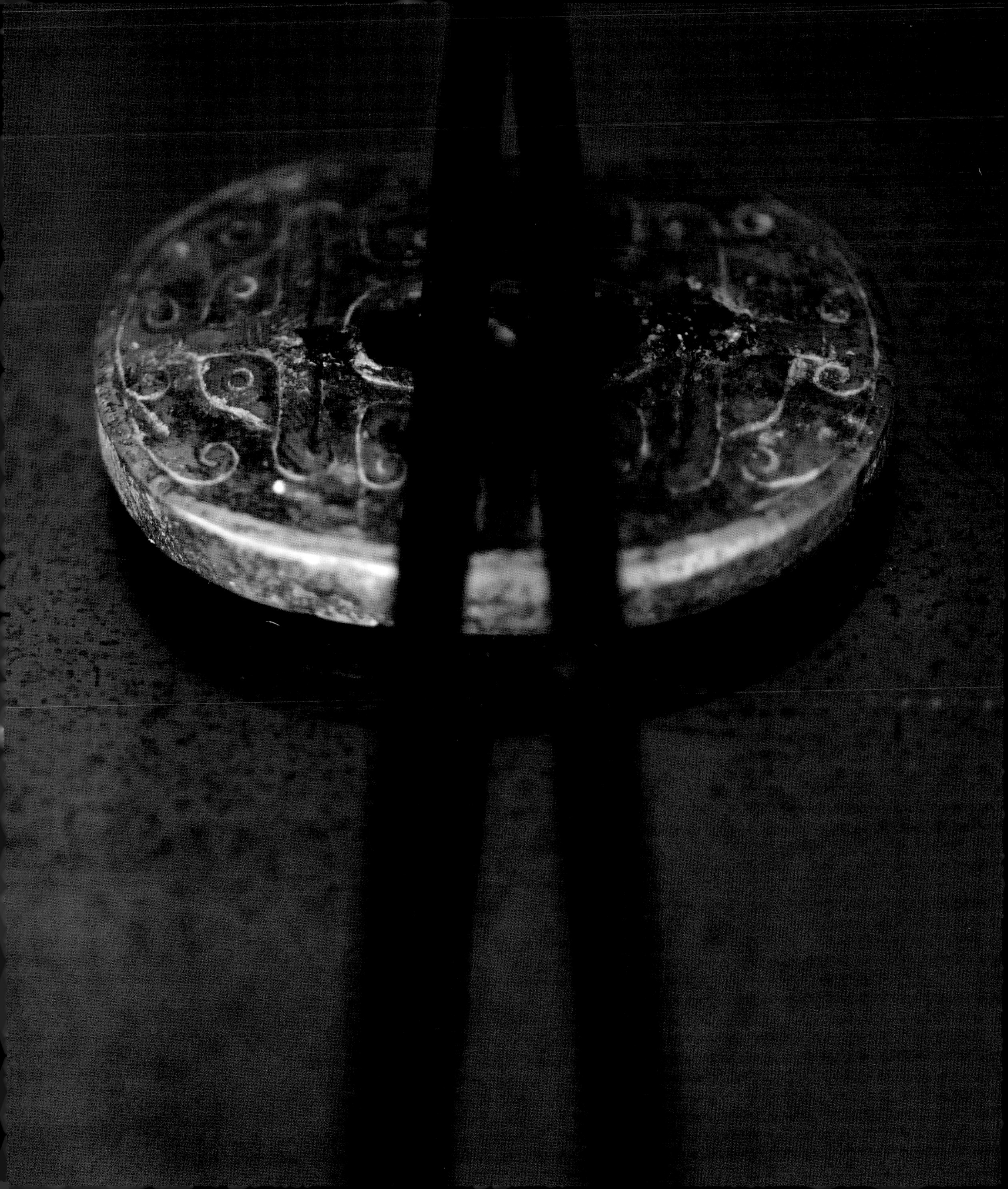

2
THE TABLE

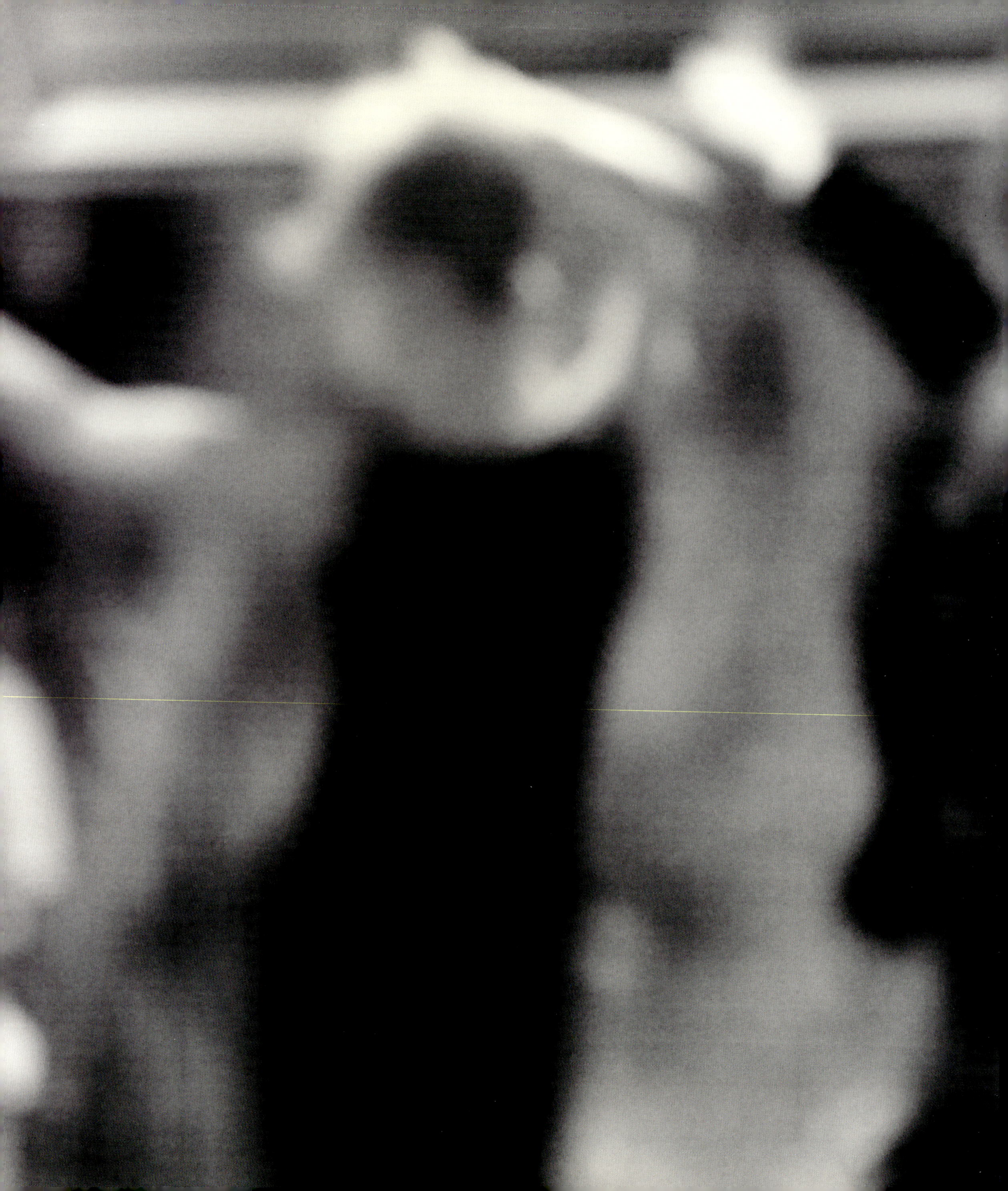

IT'S YOUR PARTY.
YOU SHOULD BE THE FIRST
TO DANCE ON
THE TABLES.

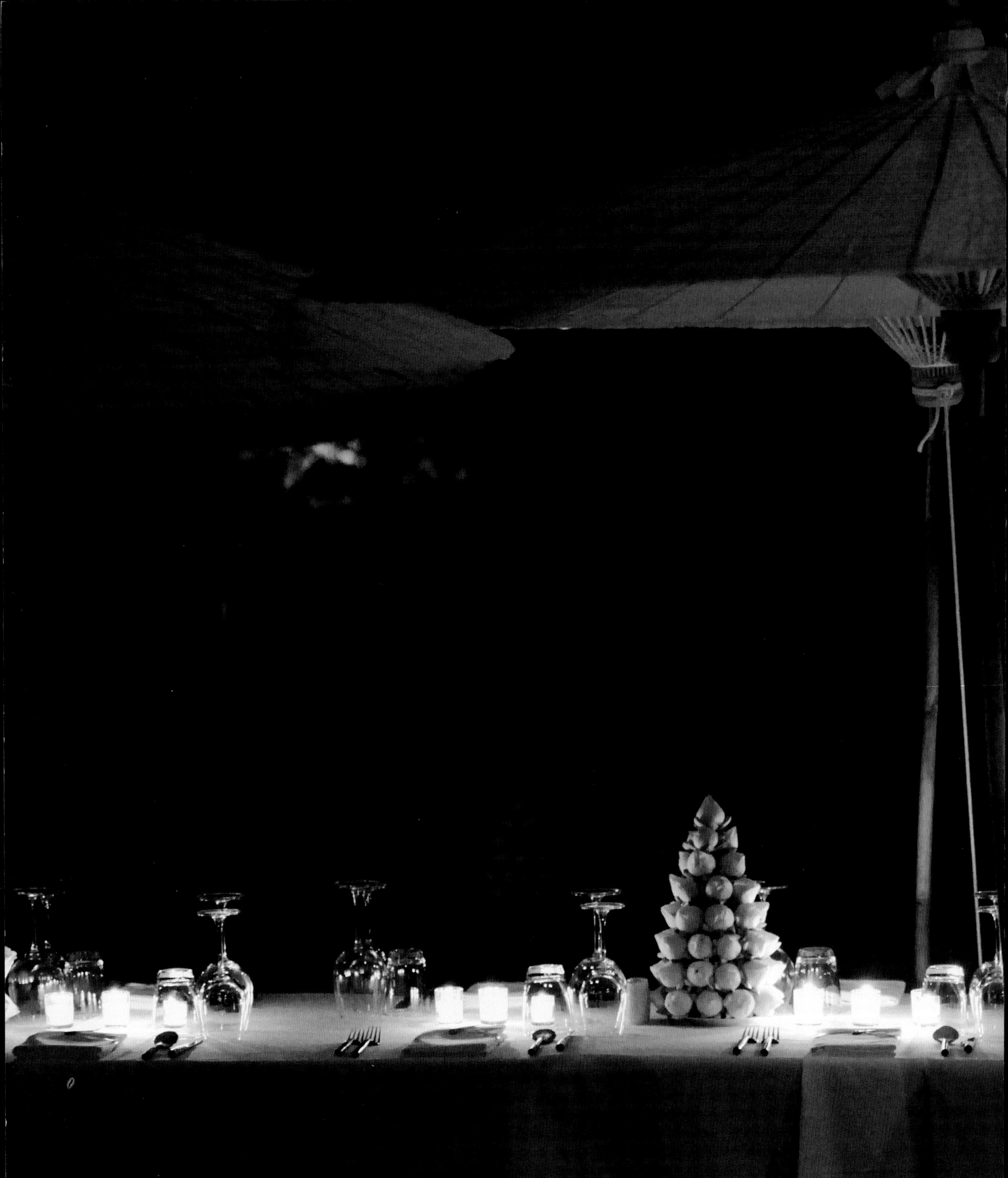

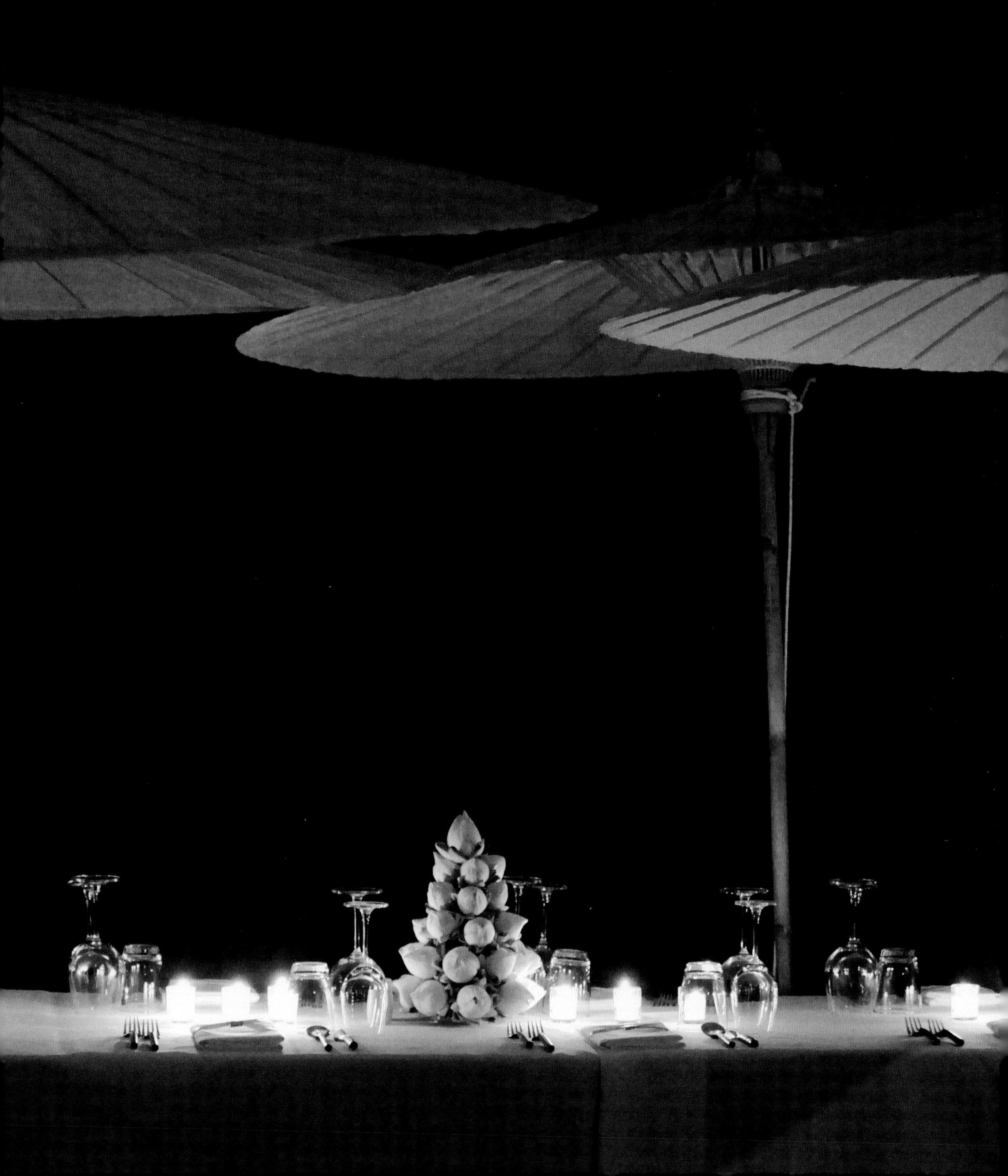

Look carefully at the picture on the preceding page. The table looks stylish, luxurious and intriguing, yet all the decoration has been done with plain, everyday objects. It's a testament to the power of simplicity in creating a beautiful and interesting table.

Simple ingredients, carefully combined, can generate tremendous glamour. The idea is to conjure maximum ambience; it is not about showing off. Inexpensive white plates, plain wine glasses, linen napkins and ordinary stainless-steel cutlery can – with the addition of flowers, candles and a few personal touches – make magic.

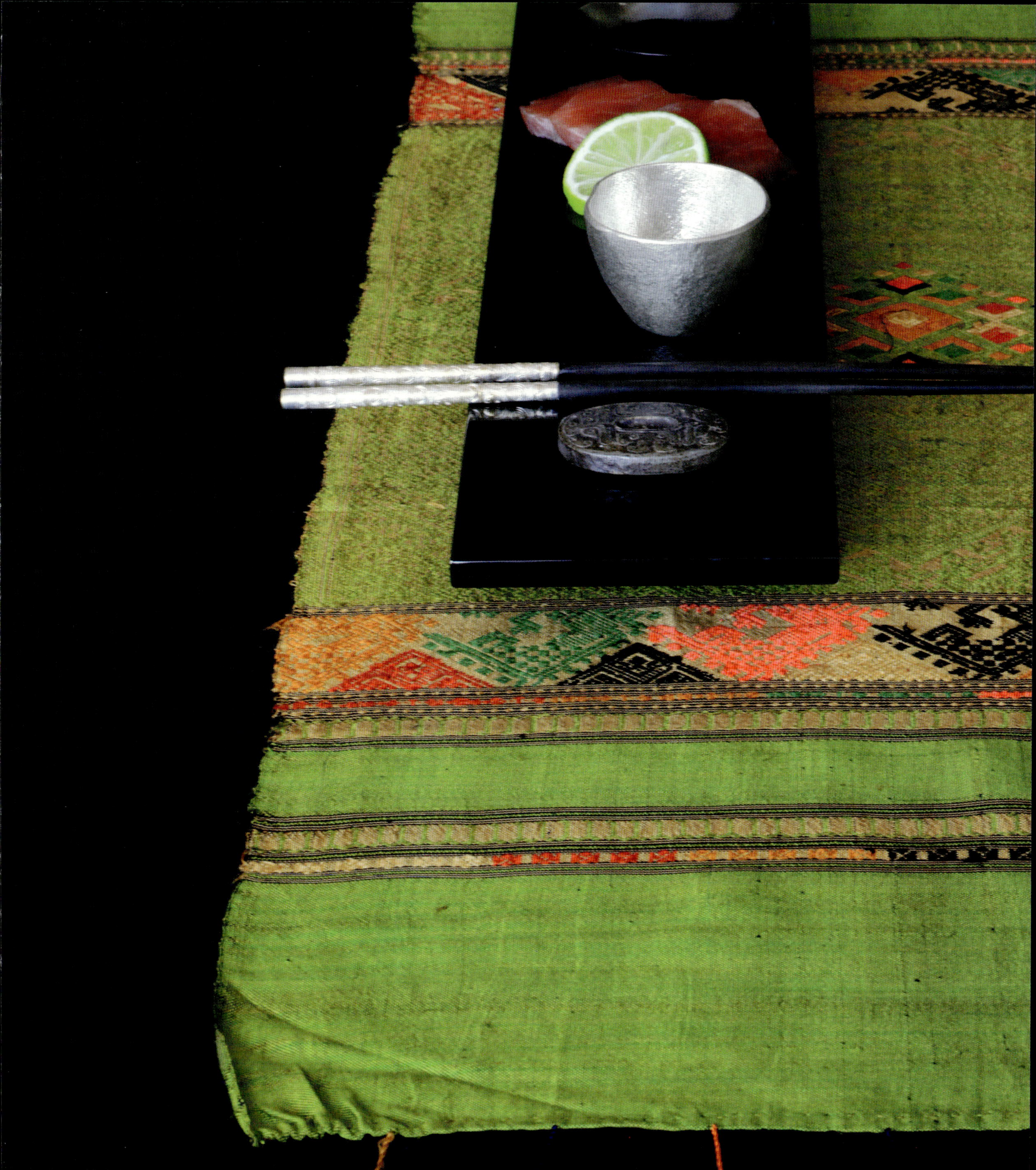

THE TABLE

THE TABLE

THE TABLE

THE TABLE

COLLECT INTERESTING THINGS
AND USE THEM ON YOUR TABLE.

THEY CAN BE A SUBJECT
FOR CONVERSATION,
AND FRIENDS WILL
ALWAYS KNOW WHAT
TO BUY FOR YOU.

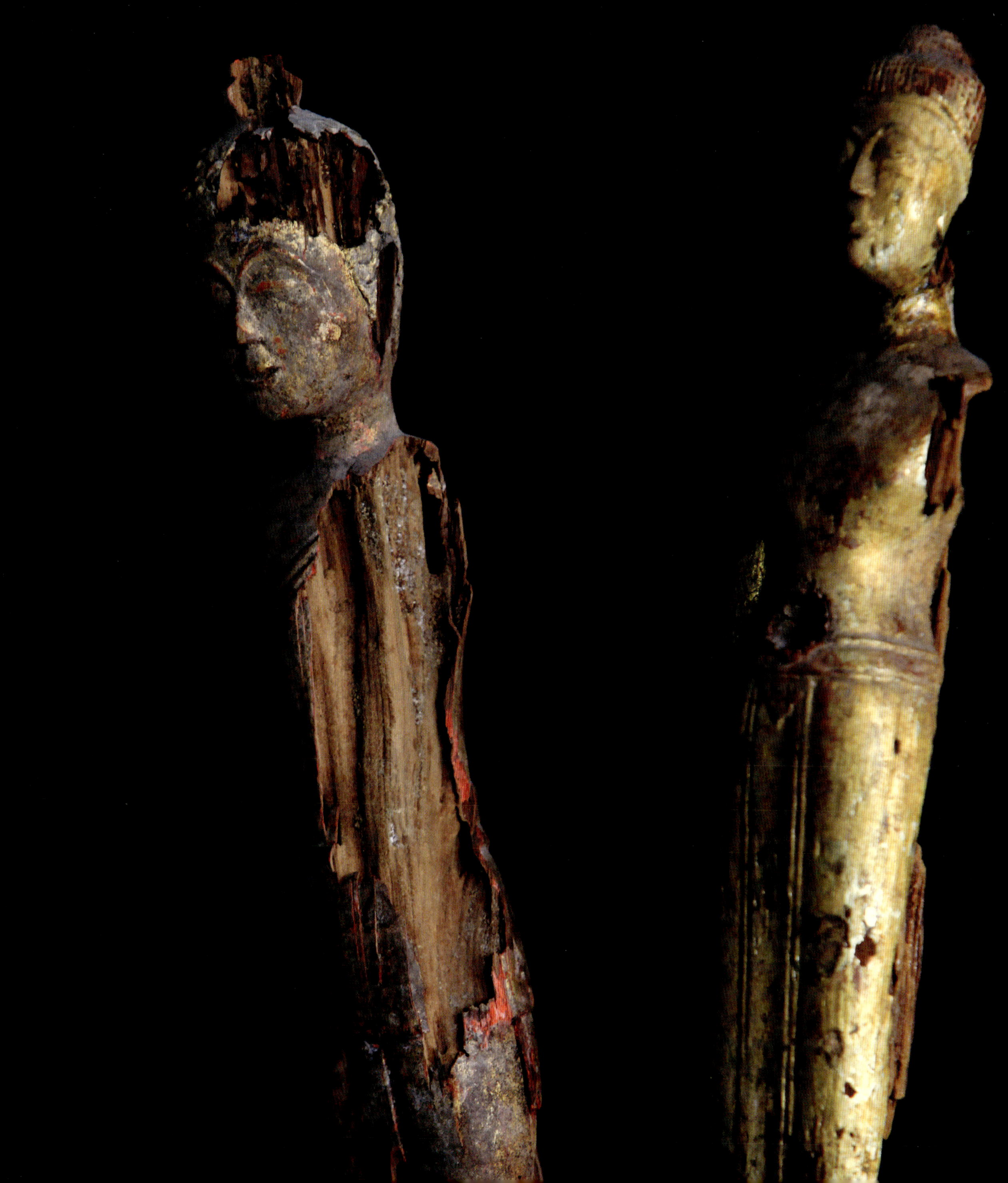

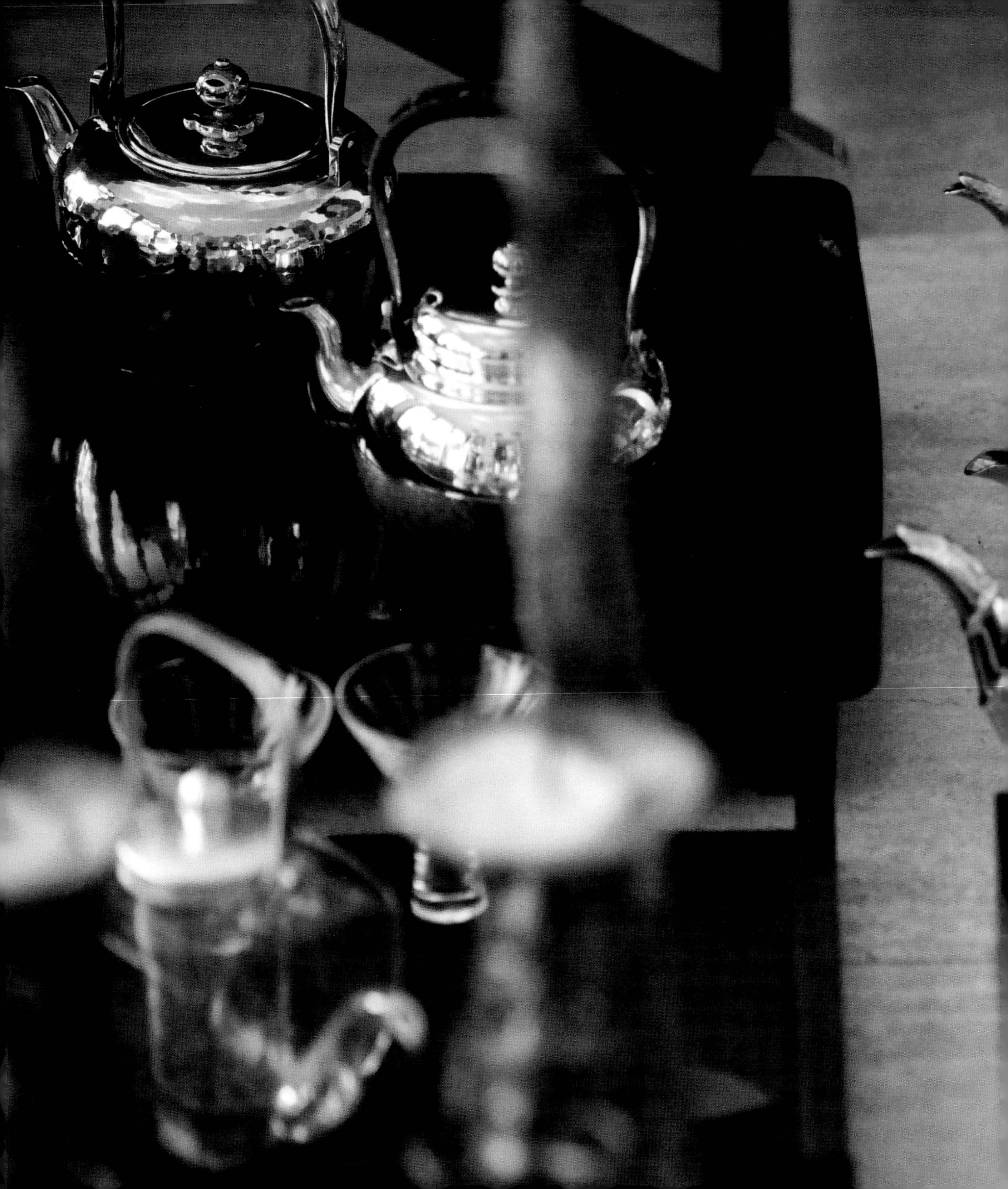

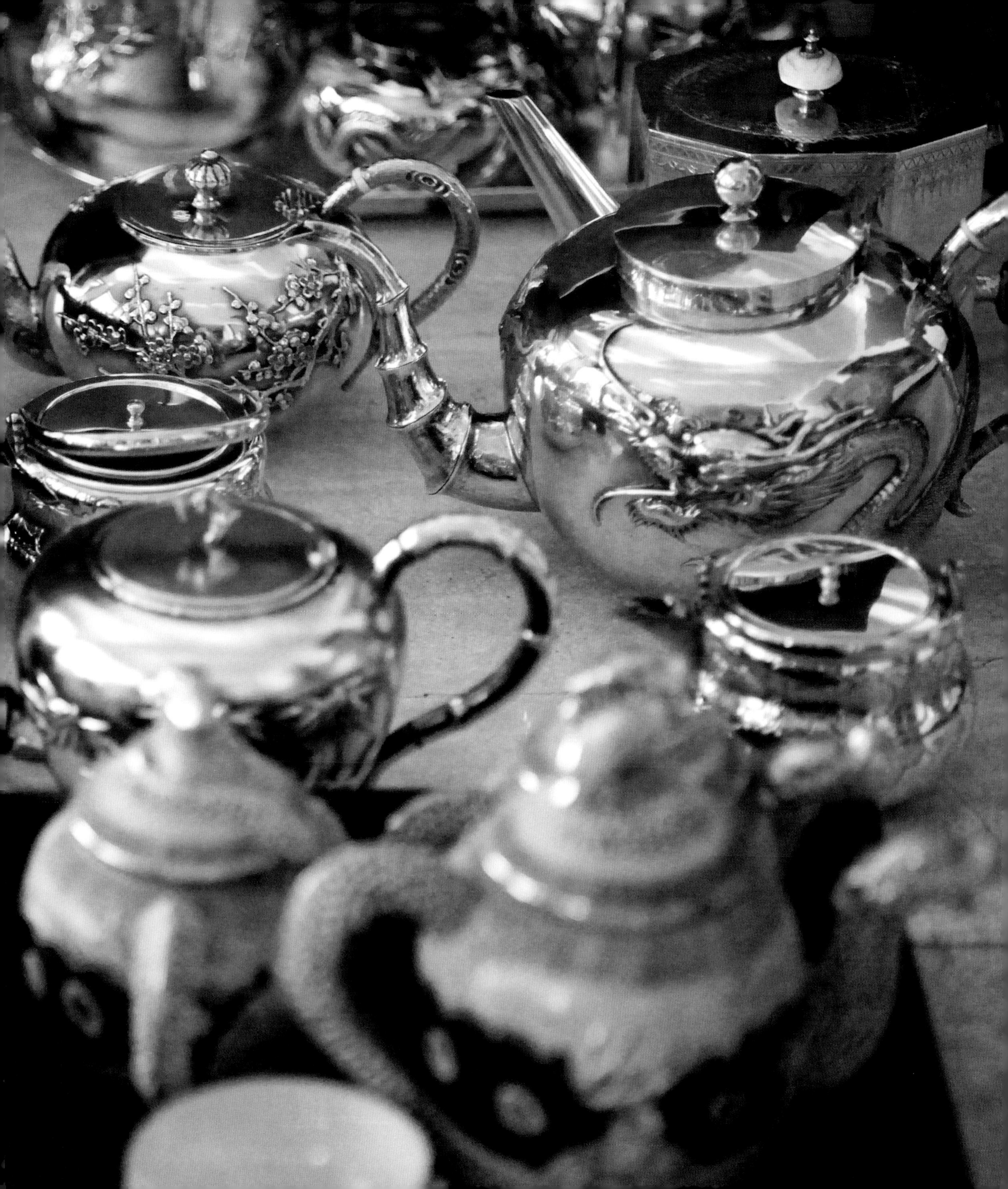

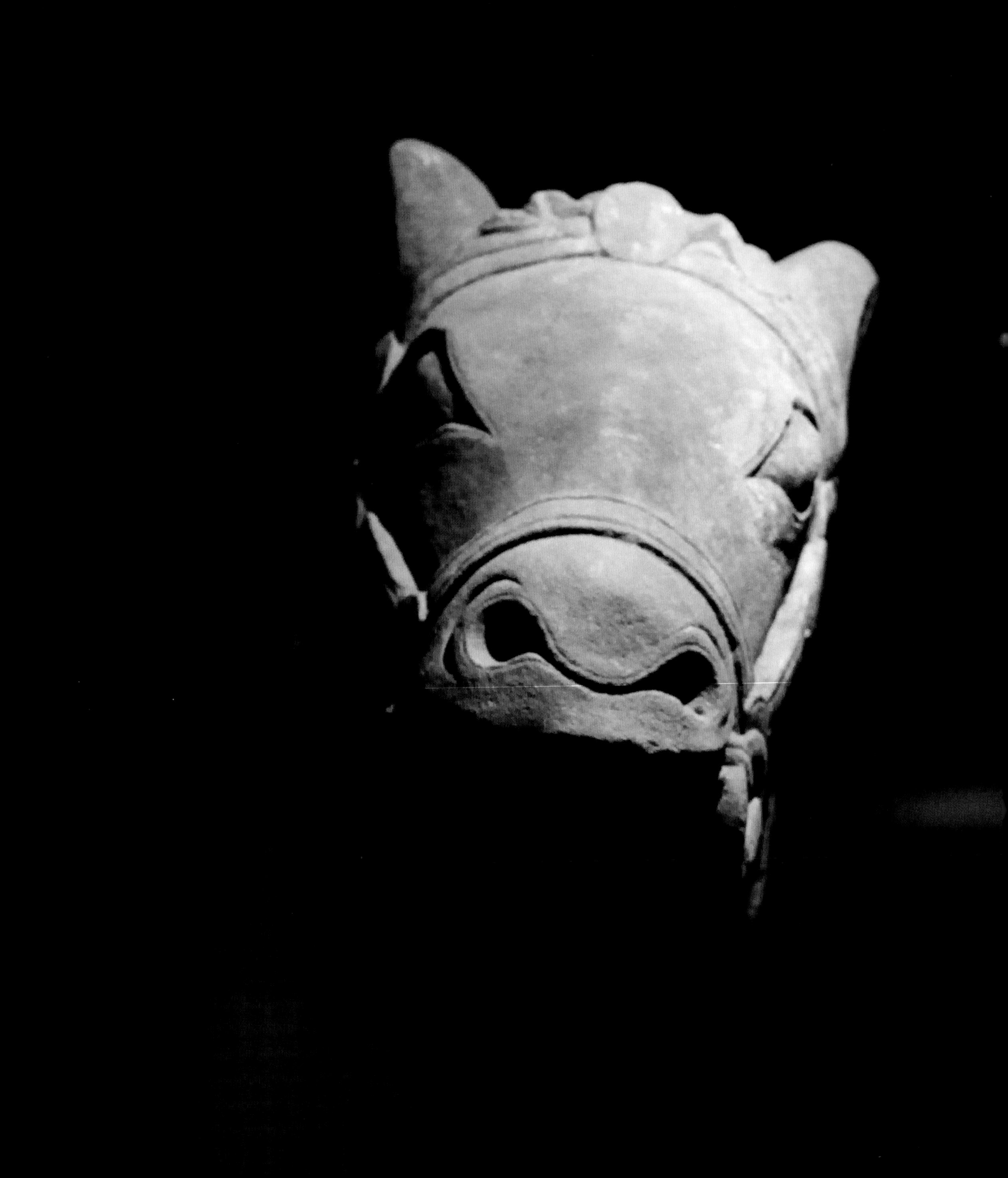

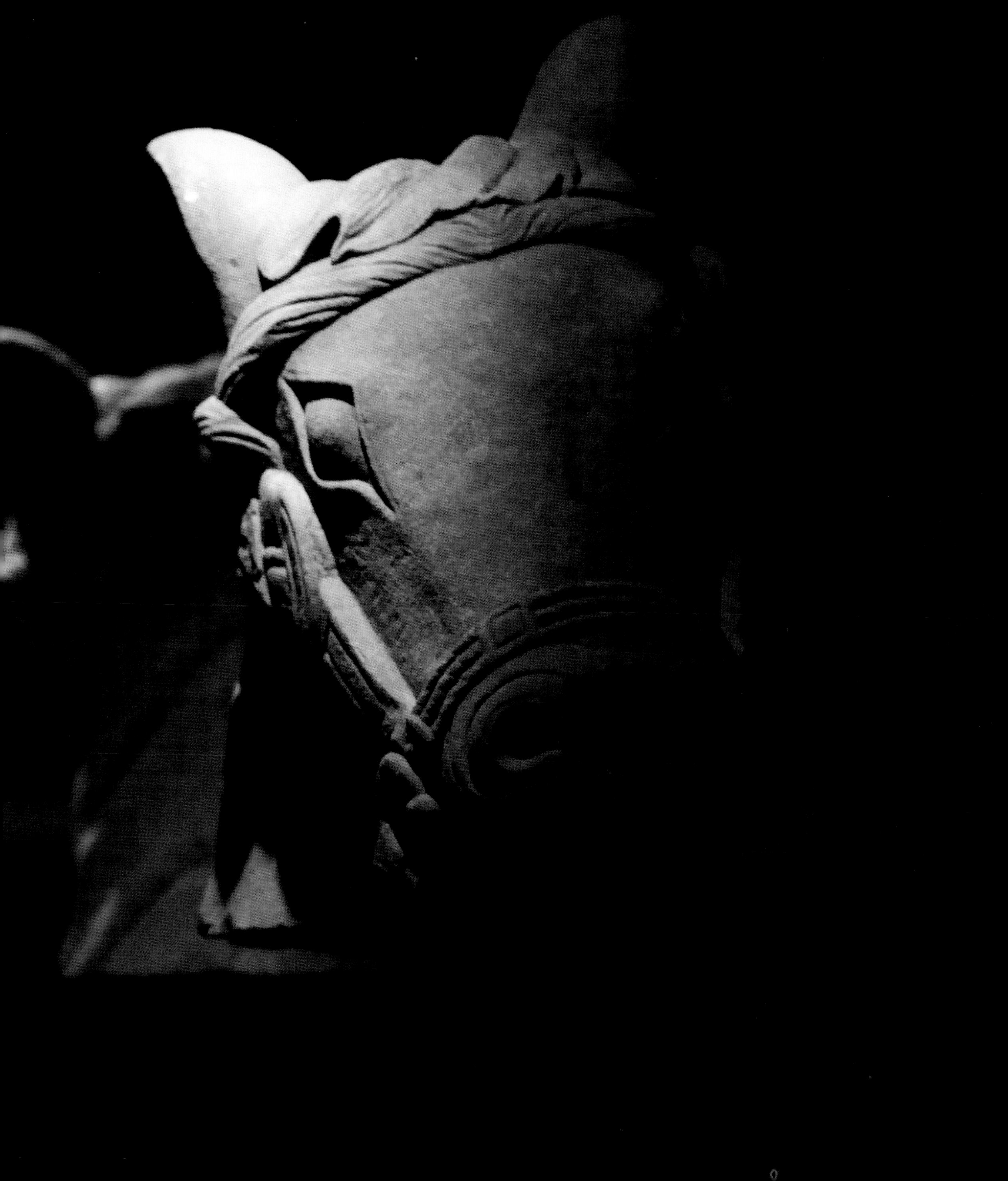

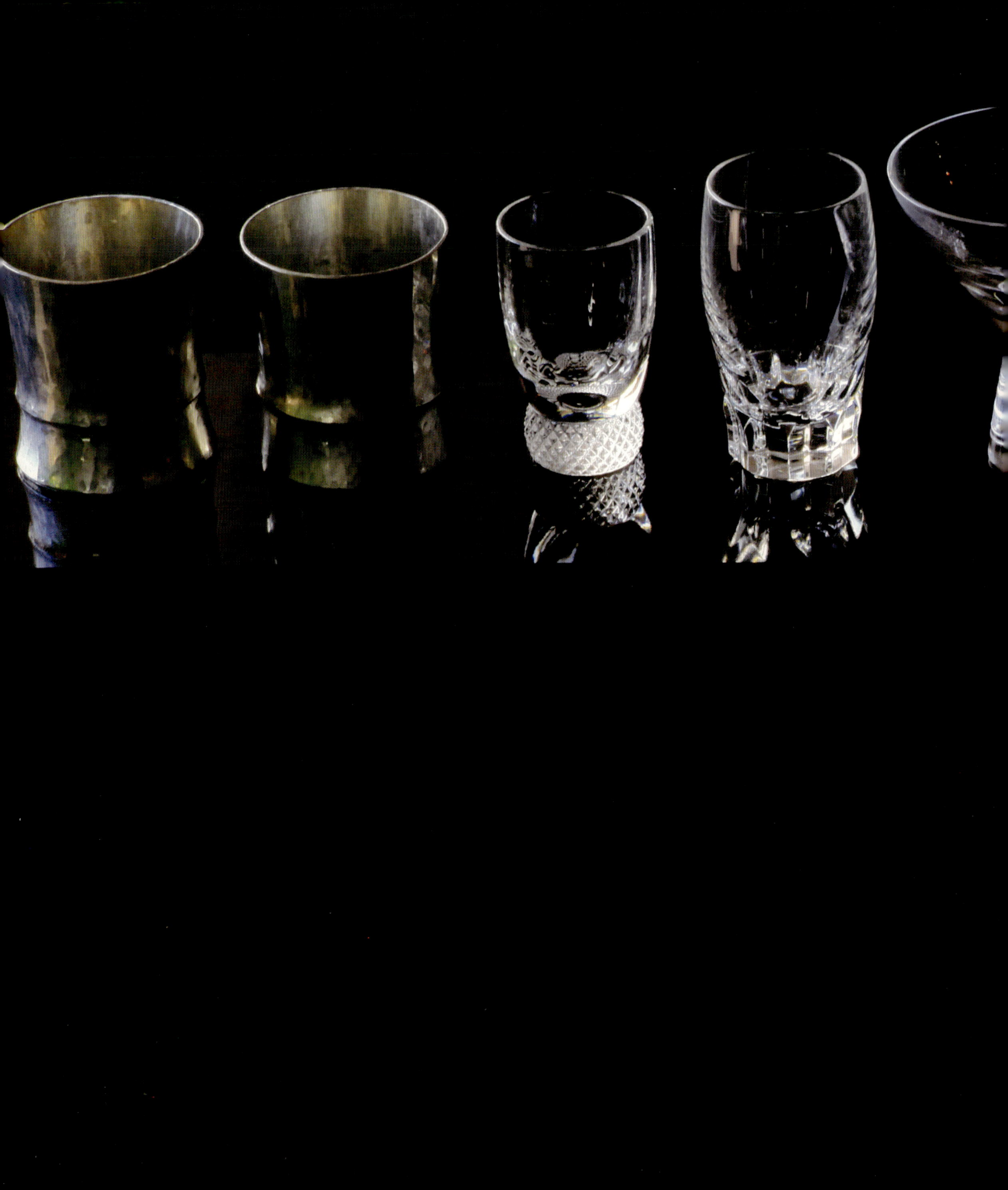

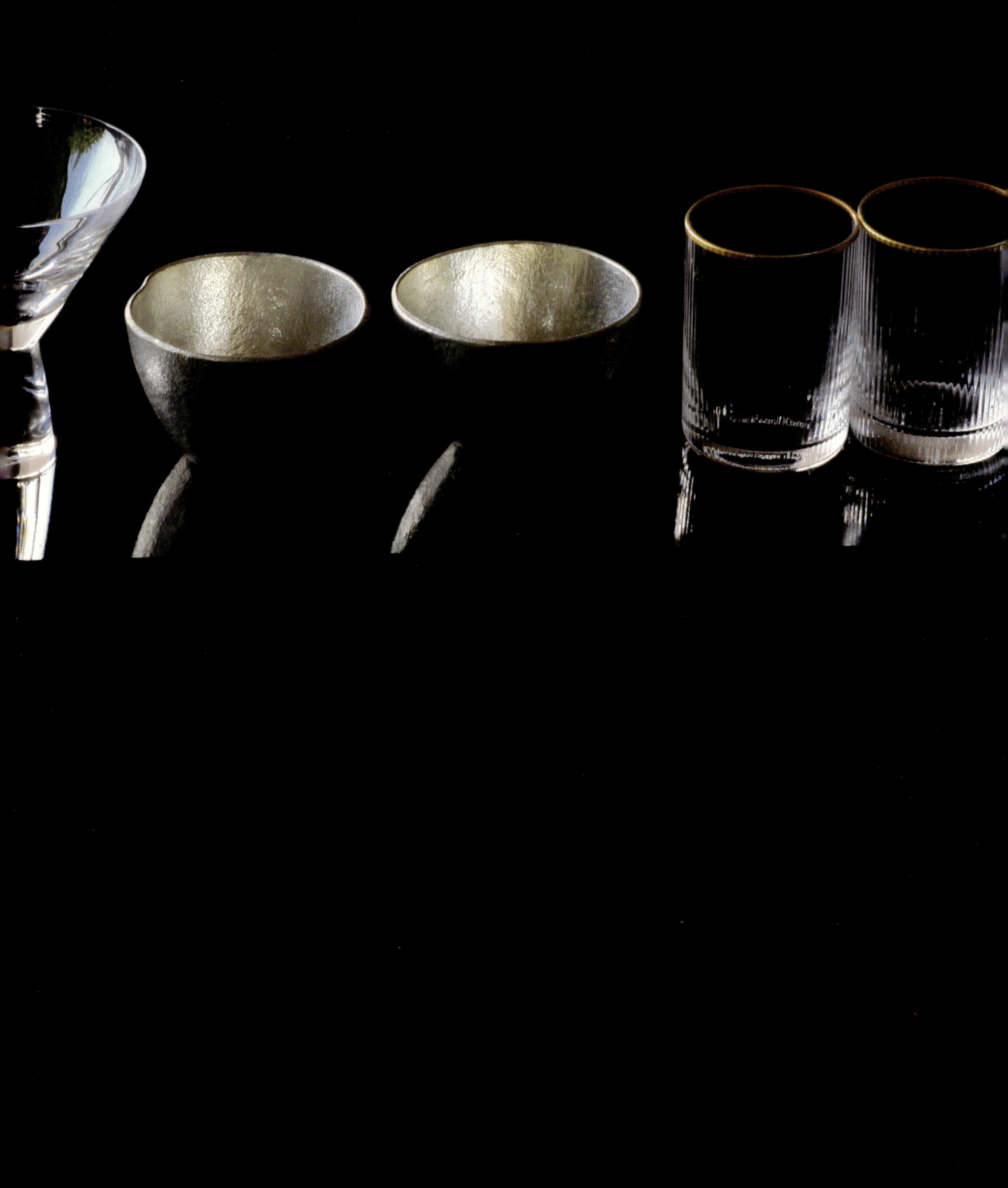

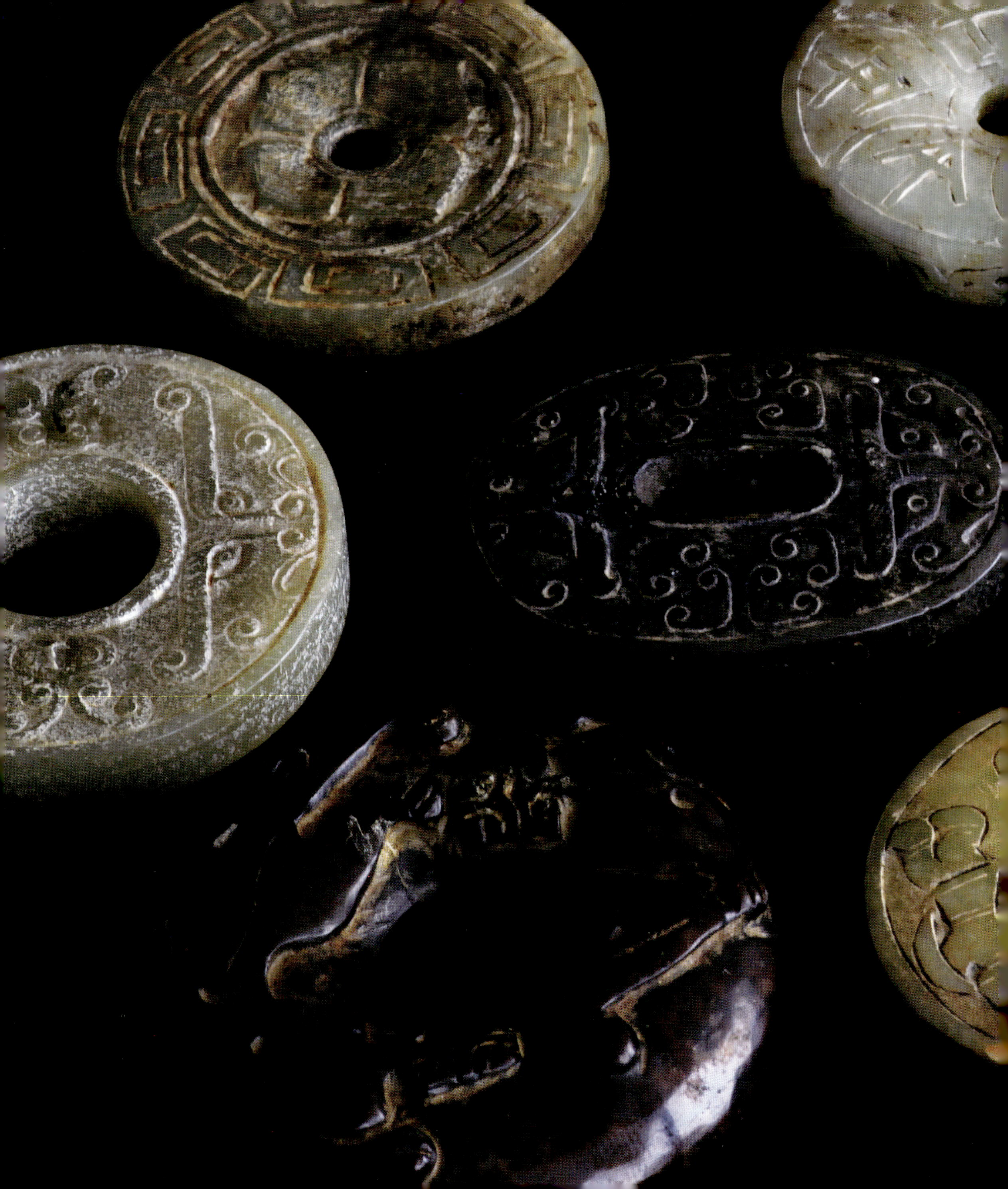

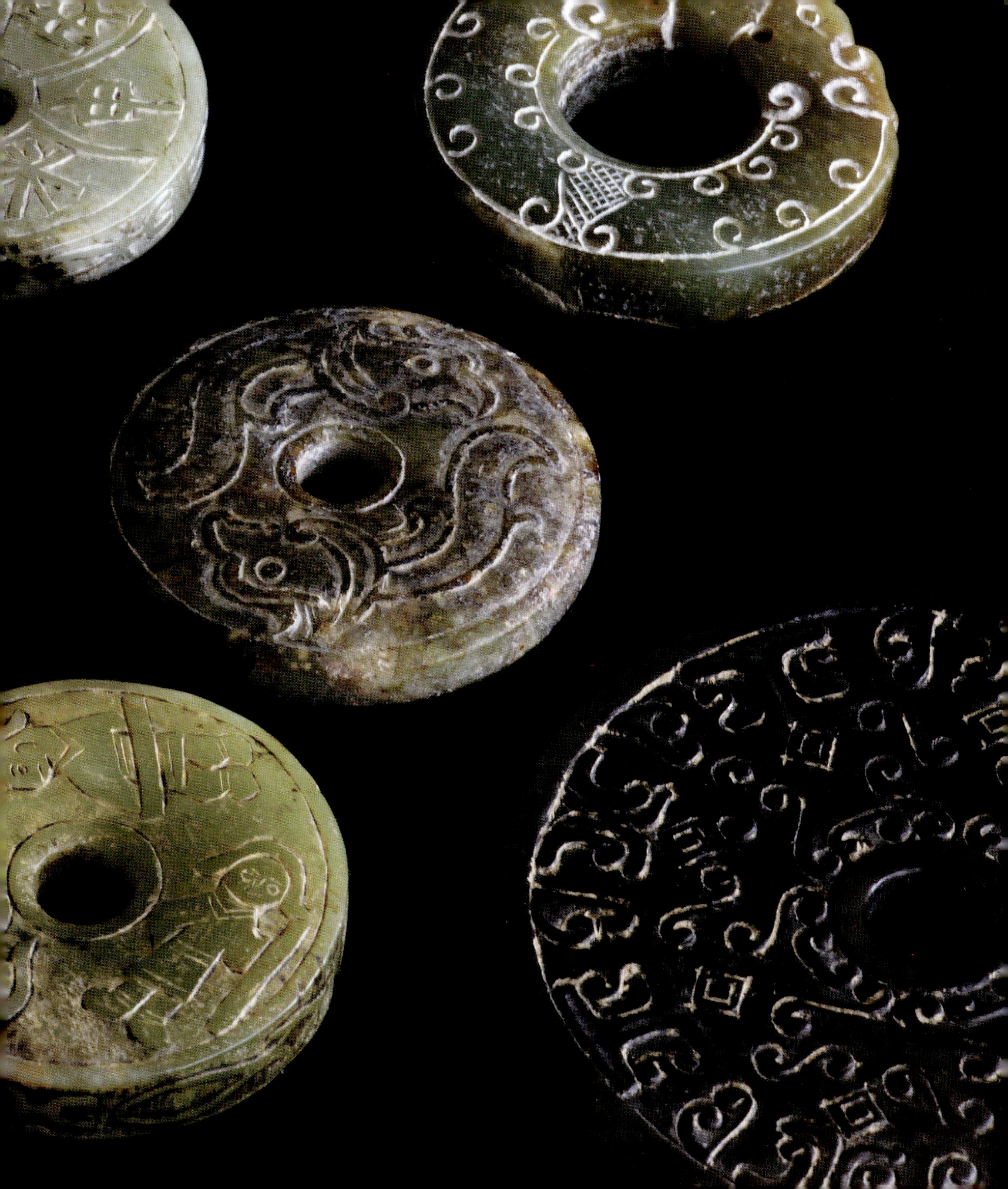

There's a shop in Tokyo that only sells chopsticks. Thousands of chopsticks. I could spend hours in there. My family hates it exactly for that reason. But you can never have too much of one good thing on a table.

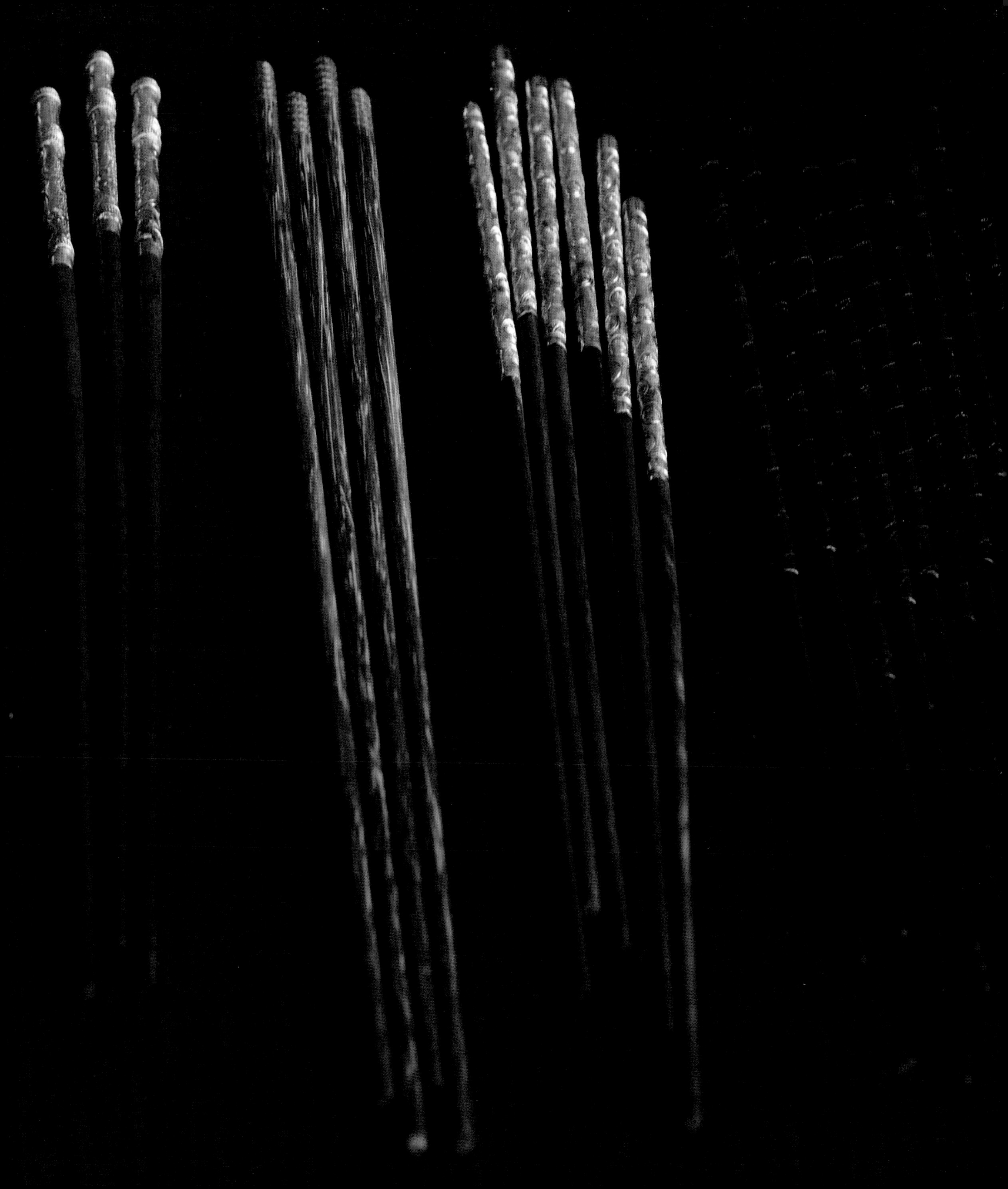

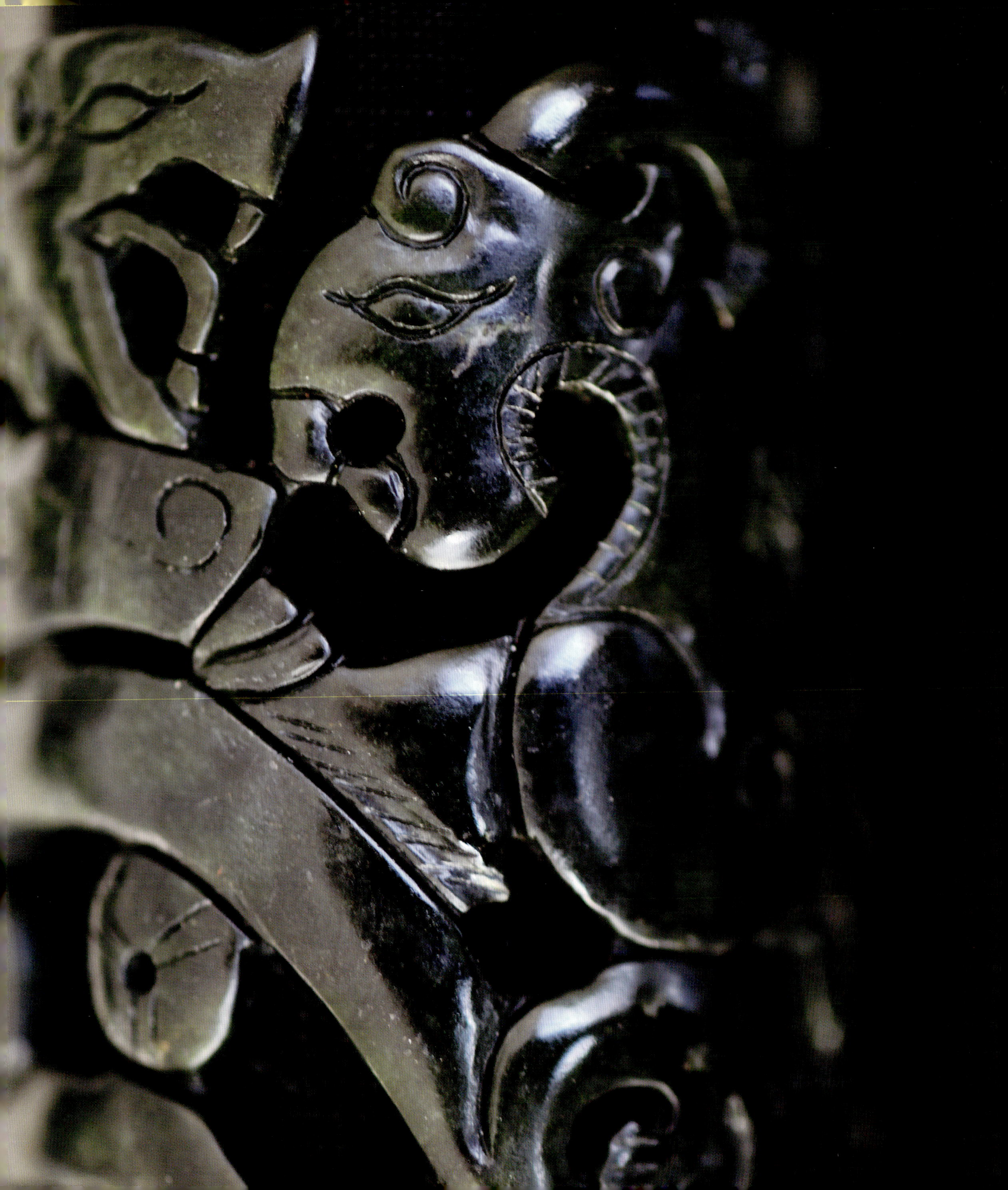

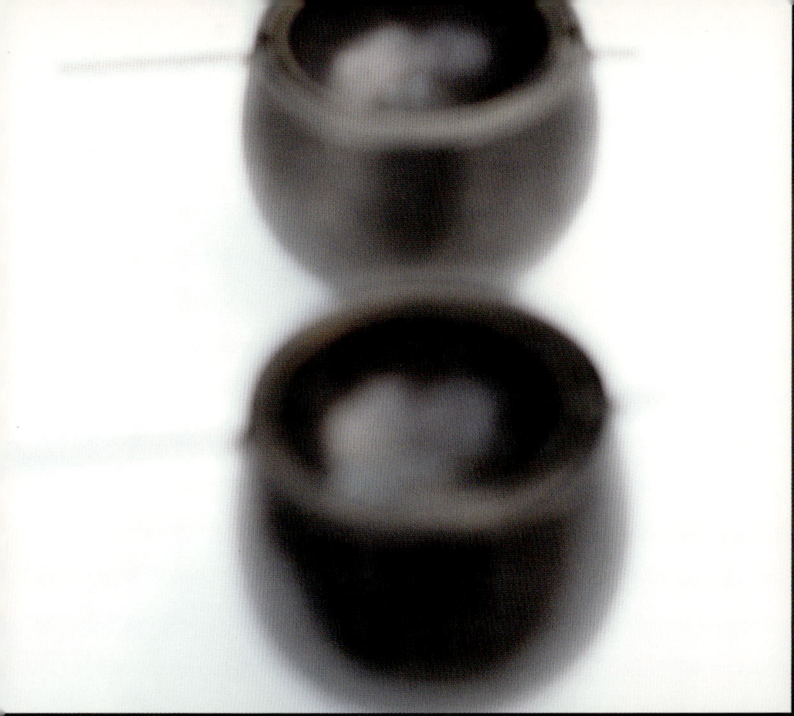
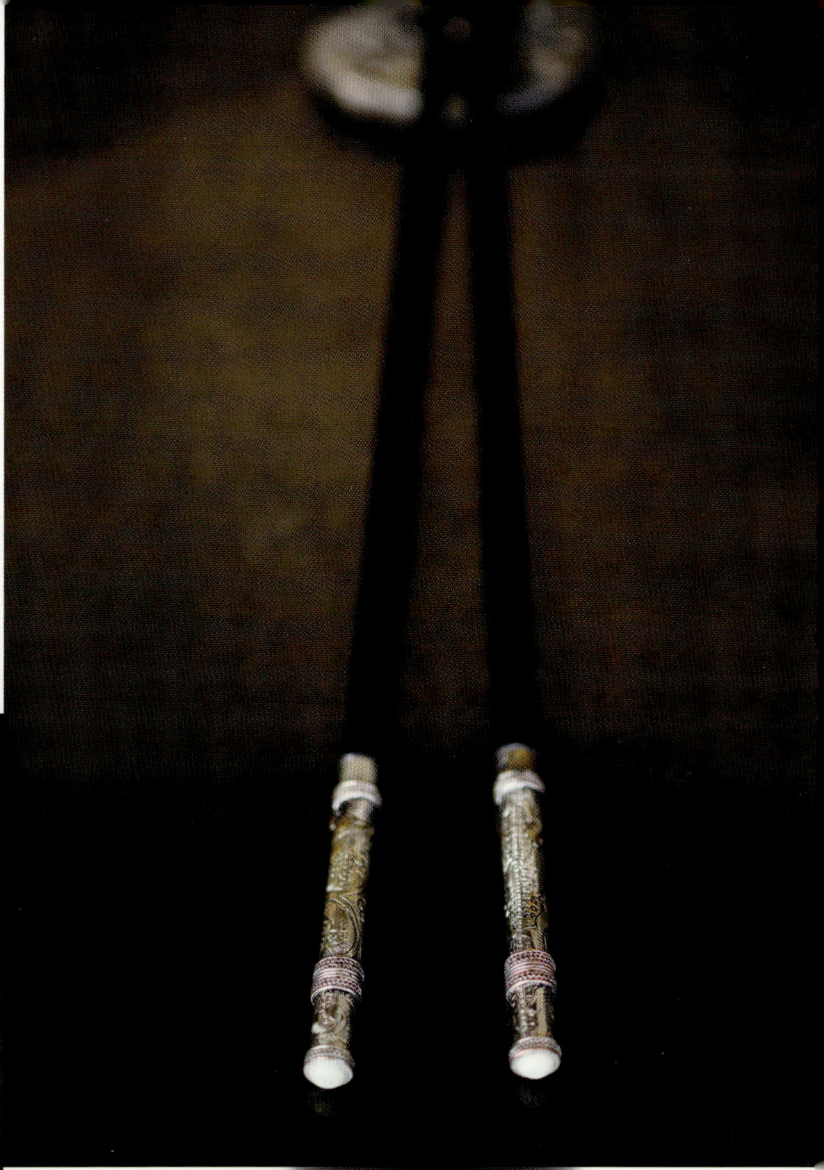
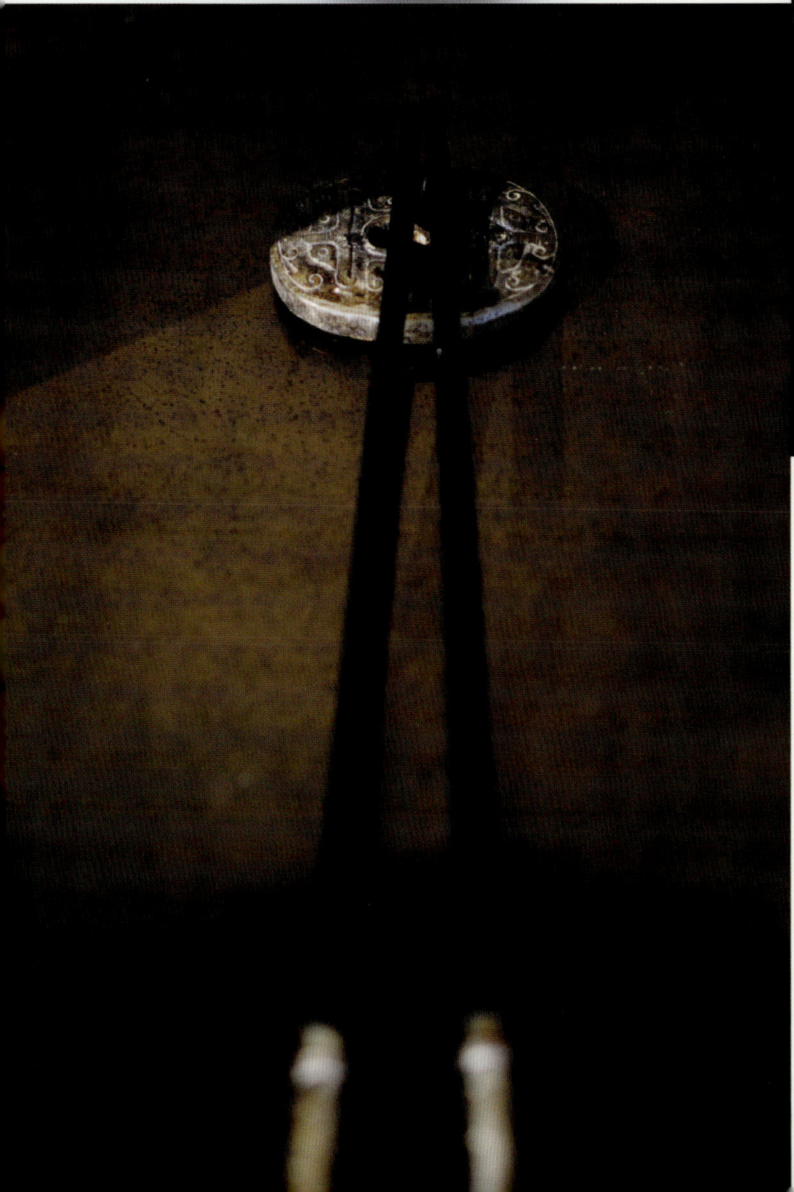
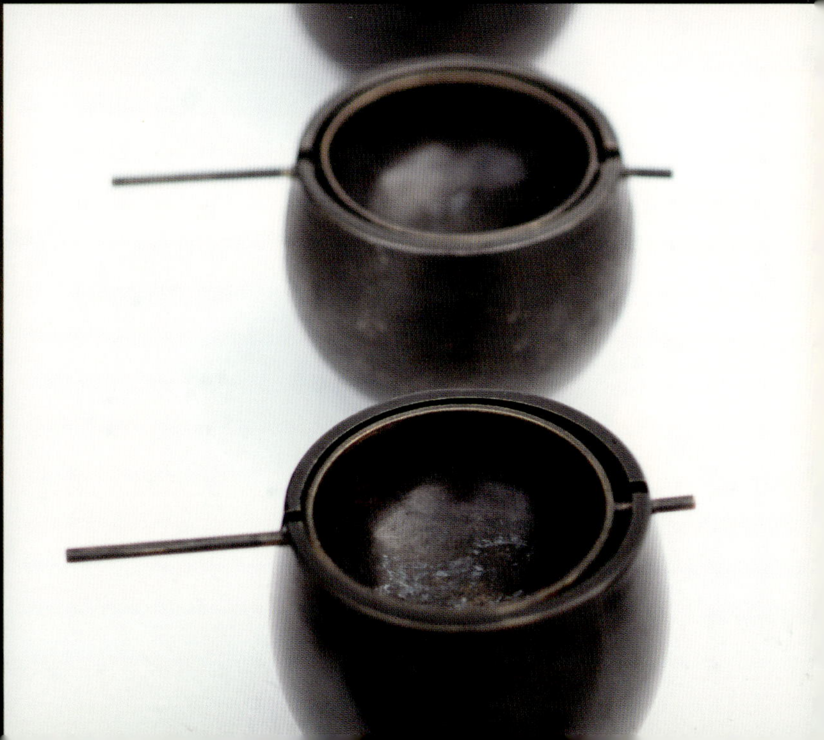

THE TABLE IN PRACTICE: NEW YEAR'S EVE POOL PARTY

Not all pool parties need to look like Spring Break.

It is possible to use a pool as an elegant setting for a memorable dinner. I did it for New Year's Eve last year. We had four tables of ten guests arranged alongside a swimming pool filled with white orchids. (This sounds extravagant, but in Asia it's not.) The tables were cheap slabs of plywood on trestles covered by tablecloths, with simple sheets of mirror laid on top. The reflection added sparkle and multiplied the effect of the flowers and the candles. The most dramatic component, as it always should be, was the lighting: moody and subdued, with a hidden ultraviolet light adding an exotic glow to the night.

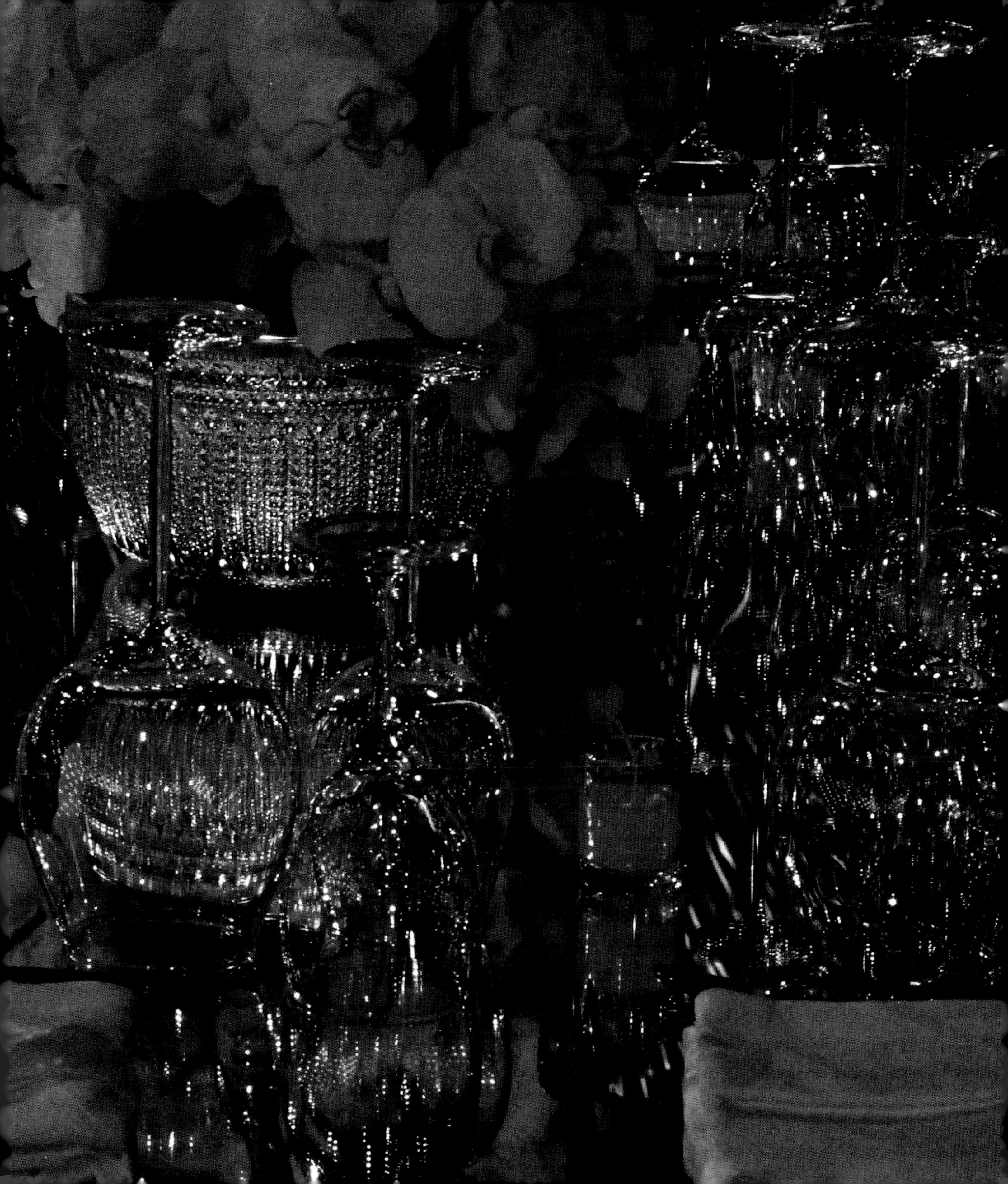

THE TABLE

THE TABLE

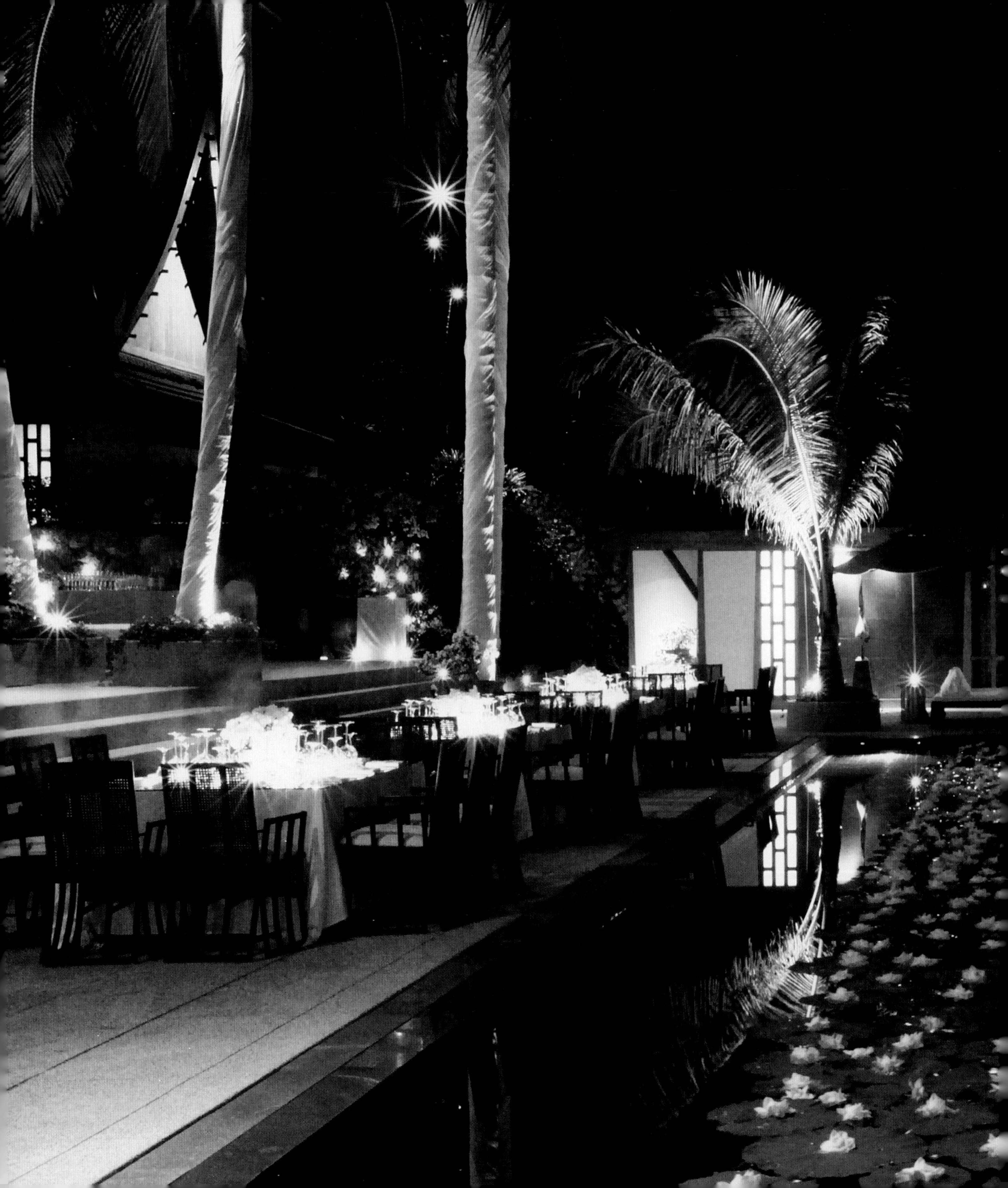

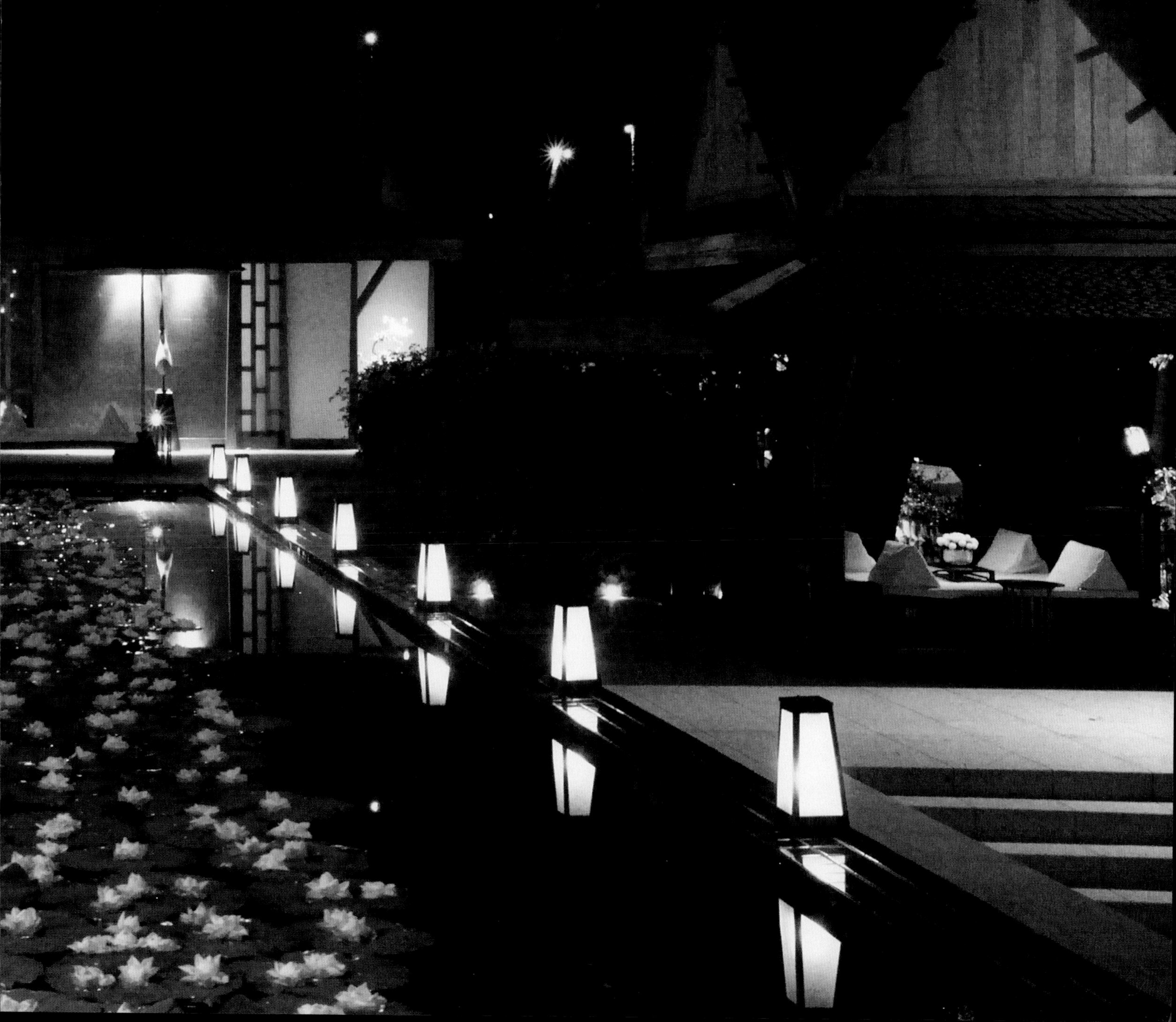

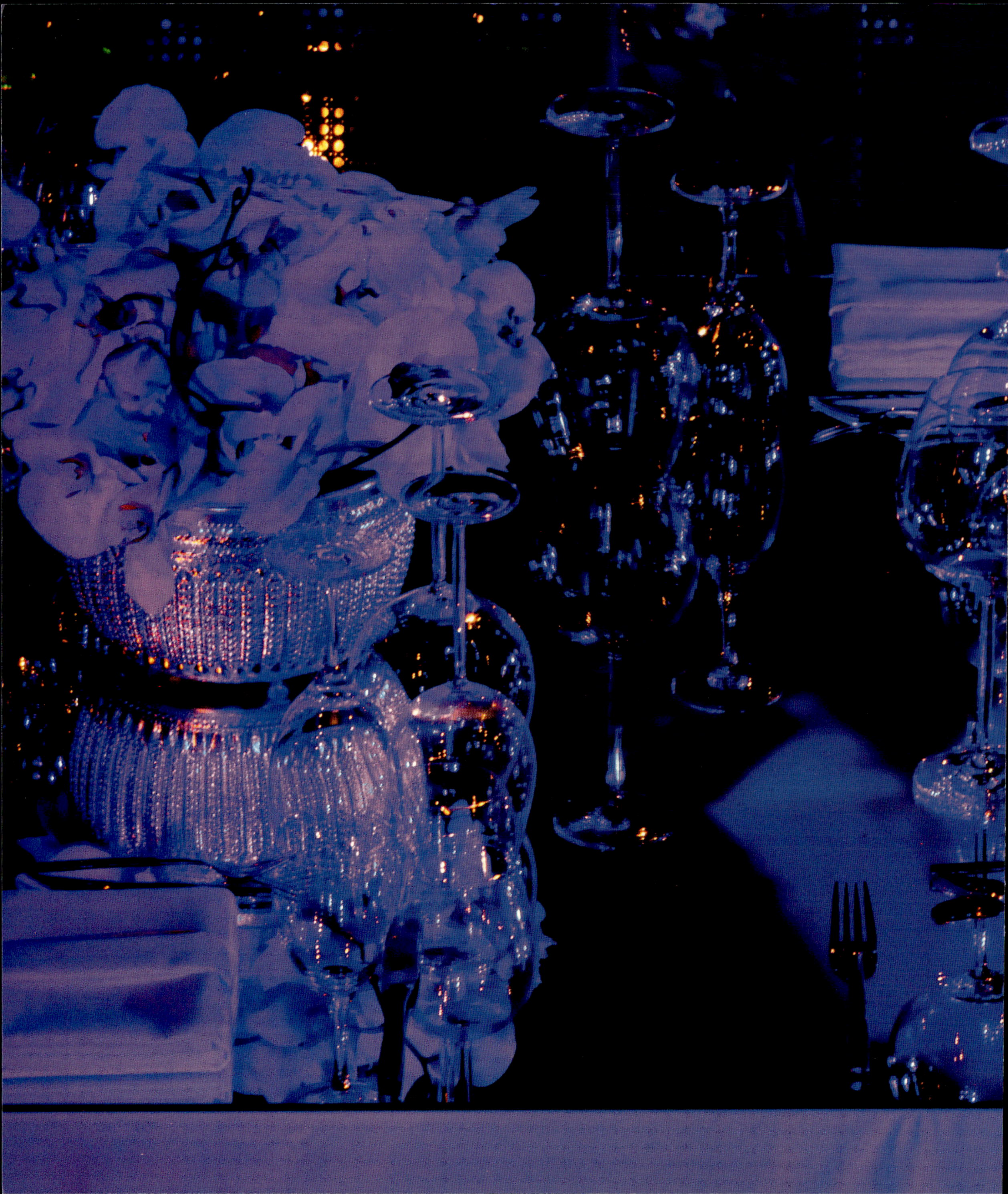

CREATE REFLECTIVE SURFACES.
A SIMPLE SHEET
OF MIRROR WILL DO.

THE TABLE IN PRACTICE: AN EIGHTIETH BIRTHDAY PARTY

There will always be a time when you have to entertain more people for dinner than your own house can hold.

Family reunions, birthdays, anniversaries, holiday celebrations: these events are too important to try to squeeze into an inappropriately small venue.

My mother-in-law had an eightieth birthday coming up and the idea was to invite thirty-four friends and family to a special sit-down dinner. No one had a room big enough and since it was in October in Belgium, having it outside was not really an option.

Even though I live in Hong Kong, I came over to Belgium to organize the event. Through friends I had heard about a small medieval manor in the area with an orangerie for rent. It sounded glamorous but the 'orangerie' was really nothing more than a brick shed with high ceilings and a wall of windows on one side. Nonetheless, it had potential!

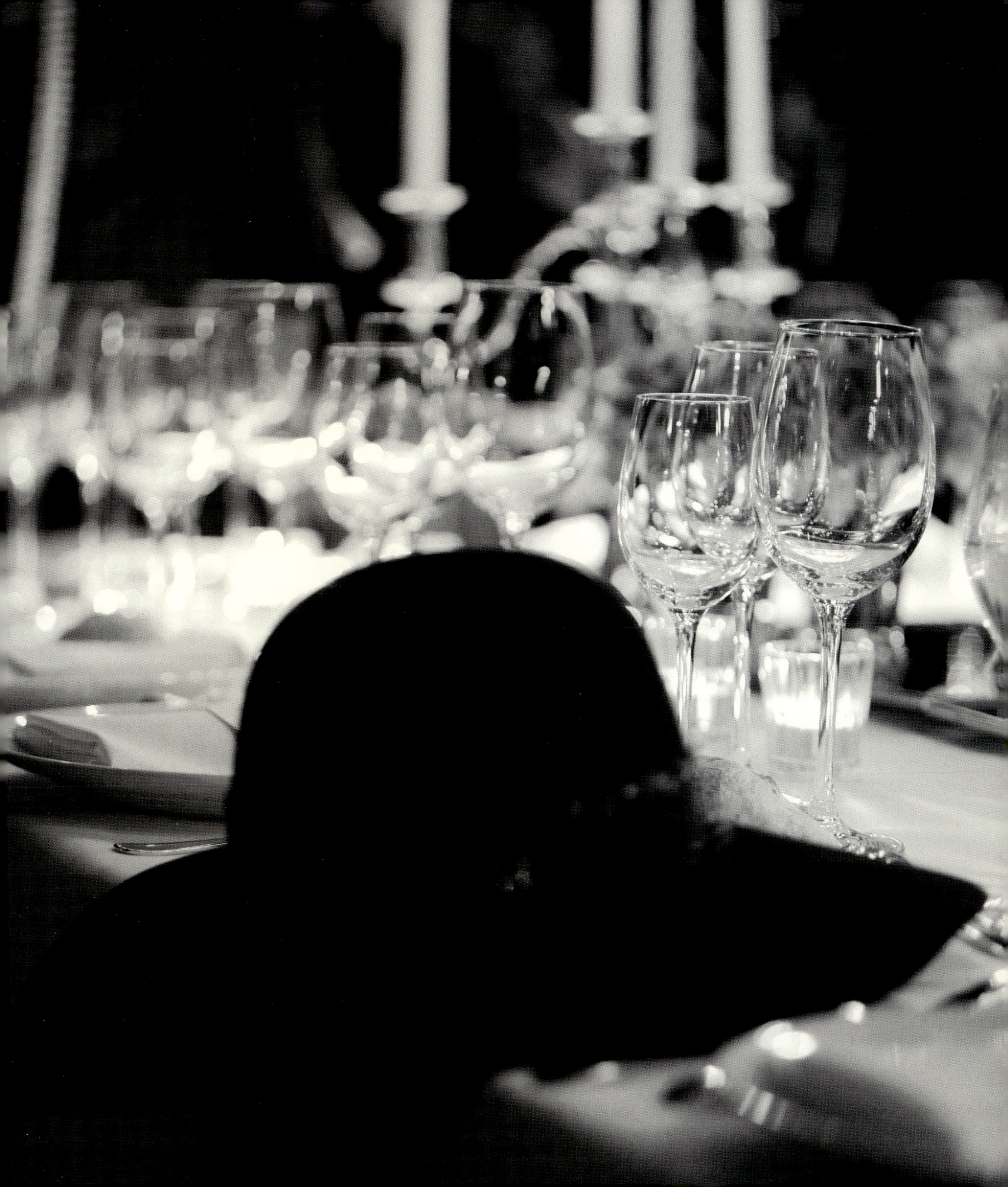

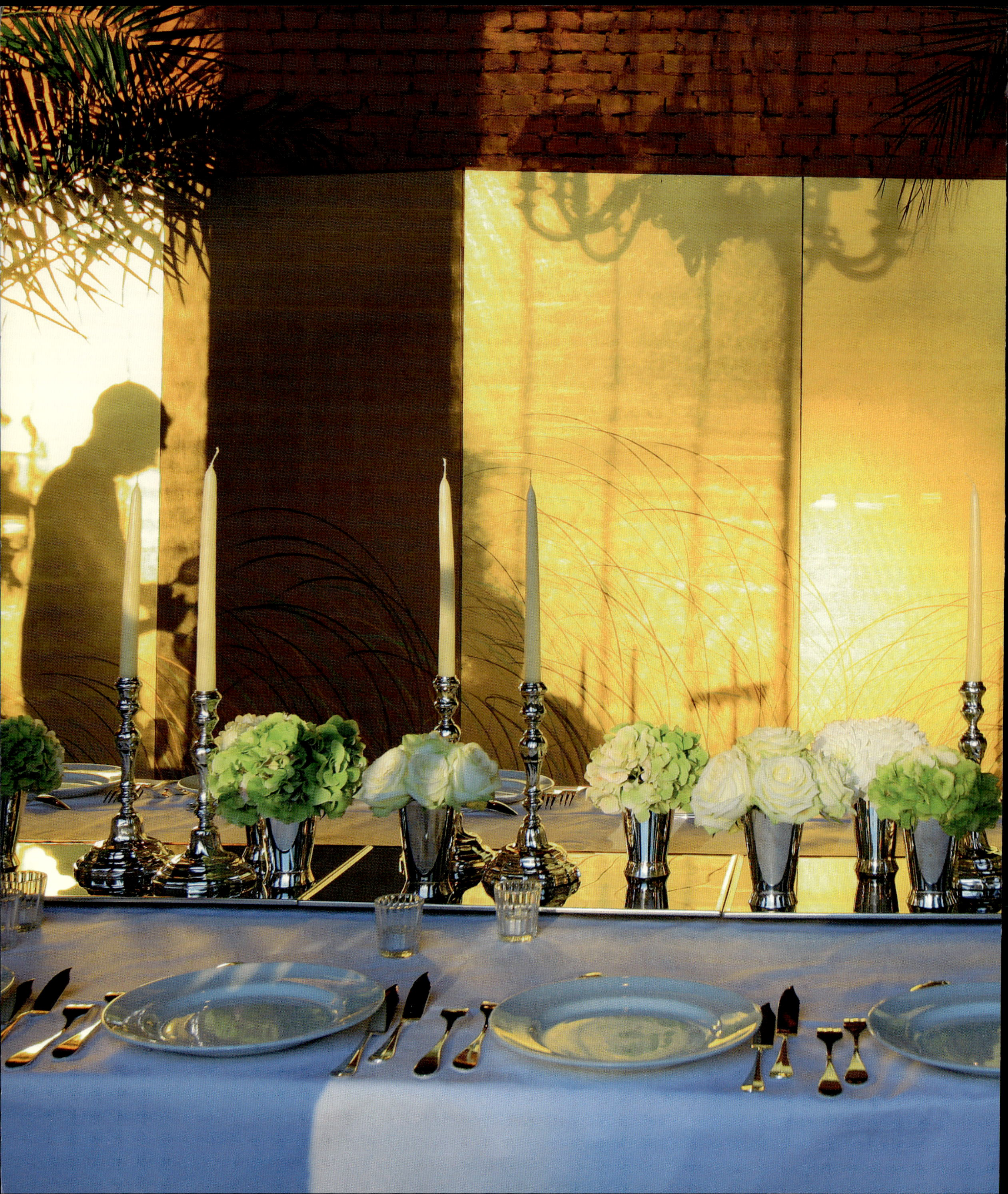

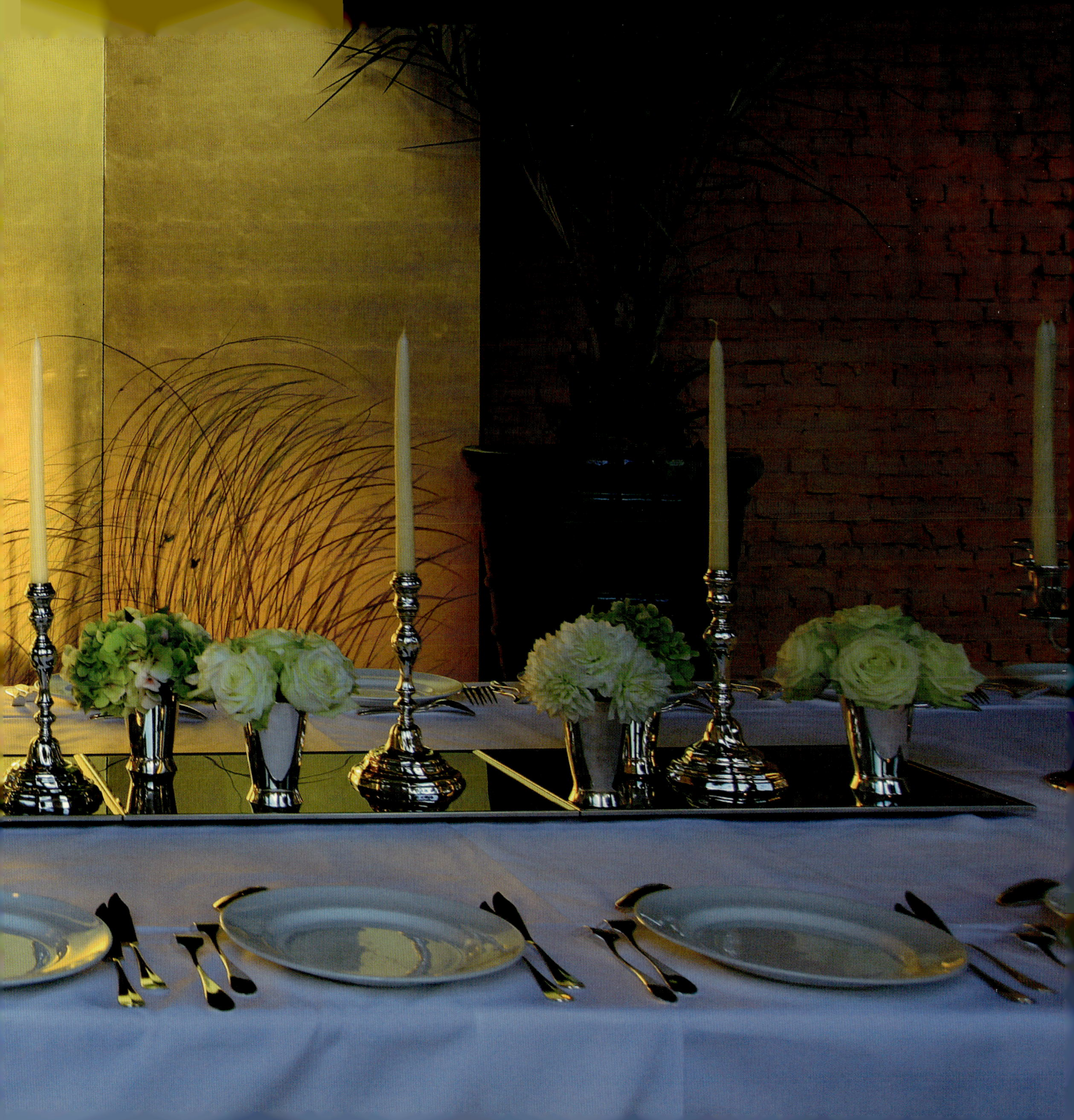

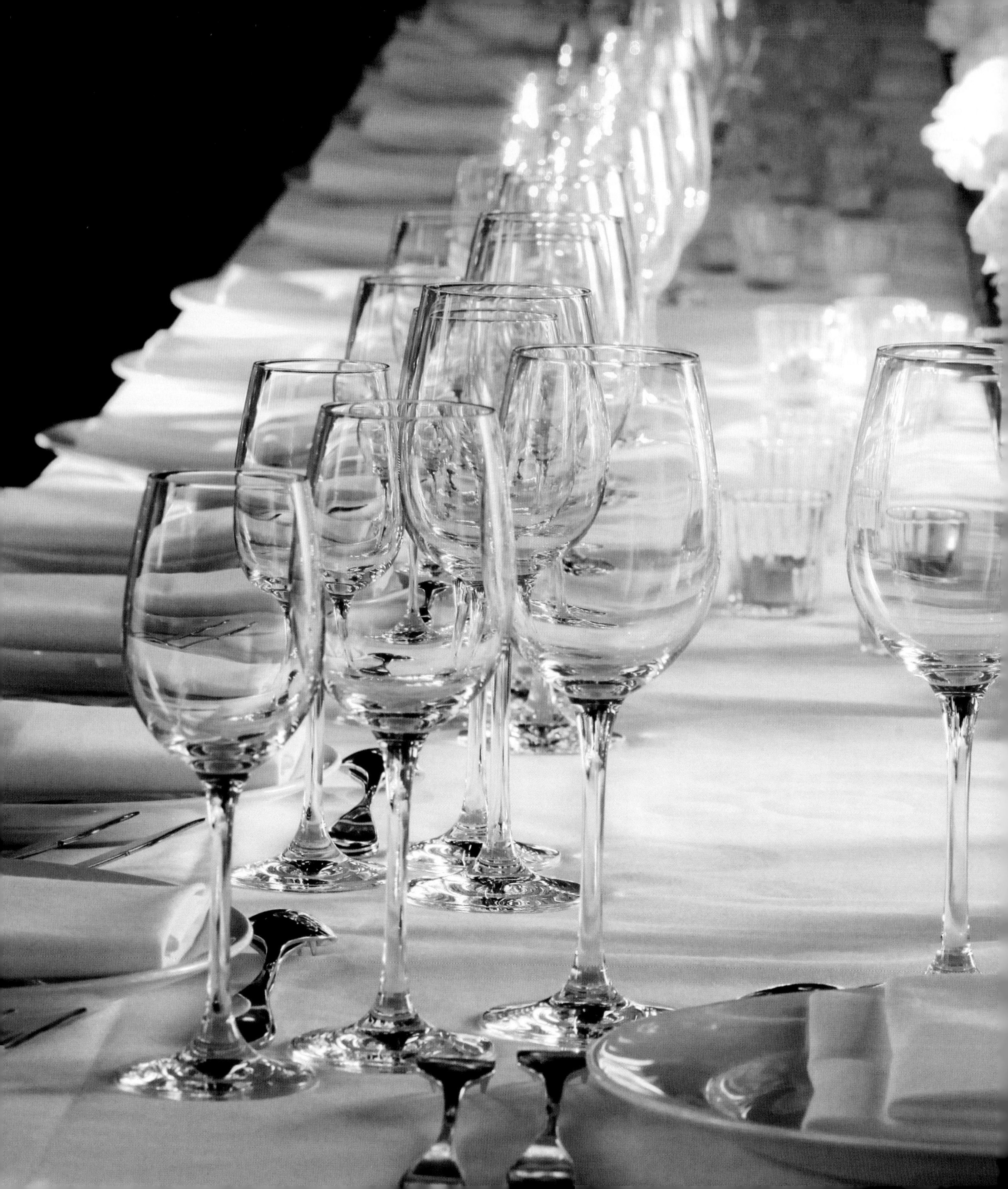

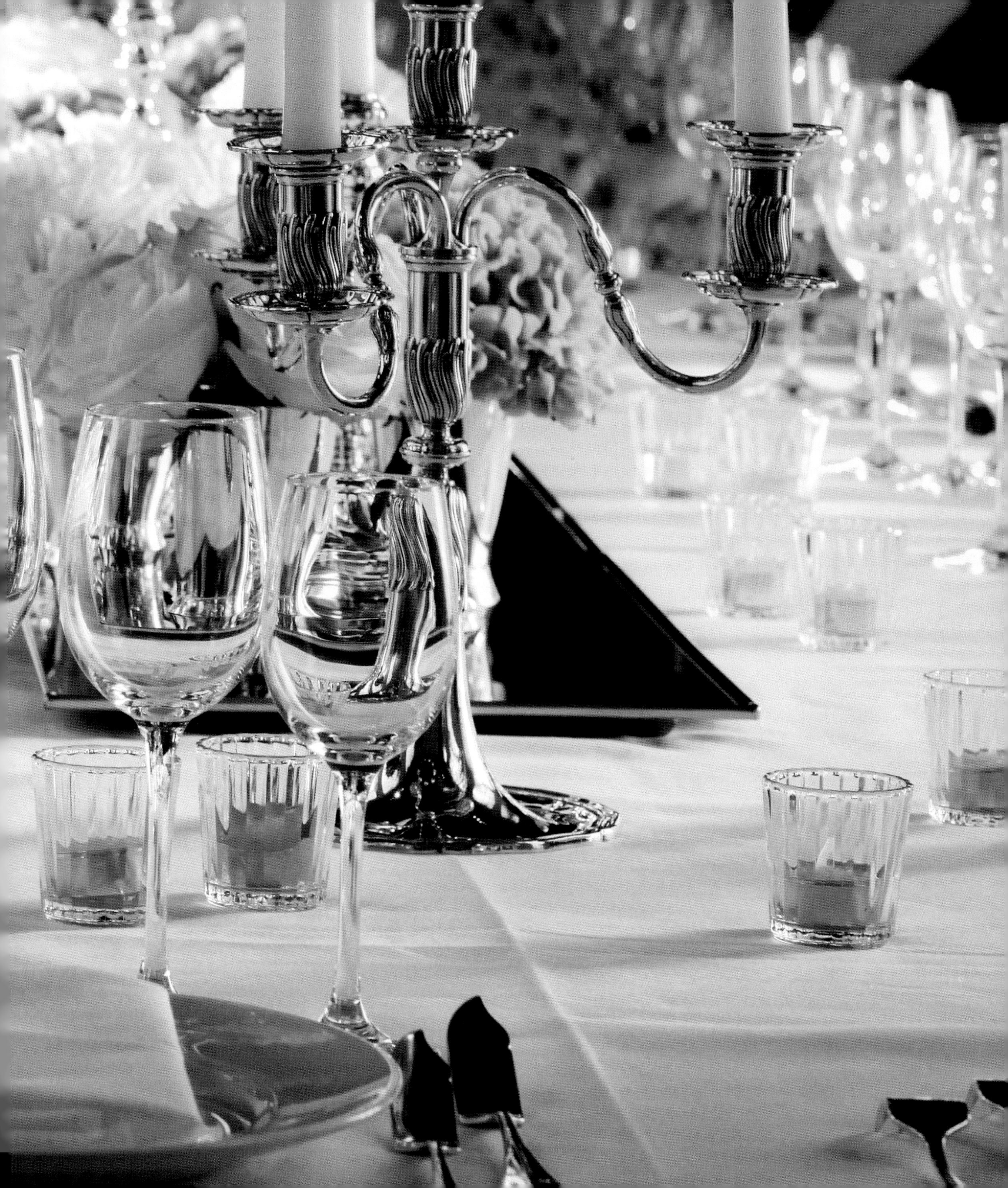

With a big wood-burning cast-iron stove for warmth, and enough space to accommodate a table that could seat sixteen on each side, all this orangerie needed was some atmosphere. Hired chairs, trestle tables, white linen, borrowed candelabra, lots of tea lights, shiny surfaces and sparkling glasses transformed the orangerie into a unique and magical place in the space of one afternoon. The entrance was dramatic: guests first crossed a drawbridge over the moat, then passed through a massive medieval gate and followed a pebble path lined with hundreds of tea lights. As they arrived at the orangerie, they could warm their hands over an outdoor fire blazing in a neoclassical iron urn.

The evening unfolded with great drama and flair and elegance. No one would have guessed that the entire venue had been conjured out of an empty shed. The party was fun; it was intimate and it left, I think, a lasting impression on everyone.

Apart from being a very memorable evening it also turned out to be a hands-on lesson in how much can be created with so little.

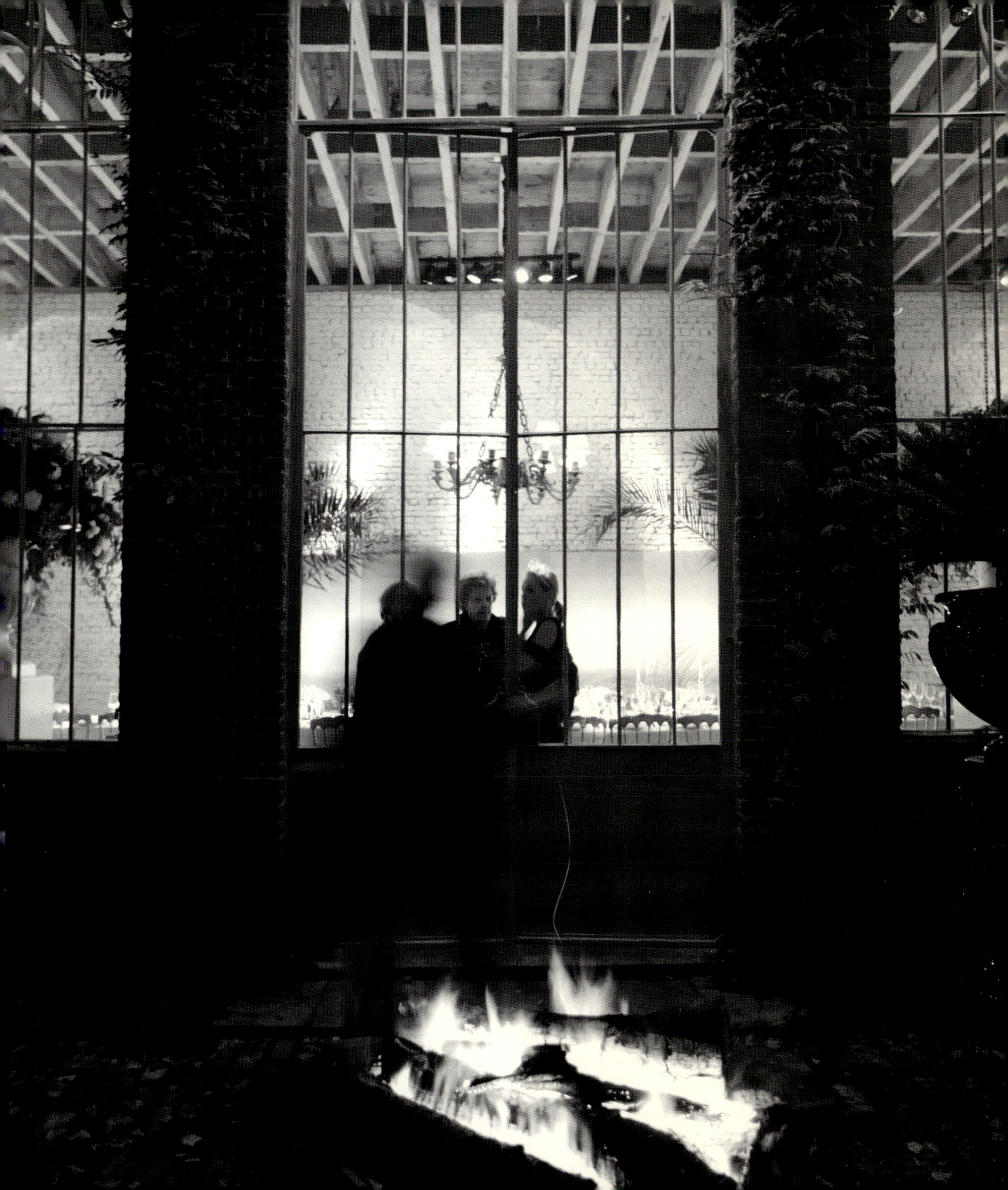

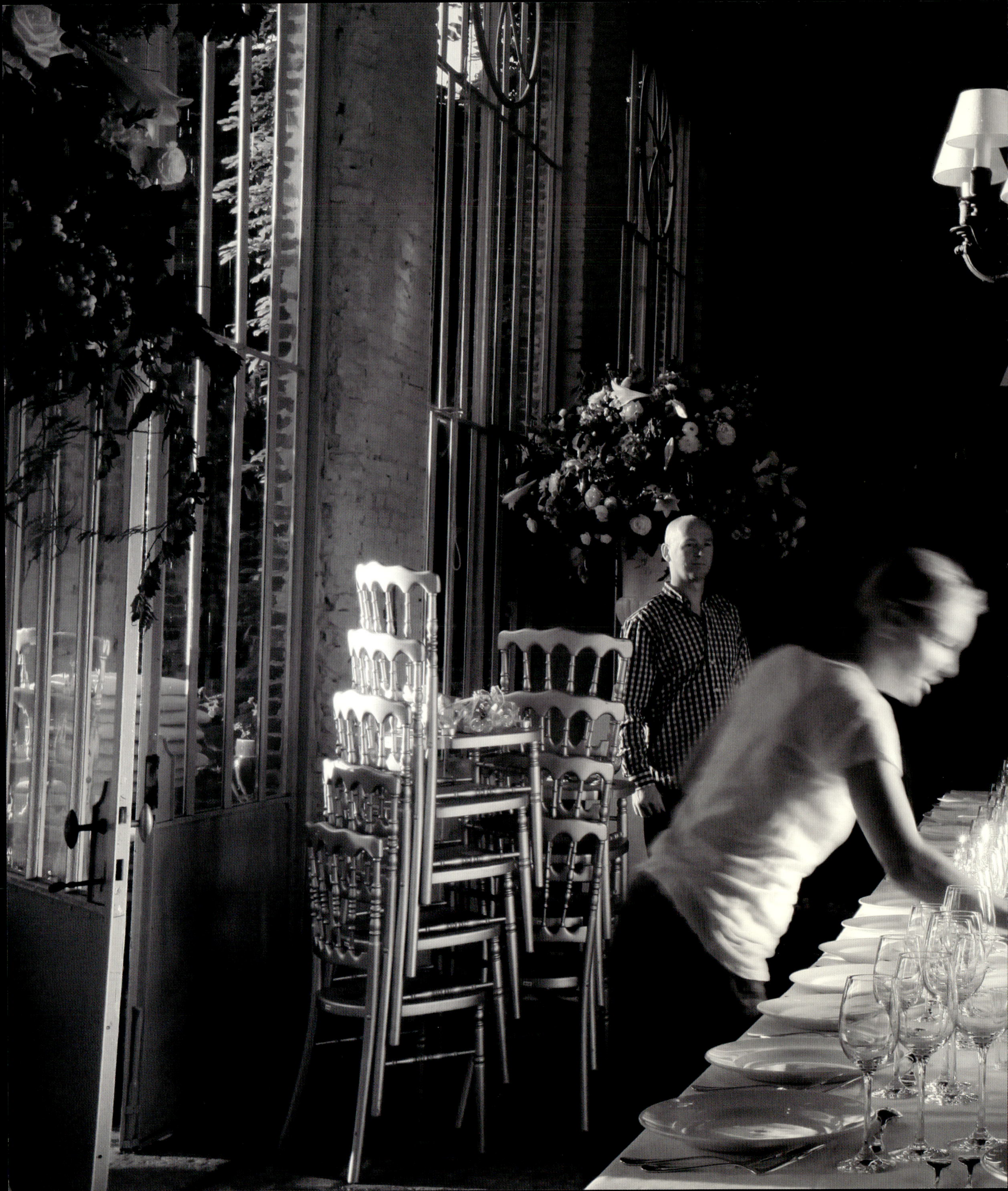

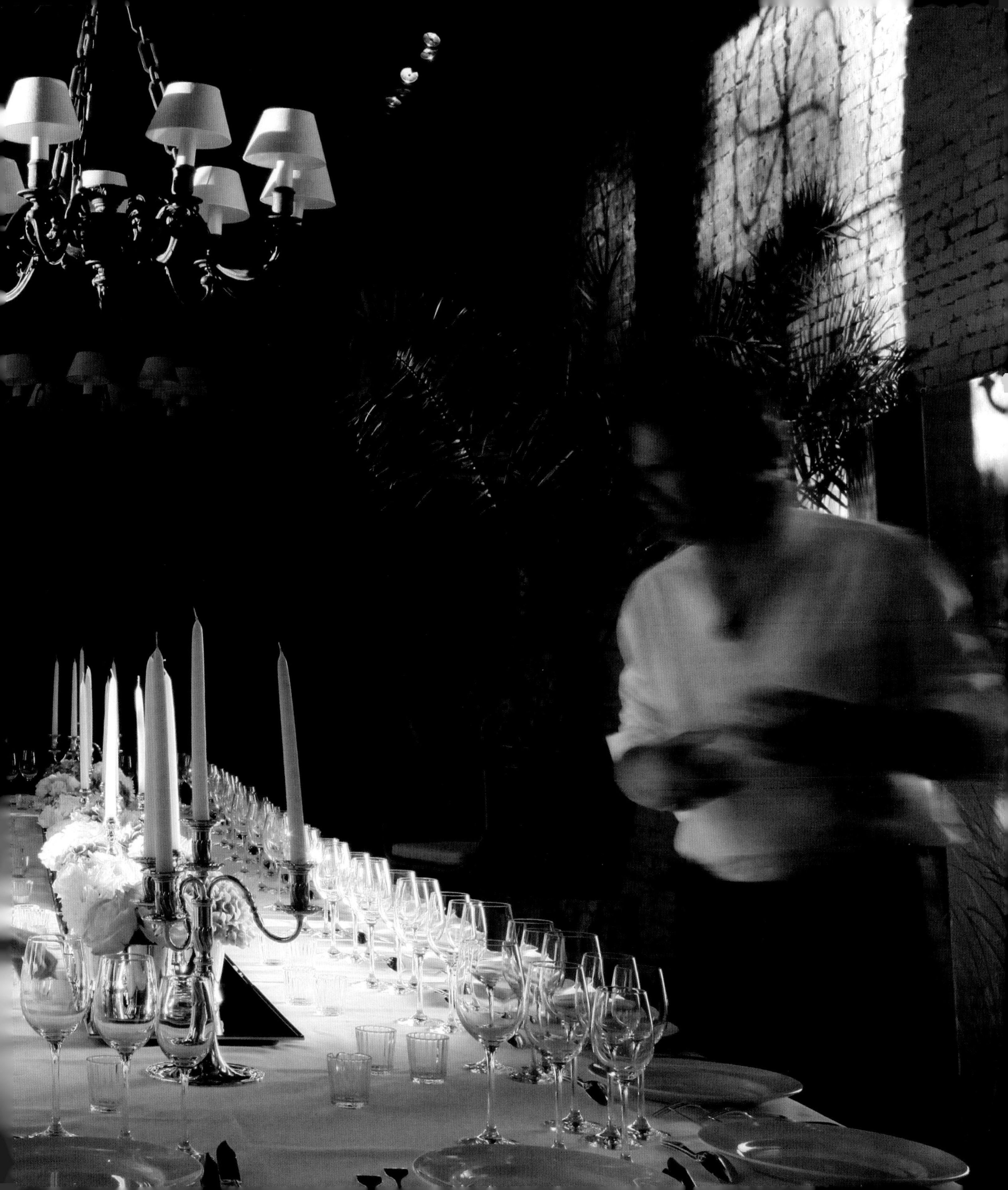

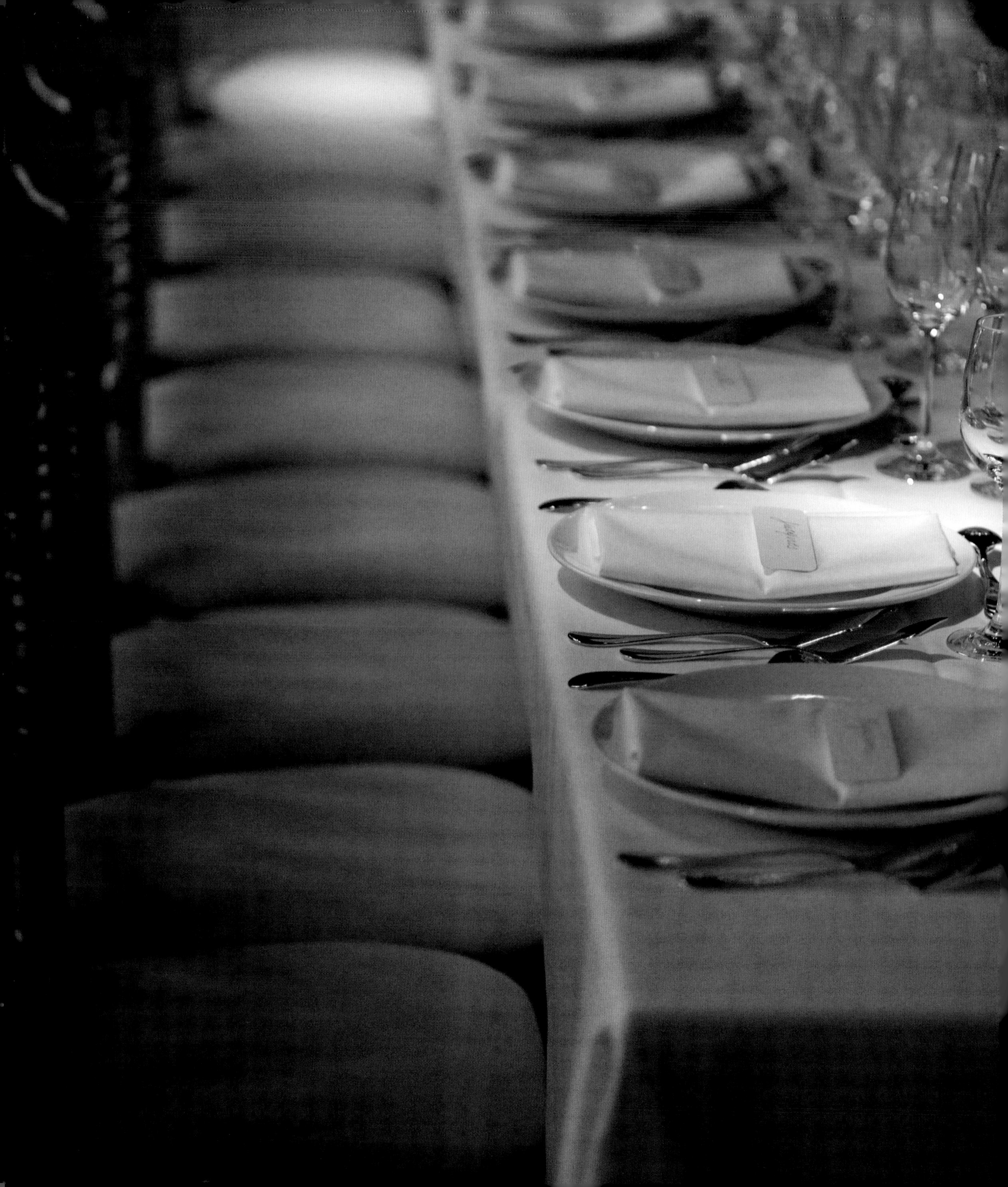

NEVER SPEND MONEY
ON NAME CARDS.
INSTEAD, CUT STRIPS FROM
A SHEET OF HEAVY PARCHMENT
PAPER AND WRITE YOUR
GUESTS' FIRST NAMES ON
THEM IN SCRIPT.

IF YOU DON'T HAVE BEAUTIFUL
HANDWRITING, FIND SOMEONE
WHO DOES.

Marc	Dominique	Pierre	Marie France
Herbert	Sacha	Valentine	Alexandre
Pauline	Fred	Nicole M.	Jacqueline
Cedric	Angelina	Patrick	Godelieve

Alex	Jacqueline	Brigitte	Pierre Paul
Paulette	André	Lisette	Charles
Maman Godelieve	Alice	Ginette	Yvan
Jacques	Myriam	Arlette	Renée

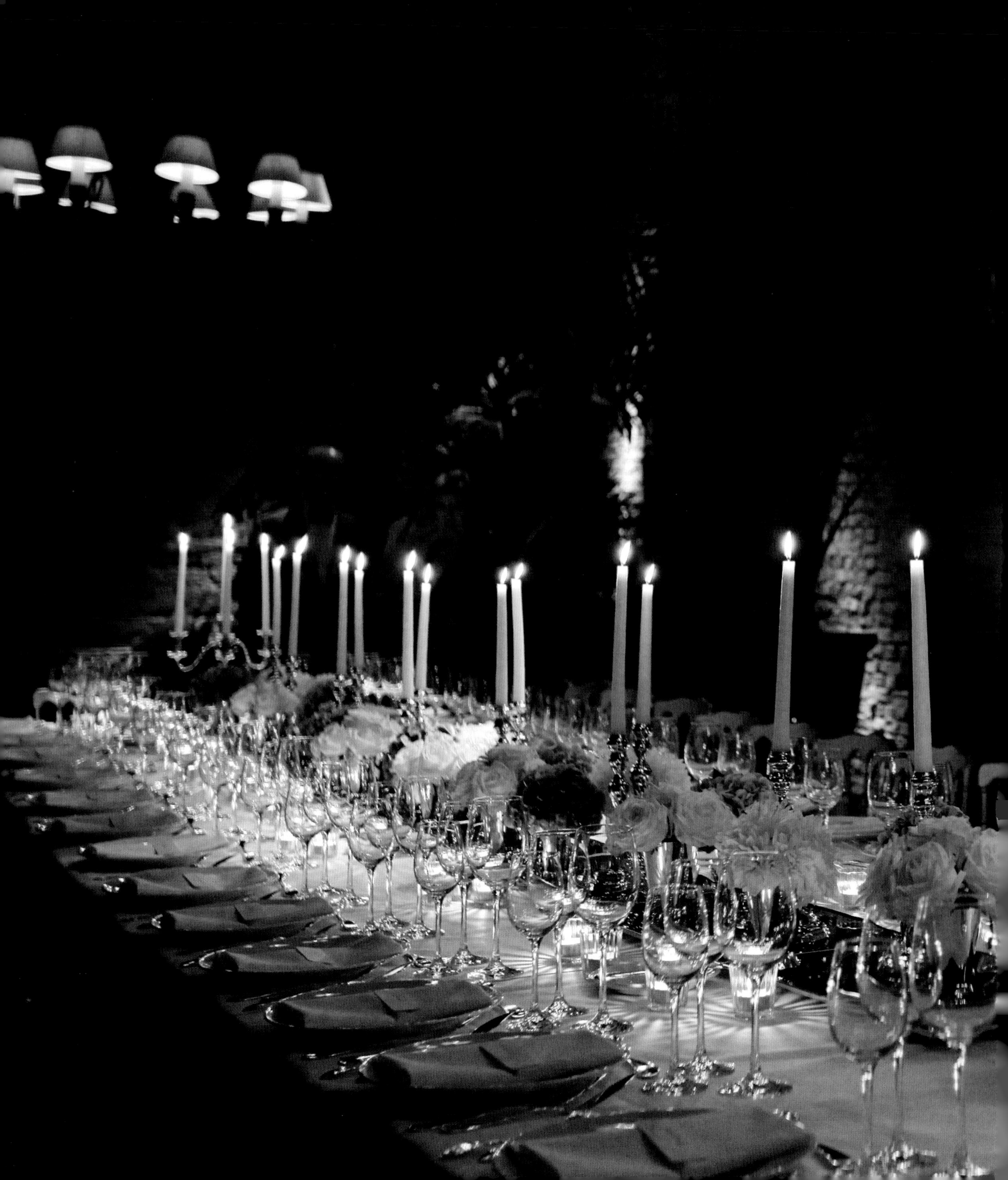

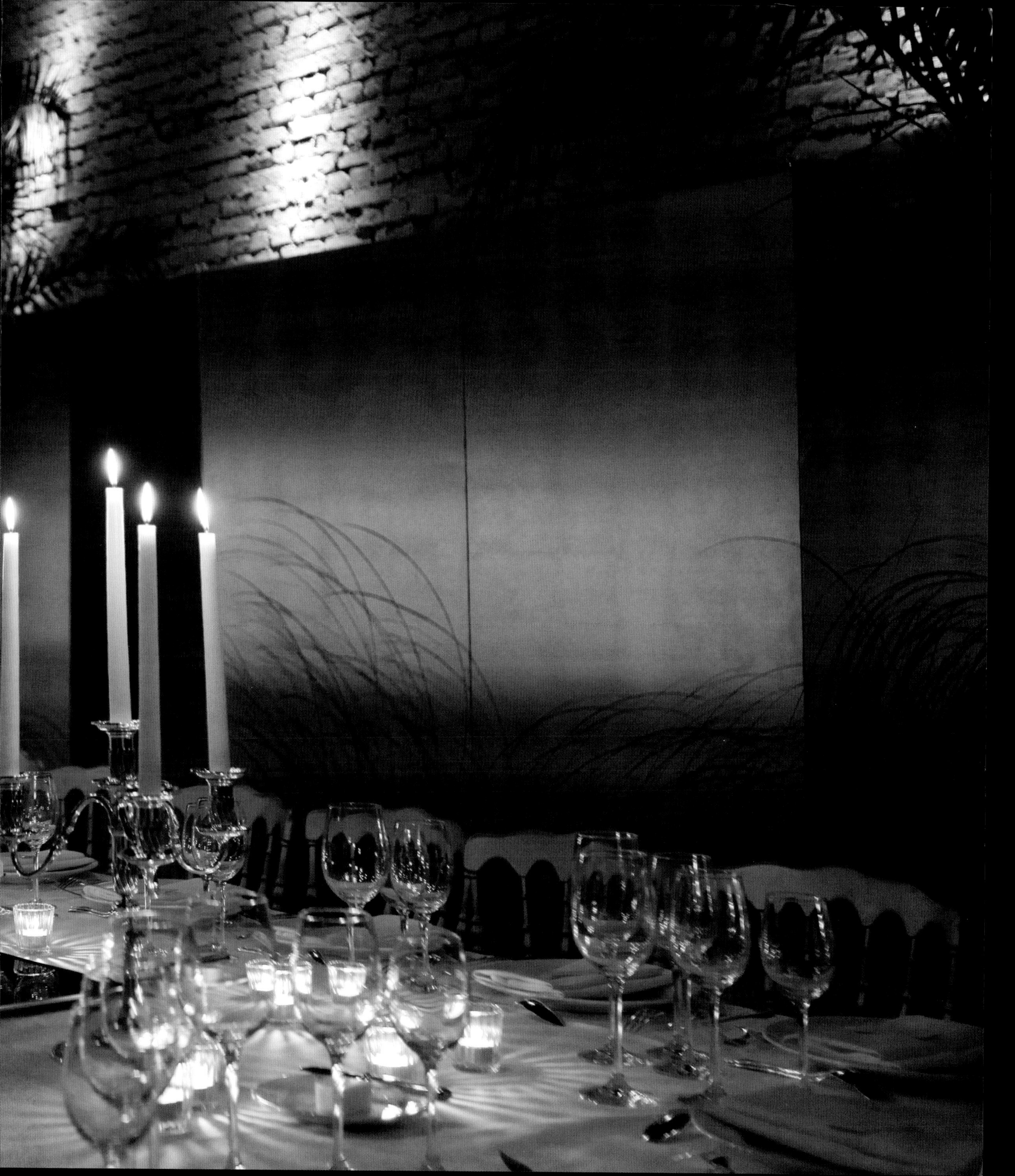

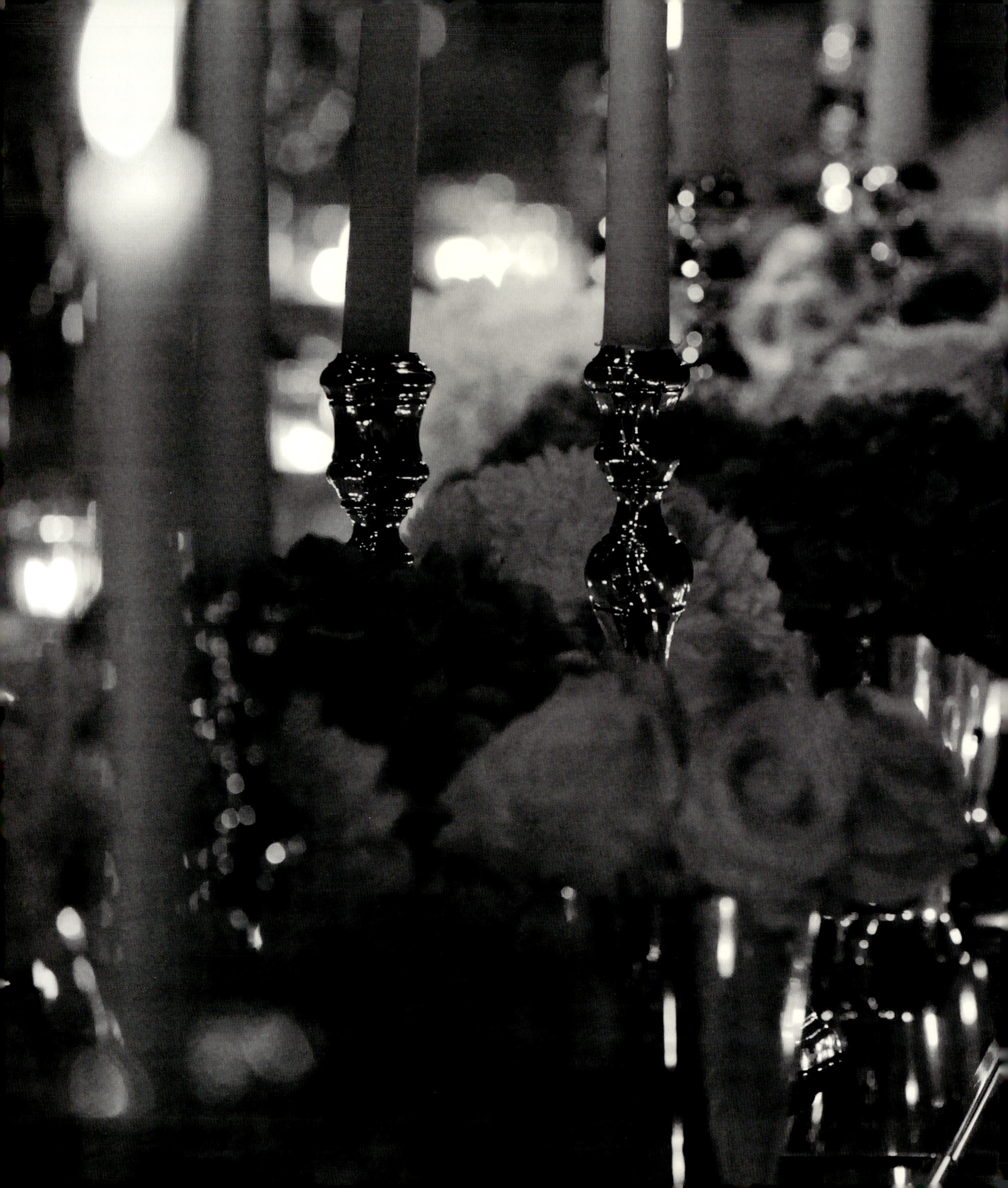

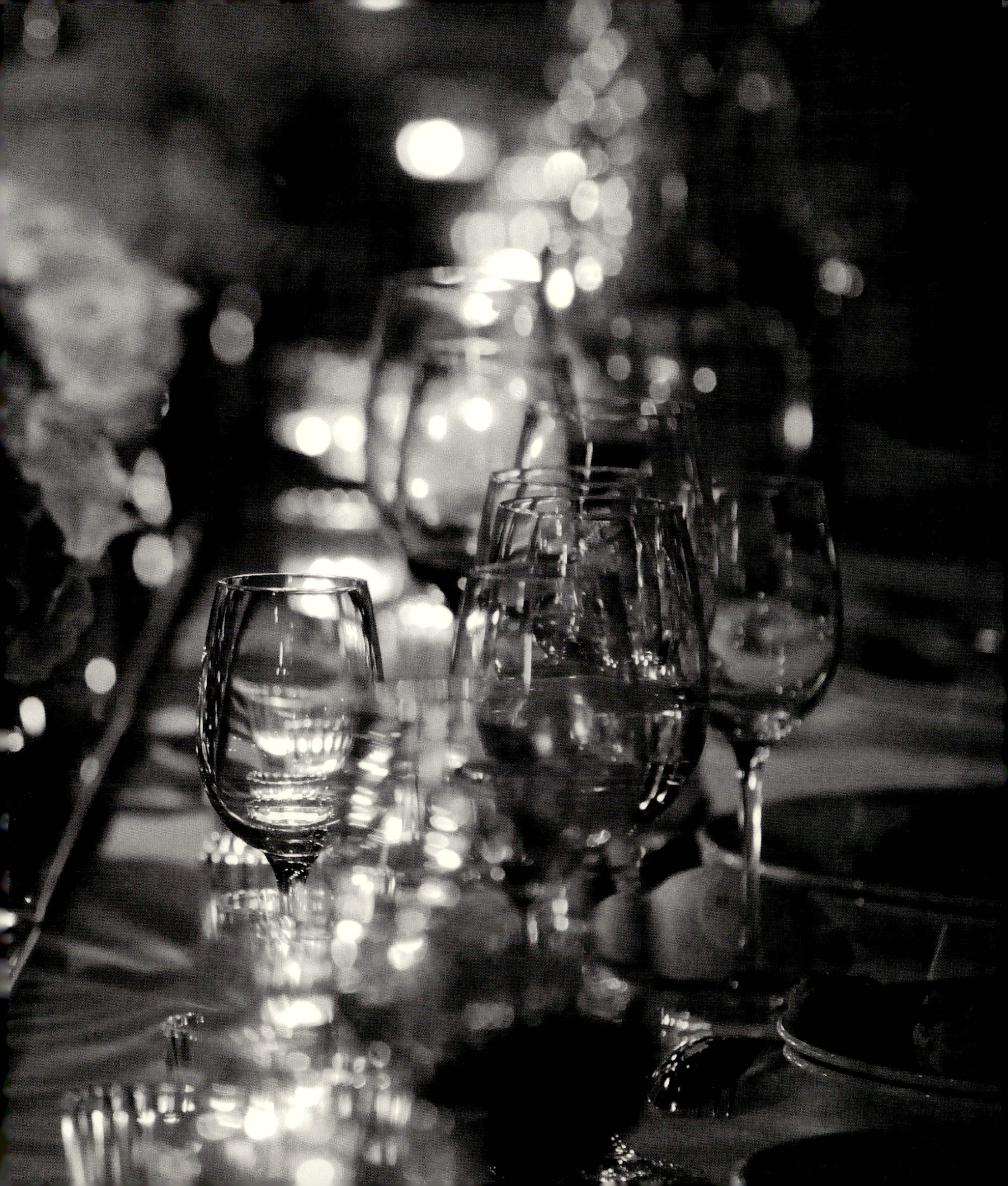

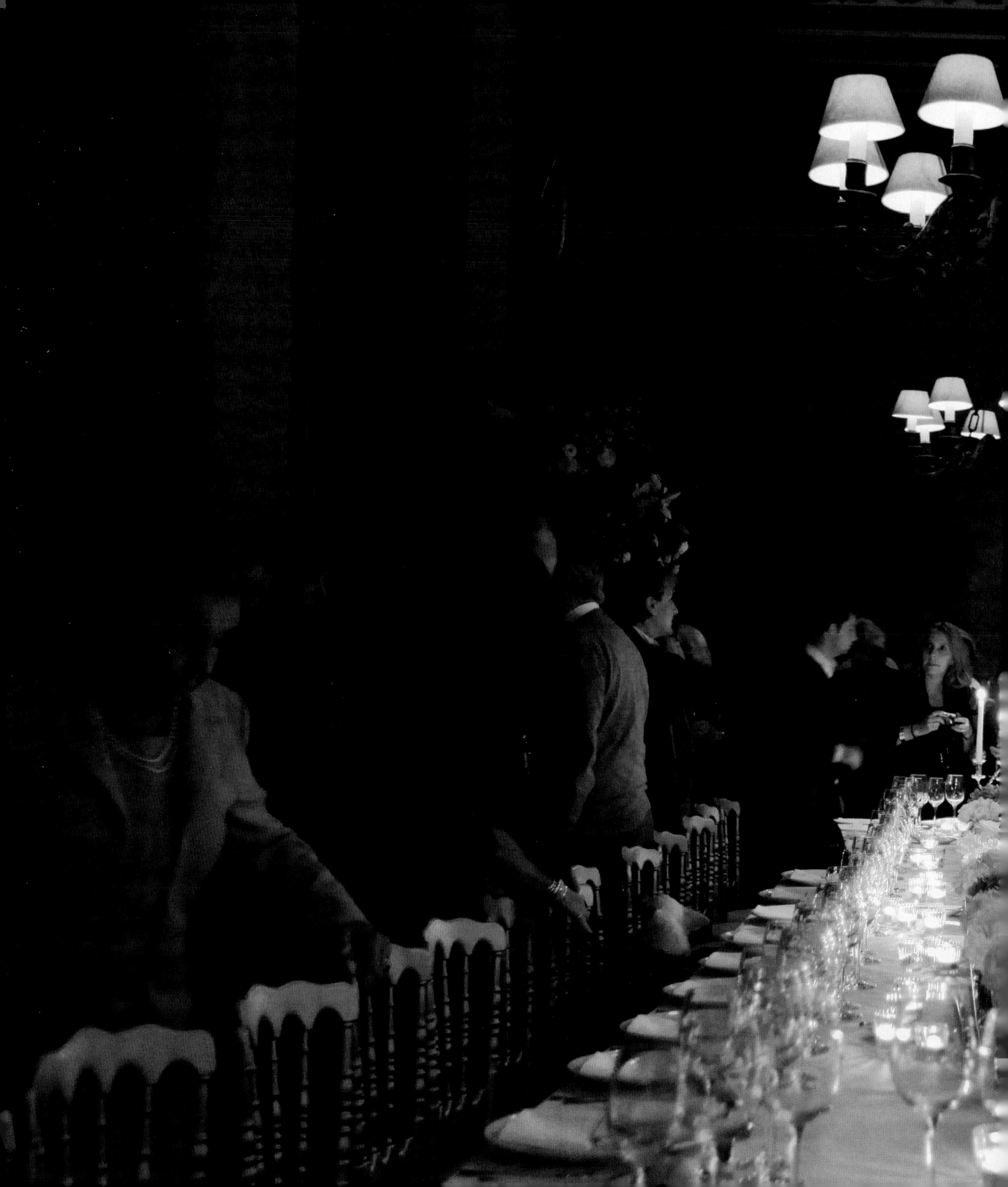

A SPEECH CAN MAKE OR
BREAK A DINNER.
TO KEEP IT SPONTANEOUS,
LET EACH GUEST
CONTRIBUTE A SENTENCE
OR TWO ACCORDING TO
A SET THEME, SUCH AS
'WHAT I LIKE ABOUT…'

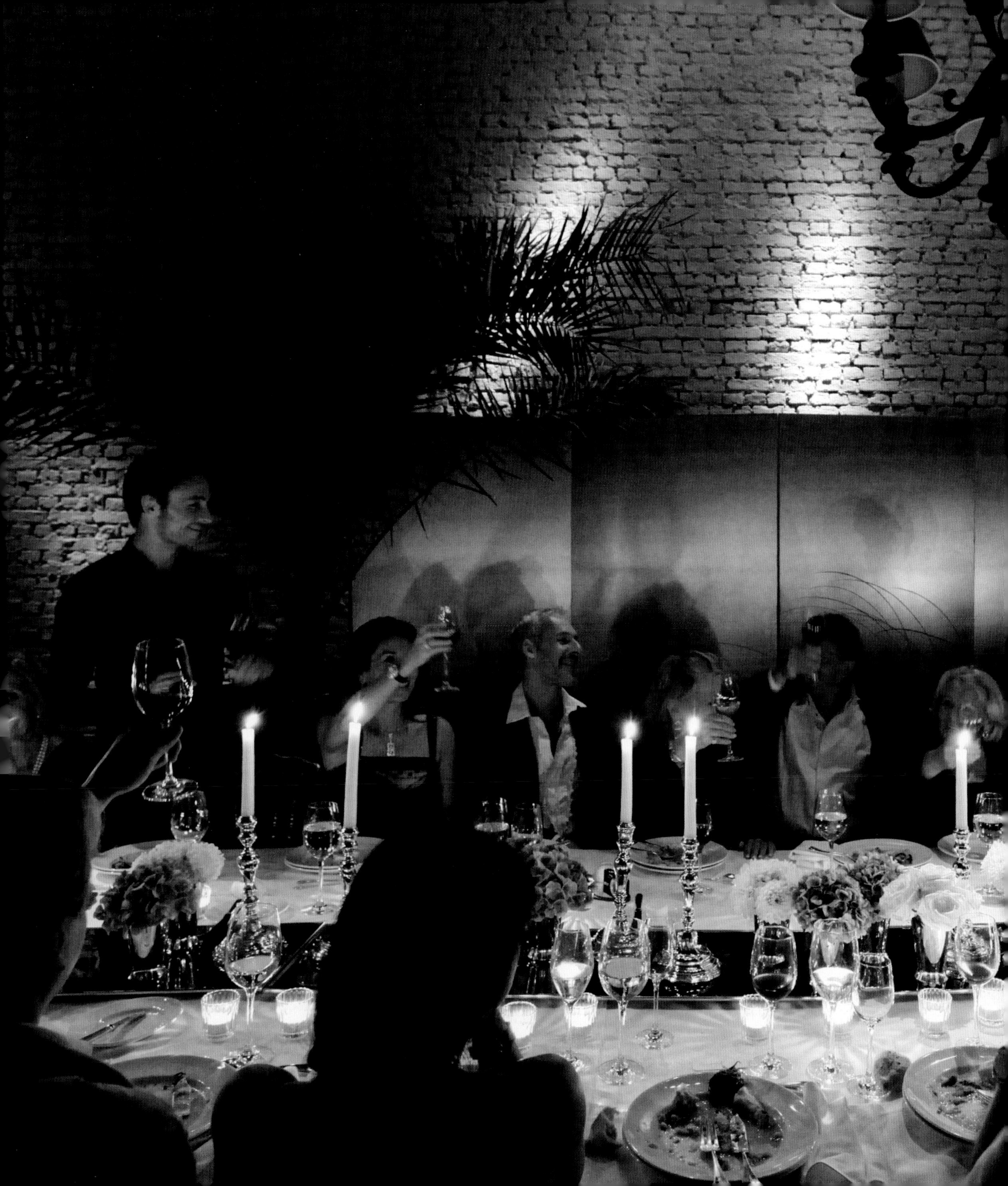

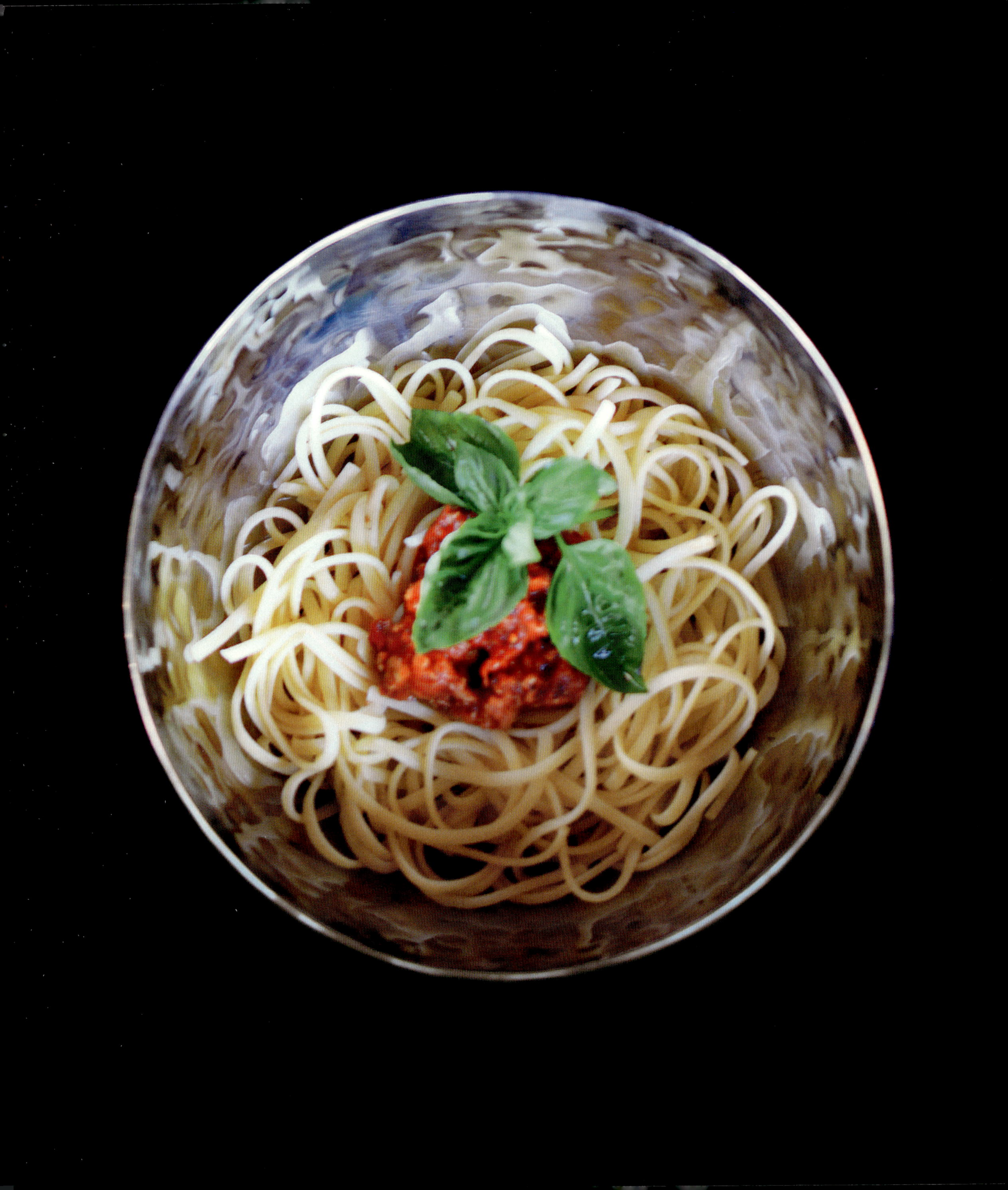

3
FOOD

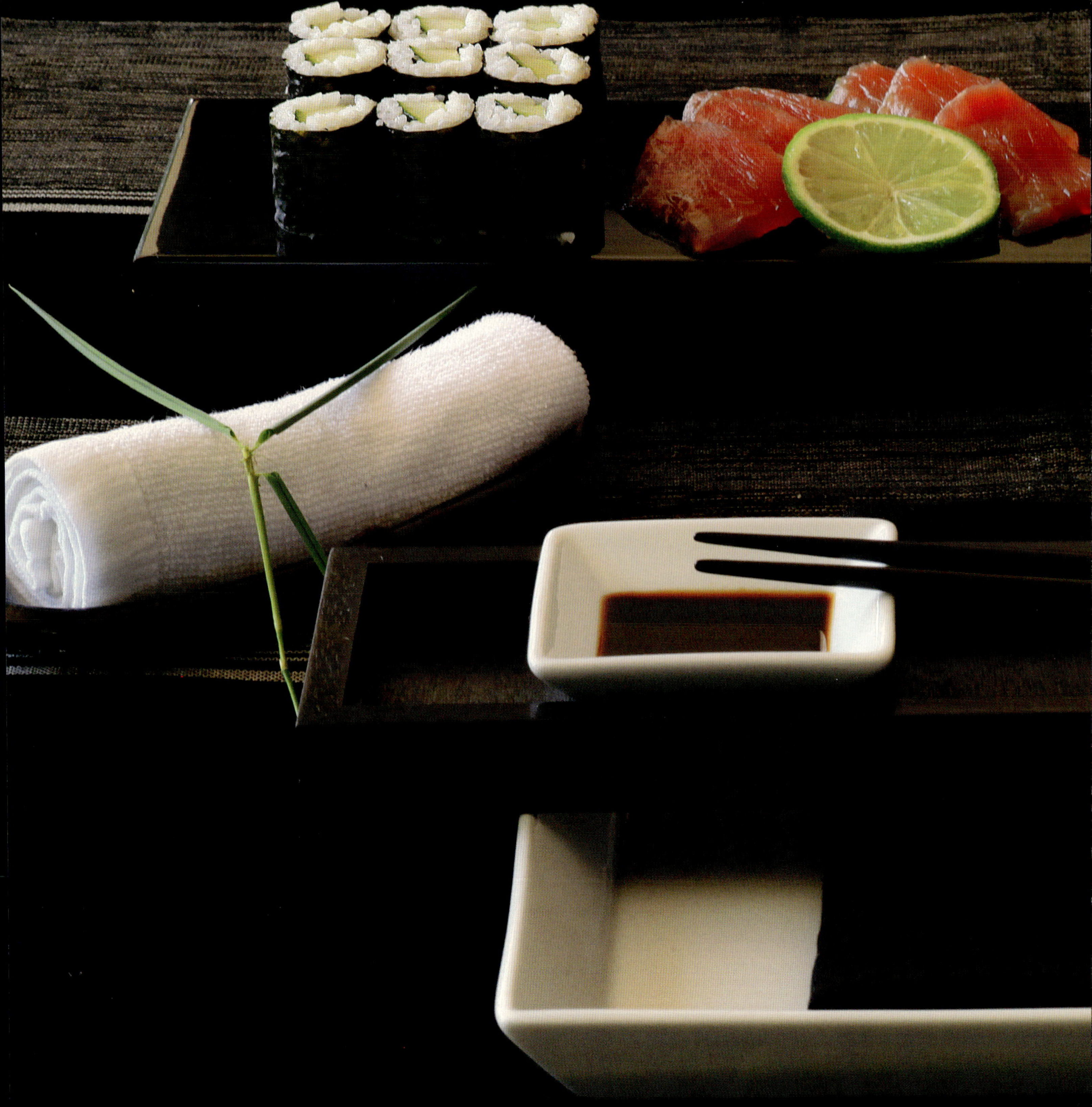

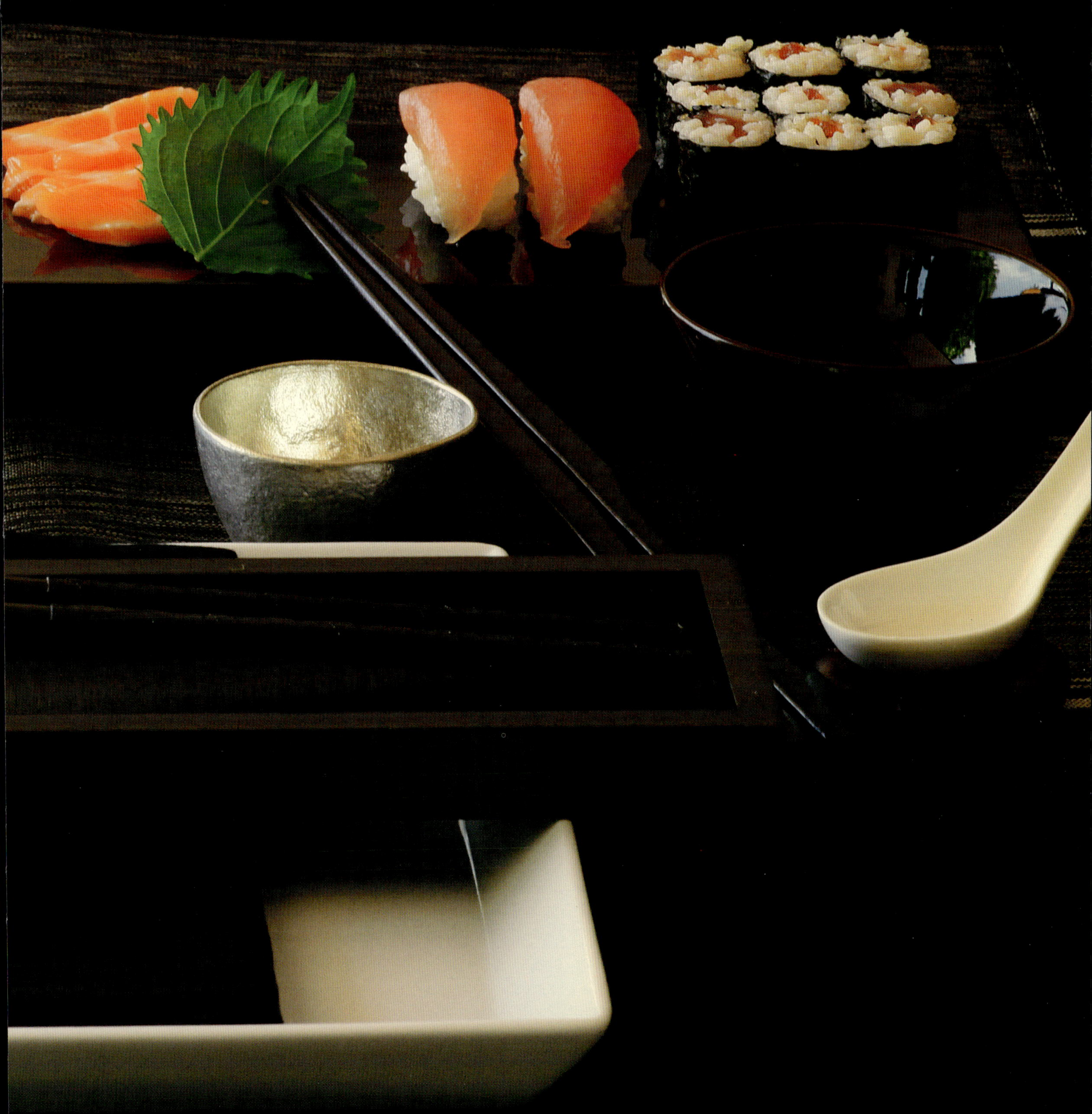

There is so much stress surrounding party food. It is probably the single biggest reason that people shy away from entertaining: 'It's too much work', 'I don't have enough time', 'I can't cook under pressure'. And so on.

Everybody forgets that entertaining is just an opportunity to bring friends and family together. That's all. Food should be the simplest part of the equation.

All you need to remember is this: 'We eat with our eyes'. If it looks good, it will taste good. A simple meal of spaghetti can look amazing. All you need is a silver bowl from the local market, some al dente pasta, tomato sauce, a sprig of parsley… and you're done.

For dessert, mixed berries in a big glass bowl can look spectacular. Add some cream or yoghurt on the side and you've created an elegant and healthy pudding.

When you entertain, you should completely enjoy the occasion and that means not having to worry about the food.

'Planning' and 'shopping' are the key words – not 'cooking'.

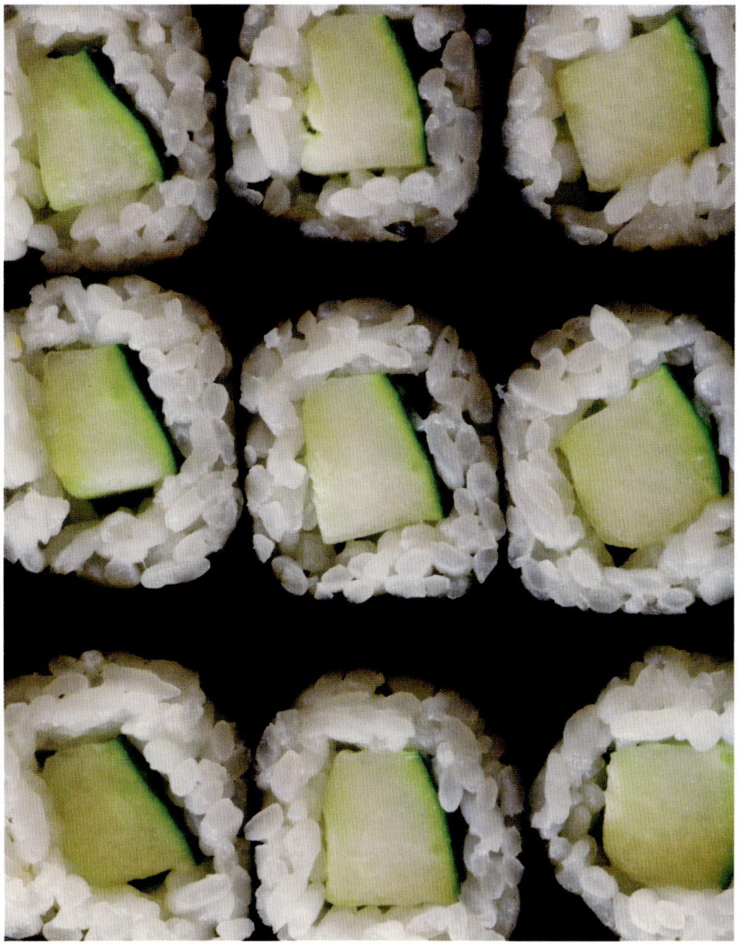

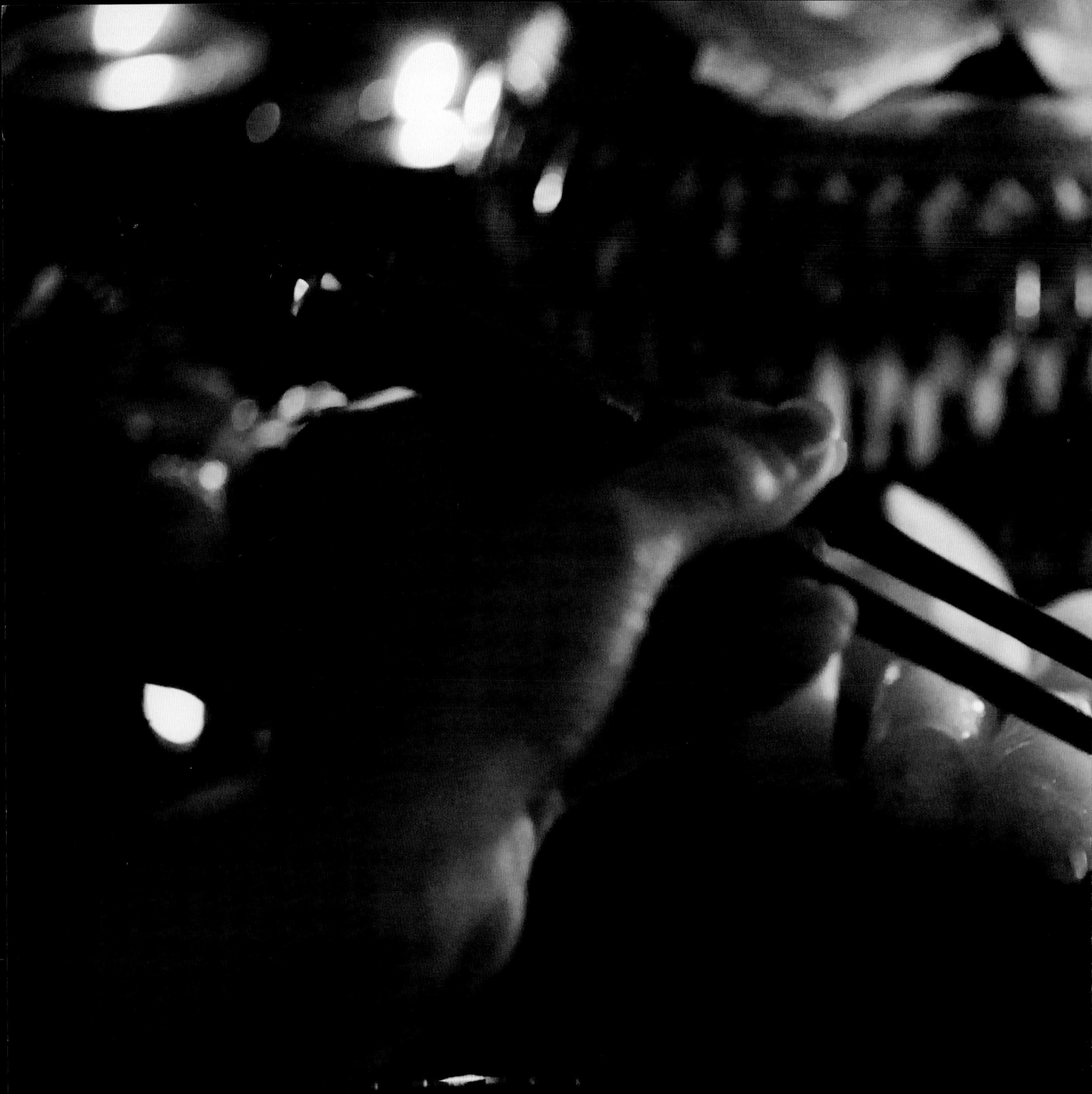

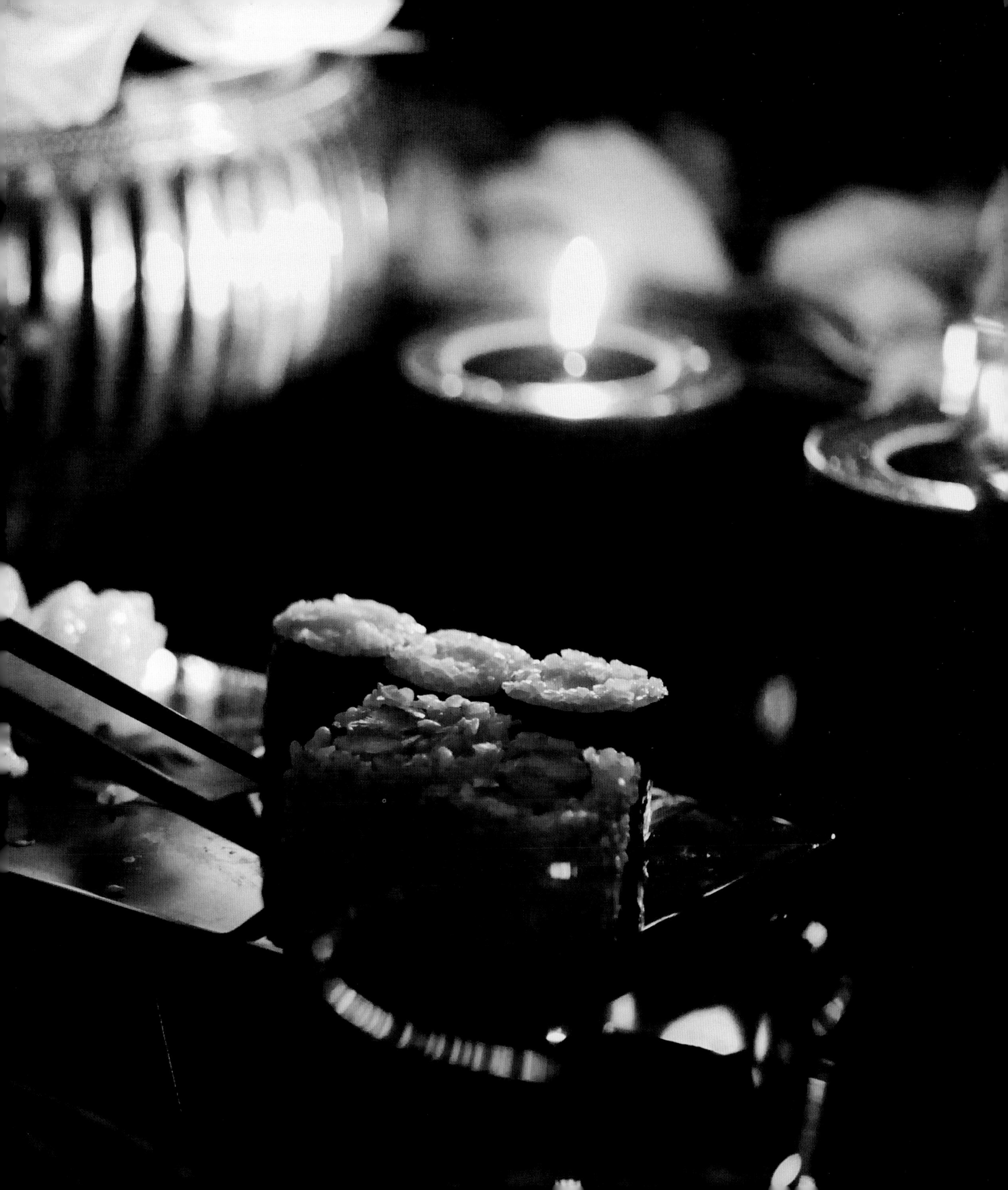

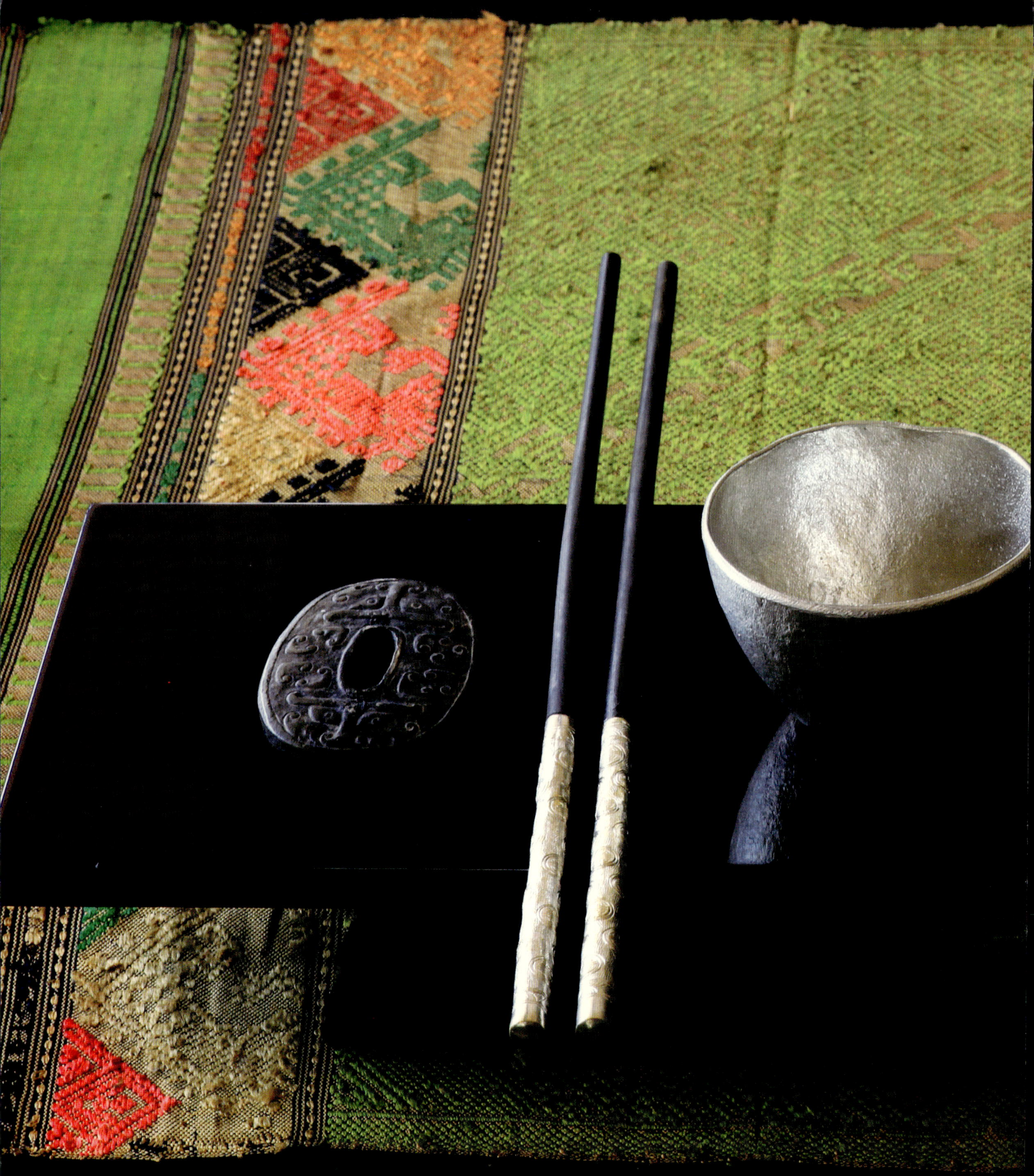

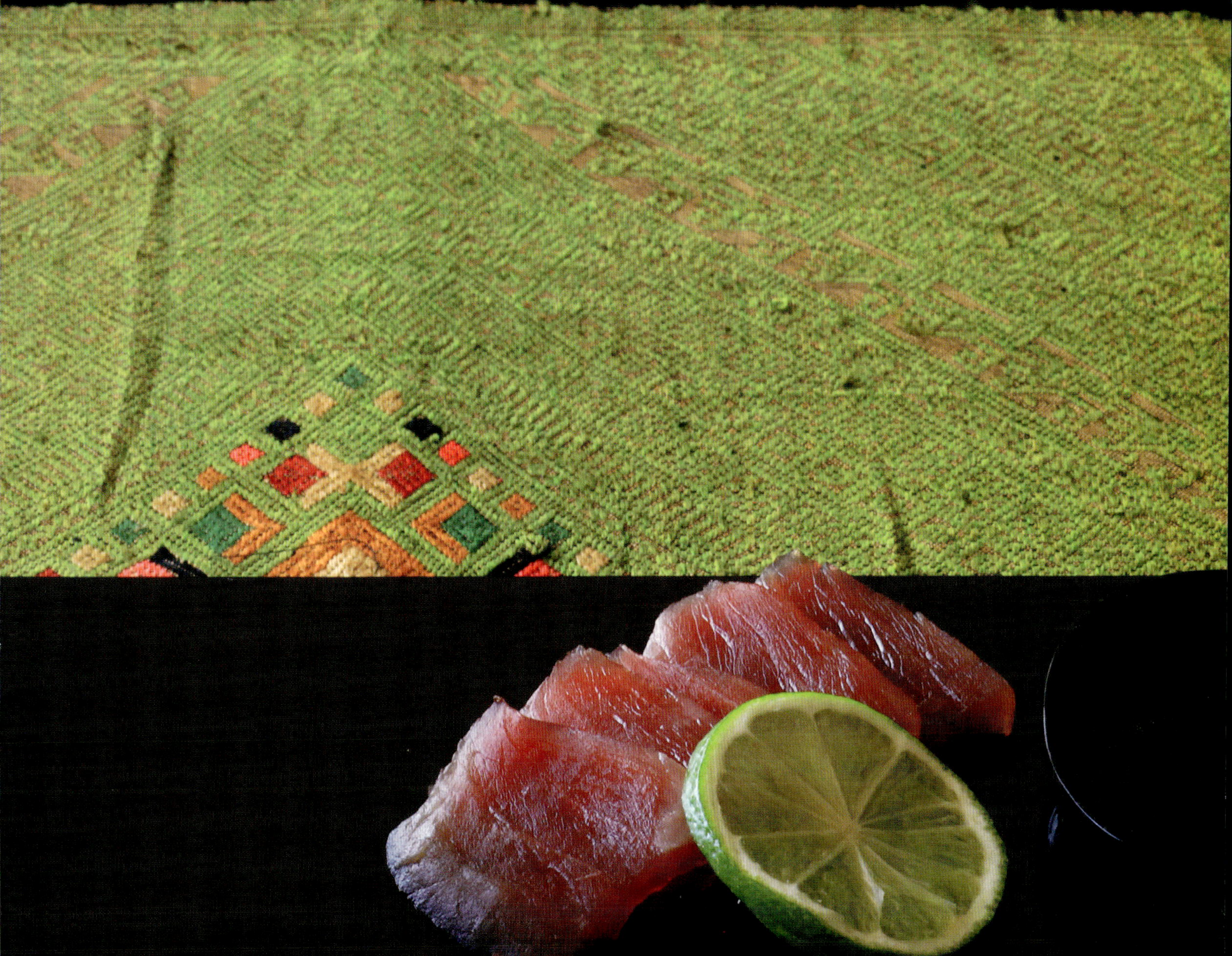

DON'T BE THE CHEF!
JUST SHOP AND ARRANGE.
IT'S AS SIMPLE AND
EASY AS THAT.

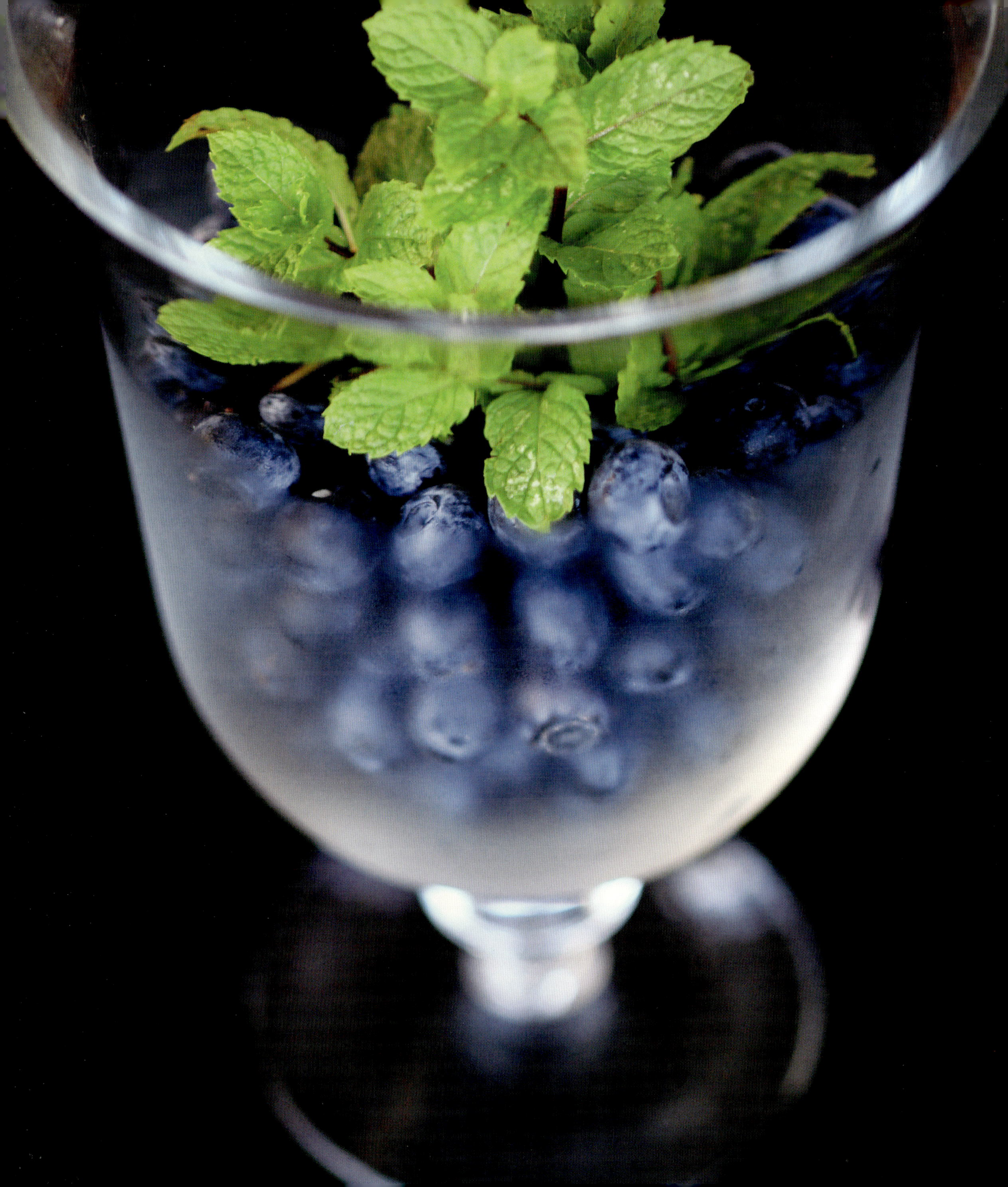

WITH THE RIGHT PRESENTATION...

FOOD

EVEN A TAKEAWAY CURRY CAN LOOK SPECTACULAR.

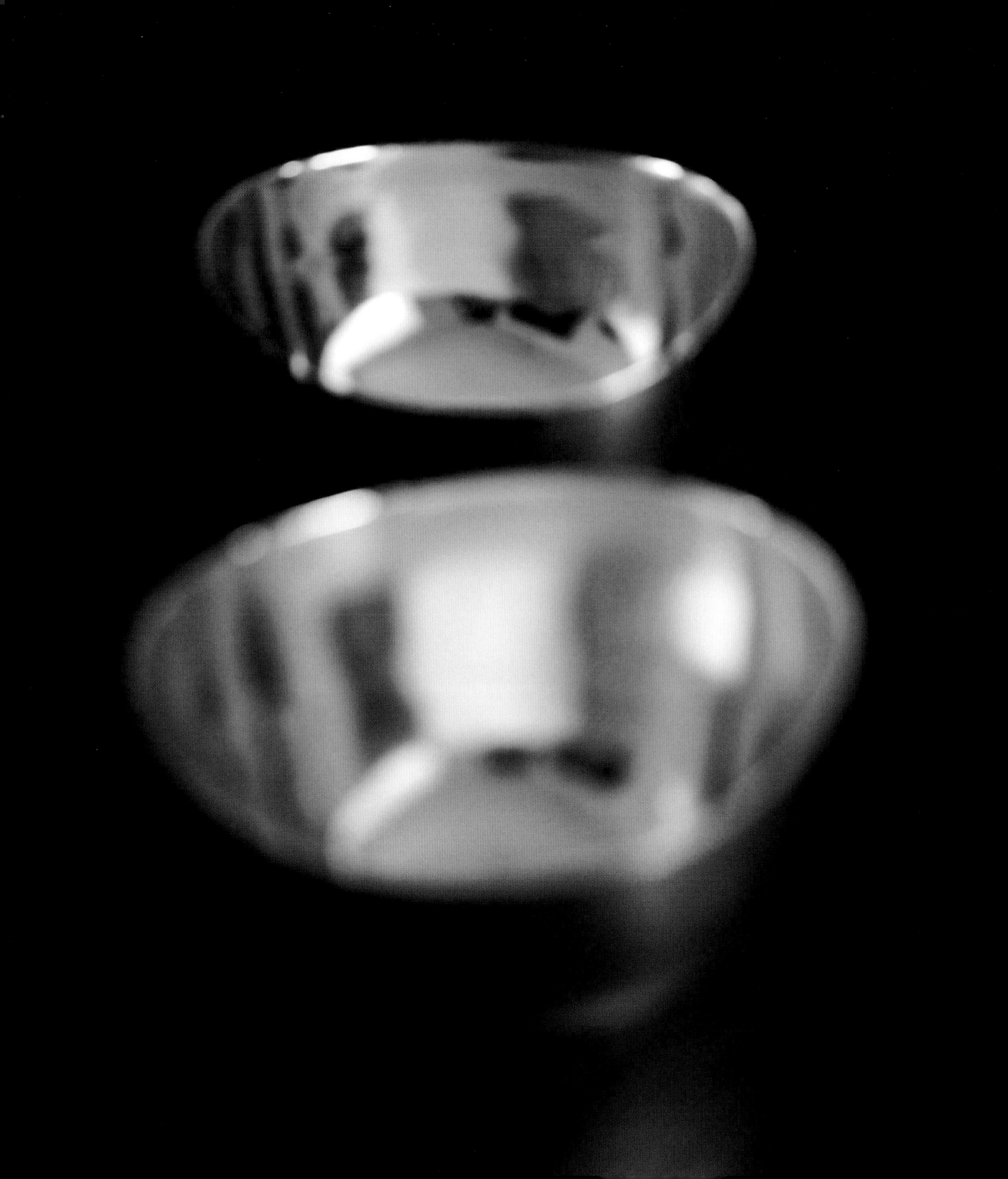

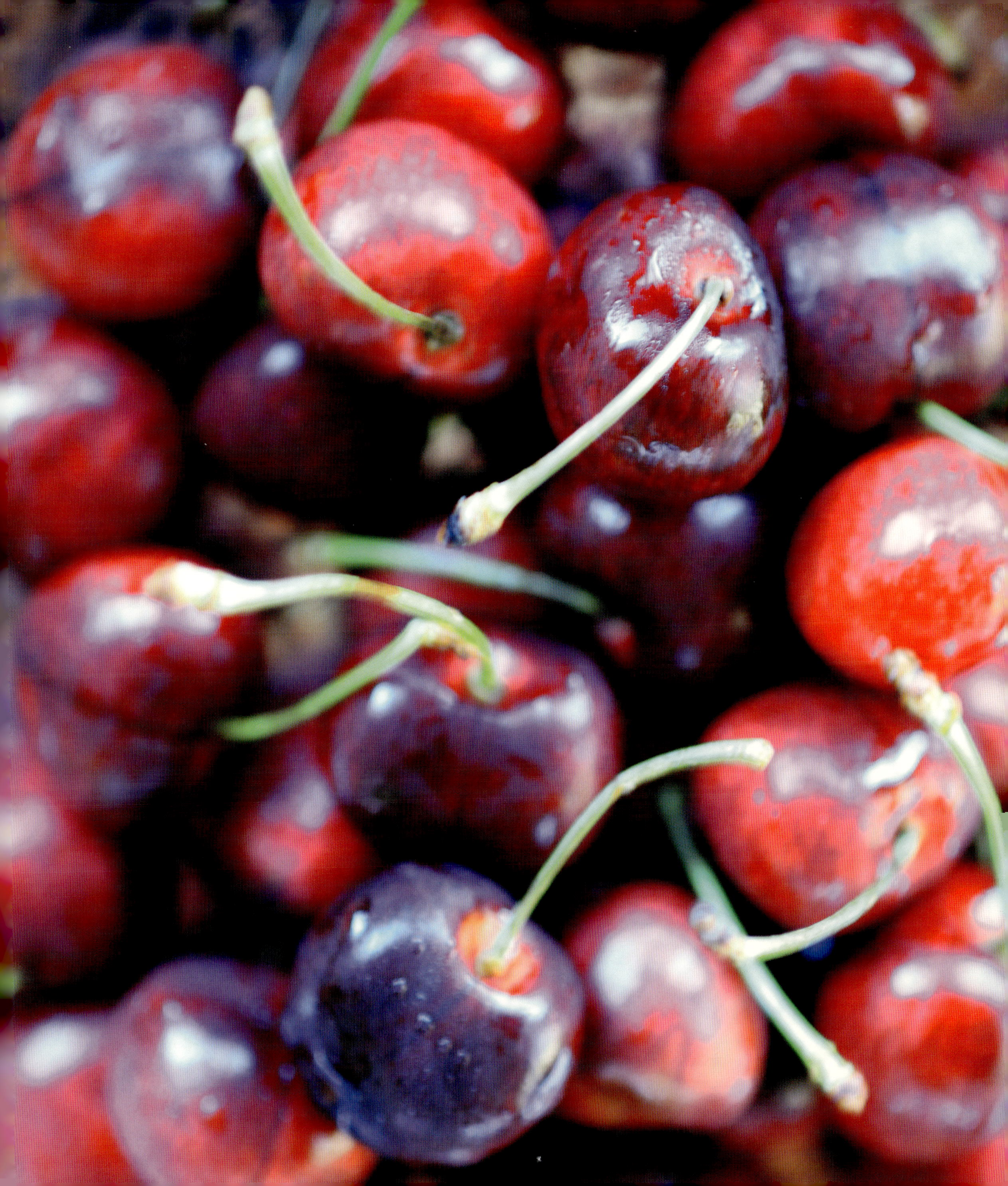

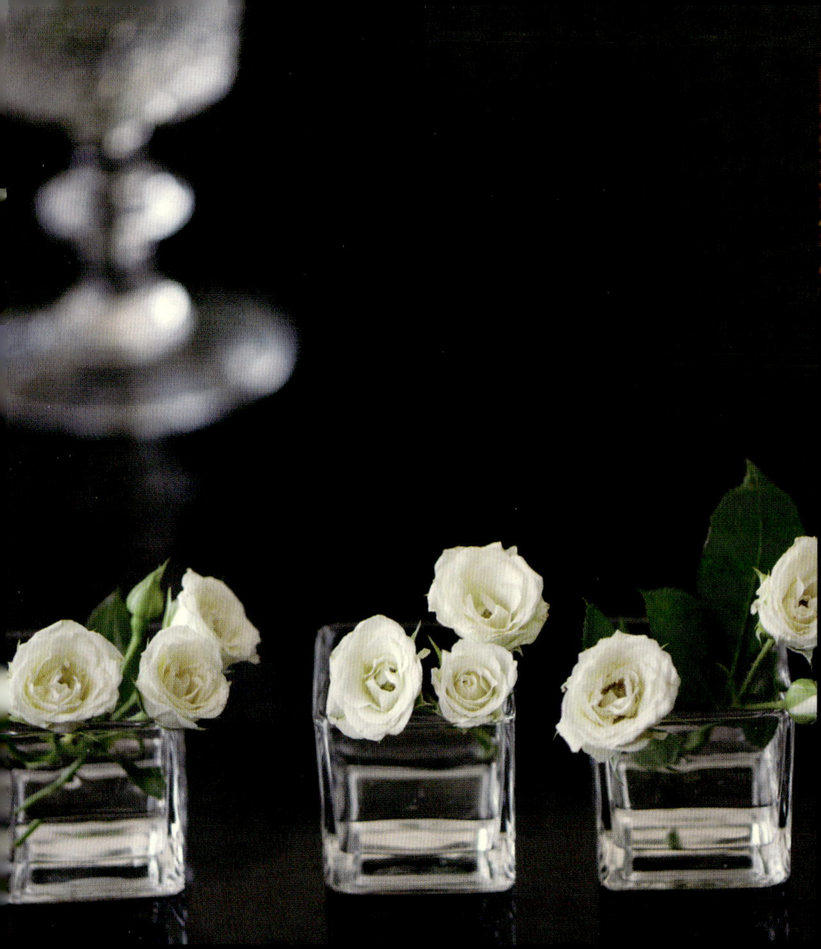
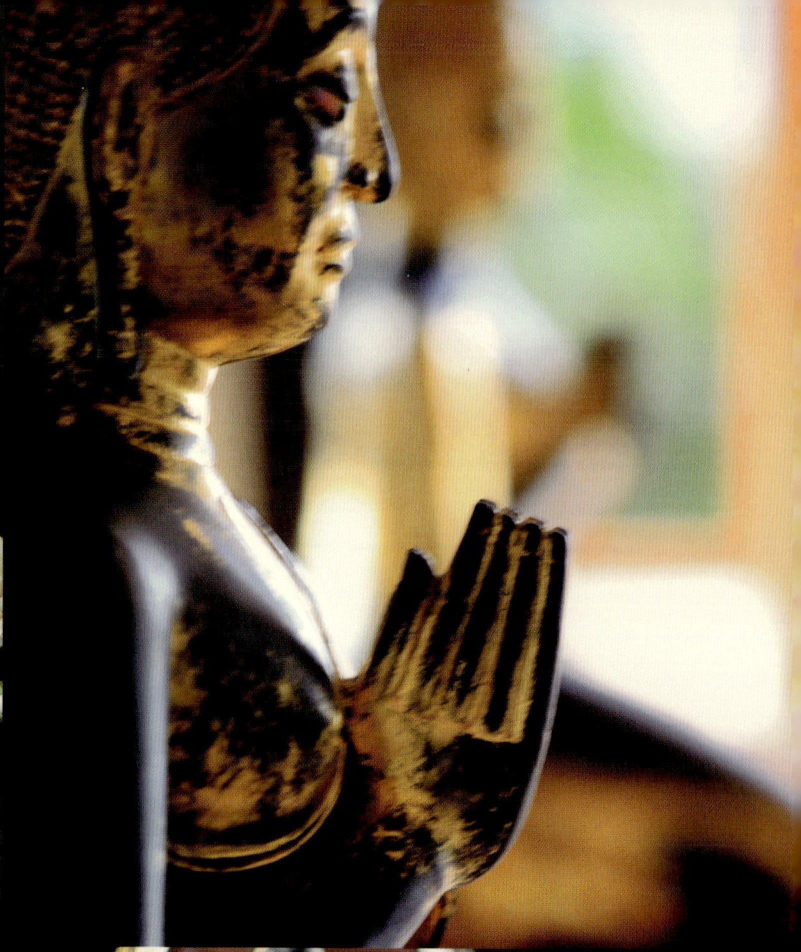
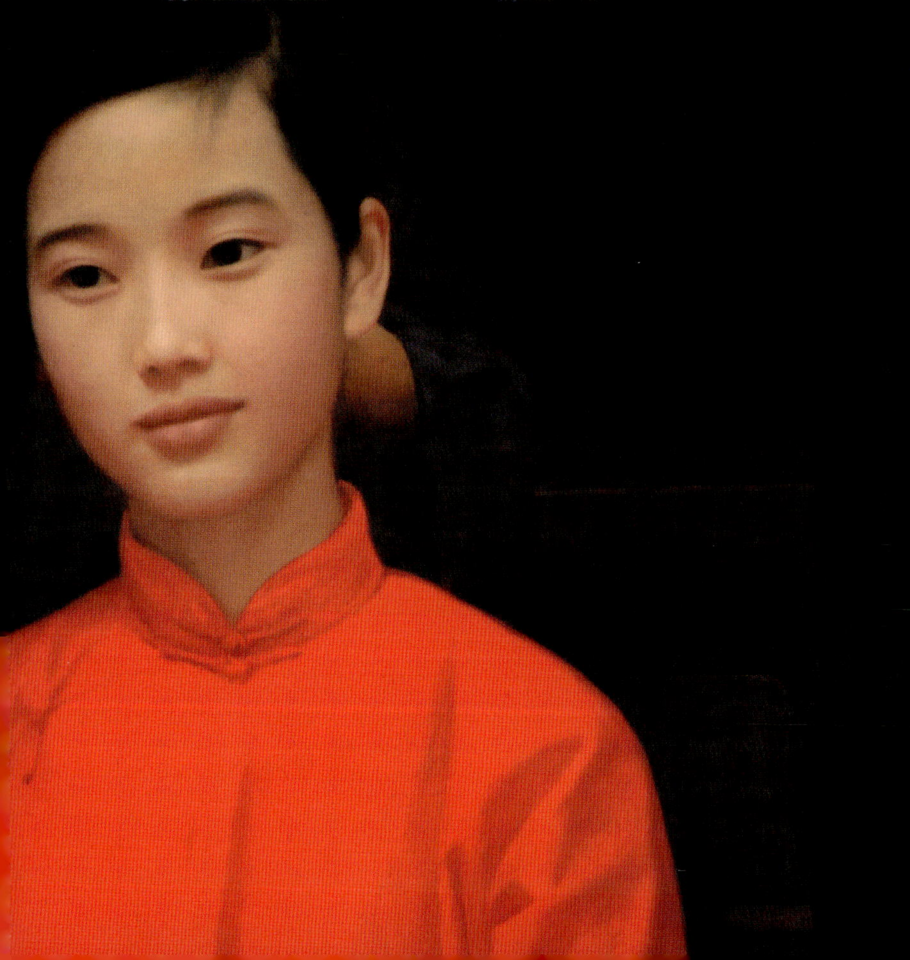
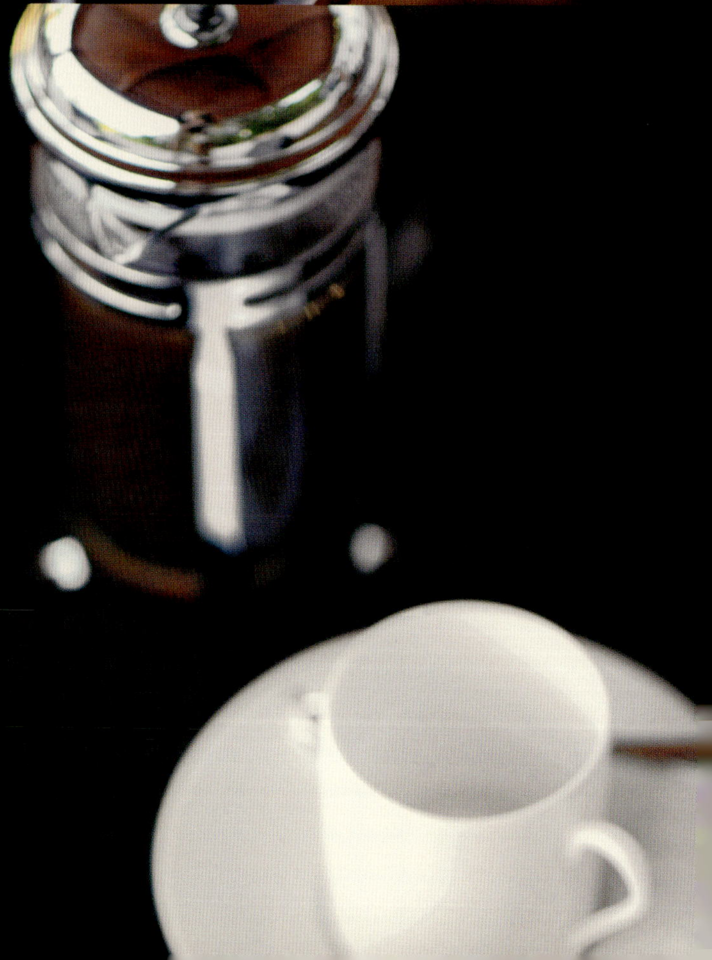

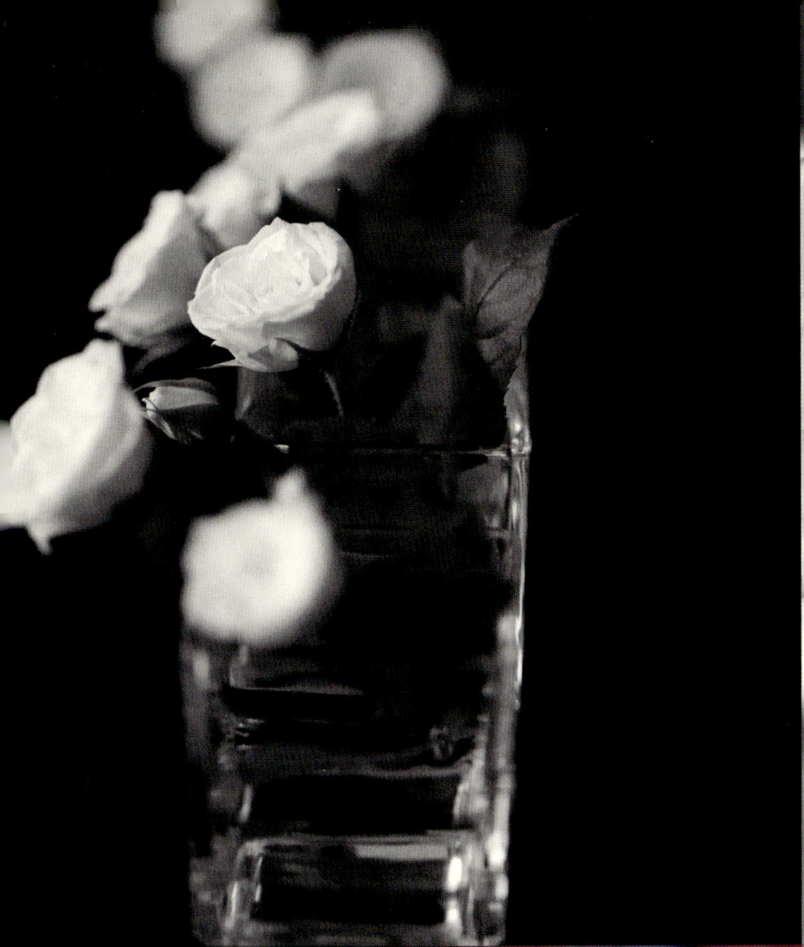
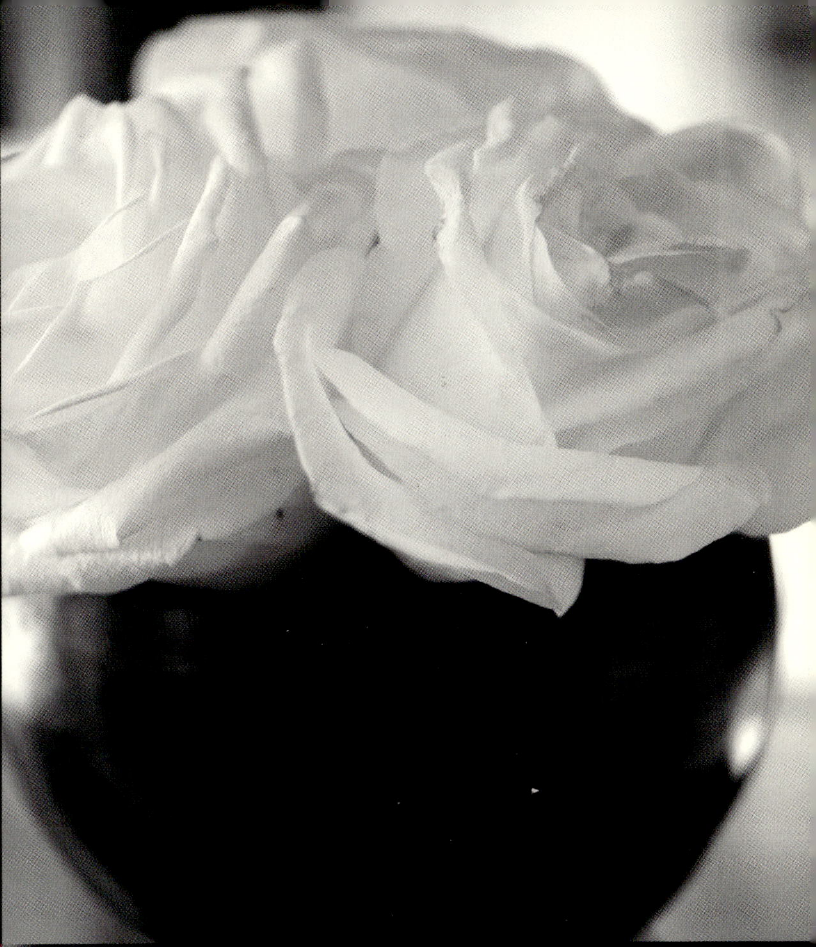
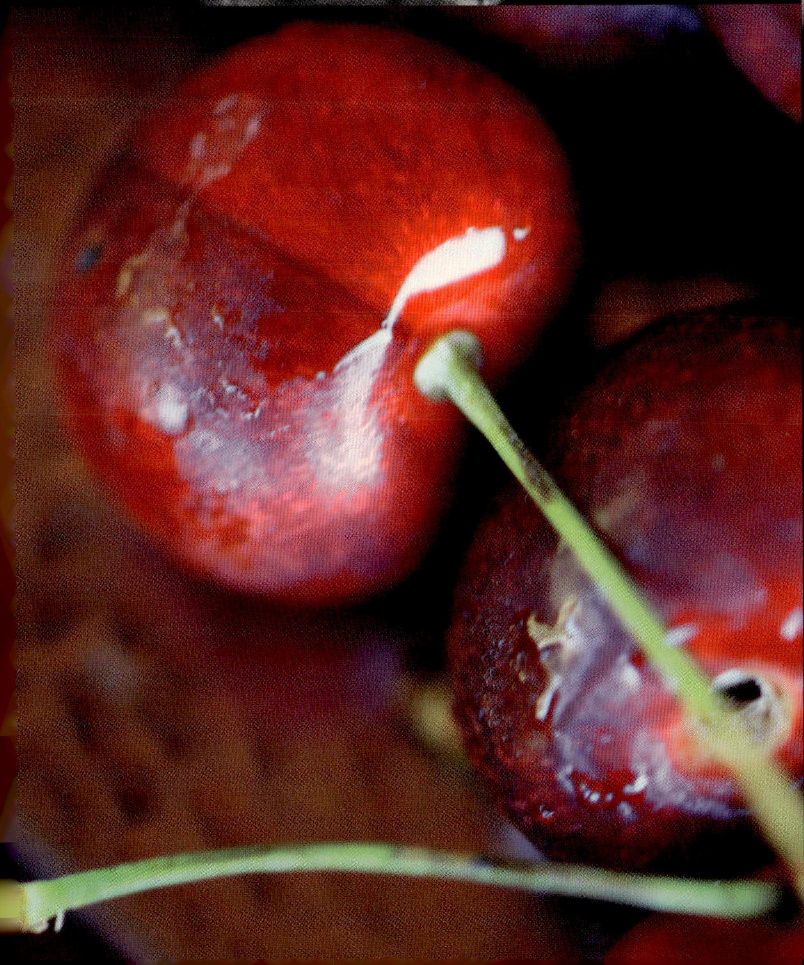
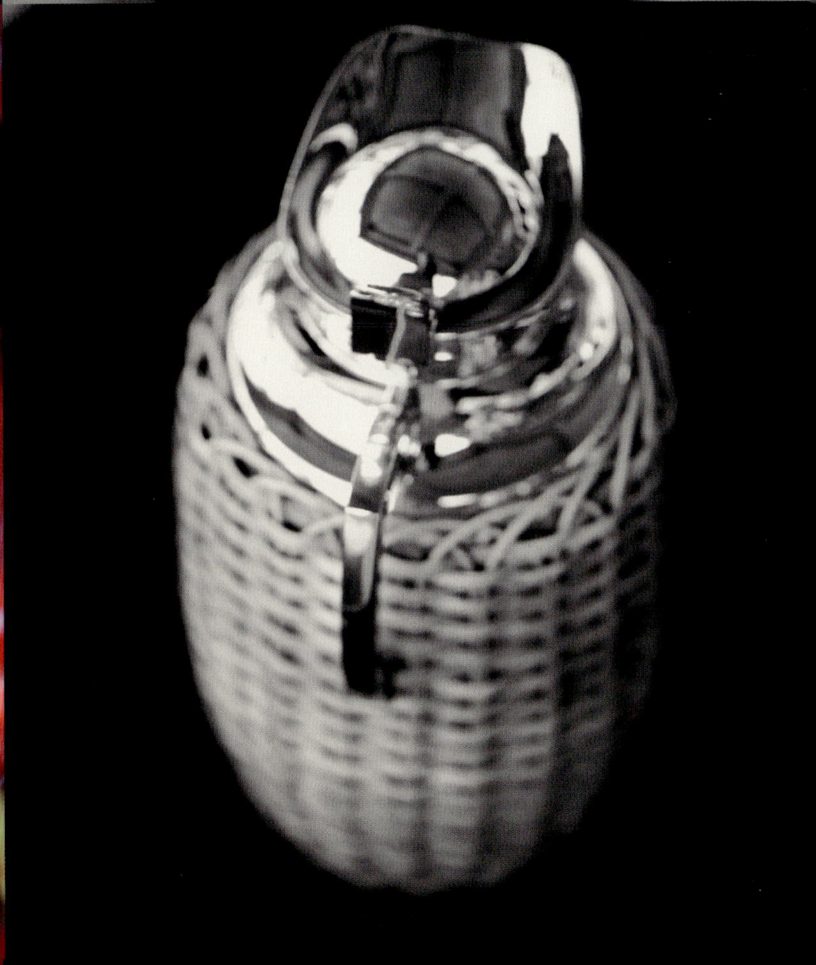

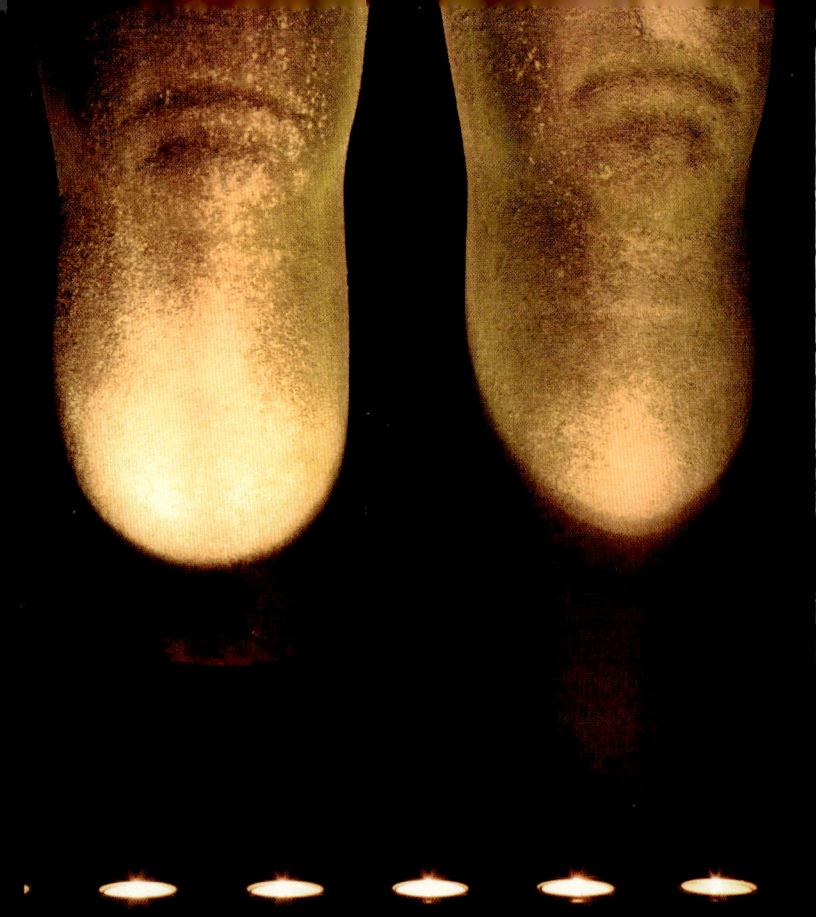
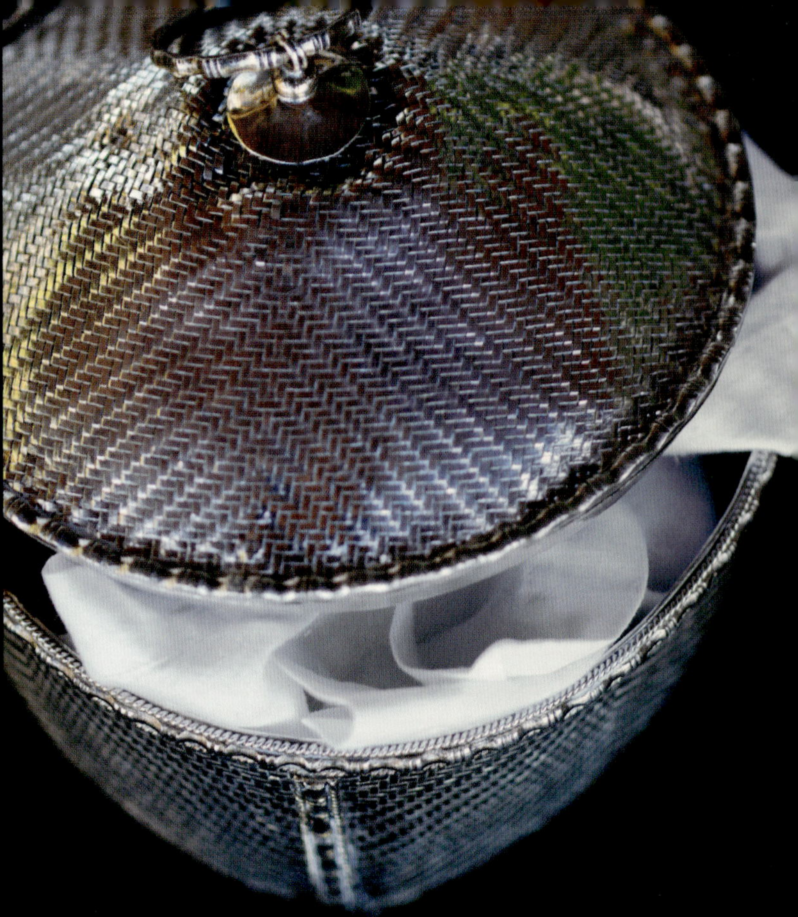
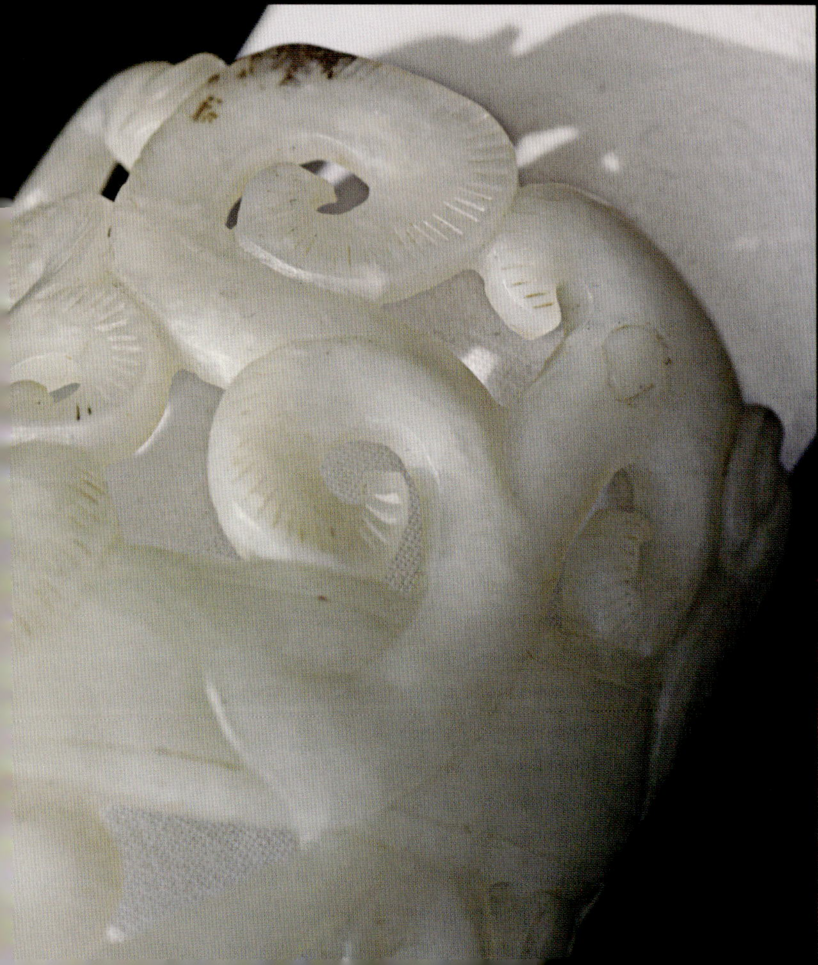
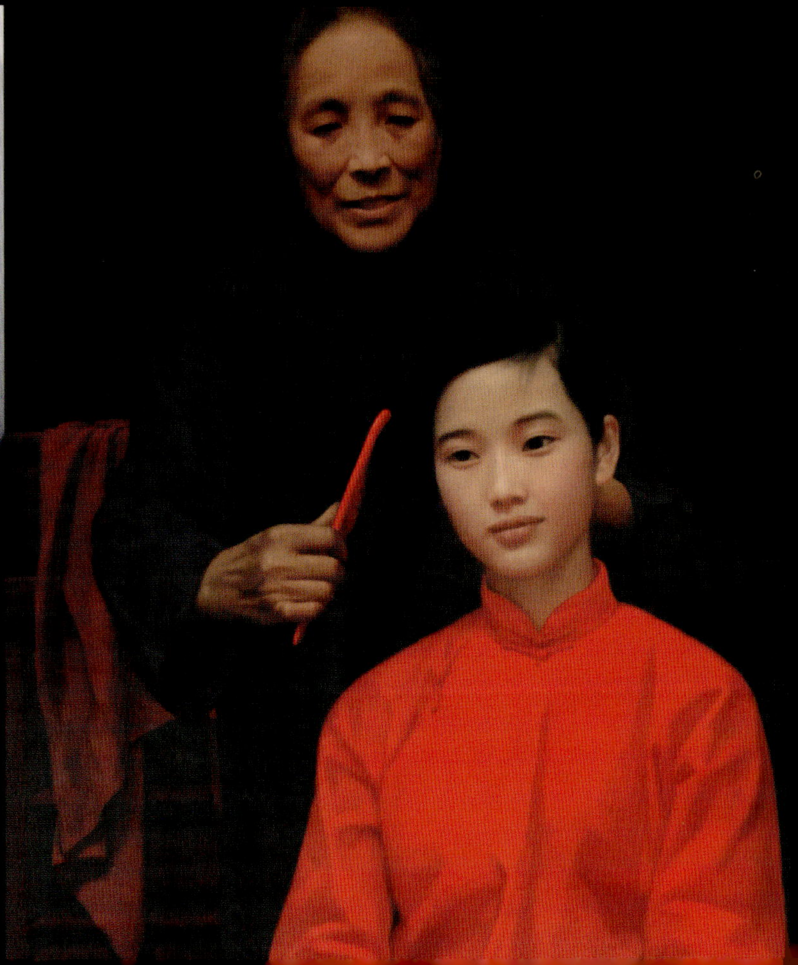

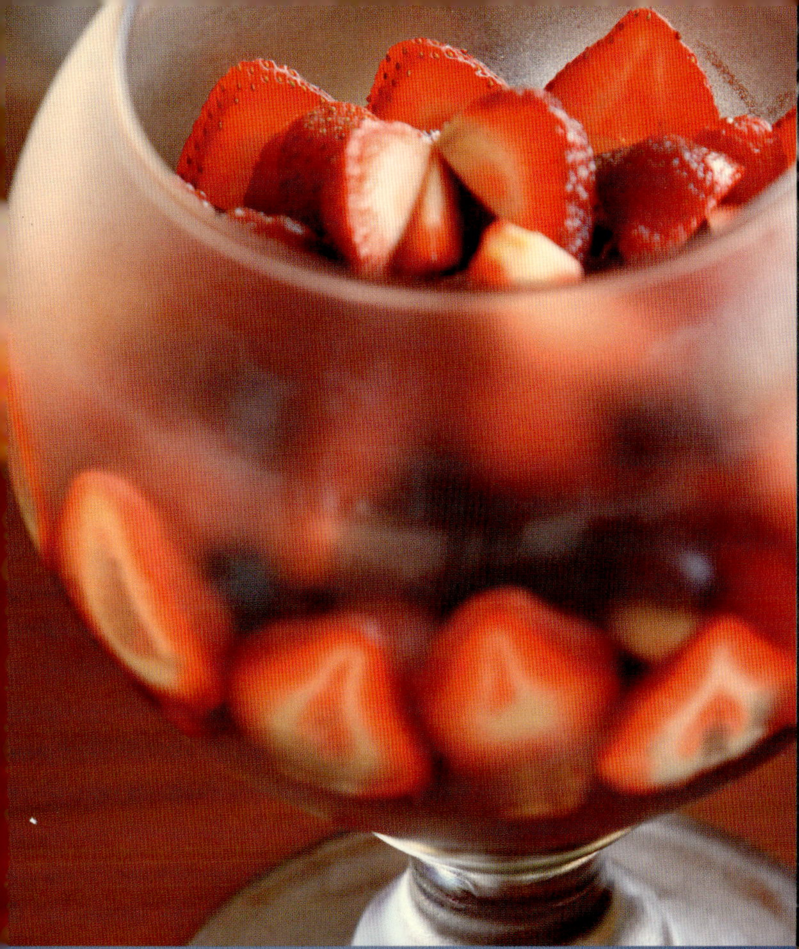
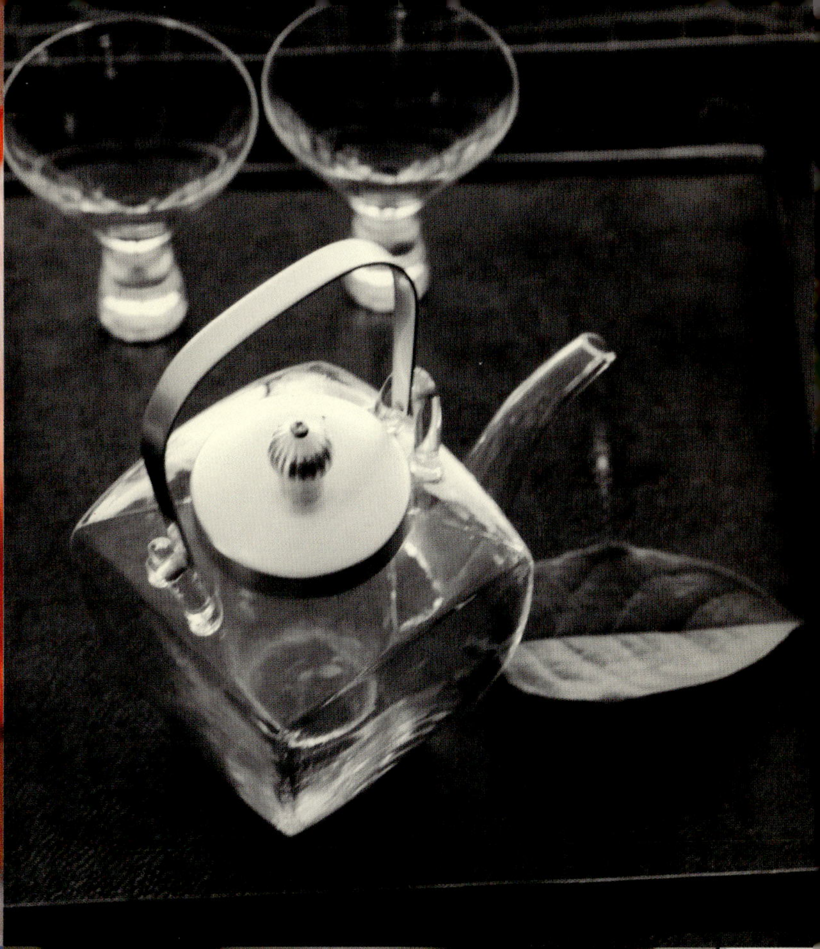
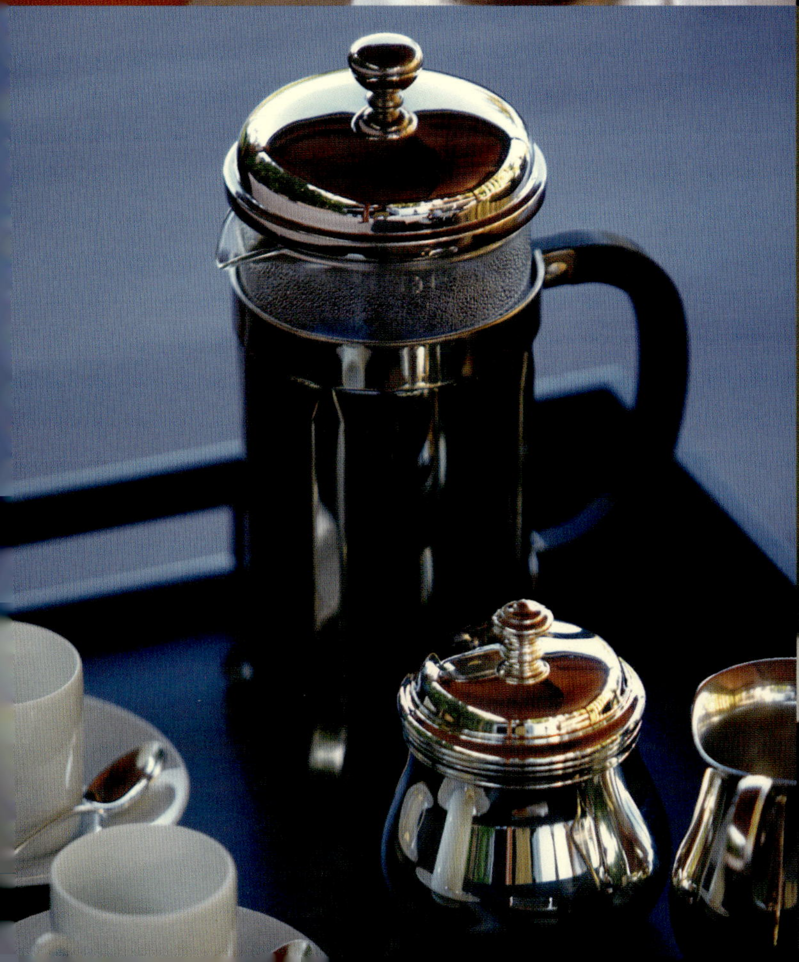
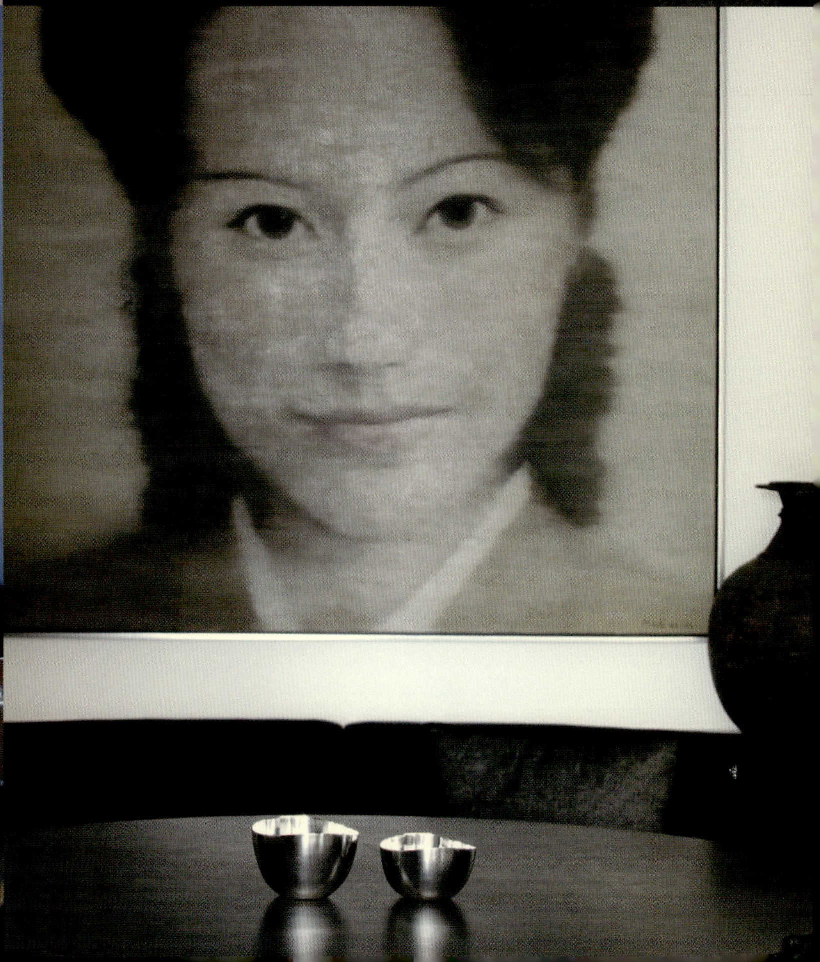

Château d'Estoublon
HUILE
VIERGE EXTRA MONOVARIÉTALE
D'OLIVE
Château d'Estoublon
HUILE
VIERGE EXTRA MONOVARIÉTALE
D'OLIVE
Huile d'olive de catégorie supérieure obtenue directement des olives et uniquement par des procédés mécaniques.
100 ML
EXTRAITE A FROID
3.38 FL.OZ

BUY FOOD THAT LOOKS ELEGANT.
IT CAN GO STRAIGHT
ON THE TABLE.

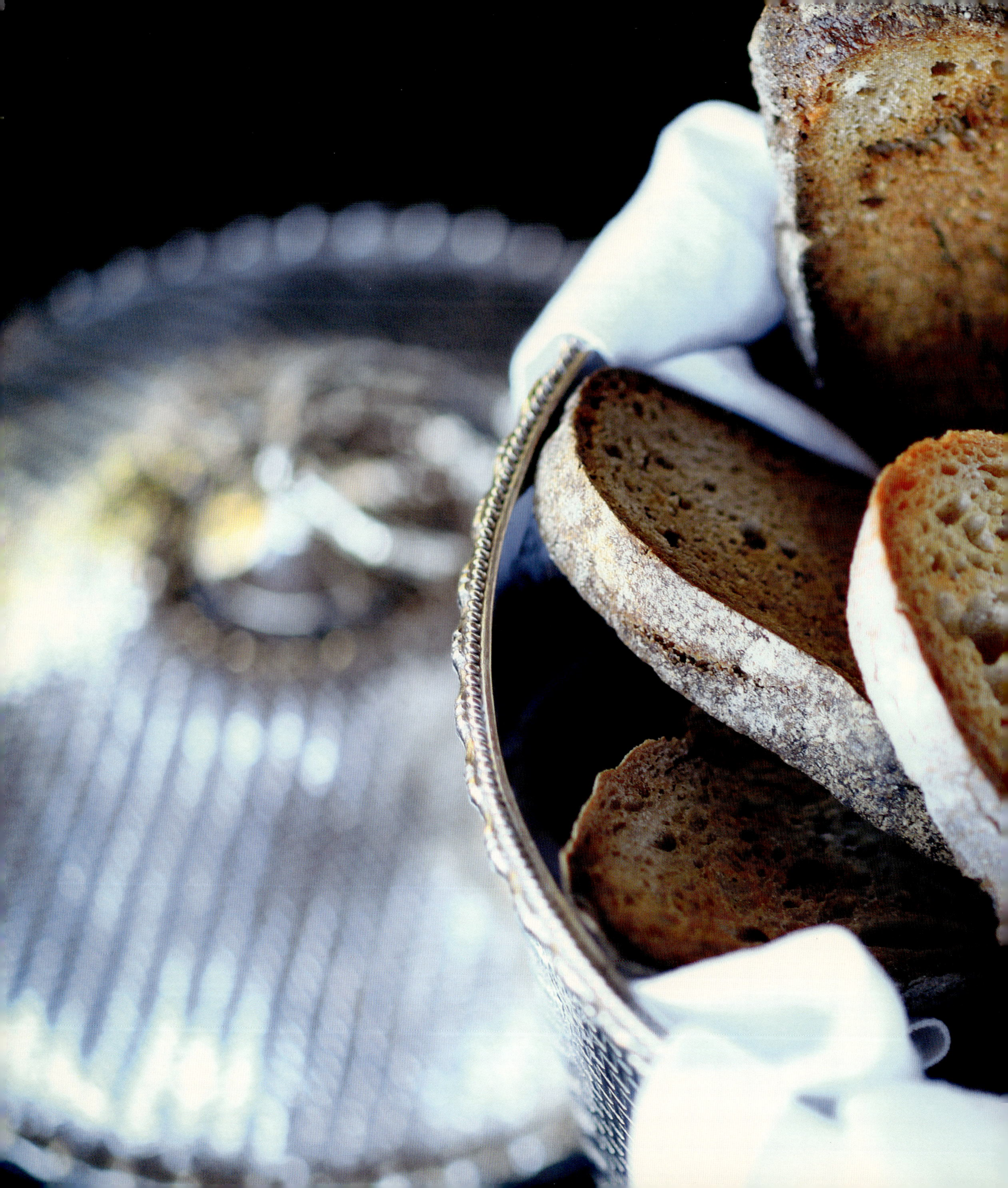

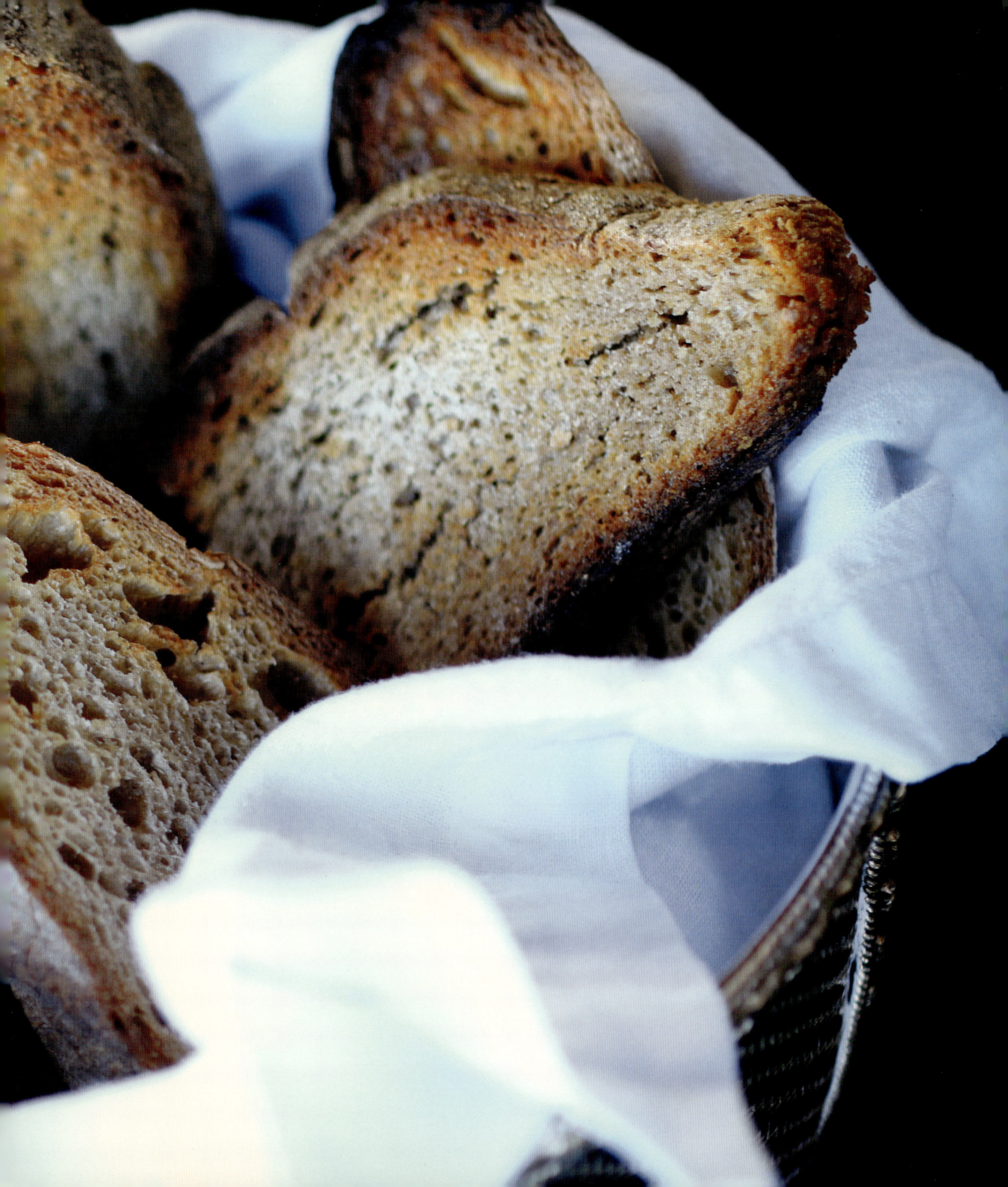

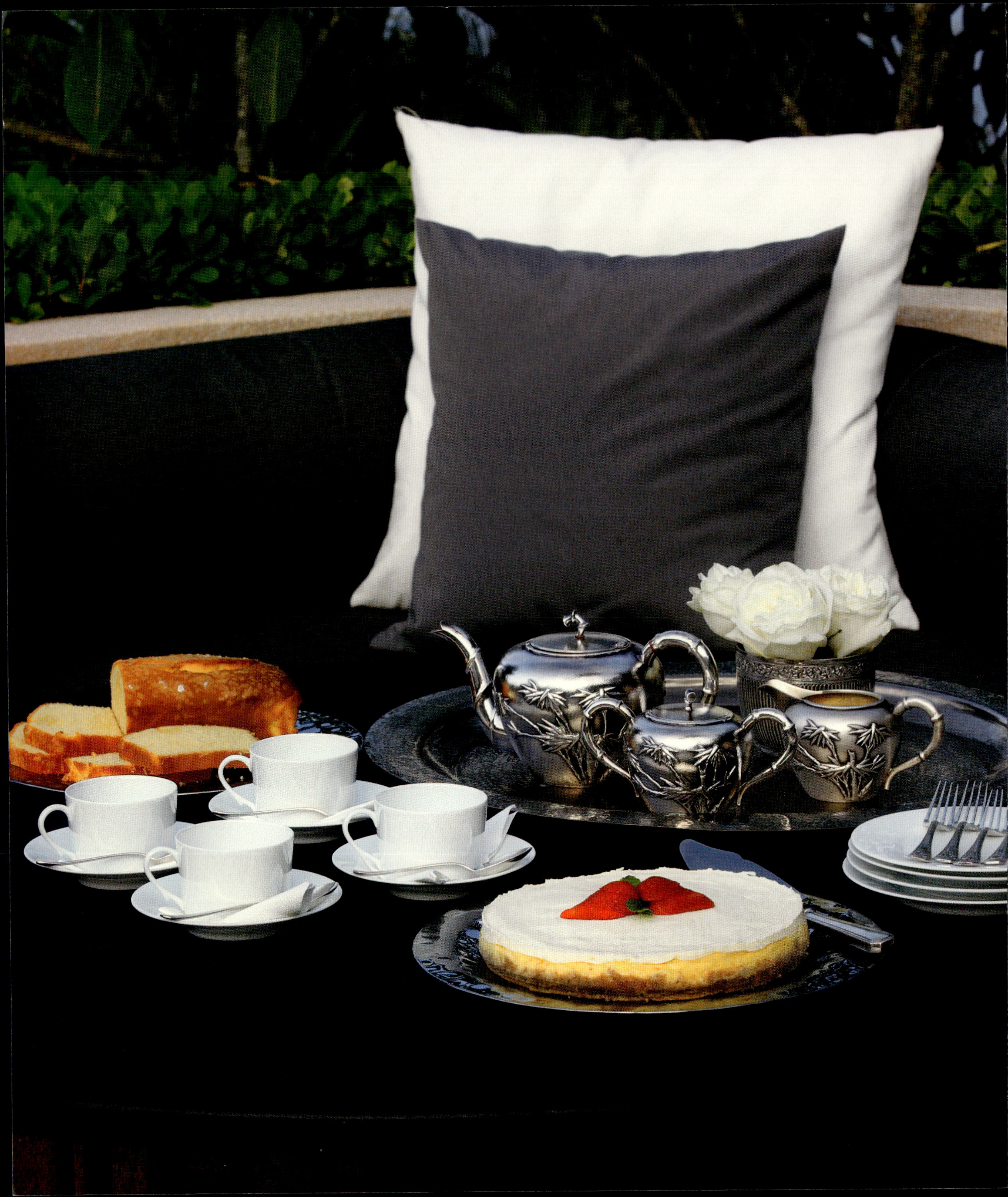

FOOD IN PRACTICE

I never miss an opportunity to entertain family. When we get together, even if it's just for afternoon tea on our terrace, I would never NOT make an effort.

But the word 'effort' is misleading. It makes it sound like afternoon tea is a chore and it is not: it is a pleasure. I enjoy bringing out my 'Dragon' or 'Bamboo Flower' silver teapots. I collect tea sets and I love having the chance to use them in different combinations. But I never change the pound cake and the cheesecake that have been my sons' and husband's favourites for so long. Why would I? It's an enduring tradition and the longer it continues, the more important it becomes.

The best part is that they think I am doing afternoon tea for them, but in fact I am doing it for myself. It makes a small part of my day special with very little effort. It takes only four cups, two cakes, a tray, a teapot and a few flowers to create a moment of pure joy.

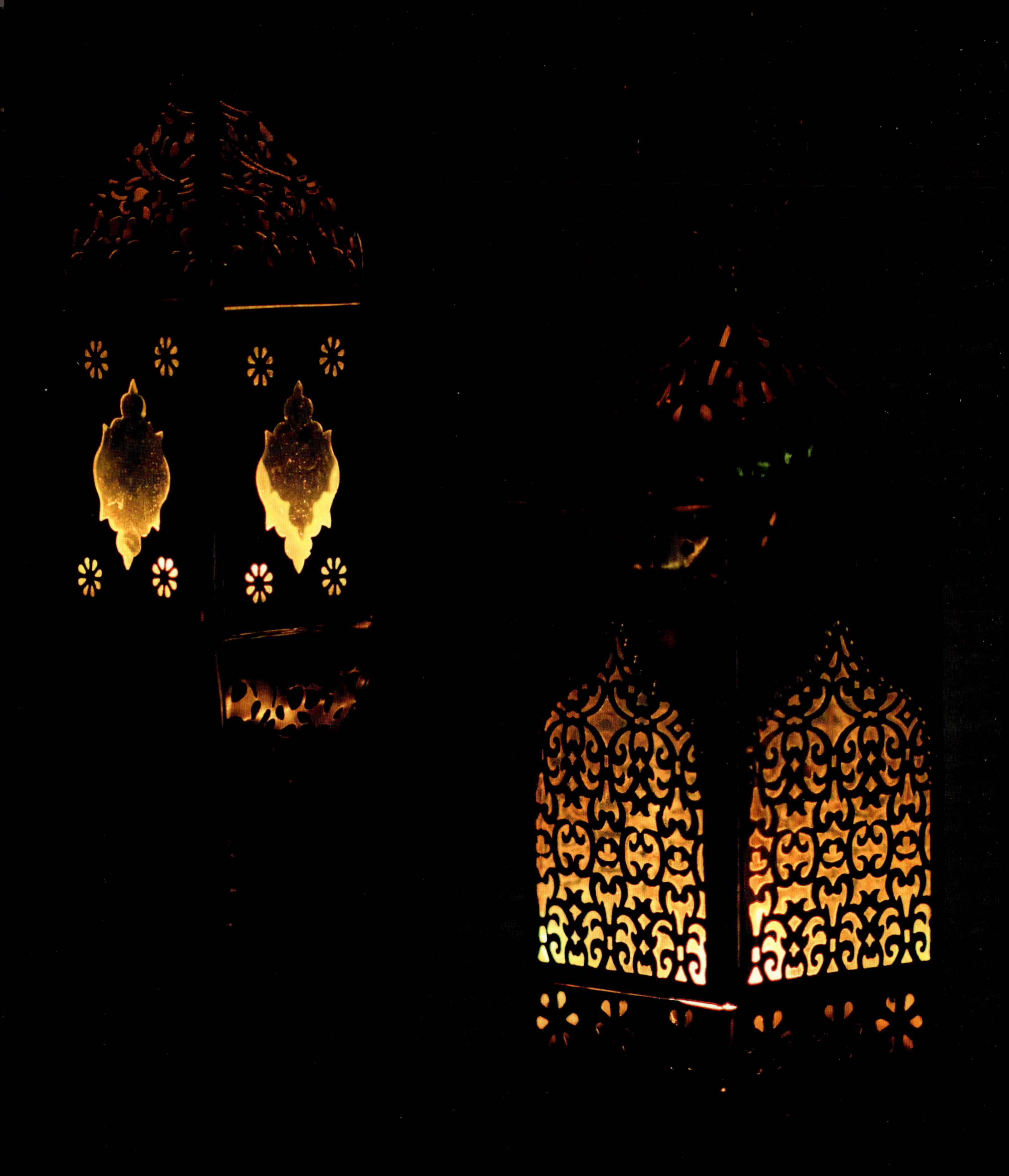

4
CANDLES

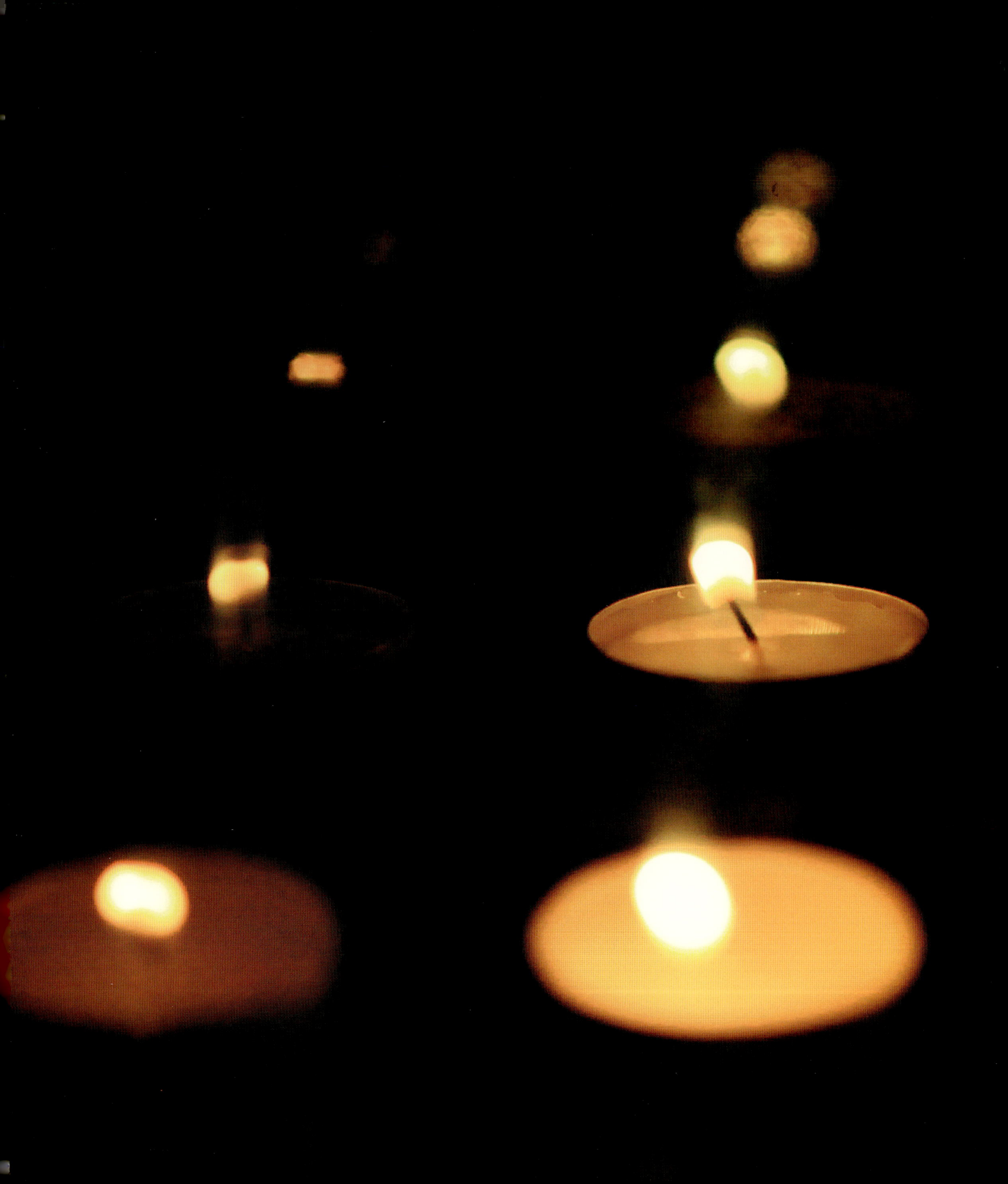

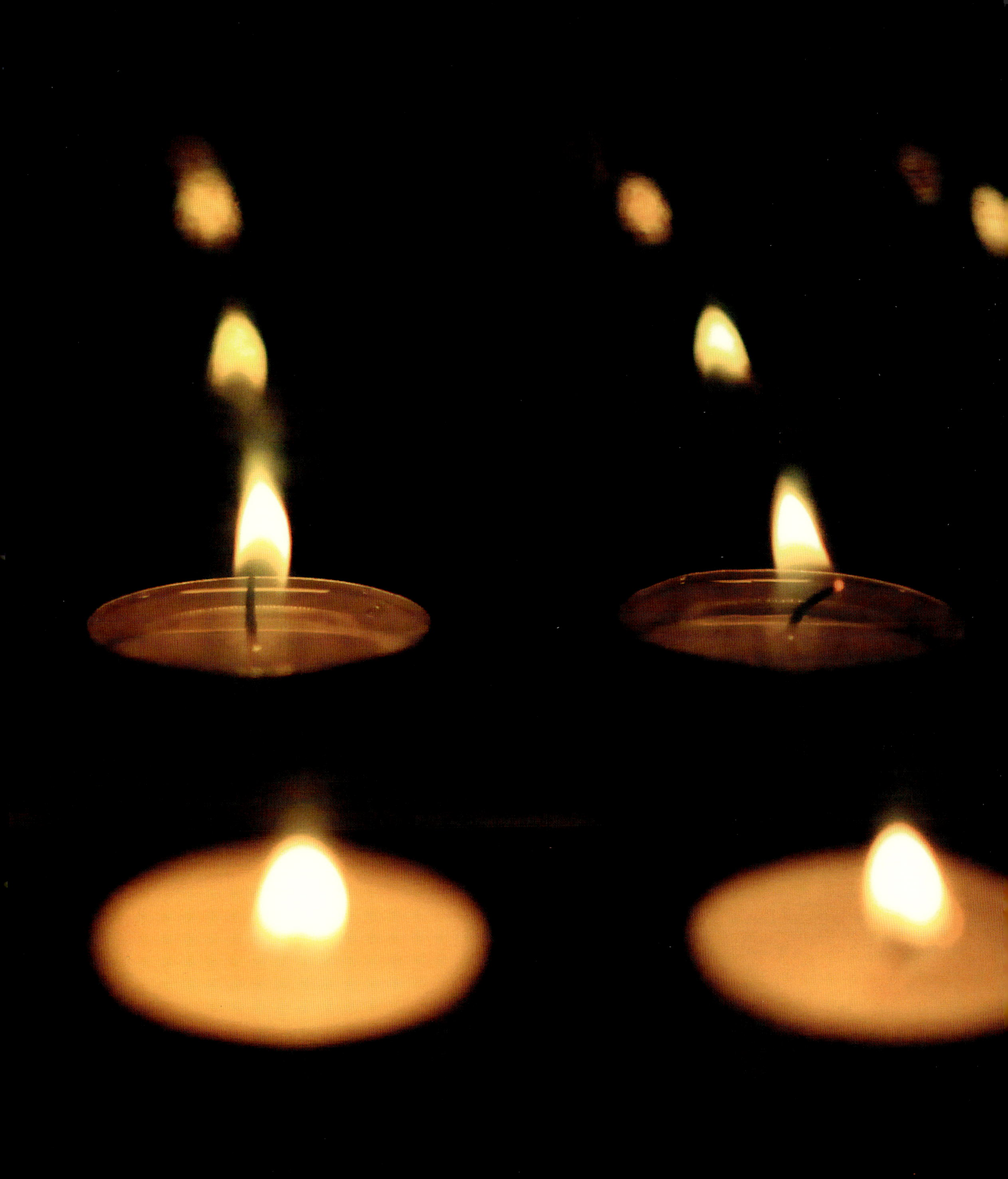

Light is so important. If the lighting at a party is harsh and unflattering, you are unlikely really to enjoy yourself.

Candles are the key to creating a seductive, pleasing ambience, and the least expensive candles are usually the best. Tea lights can be purchased in almost any supermarket; they cost next to nothing and you should use them as much as possible. With candles, and especially tea lights, it's very much a case of more is better. You can use candles to highlight features in a room or outdoors, and to create a sense of theatre. Most importantly, candles provide a level of lighting that makes everyone look good.

It's definitely not about the candles you use – it's about the effect they create.

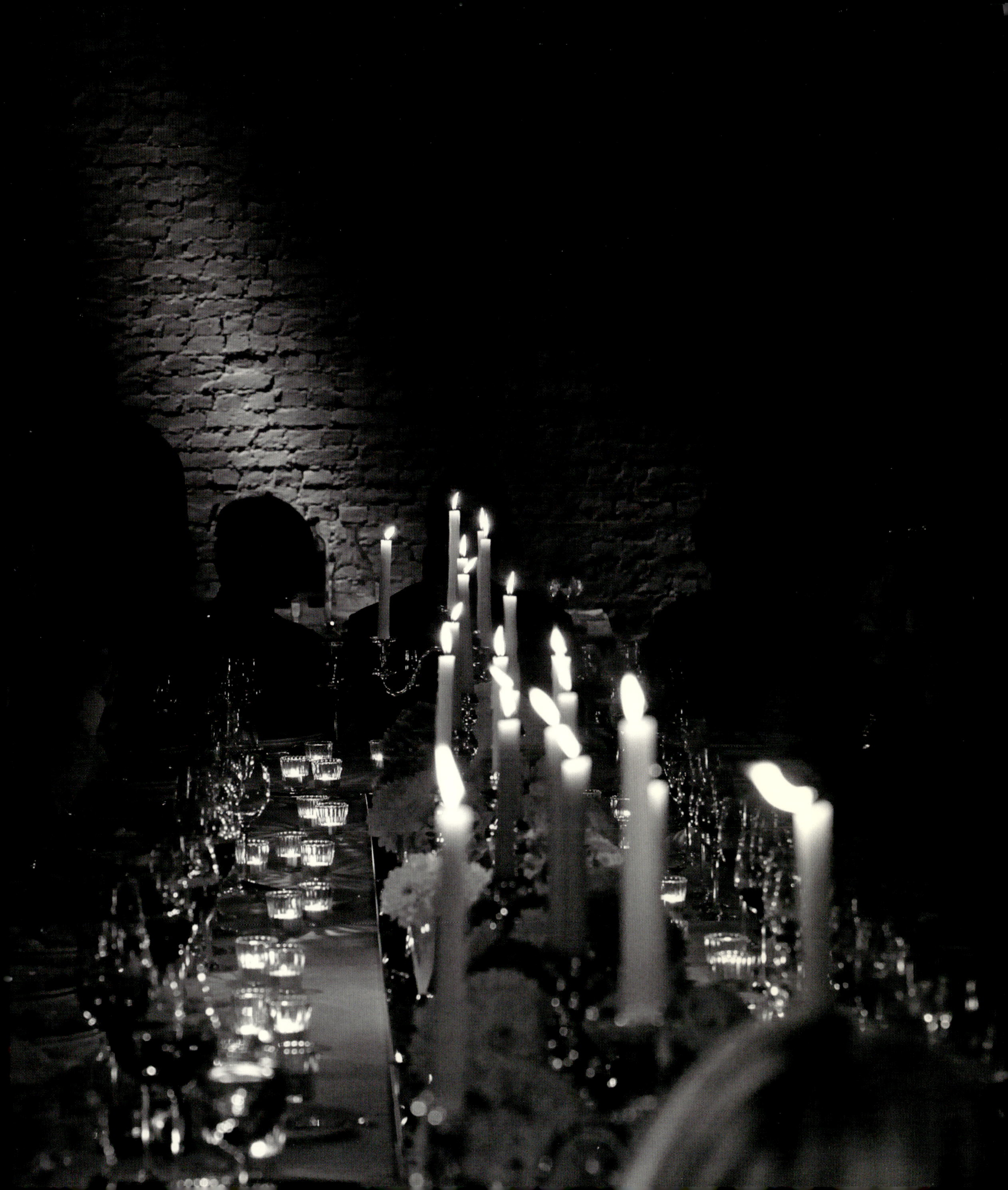

THE BEST CANDLES ALSO HAPPEN TO BE THE CHEAPEST.

TEA LIGHTS CAN BE USED EVERYWHERE, ESPECIALLY TO HIGHLIGHT SHAPES OR FEATURES.

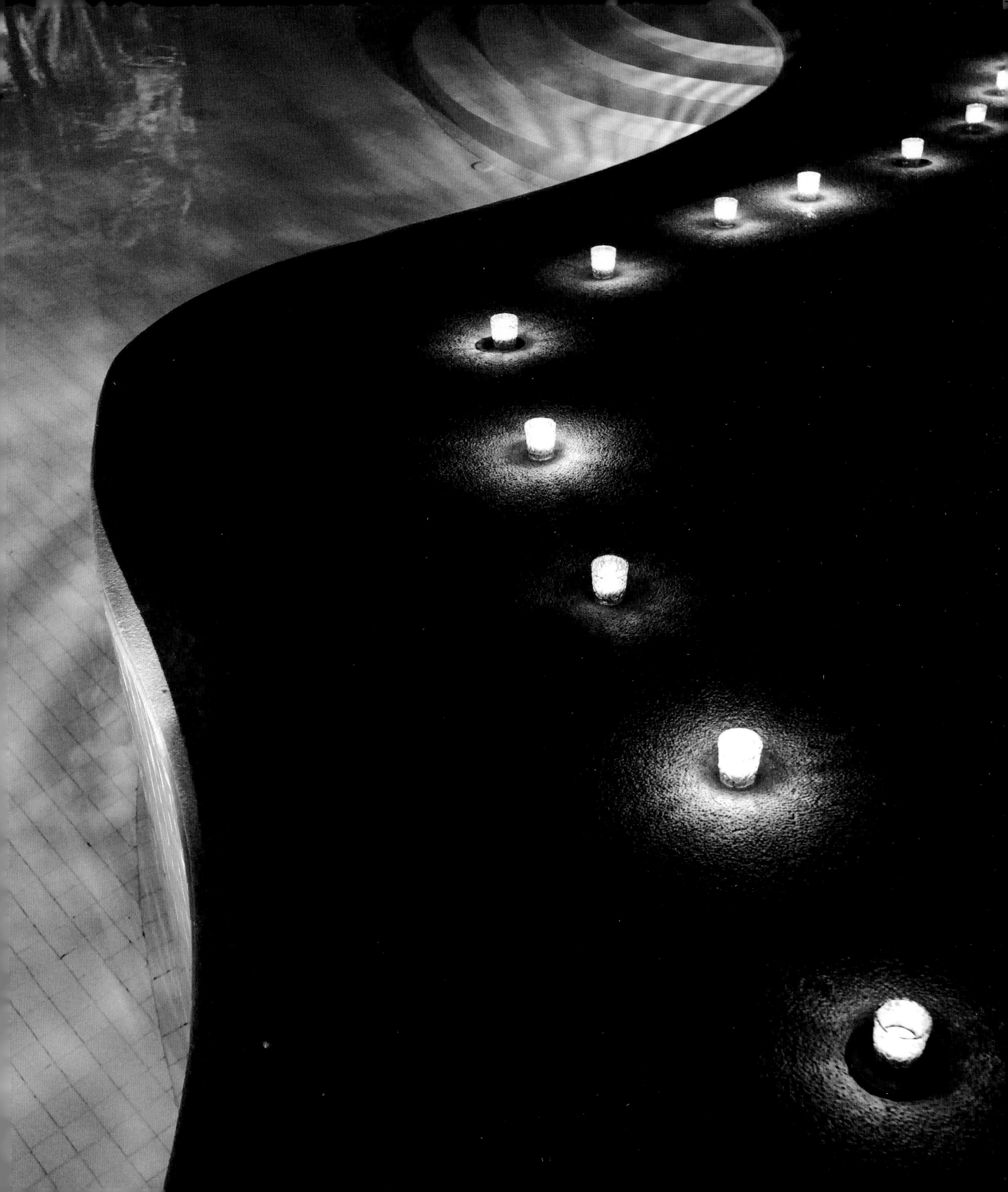

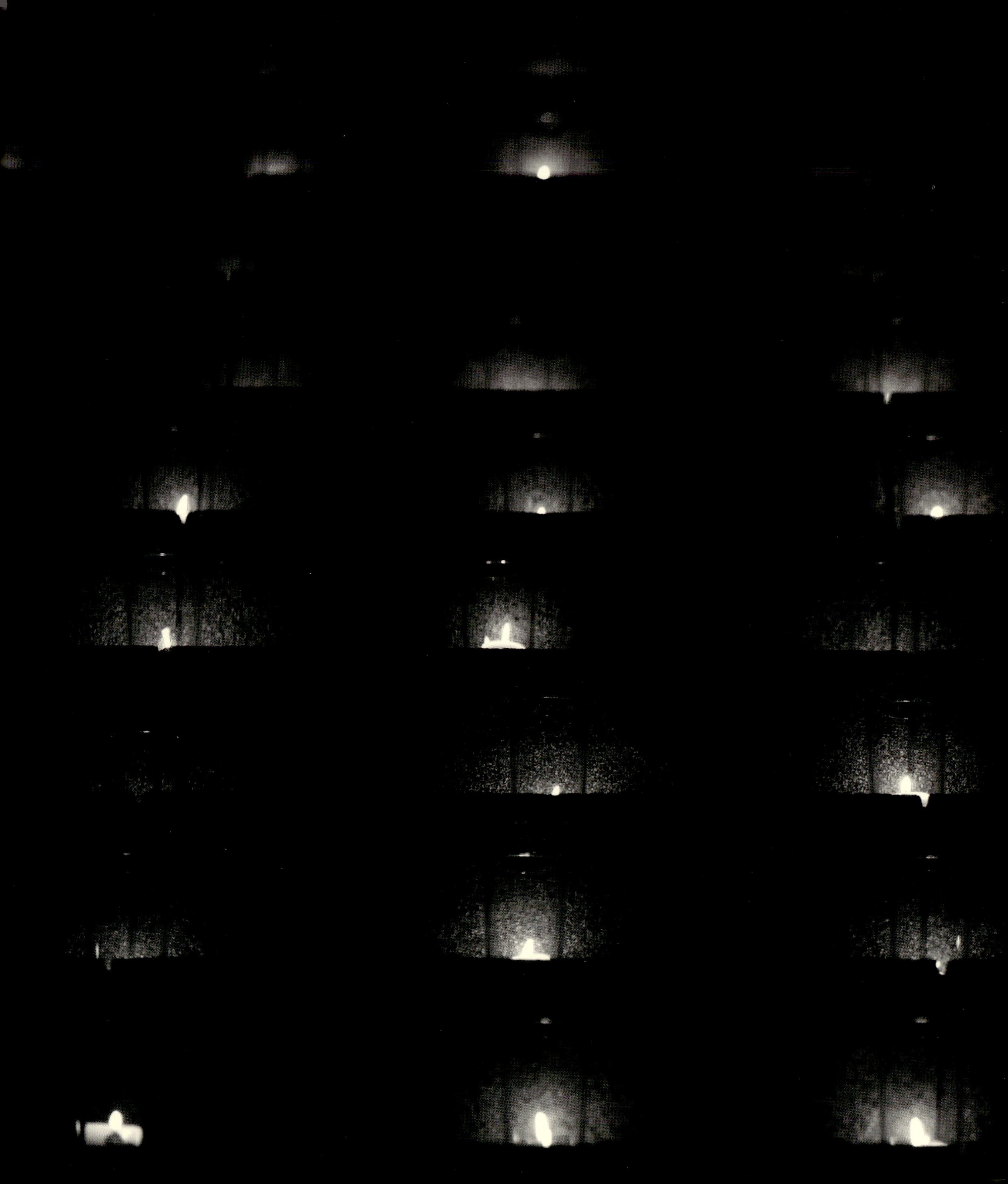

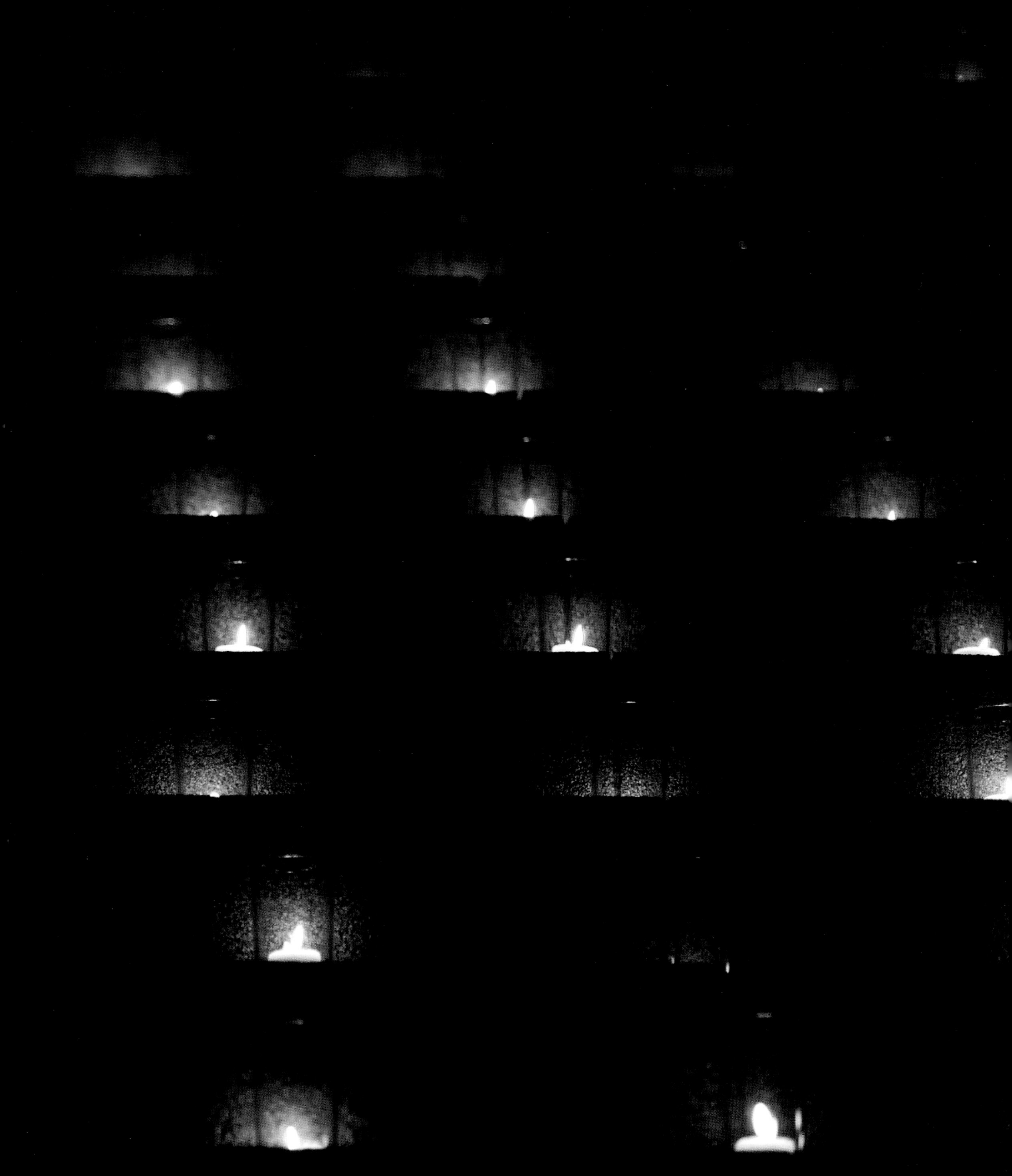

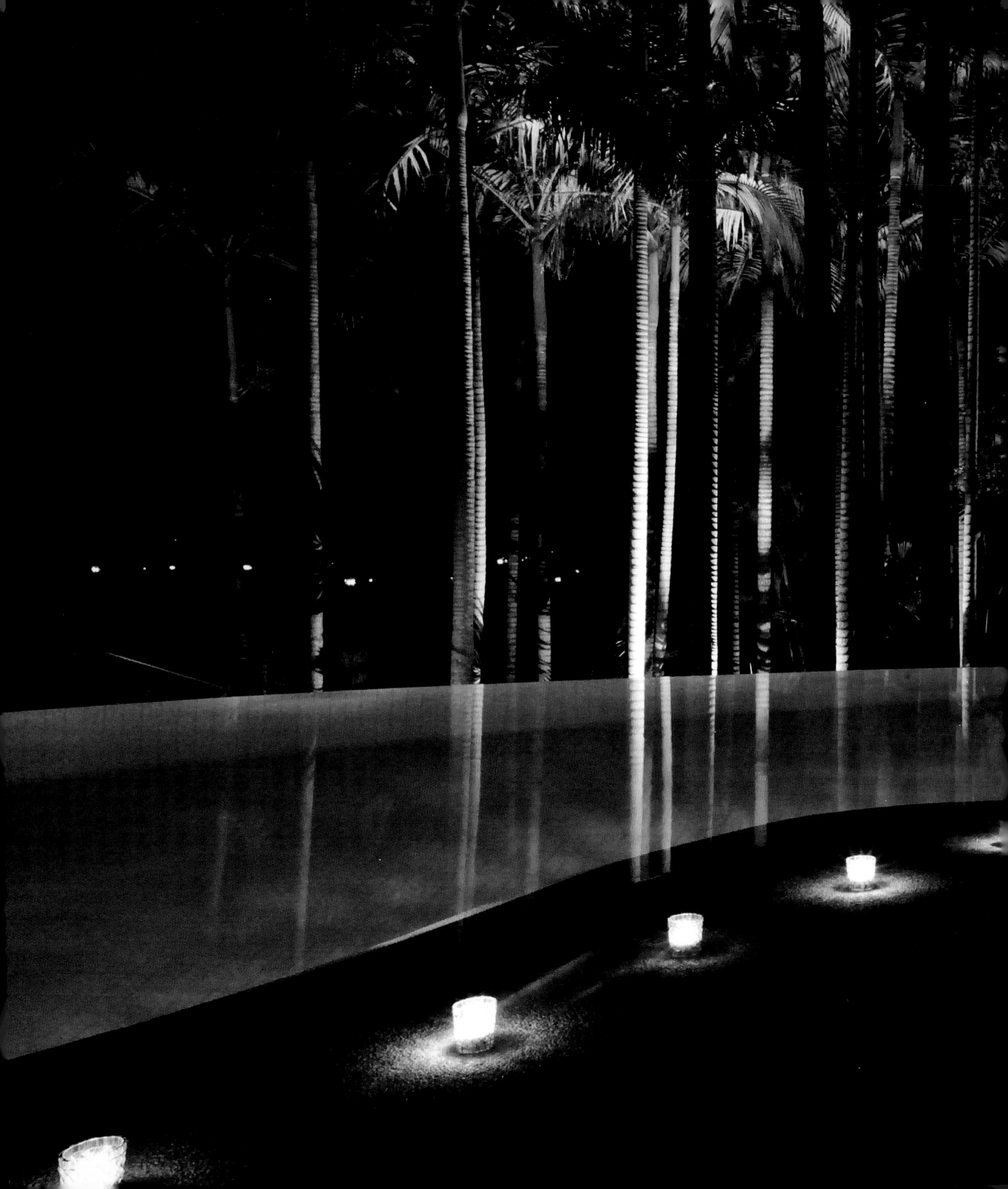

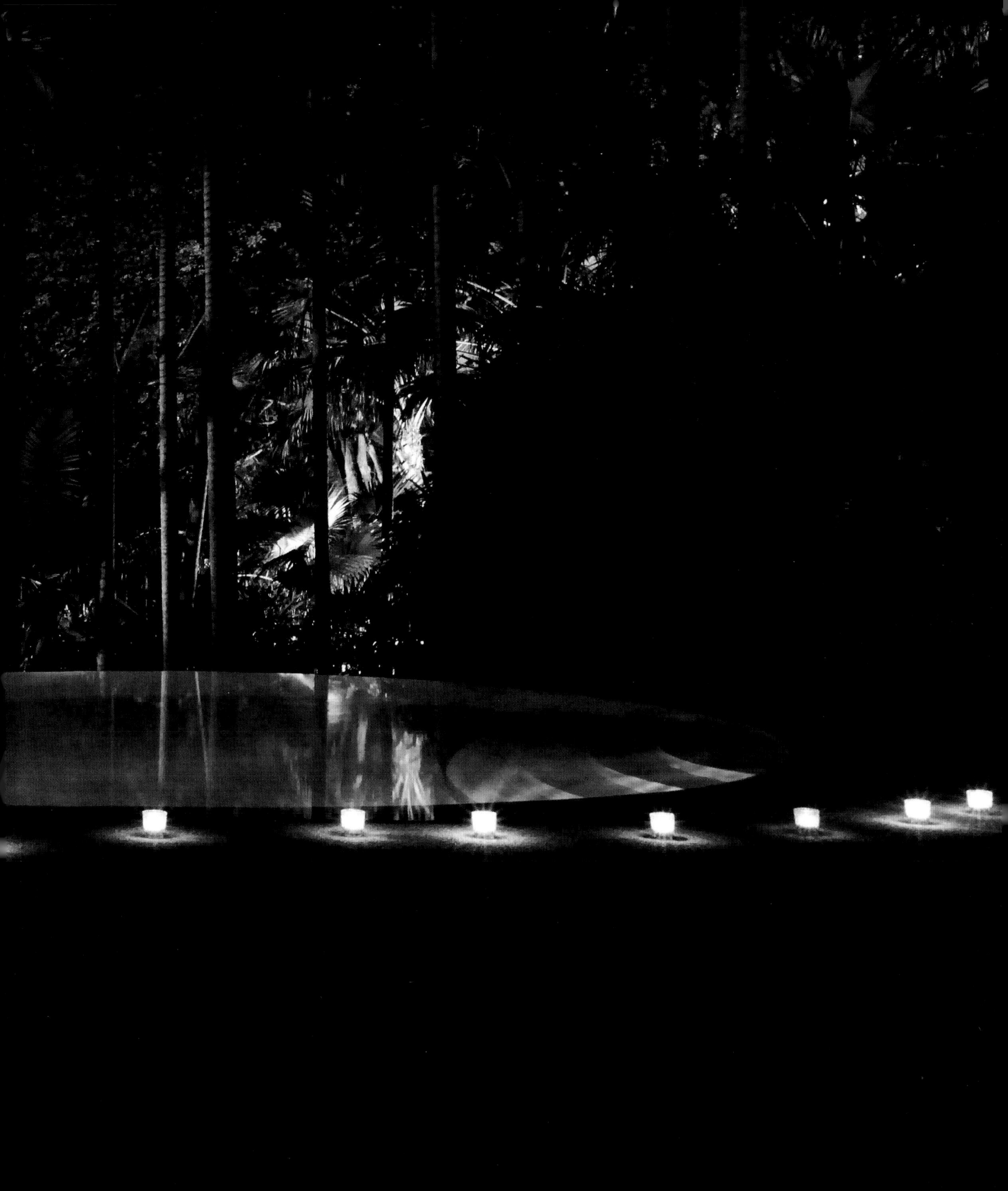

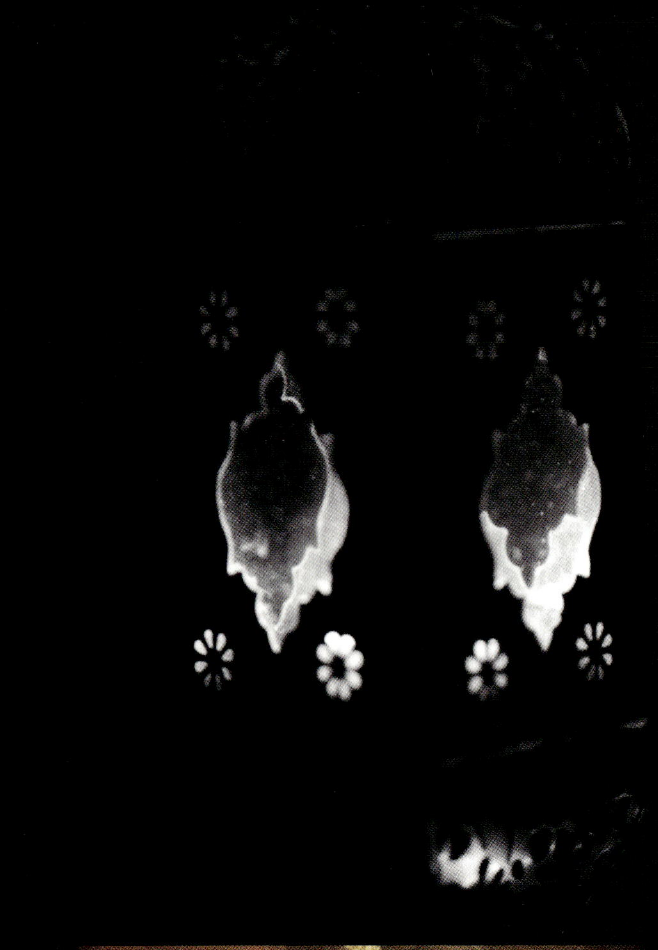
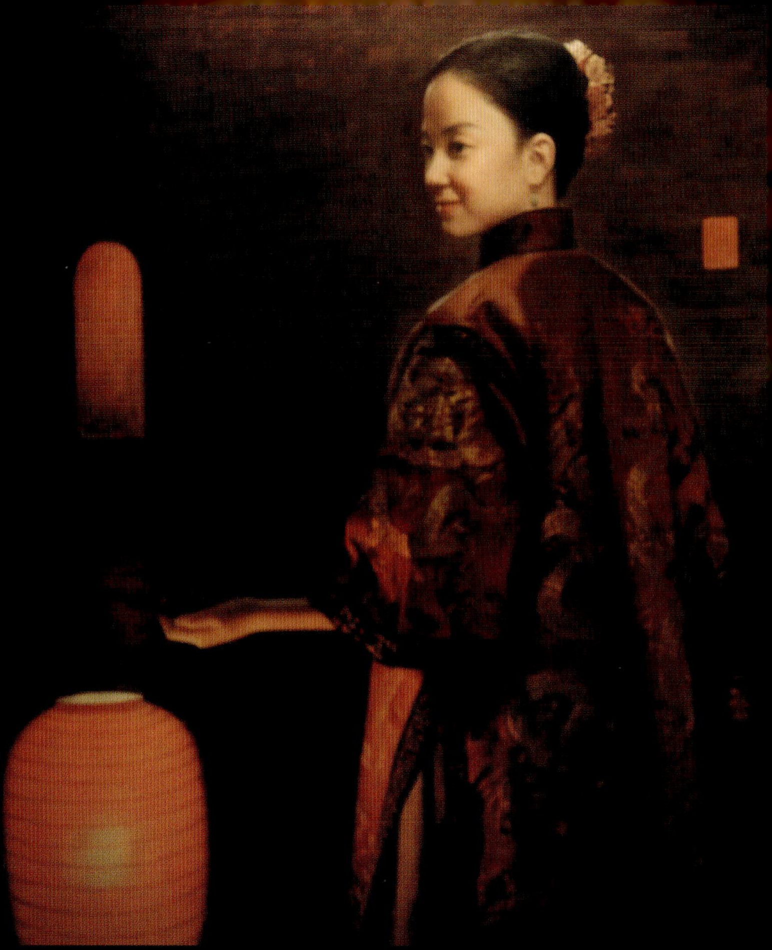
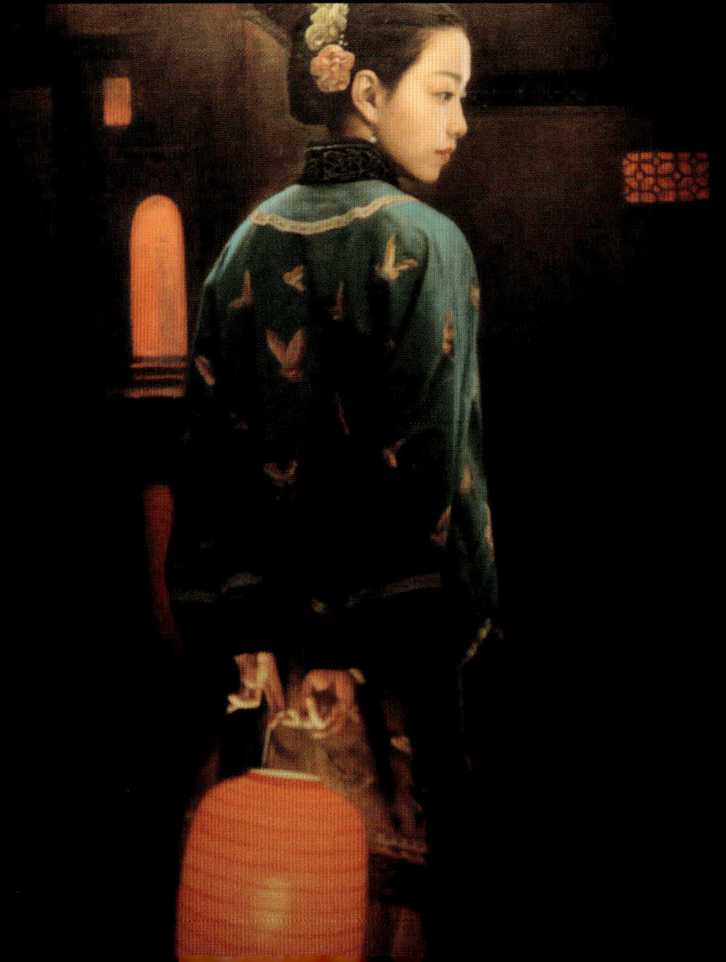
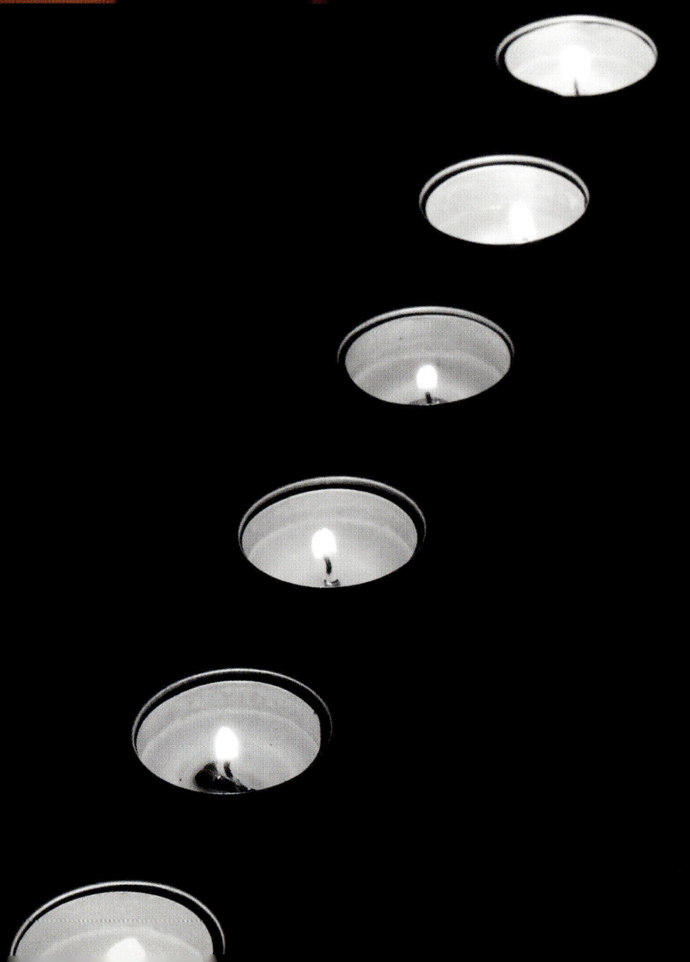

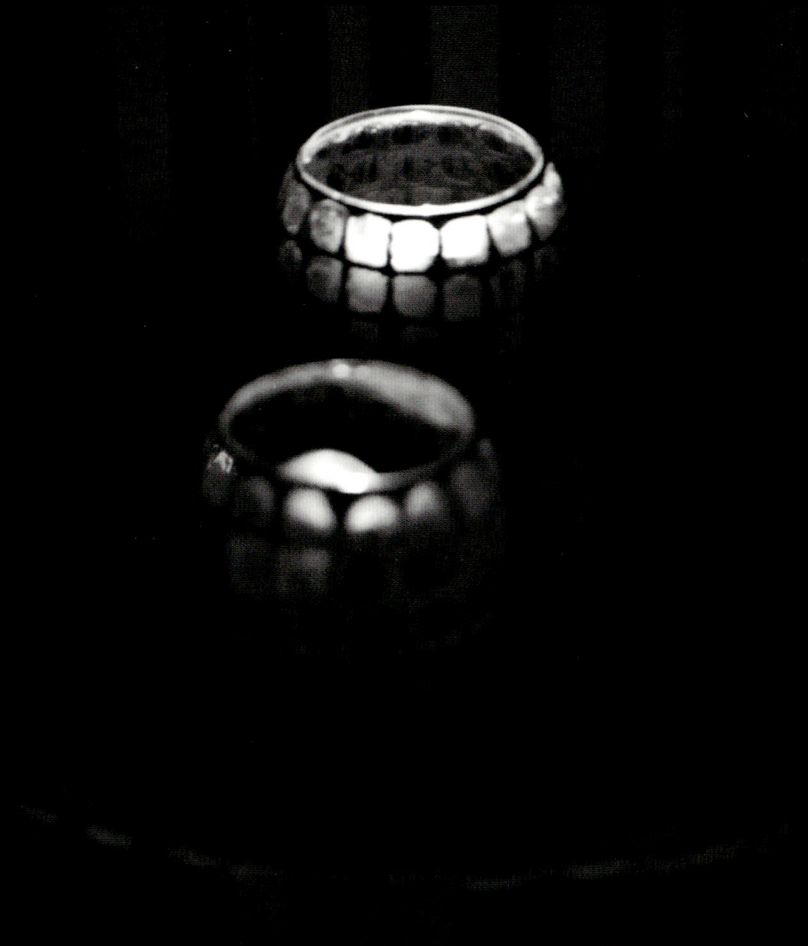
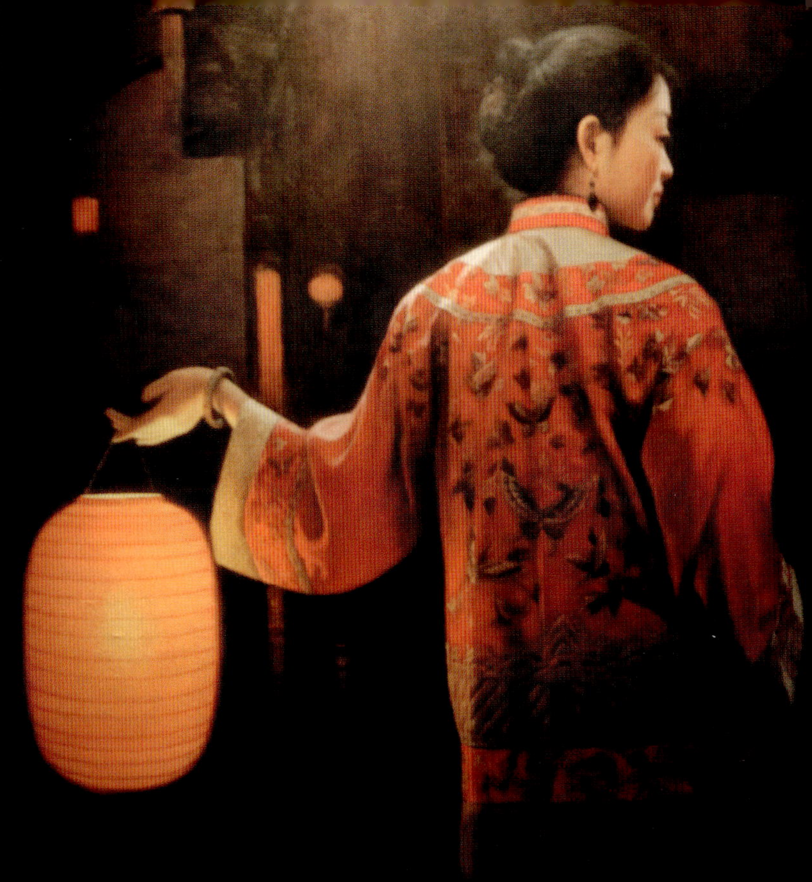
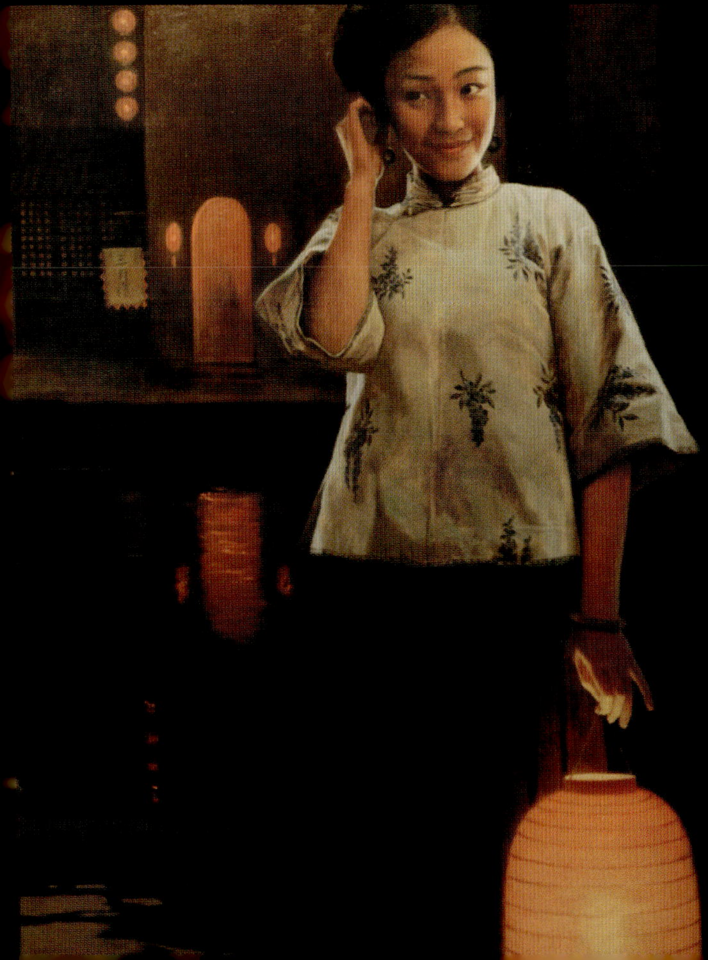
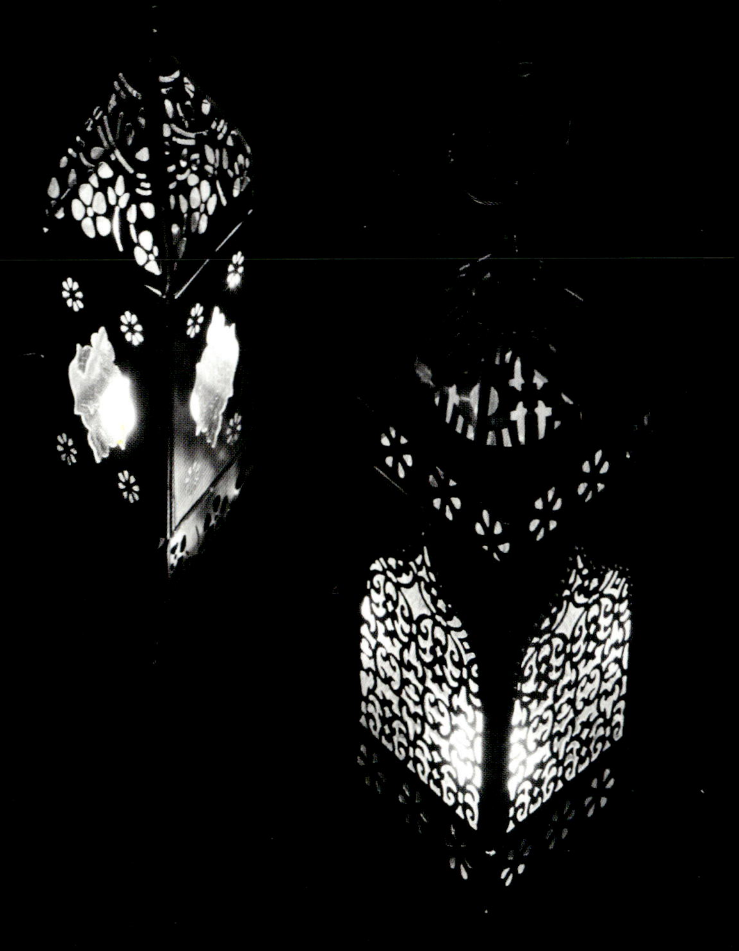

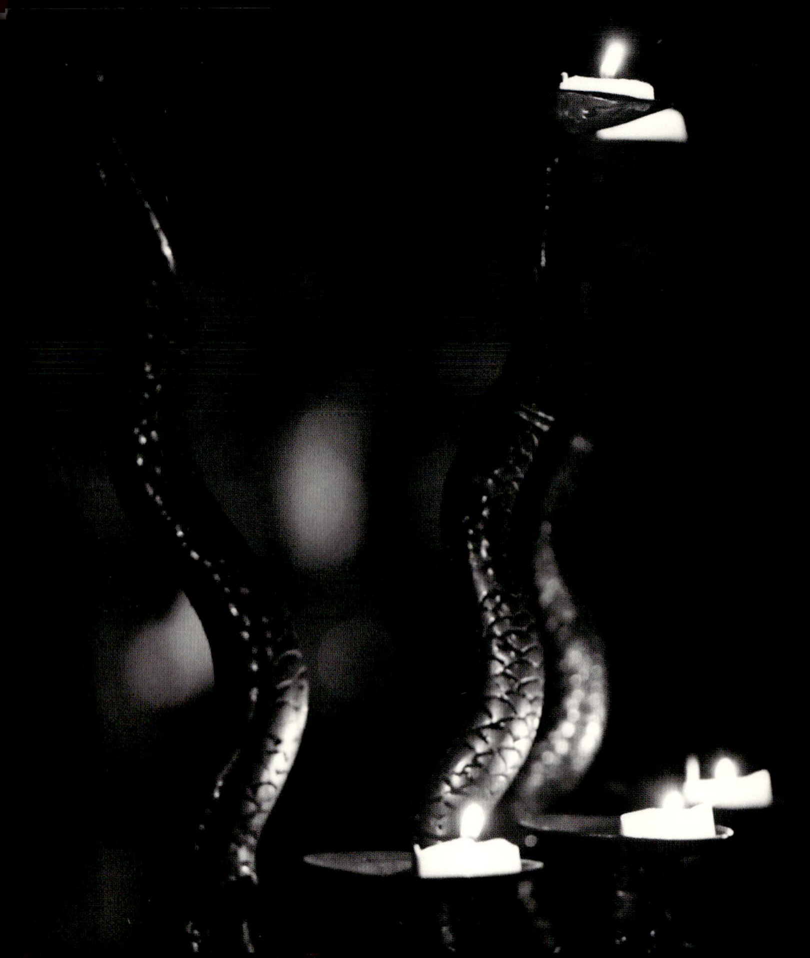
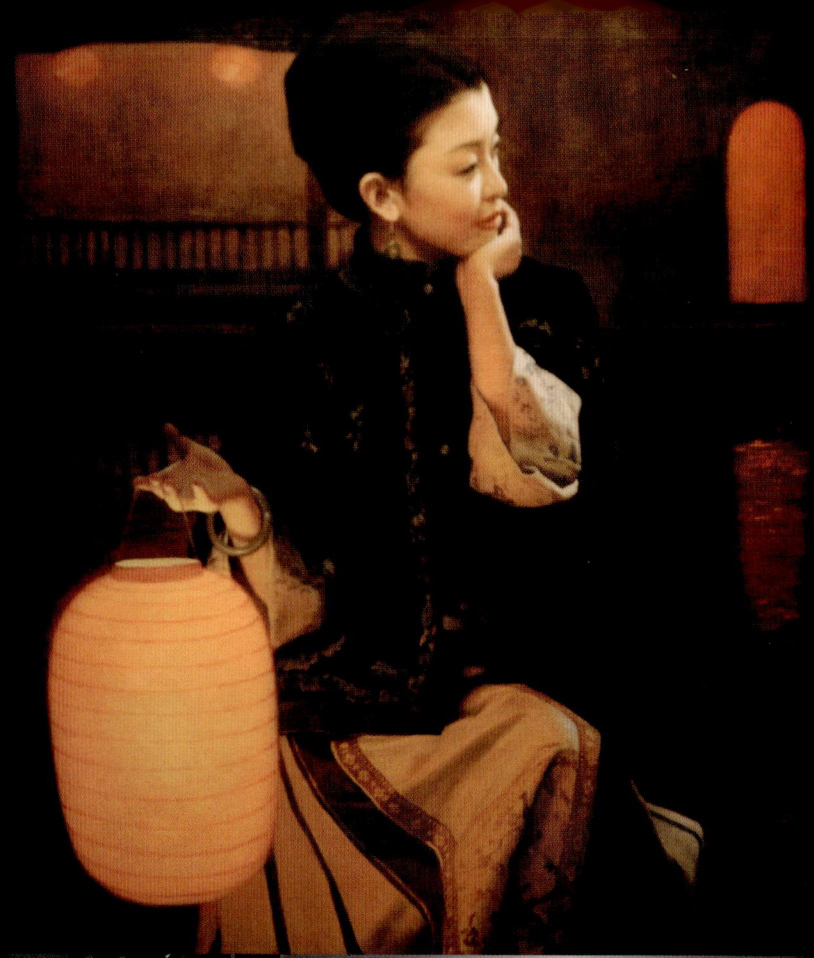
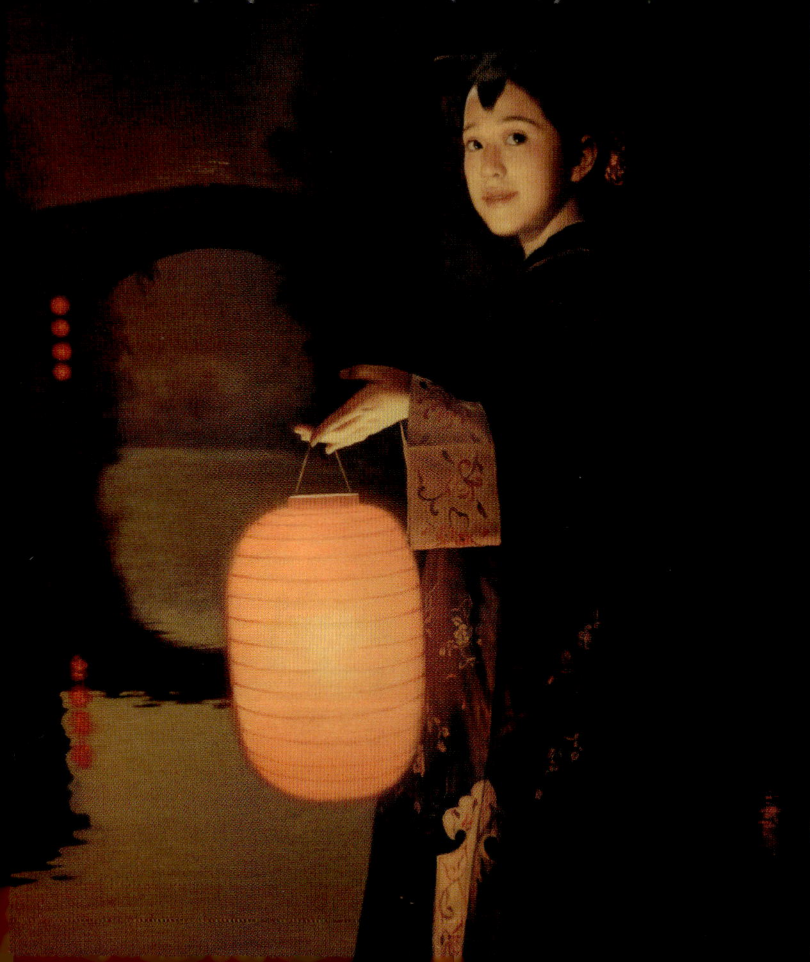
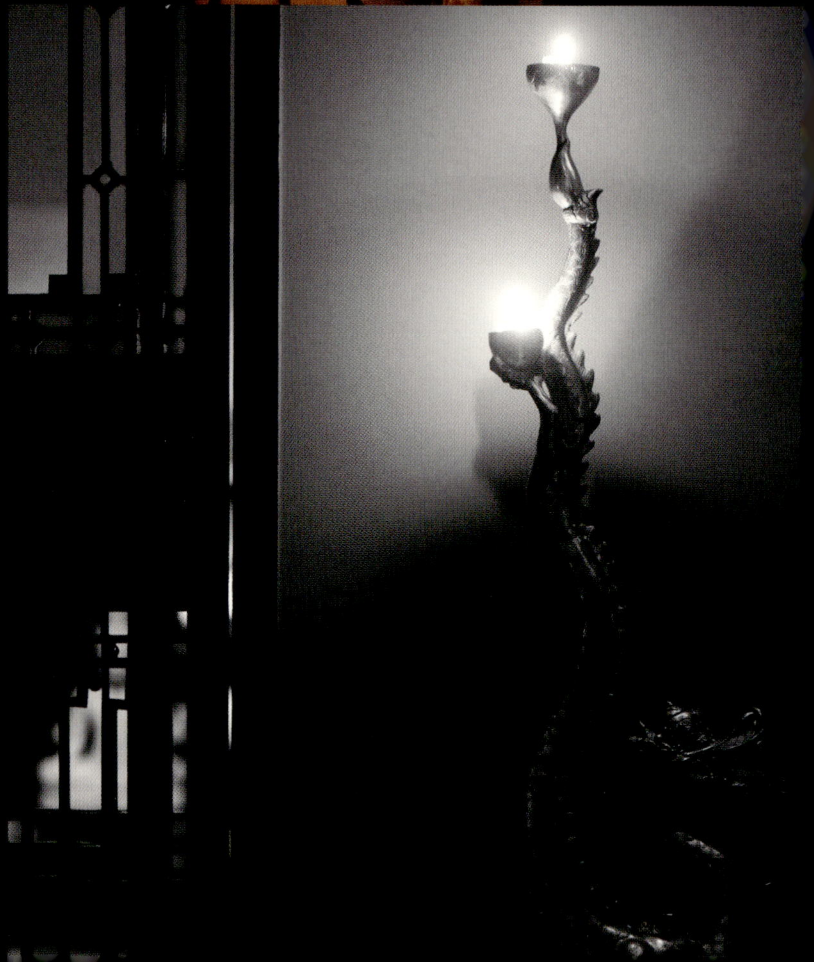

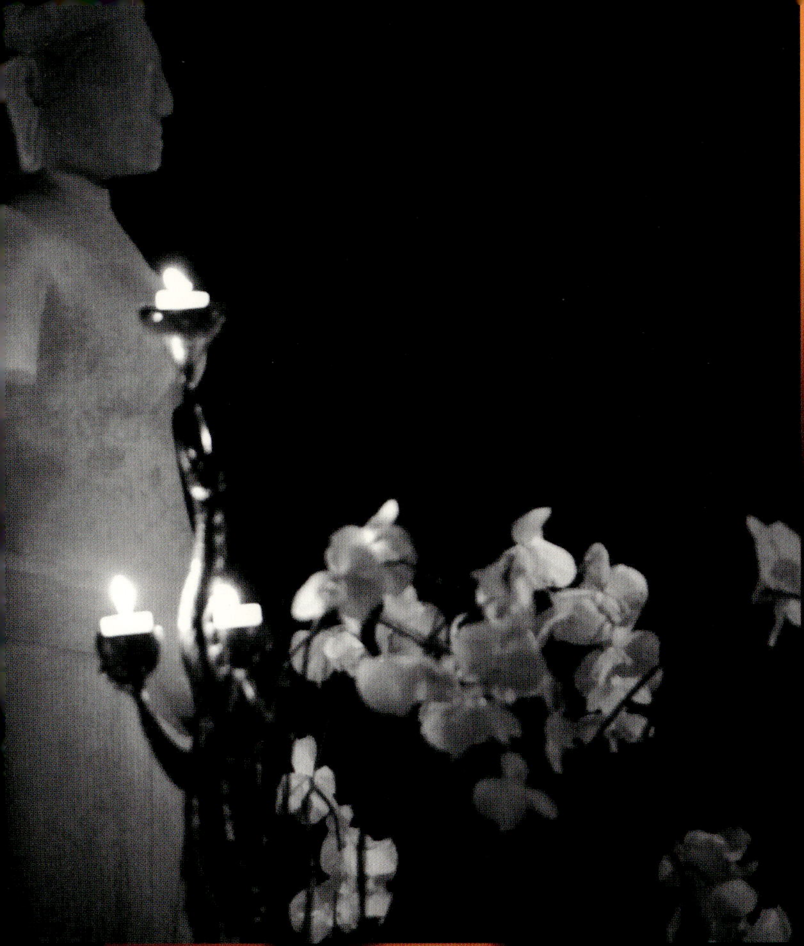

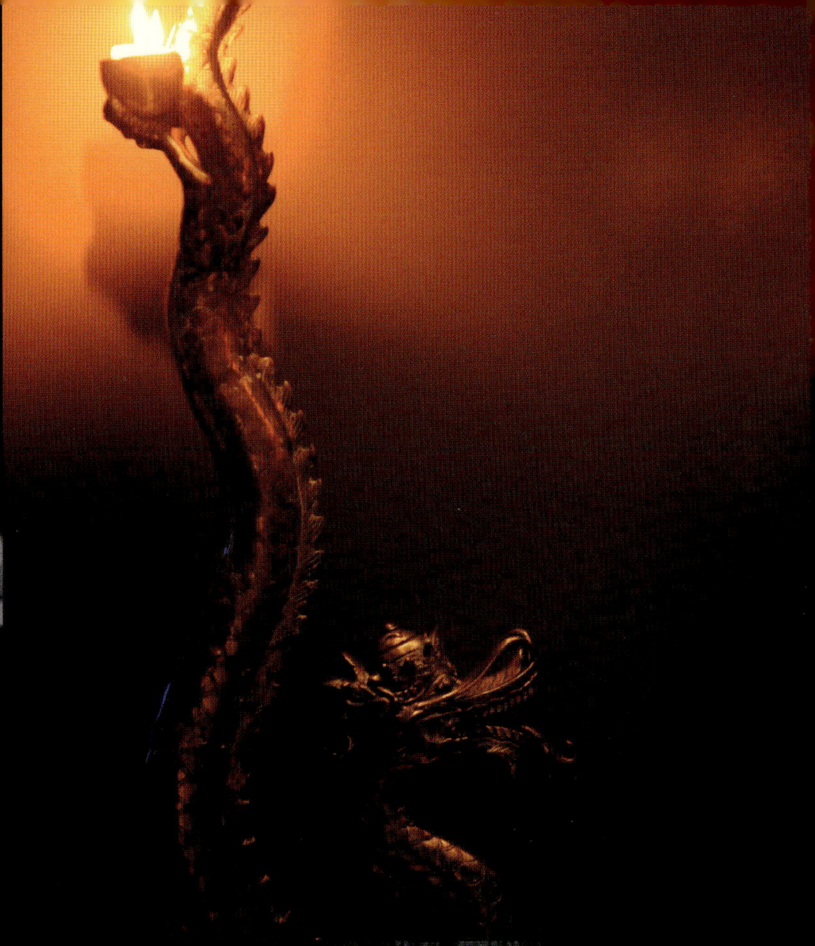

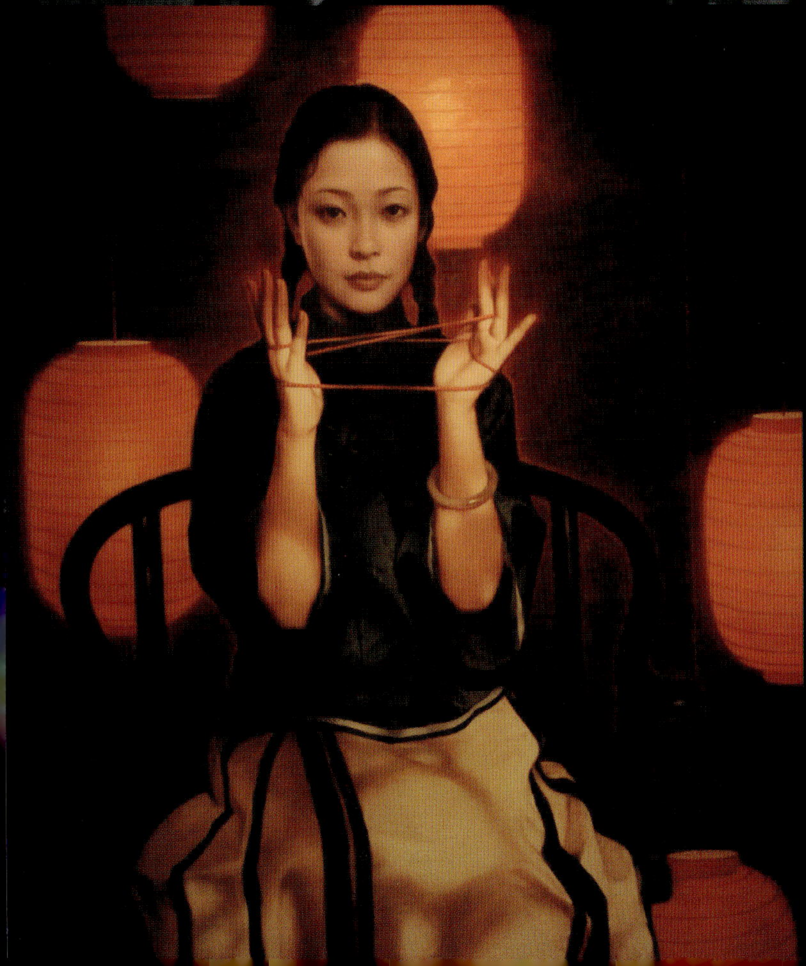

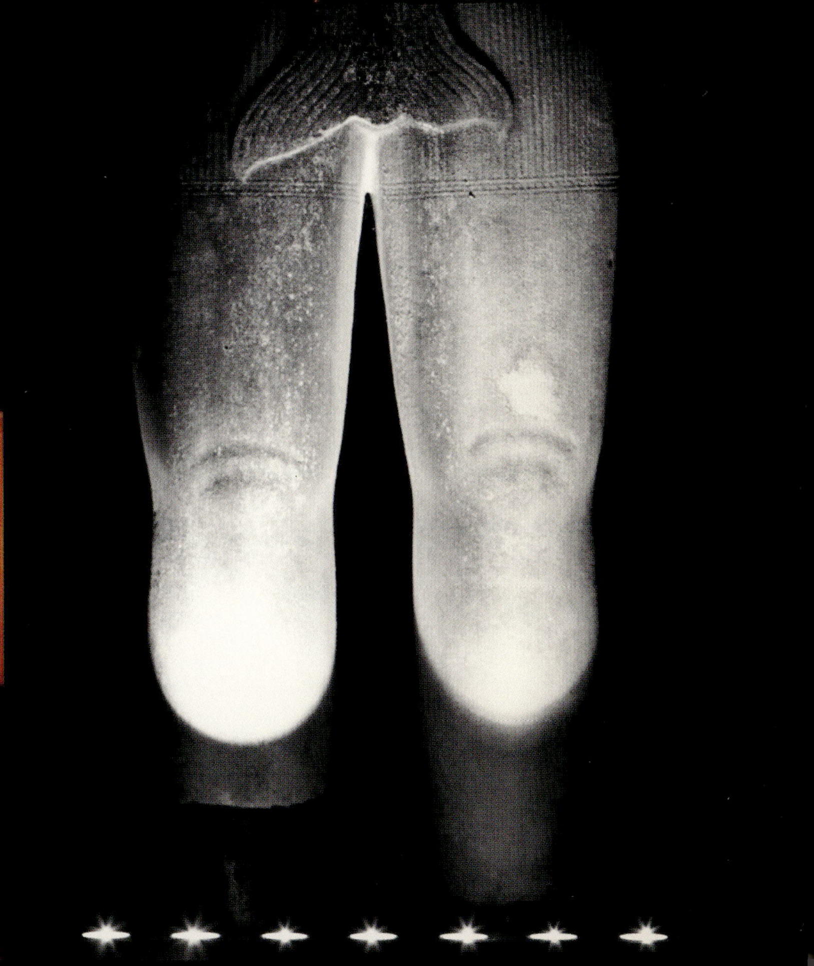

CANDLELIGHT DANCING
ON UMBRELLAS OR
AN OVERHEAD CANOPY
CAN CREATE
A MAGICAL GLOW.

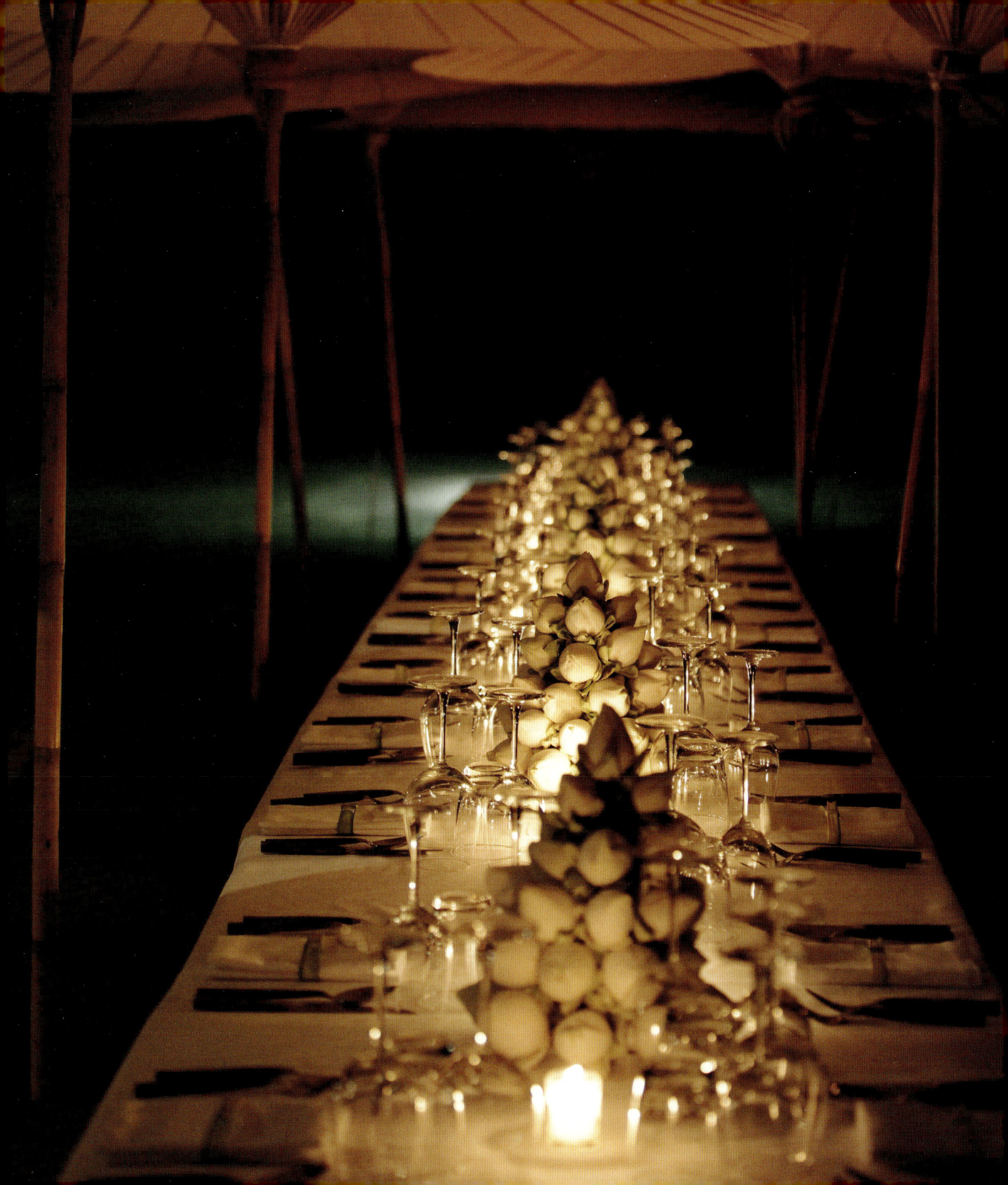

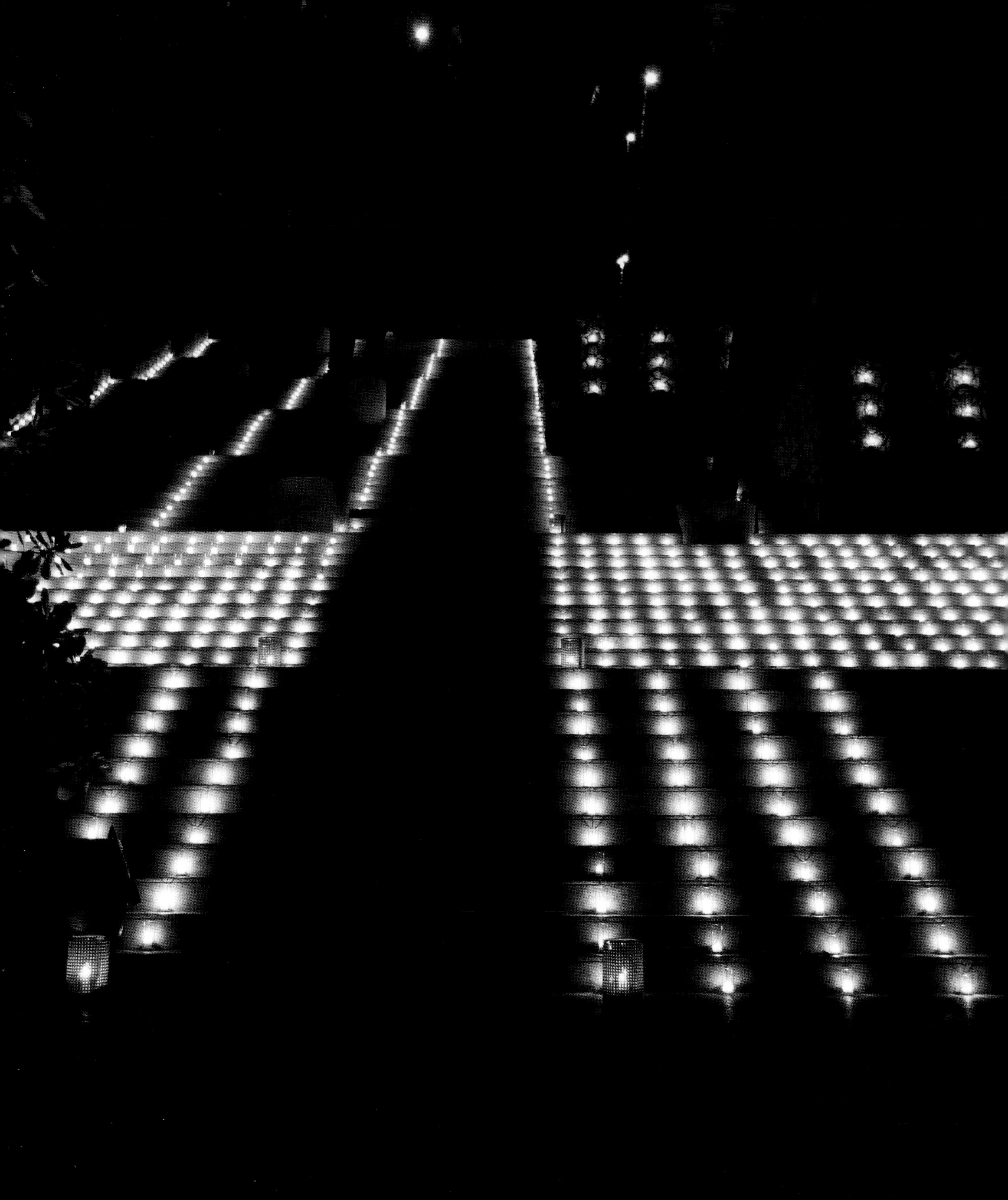

A STAIRCASE CAN BECOME
A DRAMATIC BACKDROP
TO A DINNER.

ALL IT REQUIRES IS
A FEW HUNDRED
TEA LIGHTS.

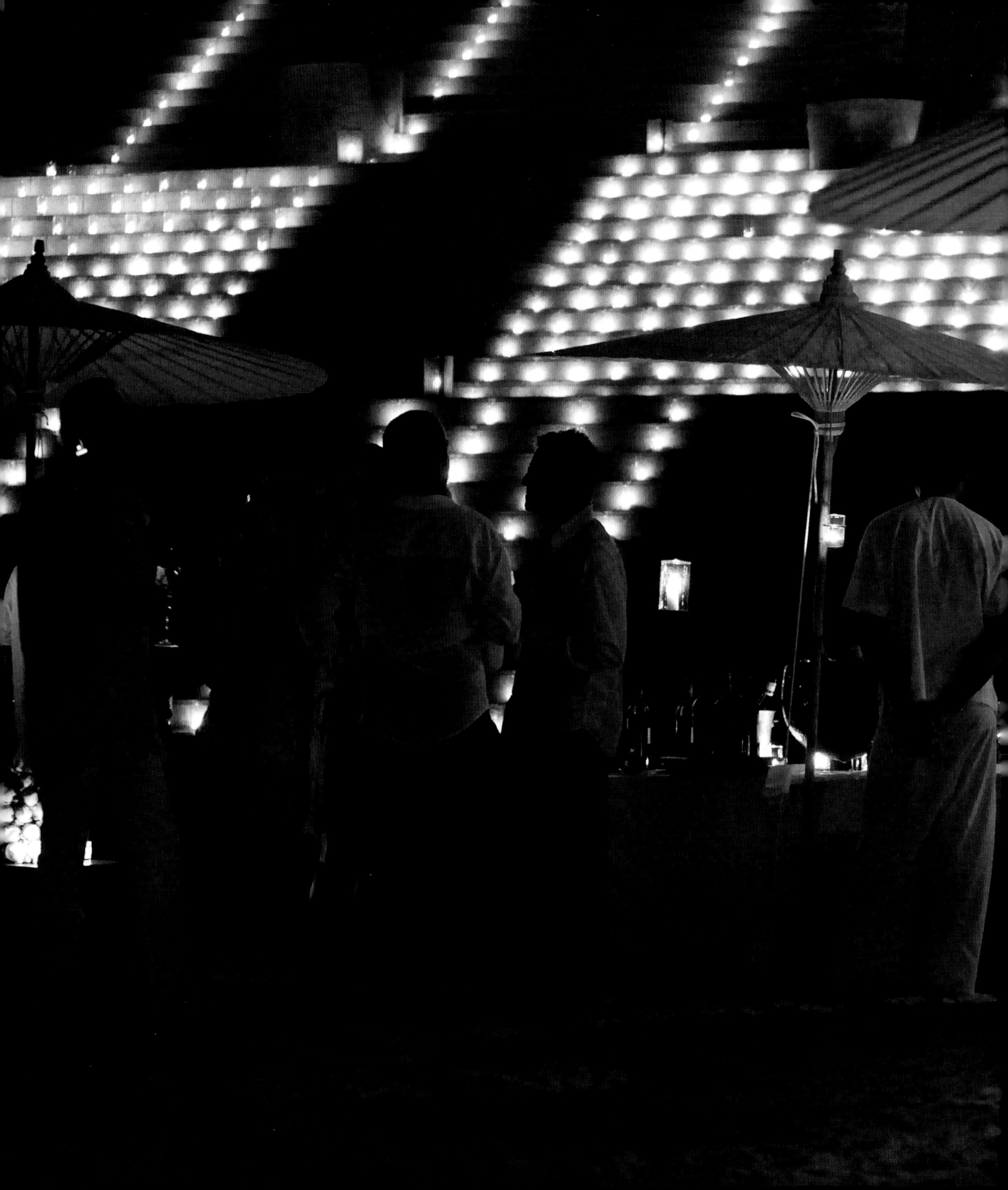

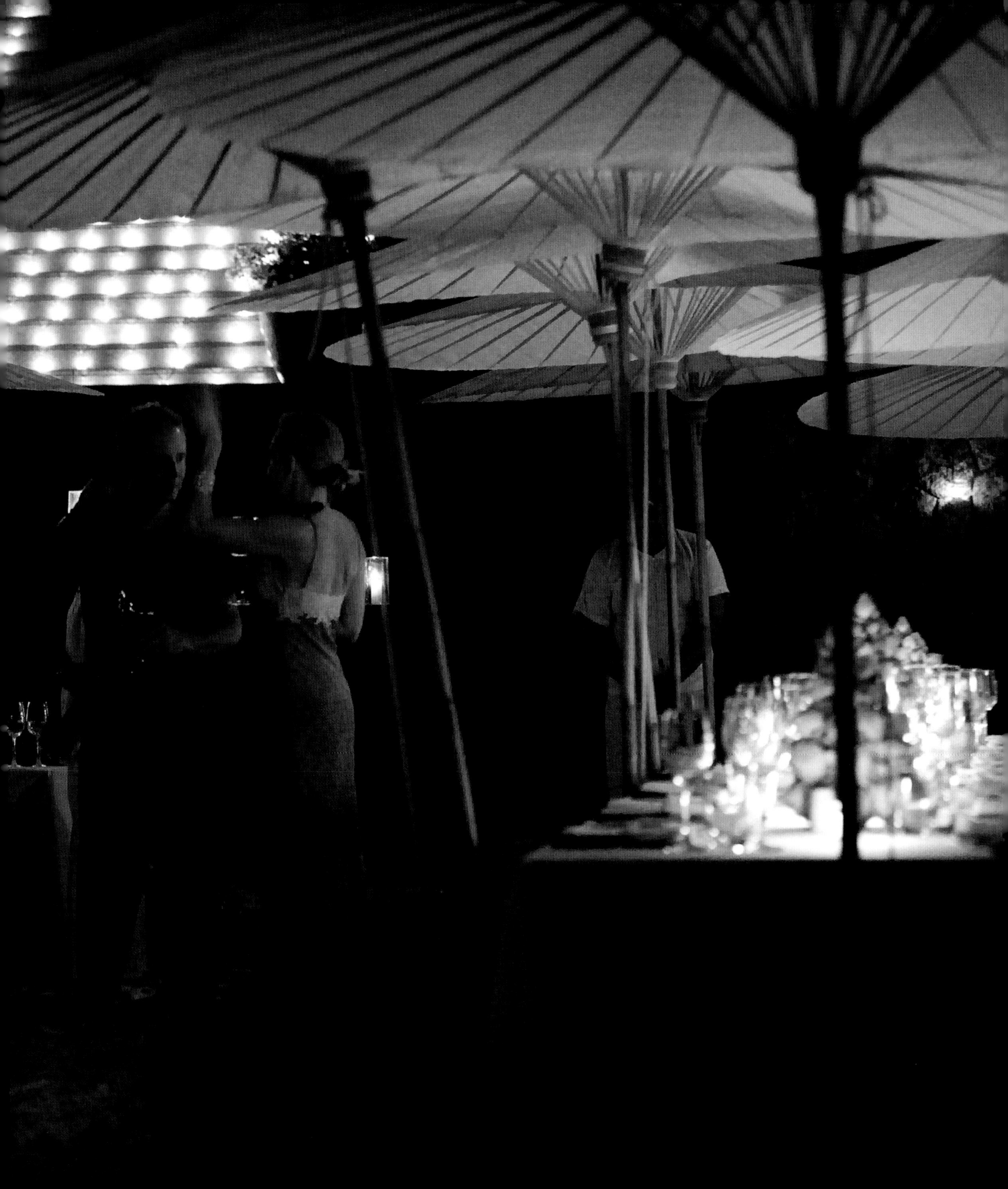

CANDLES IN PRACTICE: A BEACH PARTY

A beach picnic doesn't require much: a remote beach, a big rock, rush mats, pillows, ice, a few bottles of wine, a roast chicken, fruit, a big bag of candles and a boat to carry it all.

There is a small group of islands called the Racha in the Andaman Sea just south of Phuket. The bigger Racha is popular because it's good for diving and has some beautiful beaches. The smaller Racha is more densely vegetated, uninhabited and not popular with tourists because it has no beaches – or so most people think. It does in fact have one, a hidden gem of a beach, tucked out of view at the far end of the island. It was where I wanted to have Christmas dinner with a few friends and close family.

From the boat the beach looked perfect: turquoise water, white sand and no people. Up close it wasn't quite so promising. The beach faces the open sea and the currents and prevailing winds wash all the debris in the water onshore, so there was a lot of cleaning up to do before we could set up our 'Christmas Dinner à la Robinson Crusoe'. We built a big fire and threw everything on it, including things you're not supposed to throw on fires, such as aerosol cans. The bonfire burned and exploded all day long. By the end of the day, the debris had been transformed into a pile of white ash and Paradise had been restored.

Getting ready for dinner was the easy bit. We piled all the components of dinner for ten into an inflatable dinghy and ferried them to shore. A big granite rock, poking out of the sand as if it had just washed up on the deserted beach, became our private dining room. The pillows rested against its base and the tea lights outlined its shape in the dark, giving a cosy sense of space. With the addition of flowers, white plates, plain wine glasses and lots and lots of candles, we created a memorable Christmas dinner that could not be surpassed anywhere, at any price.

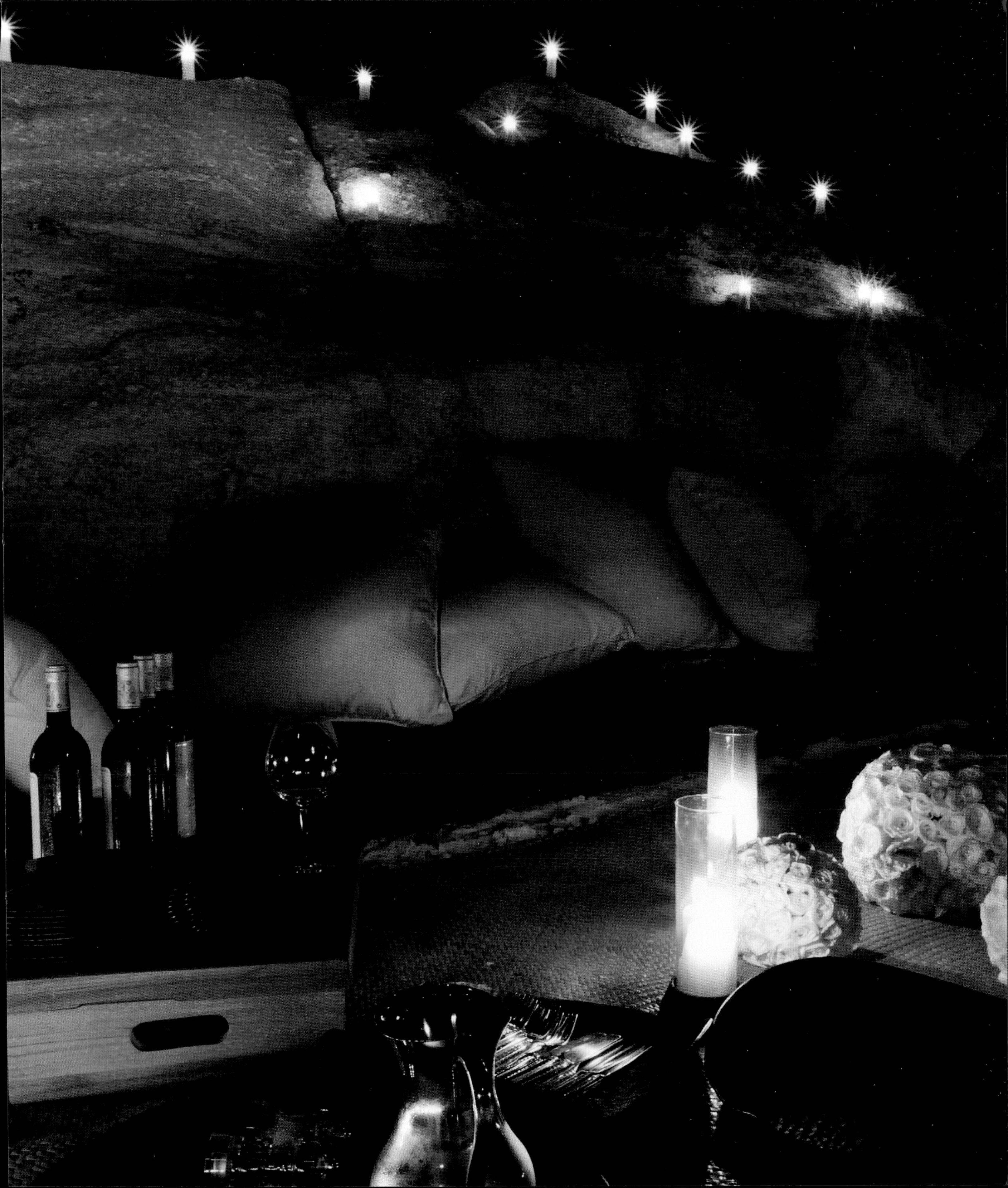

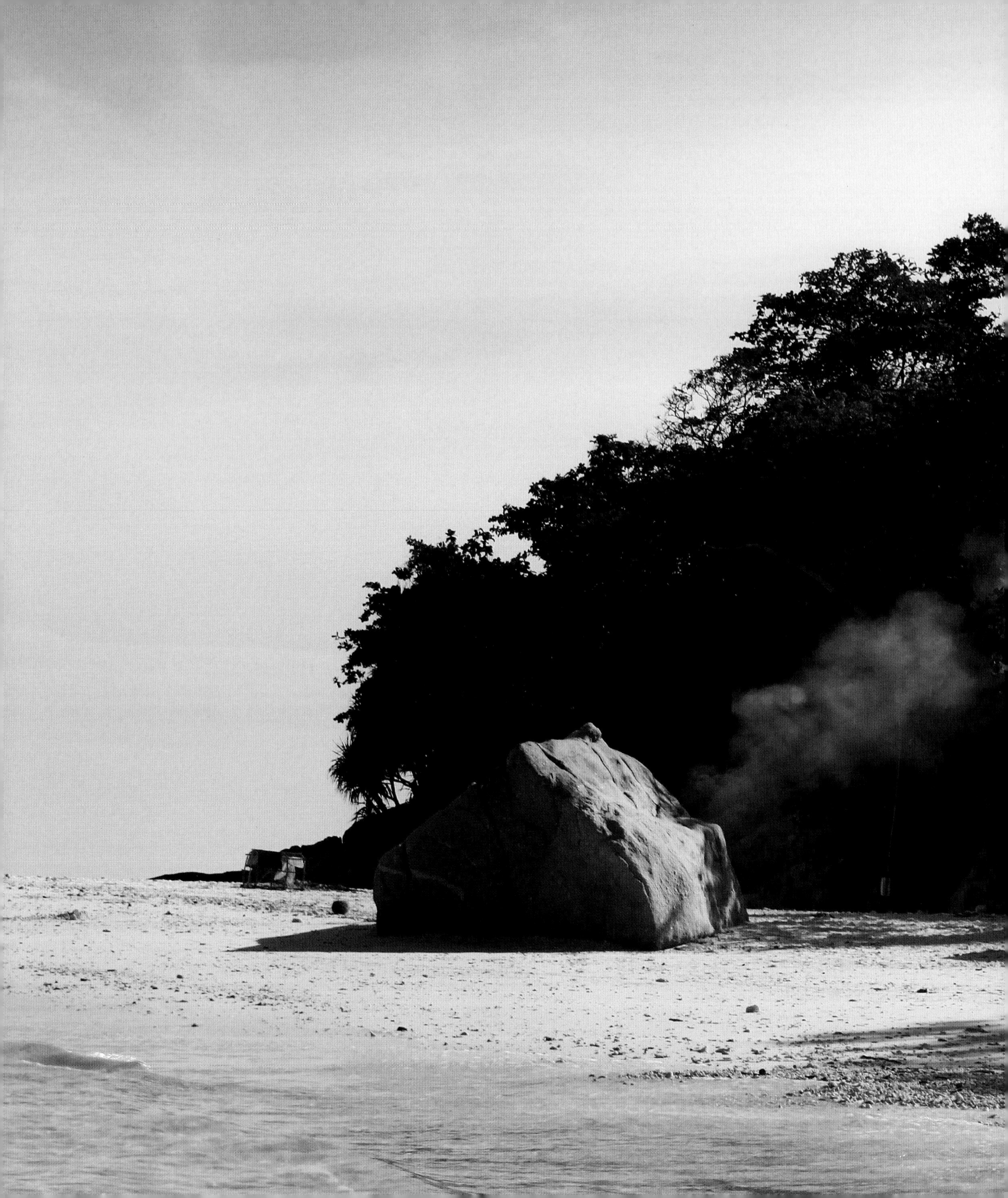

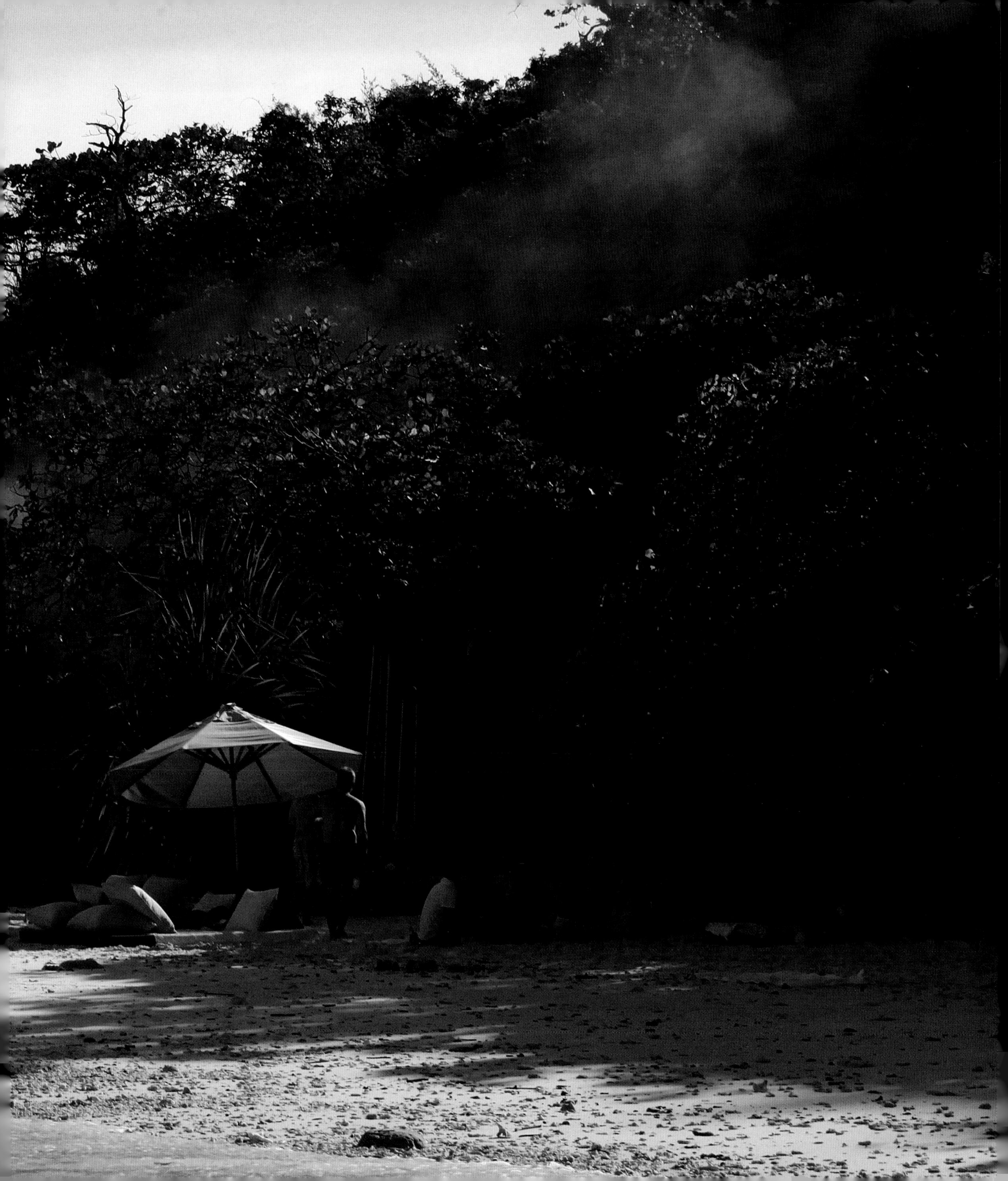

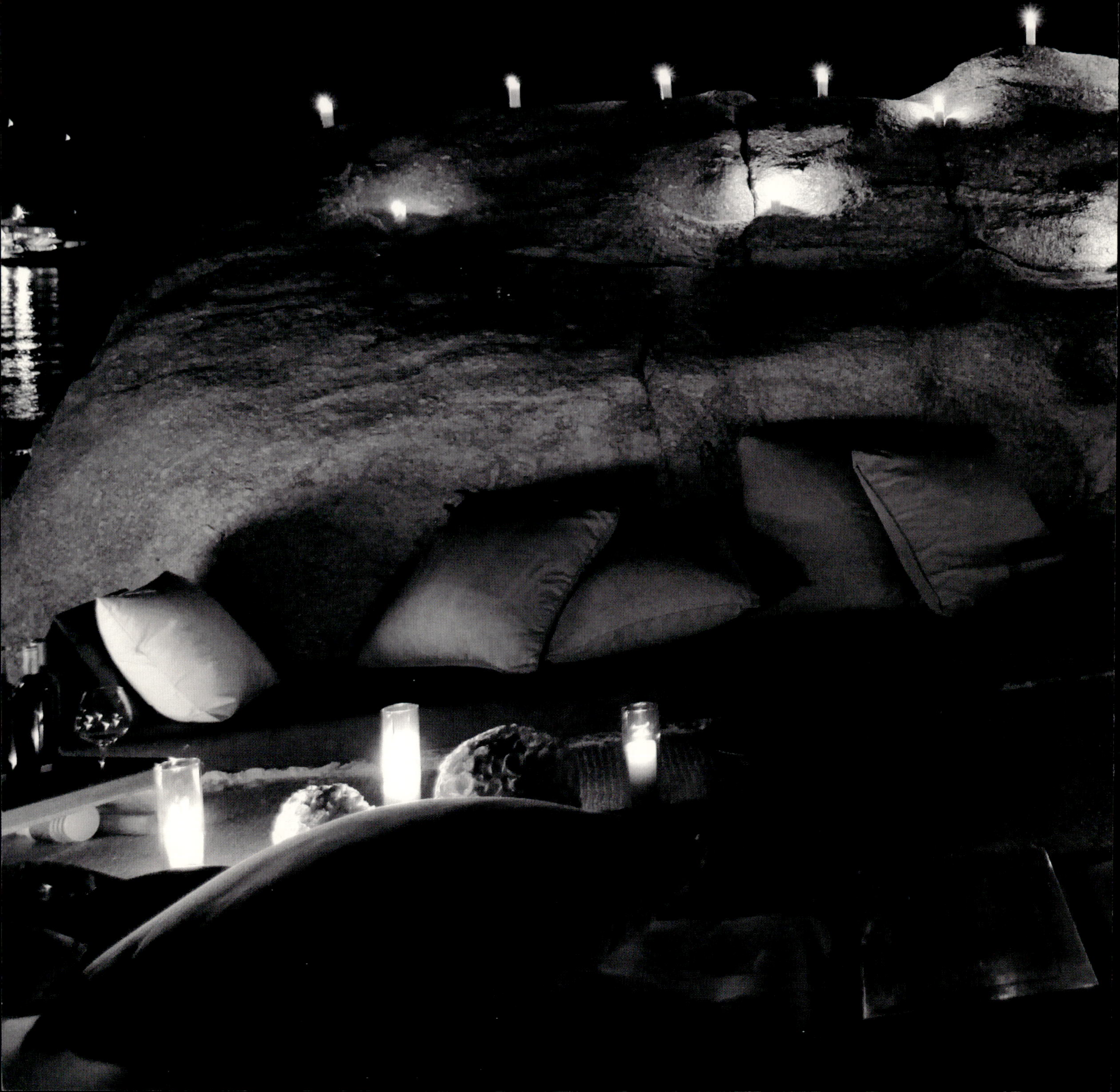

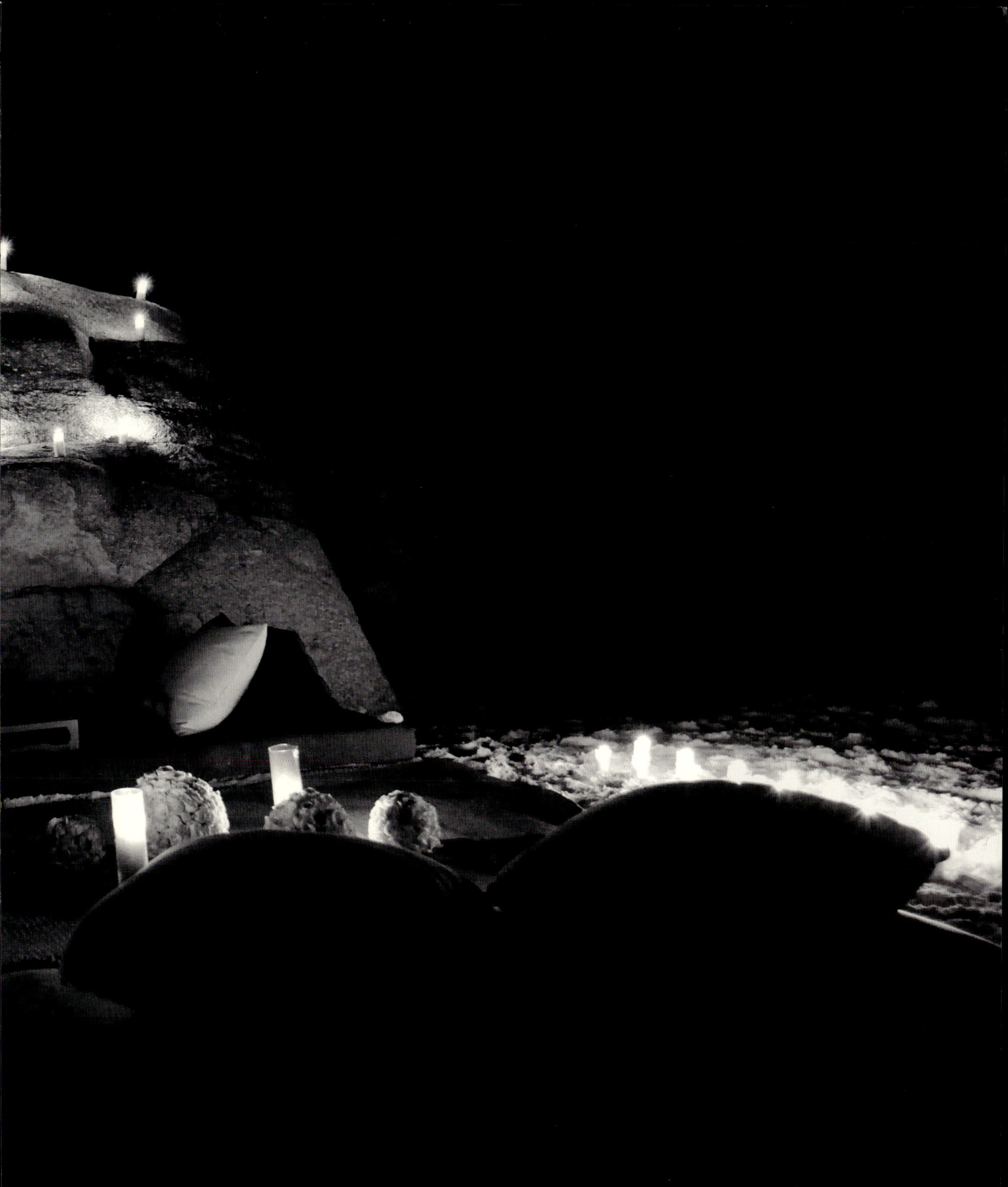

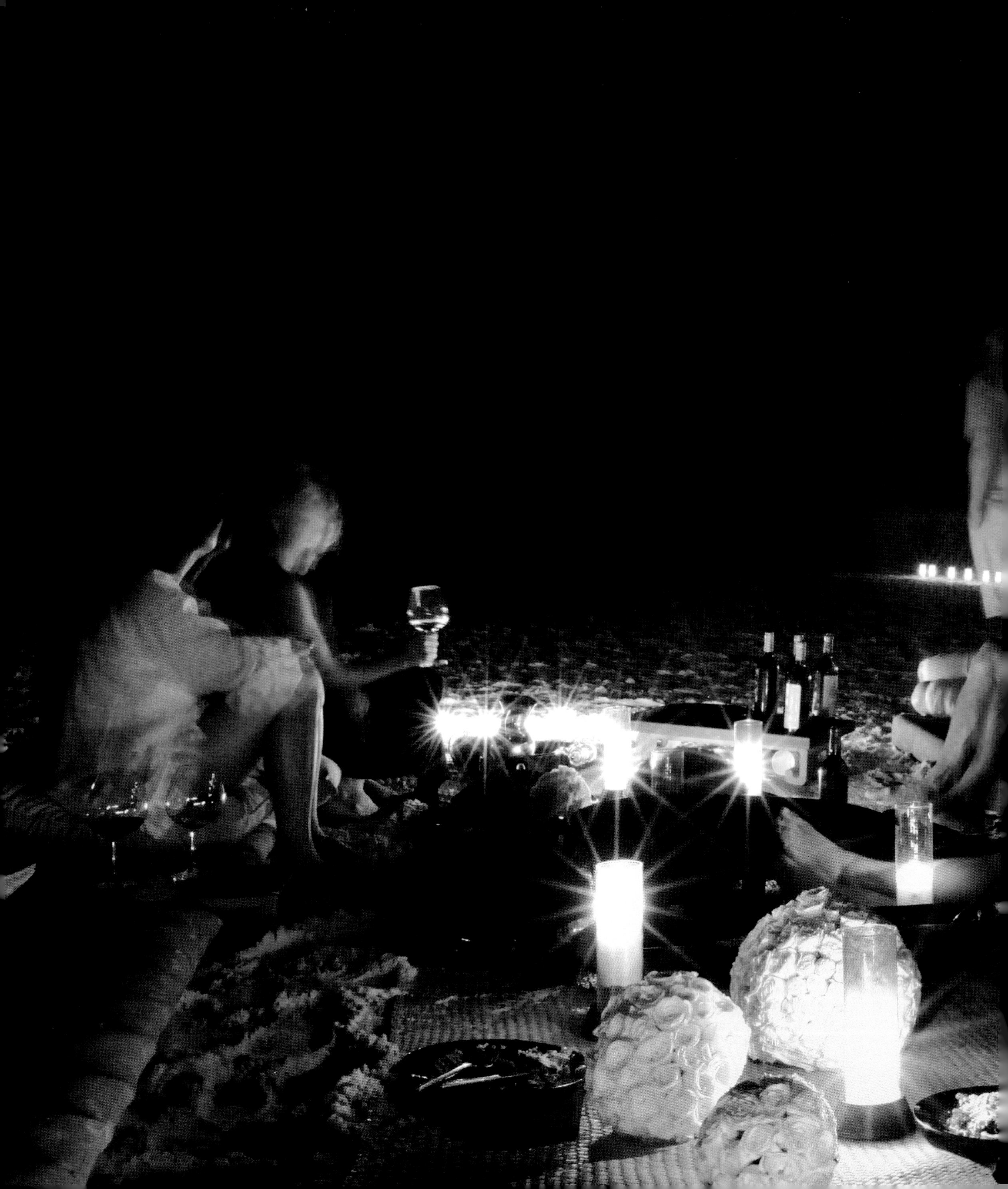

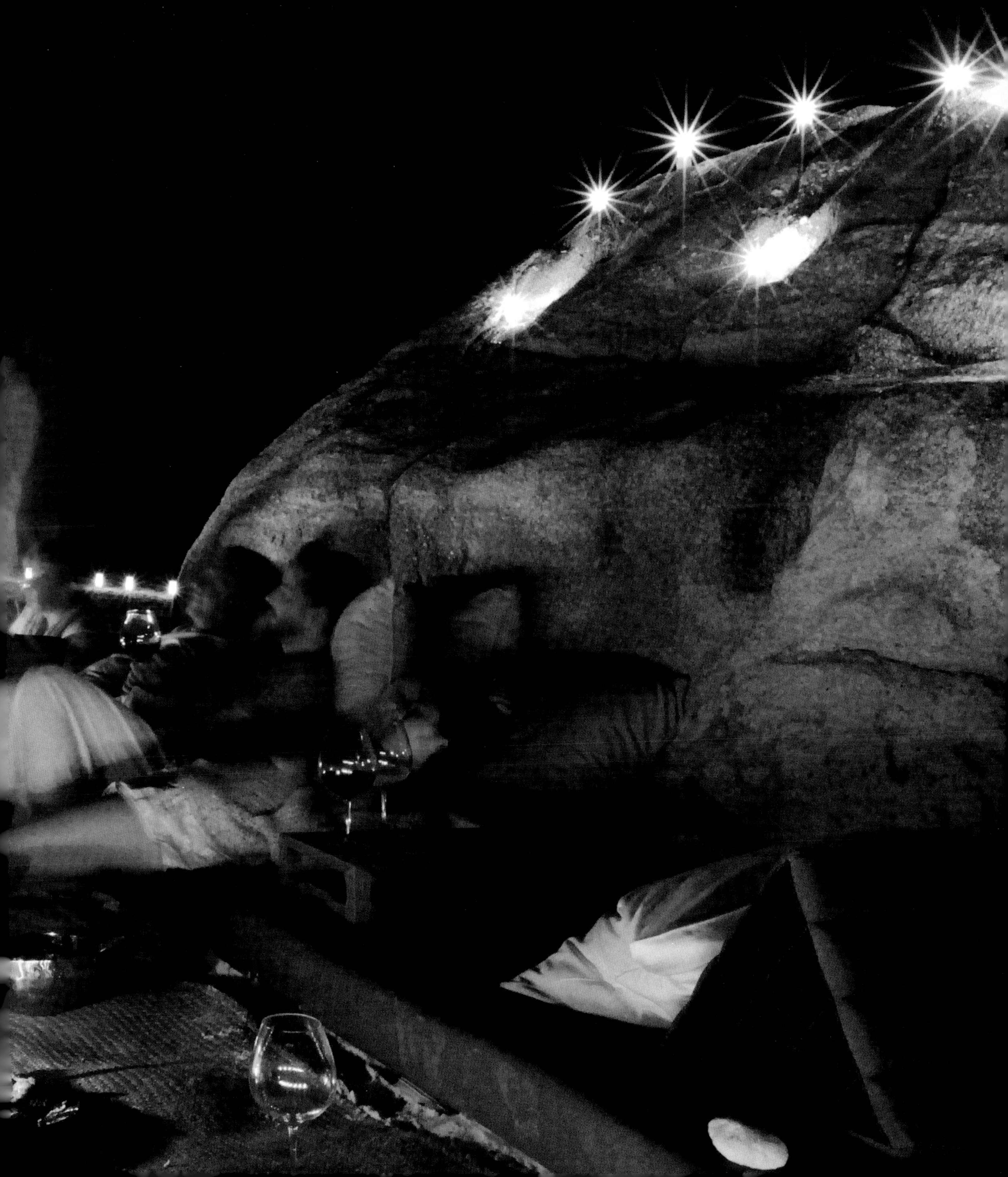

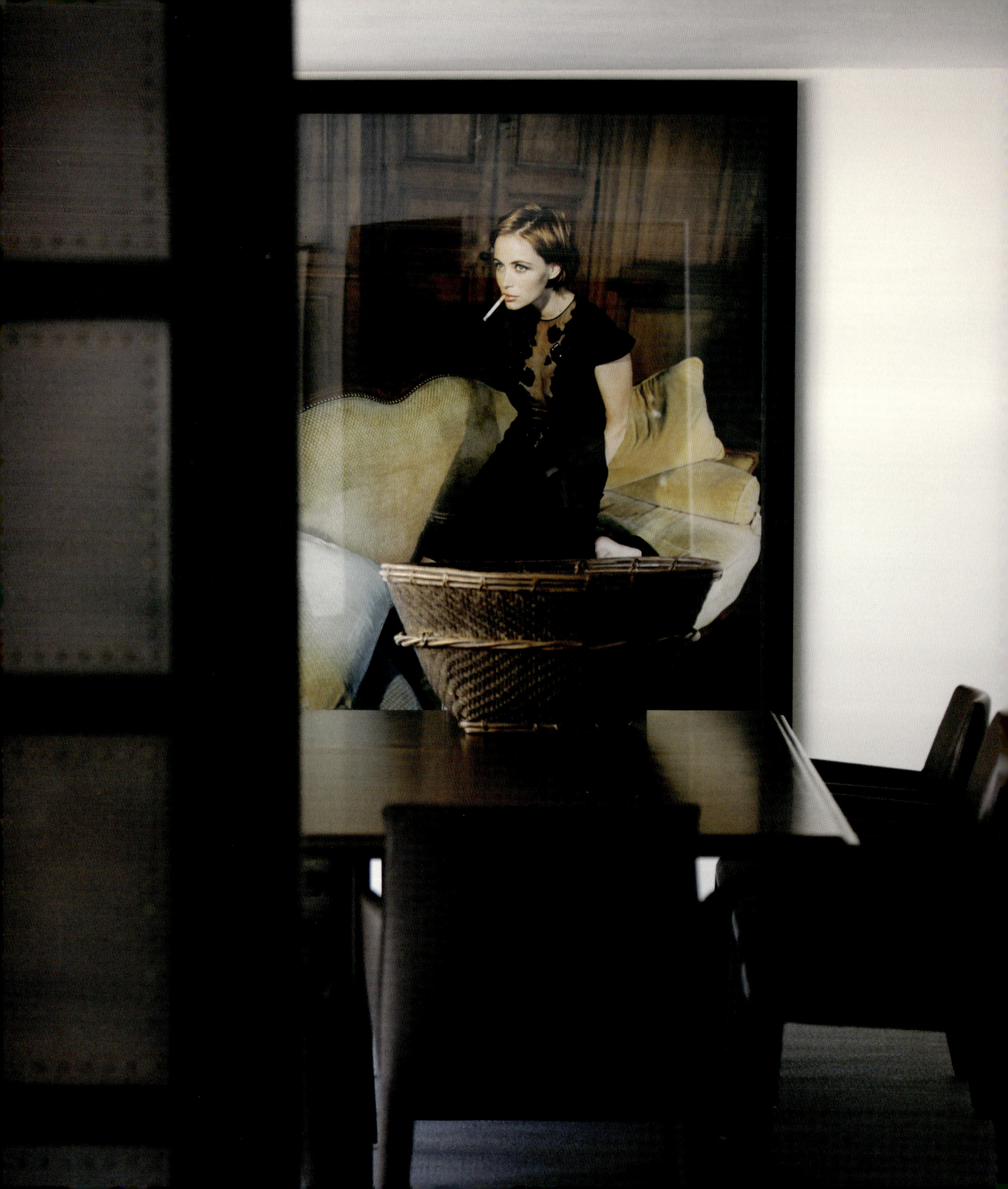

5
ART

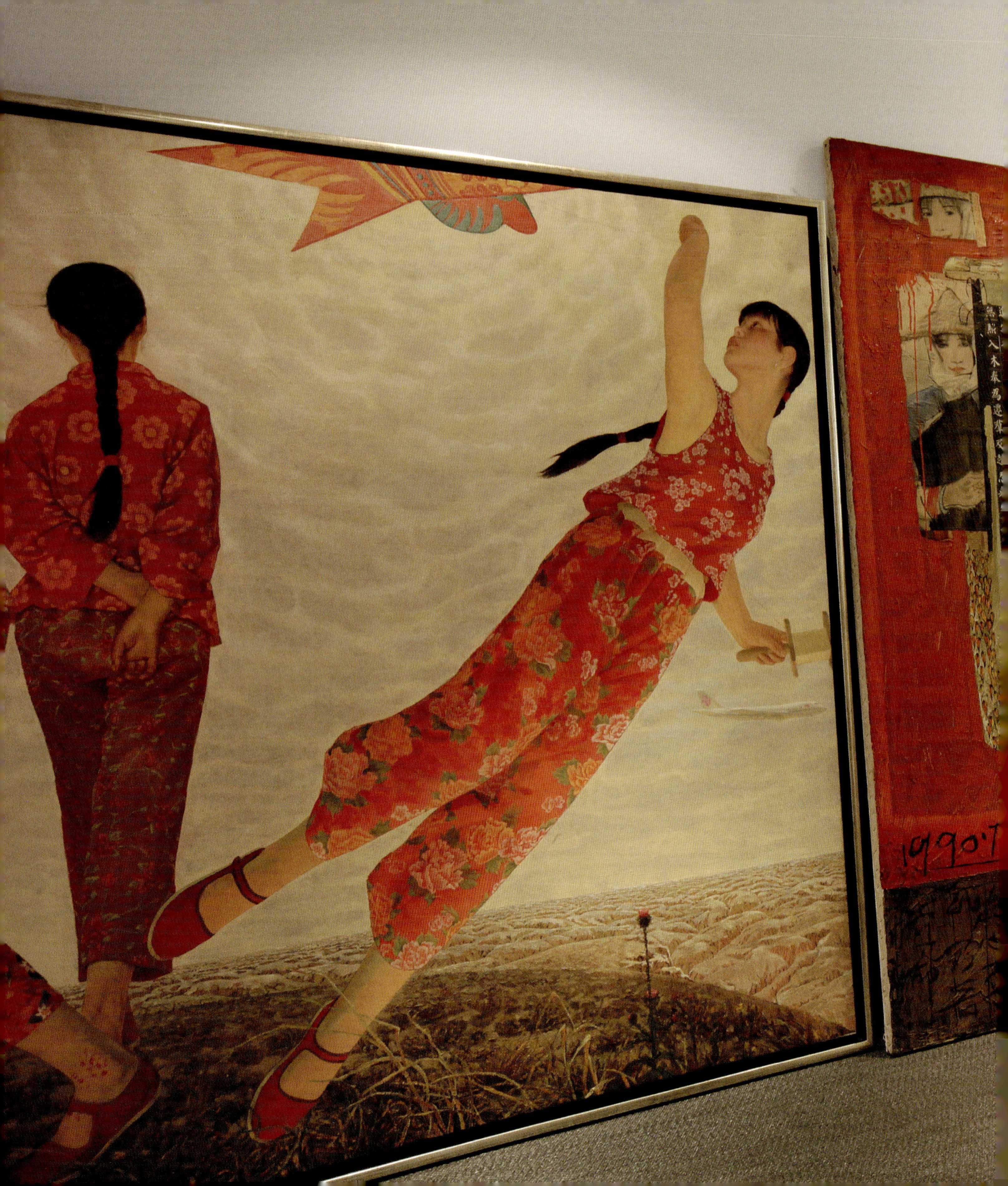
1990·7

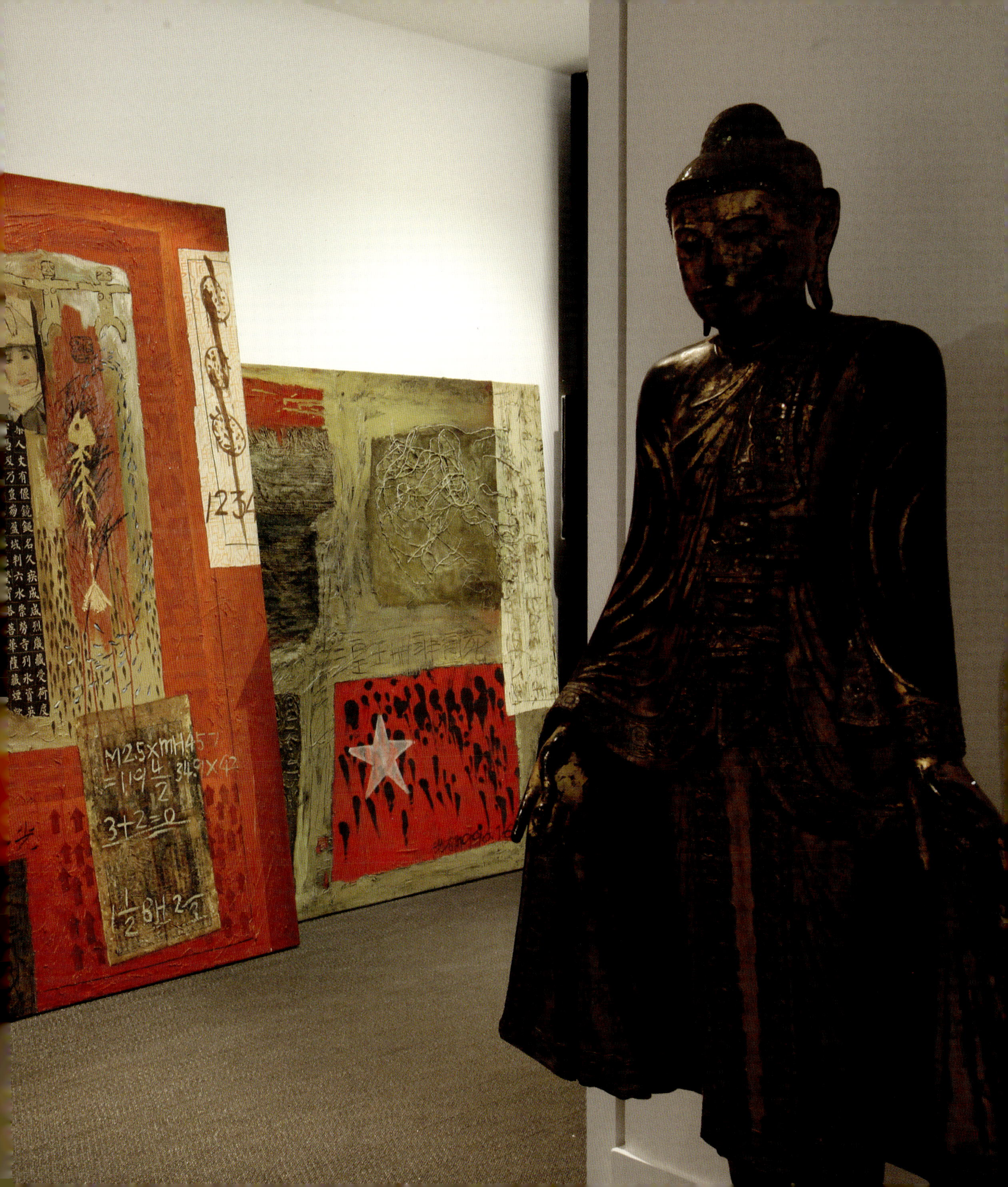

Art is a crucial – though easily overlooked – component of entertaining. It says something about you: what you like, how you think. But nobody cares – or ought to care – how much you paid for it. Art should be about one thing: what you like. Don't buy art as an investment; don't buy it to impress and don't imagine that owning an important work will somehow make YOU important. It won't.

Not long ago, the art that I bought was not taken seriously. No one knew the artists, and their work didn't come from famous galleries. But I didn't care because these were pieces I loved and I wanted them around me, both in my house and in my office.

The personality and individuality of my home comes from my art. I get enjoyment from it every day and it's a bonus when I entertain and guests ask questions about my collection. To hear the words 'I love your home, I love your art' is deeply satisfying, like being told that your children are beautiful and well behaved.

Buying art should be an adventure. Visit small, offbeat galleries; go to school and institute shows and keep your eyes and ears out for new talent. The process of finding good art not only adds depth and interest to the pieces themselves, but also gives you stories to share with friends and family when you entertain.

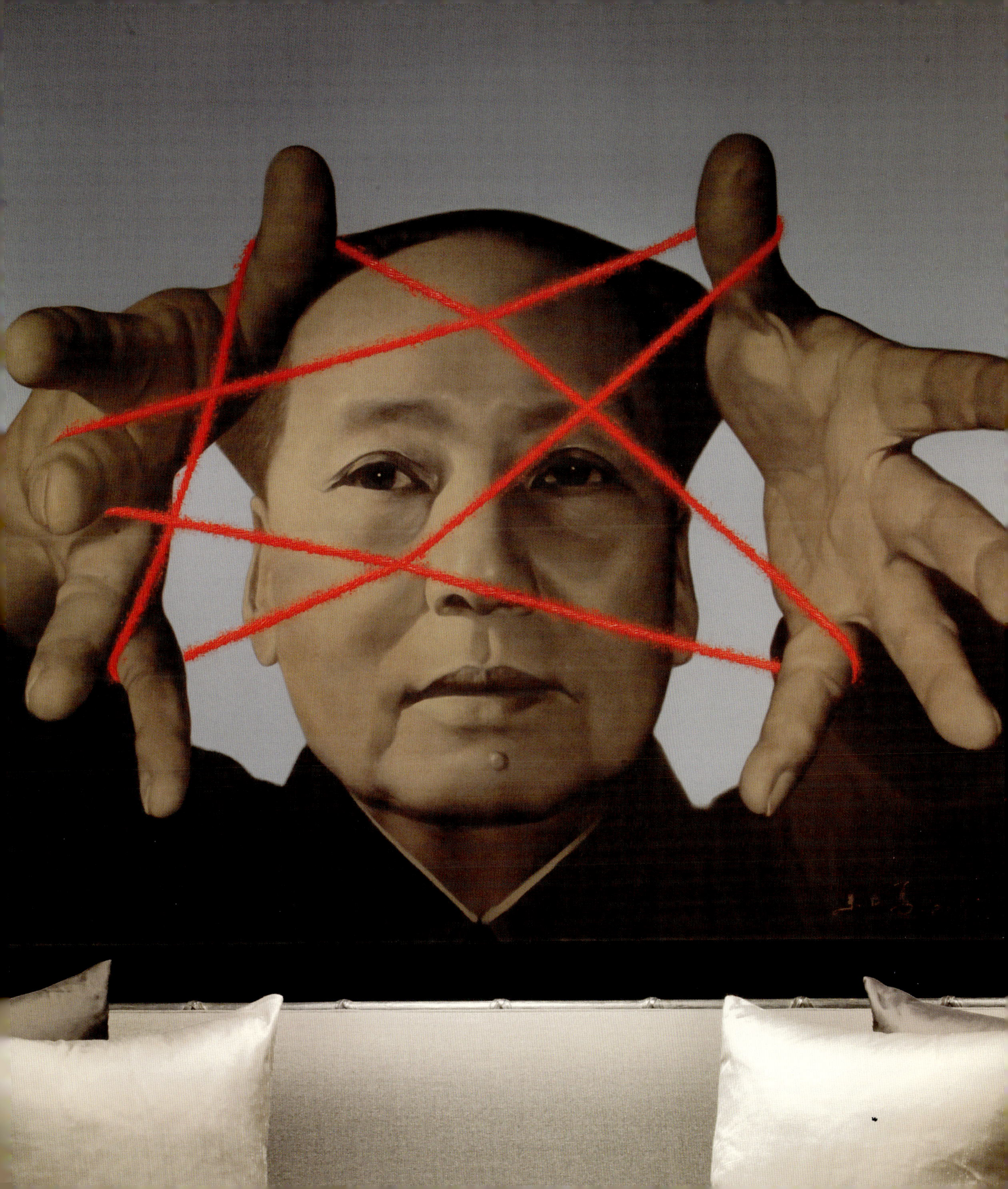

ART IS IMPORTANT,
AND THE MOST IMPORTANT
THING ABOUT ART IS TO
BUY WHAT YOU LIKE.

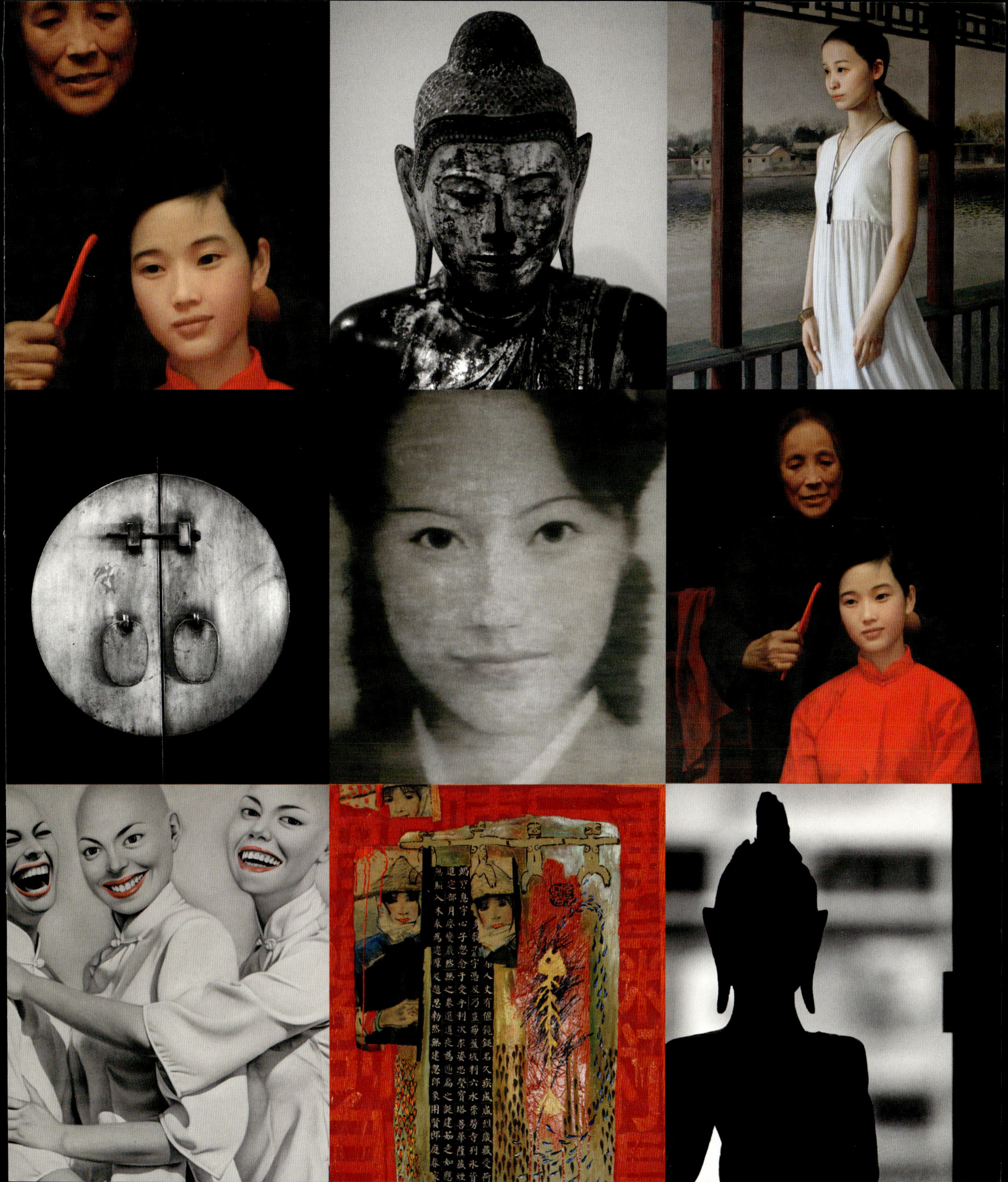

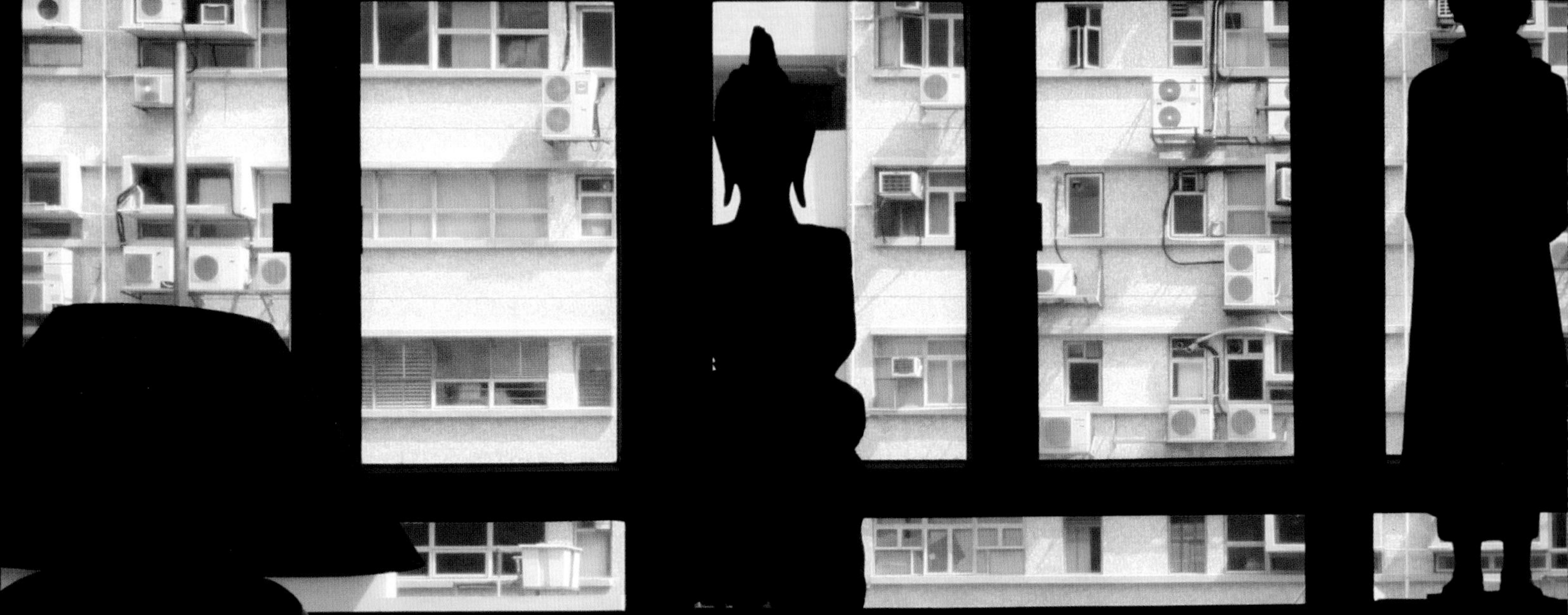

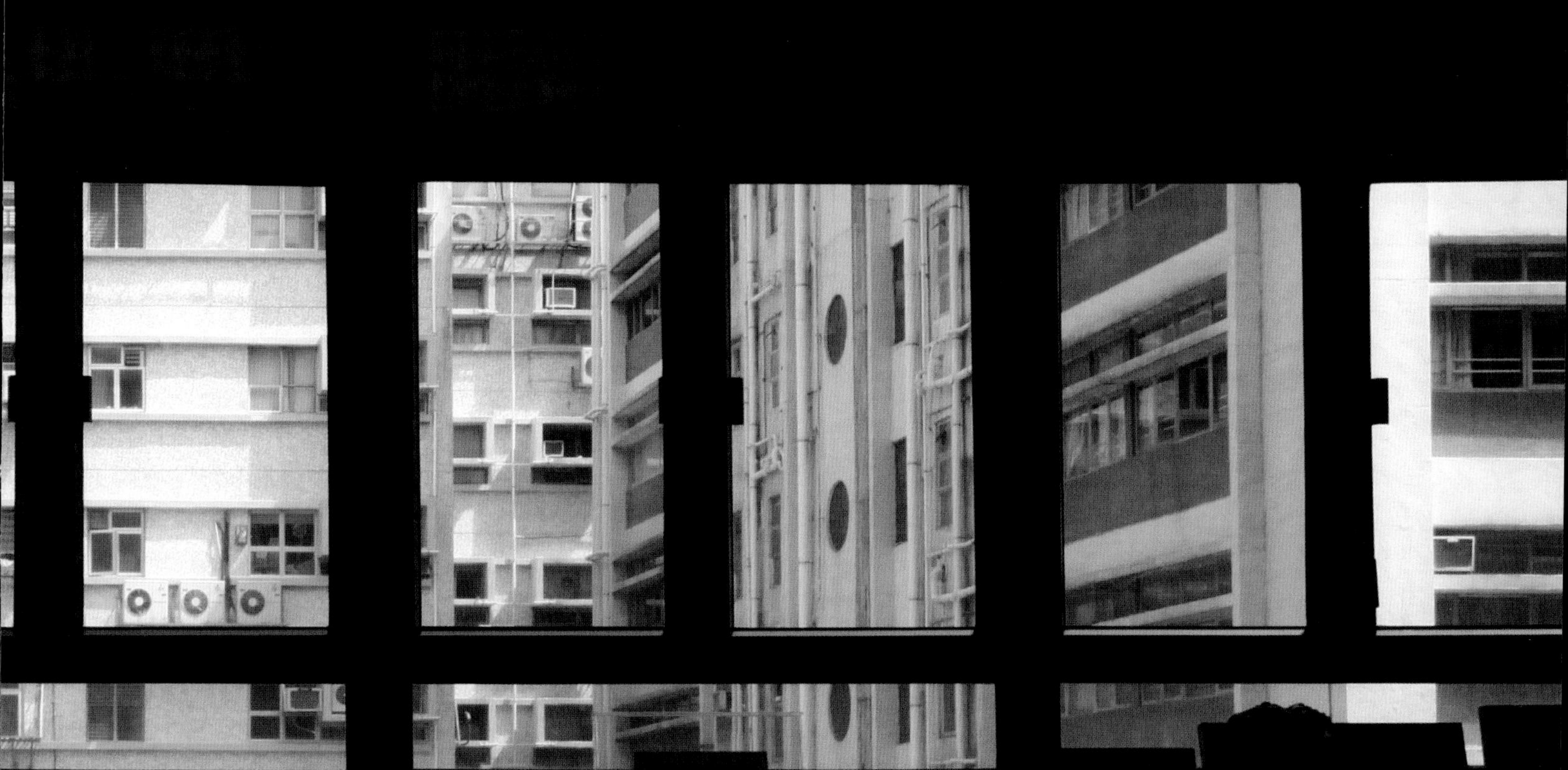

ROSE

Resort
Fashion

BAECHLER
MORRISON

WANG KEPING

WANG KEPING

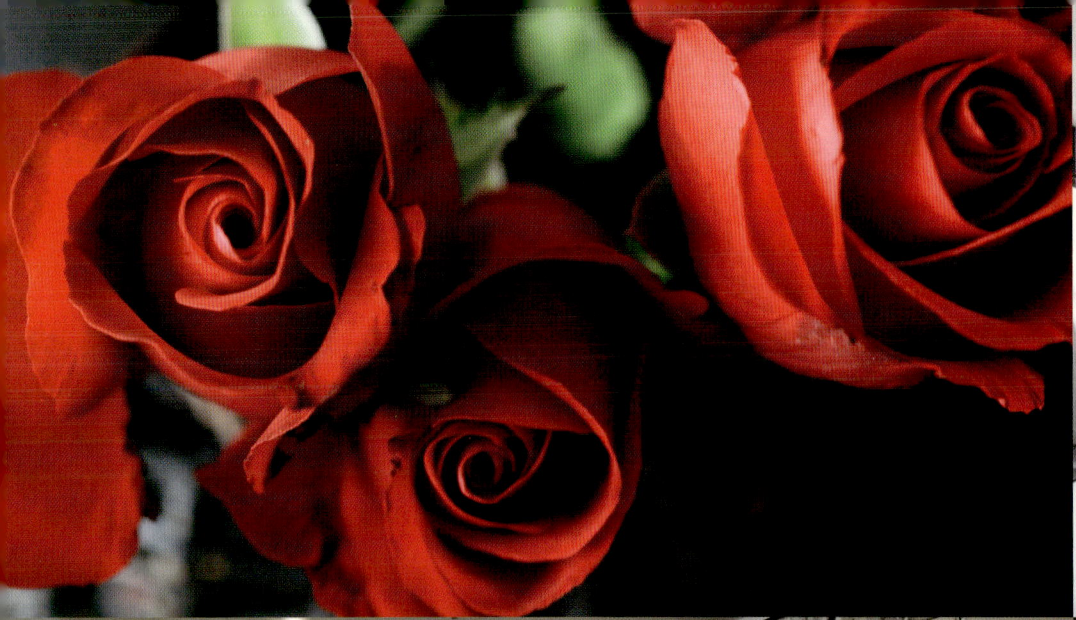

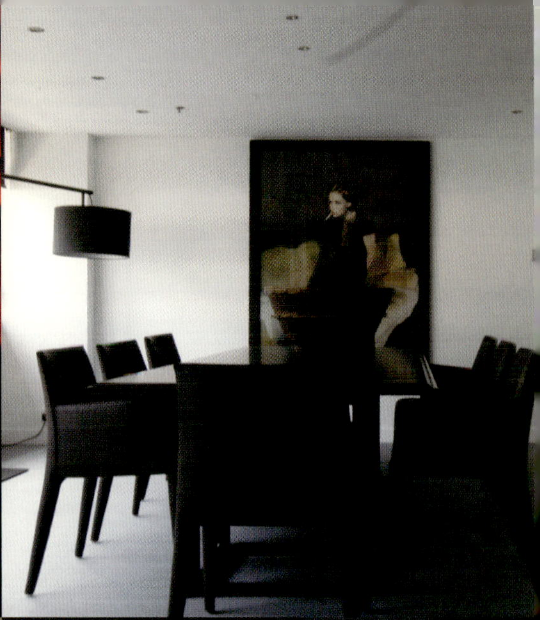

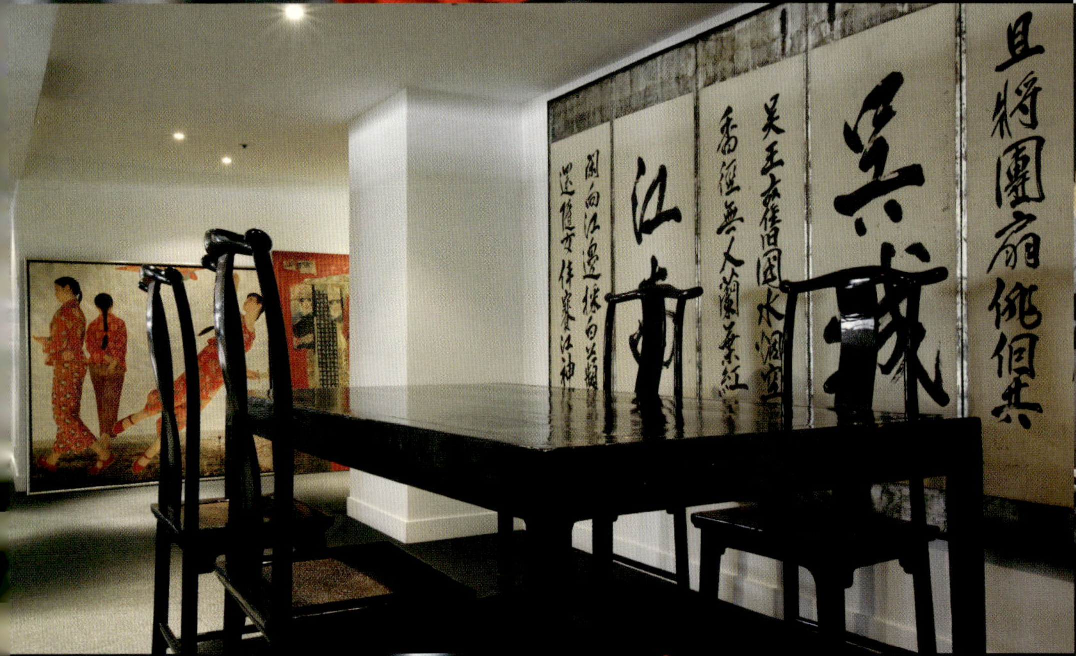

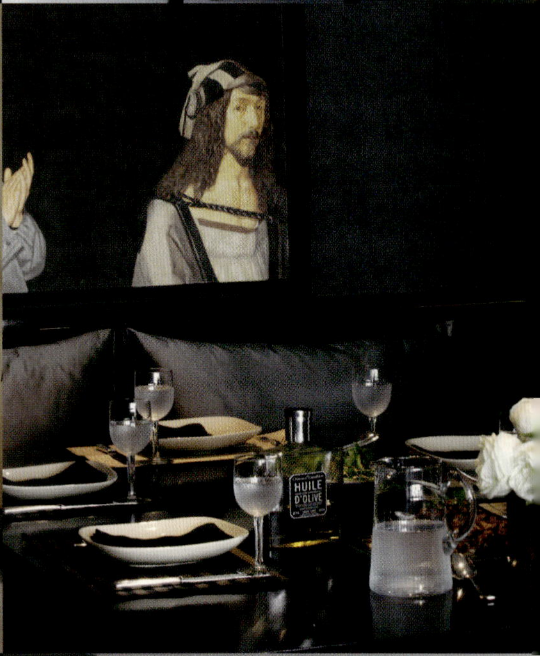
HUILE
D'OLIVE

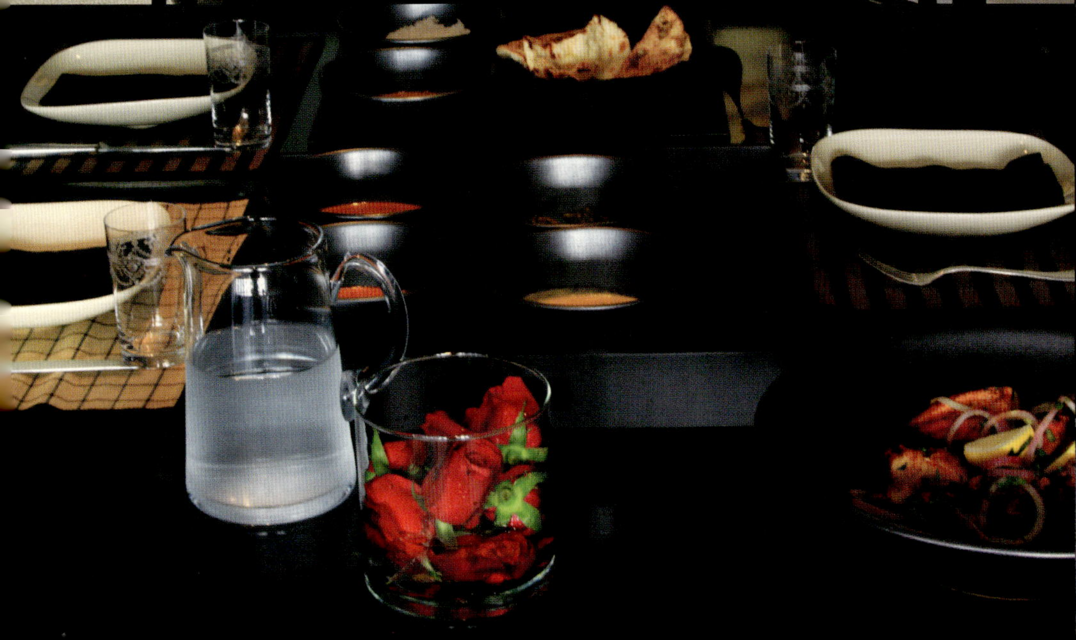

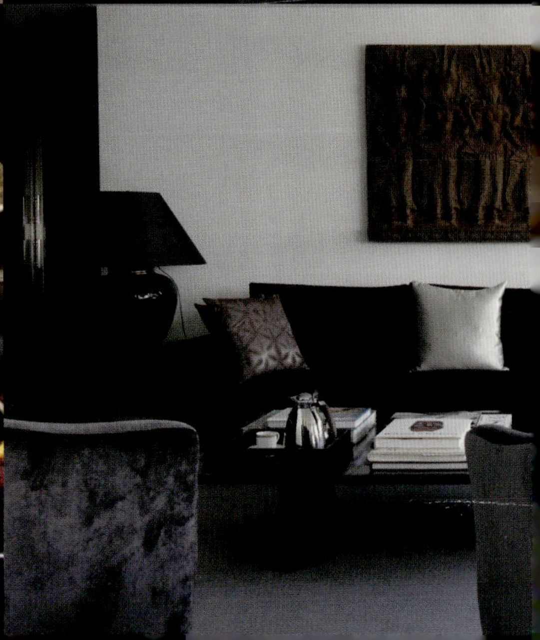

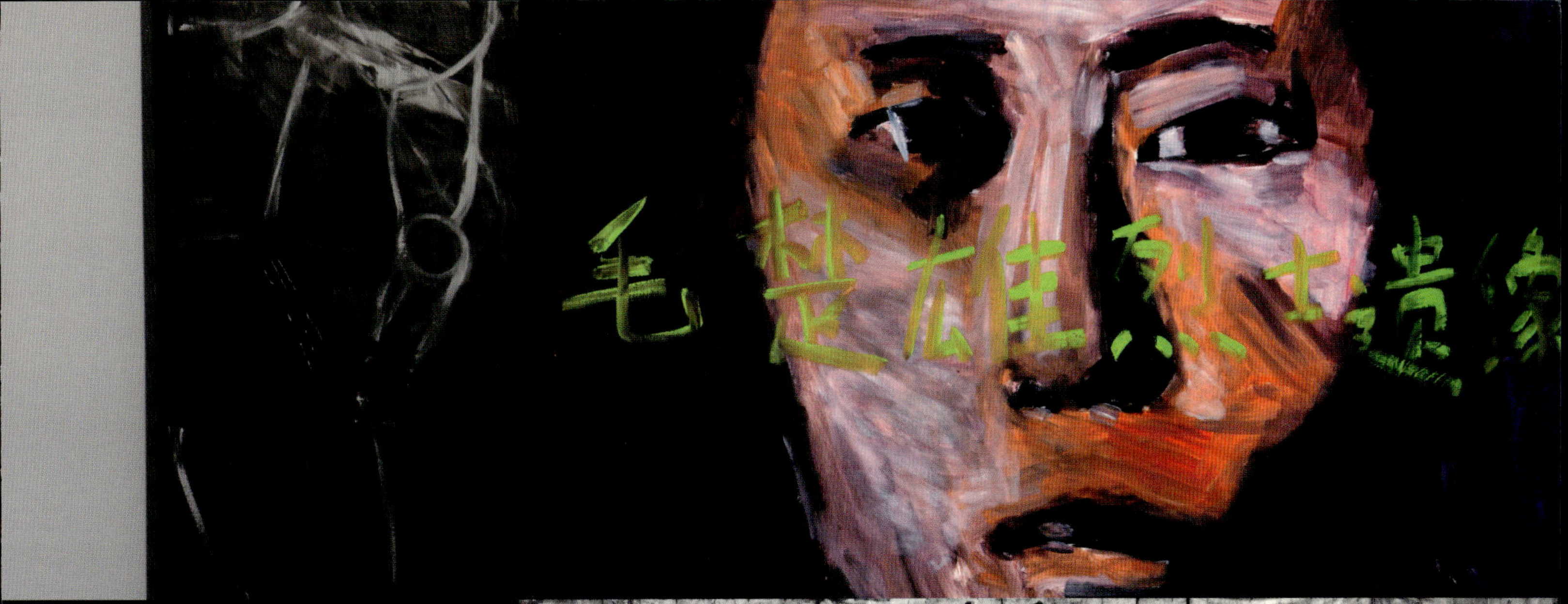
毛楚雄烈士遺像

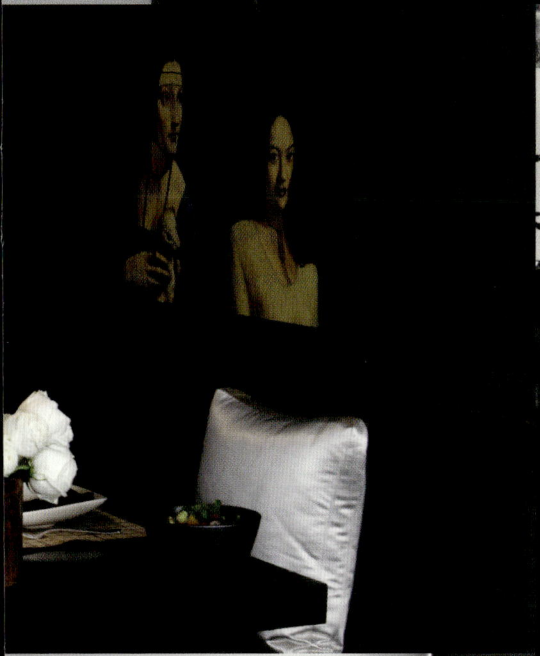

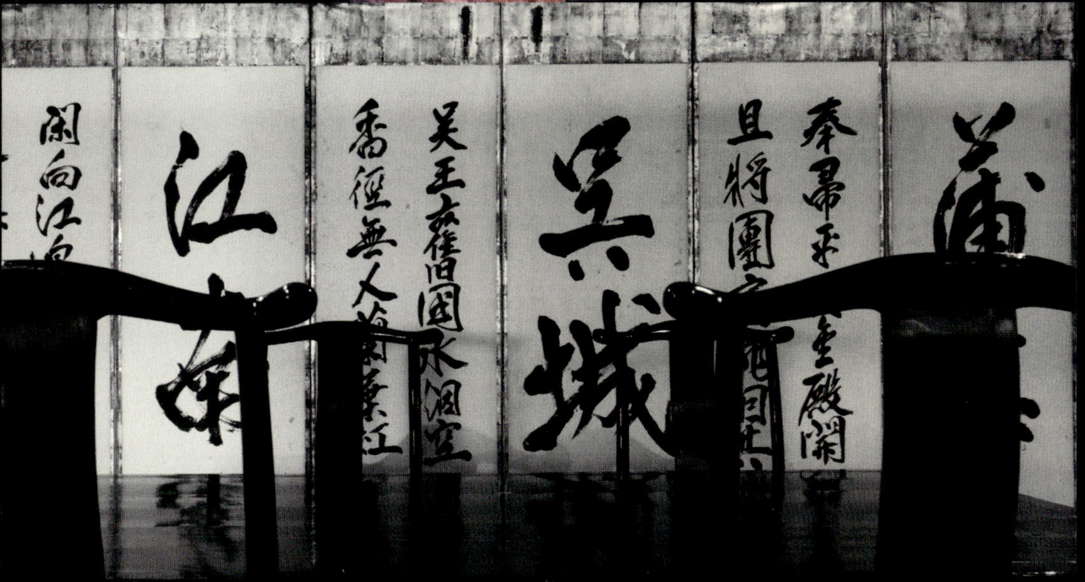

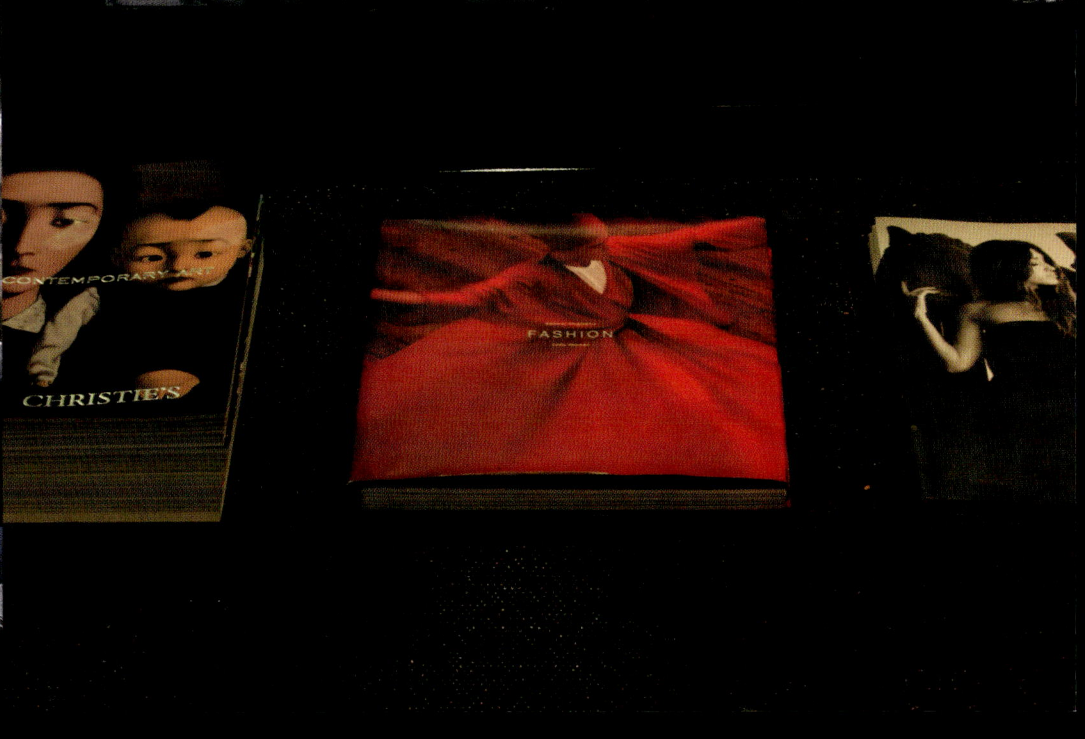
CONTEMPORARY ART
CHRISTIE'S
FASHION

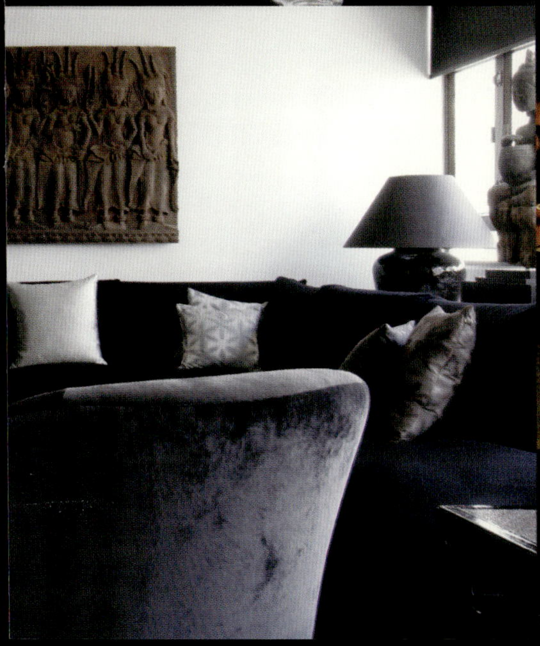

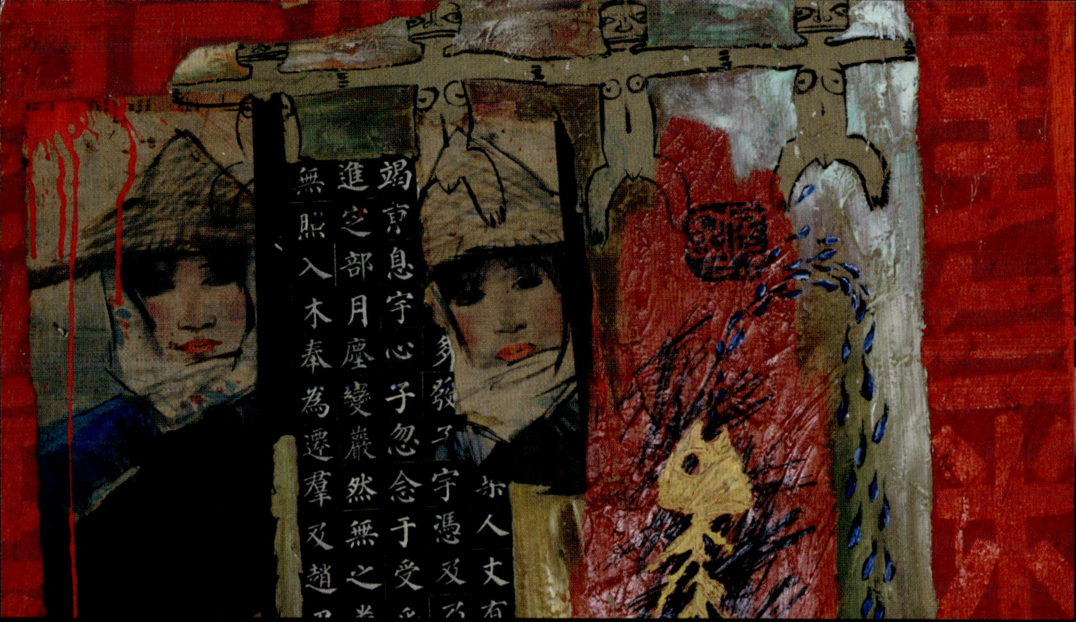
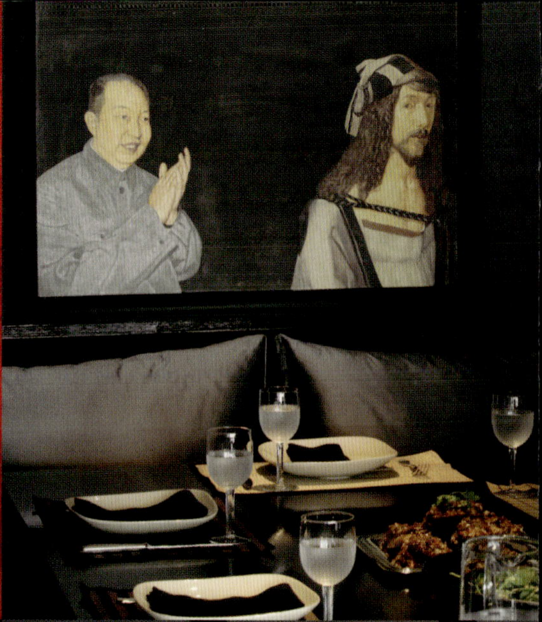
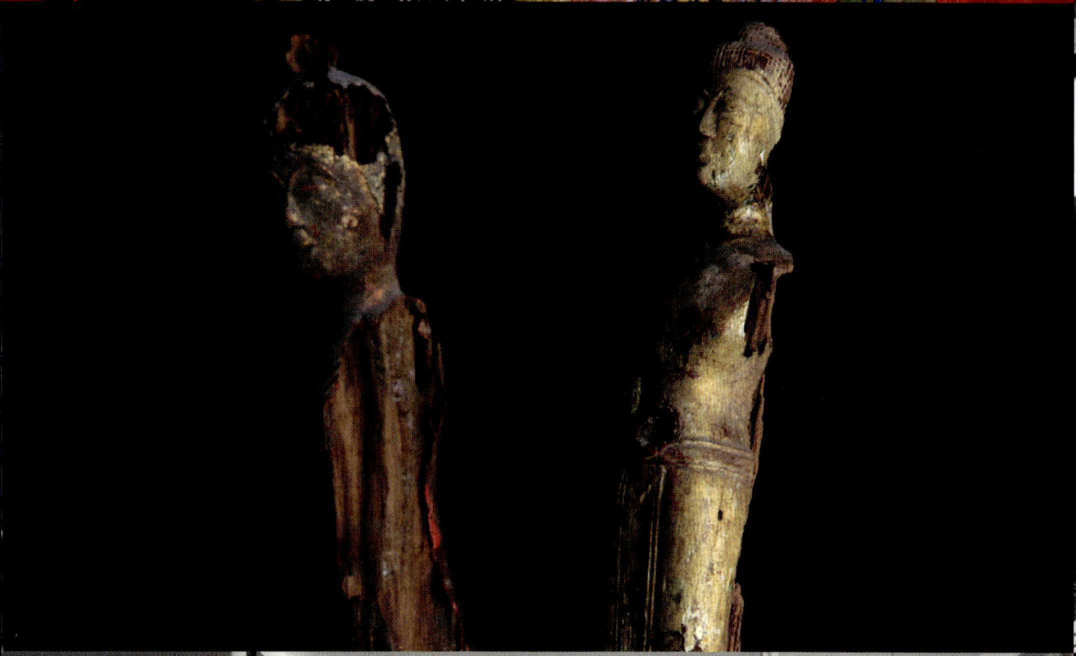
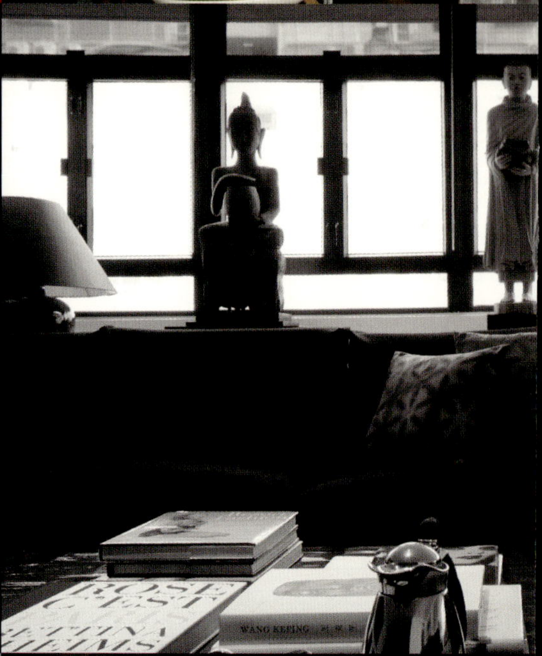
WANG KEPING
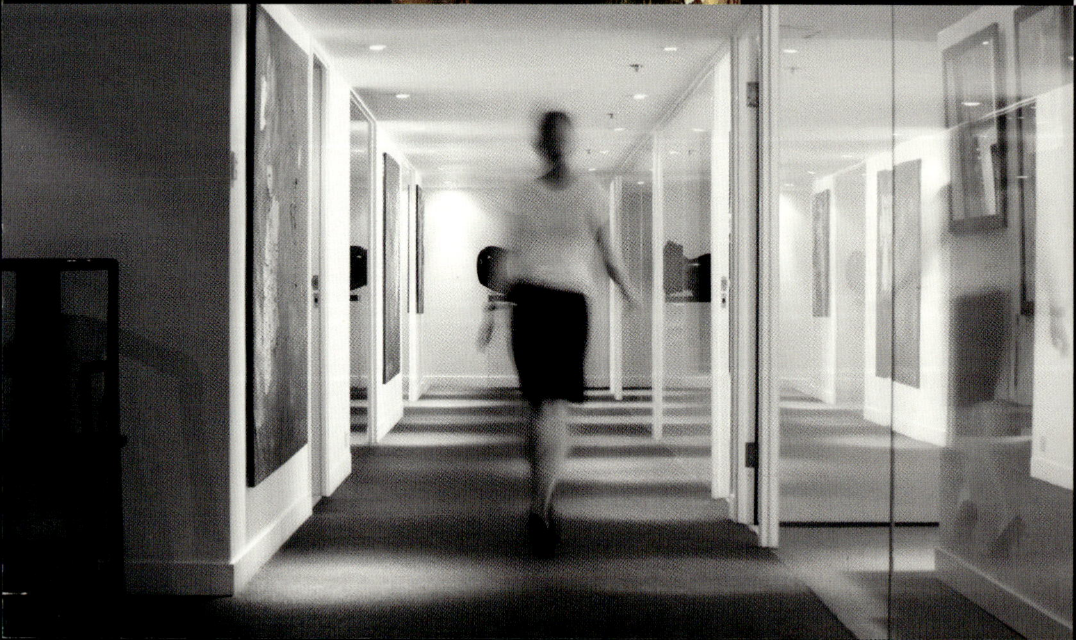
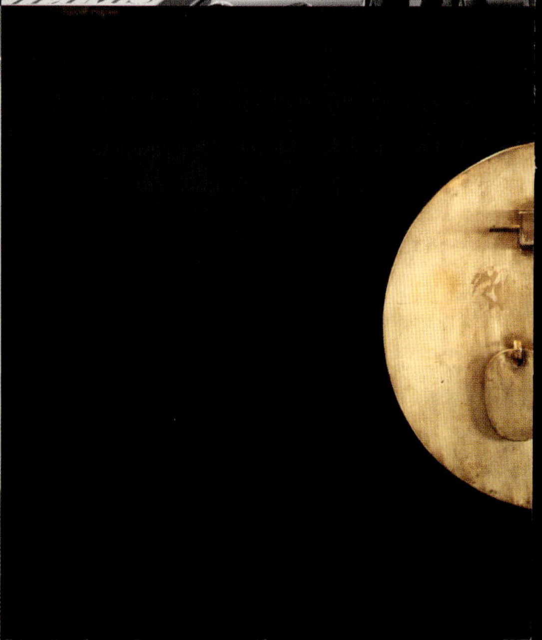

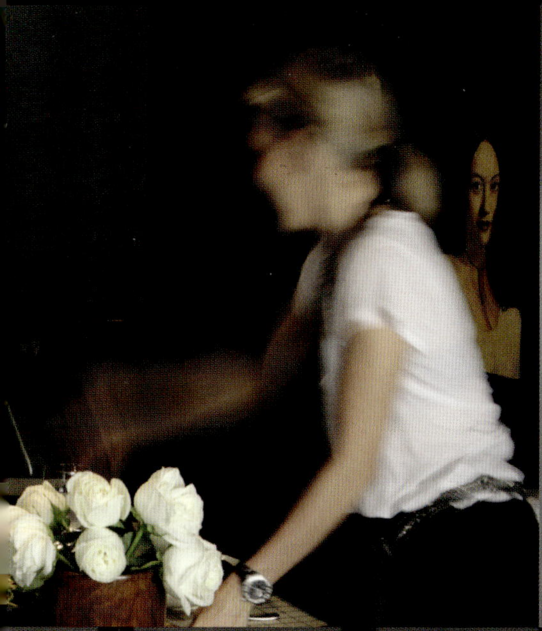
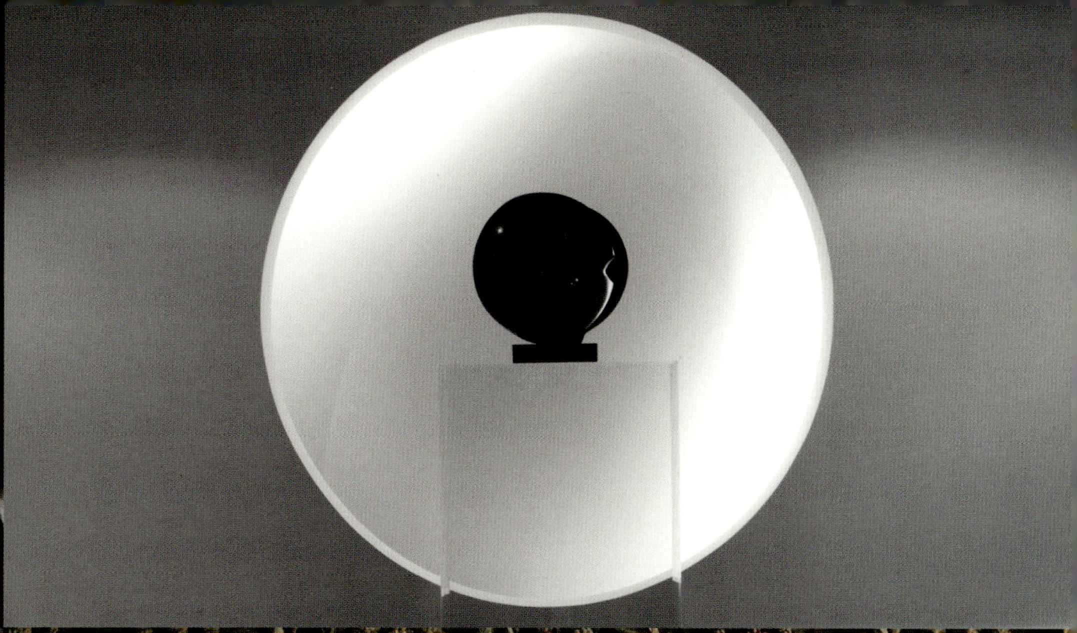
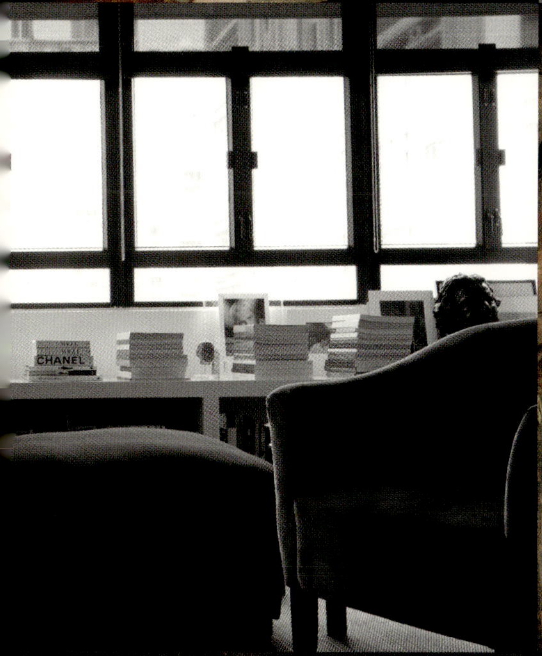
CHANEL
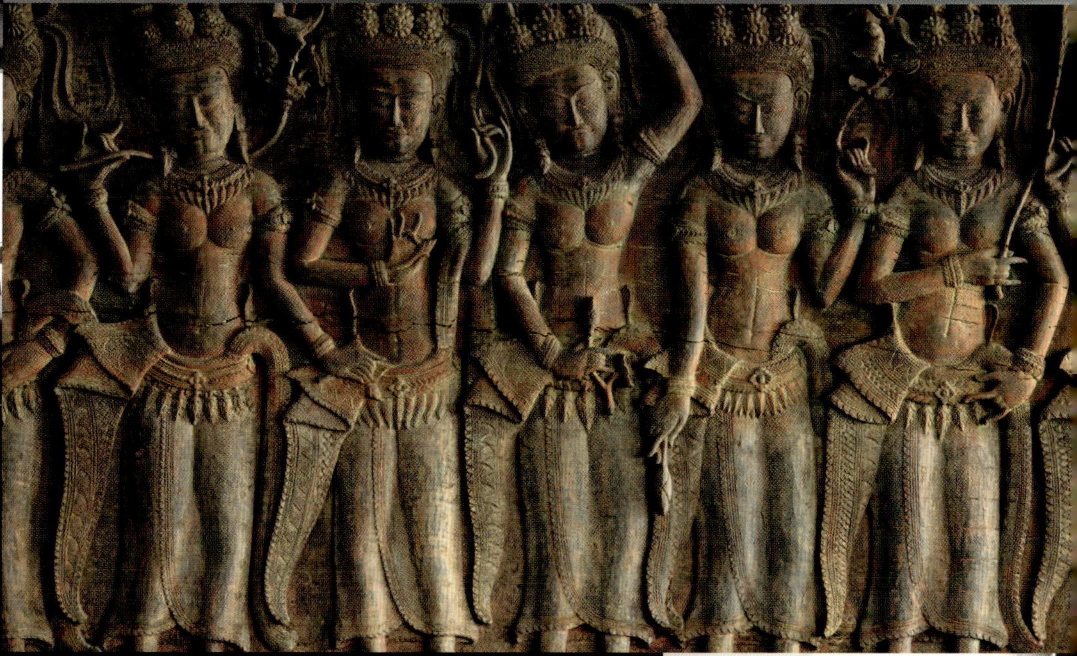
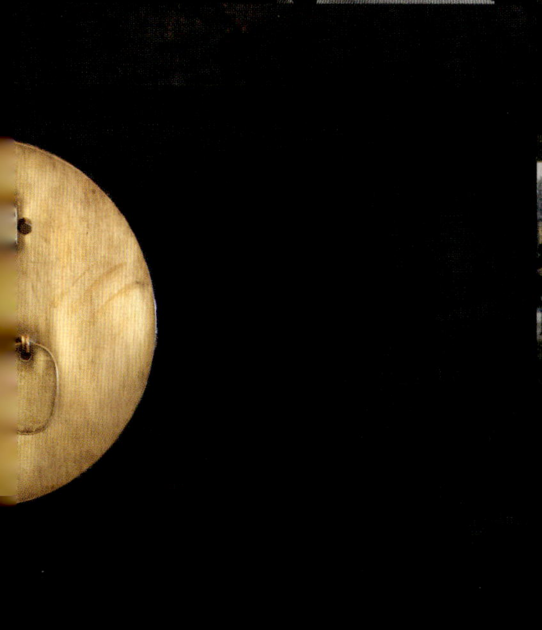
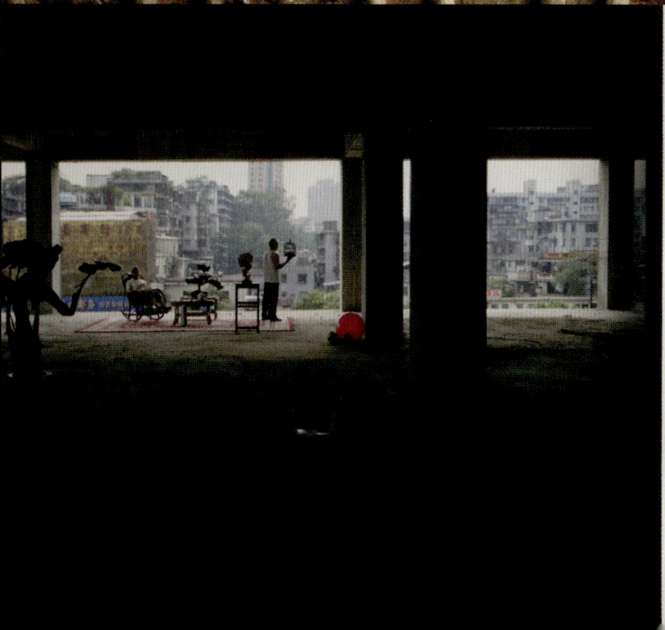
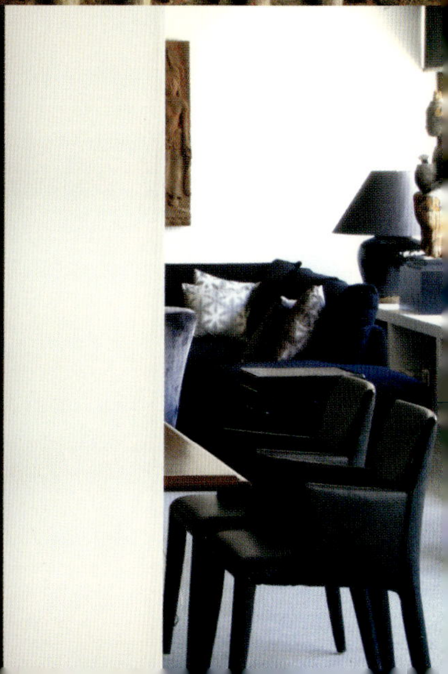

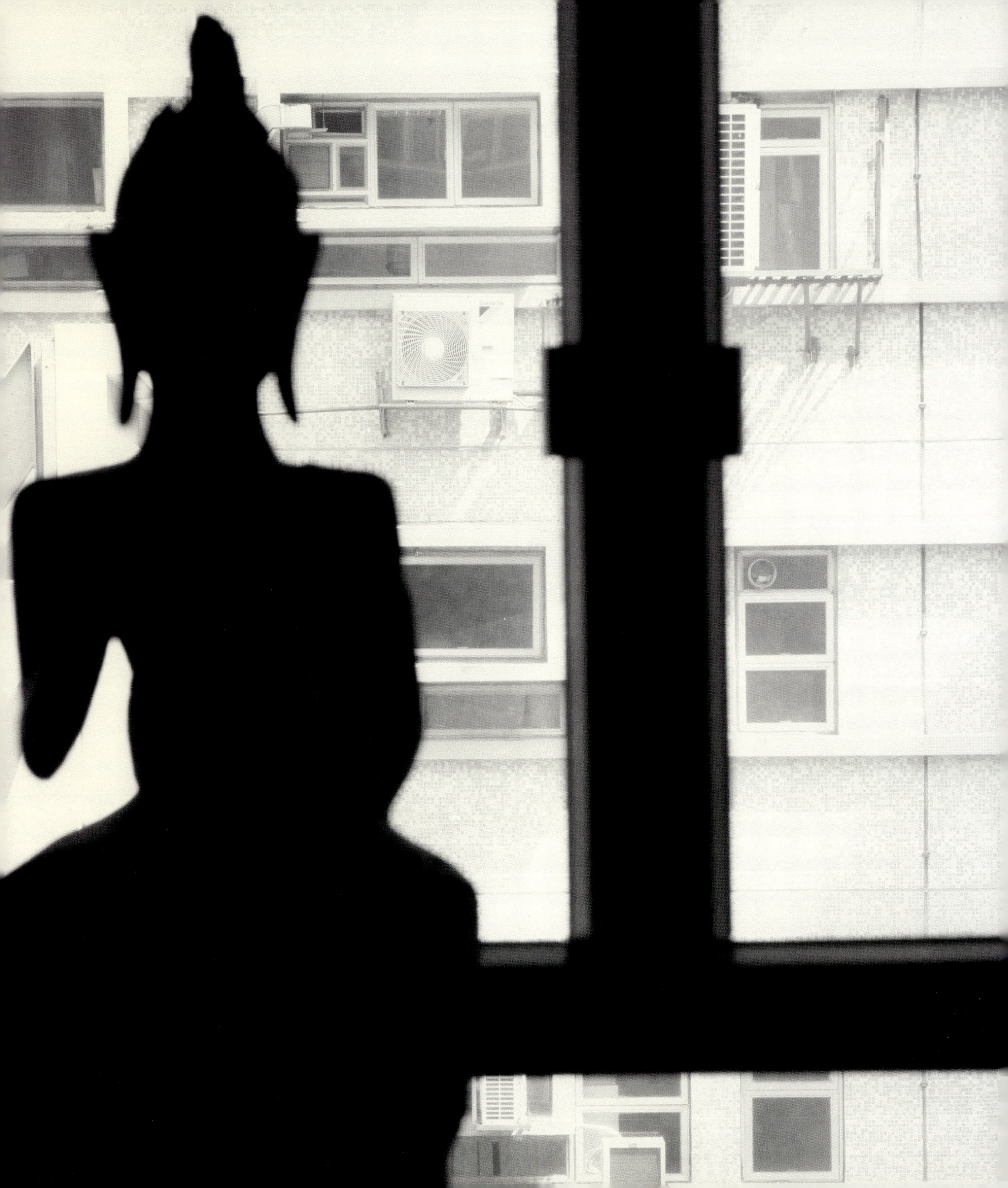

ART IN PRACTICE: THE WORKING LUNCH

My office is in the worst part of Kowloon. The surrounding buildings are semi-industrial workshops with air conditioners randomly protruding from the windows. The lobby – if you can call it that – is a loading dock with a few parking spaces, guarded by a bunch of cranky guys who are always smoking.

But I wouldn't have it any other way. I love the juxtaposition it creates. Clients arrive with certain expectations because we're a fashion business, and if they are shocked by the state of the lobby, a ride in the rickety goods elevator sets them up for an even bigger surprise when they enter our offices, which are clean, white and contemporary, decorated with beautiful modern Chinese paintings and sculptures. Contrast is a powerful aesthetic tool and I'm convinced that my art collection works better in these spaces than it would if I were based in a swanky office in Hong Kong Central.

I regularly host lunches in my office and I always get a kick out of how people respond to the contrast between the outside and the inside. But I didn't buy my art to get a reaction; I bought it because I like it and because it helps to make my workspace a more enjoyable place. If it creates a bit of theatre for my visitors in the process, I'm thrilled. I can't imagine how boring a working lunch would be without it.

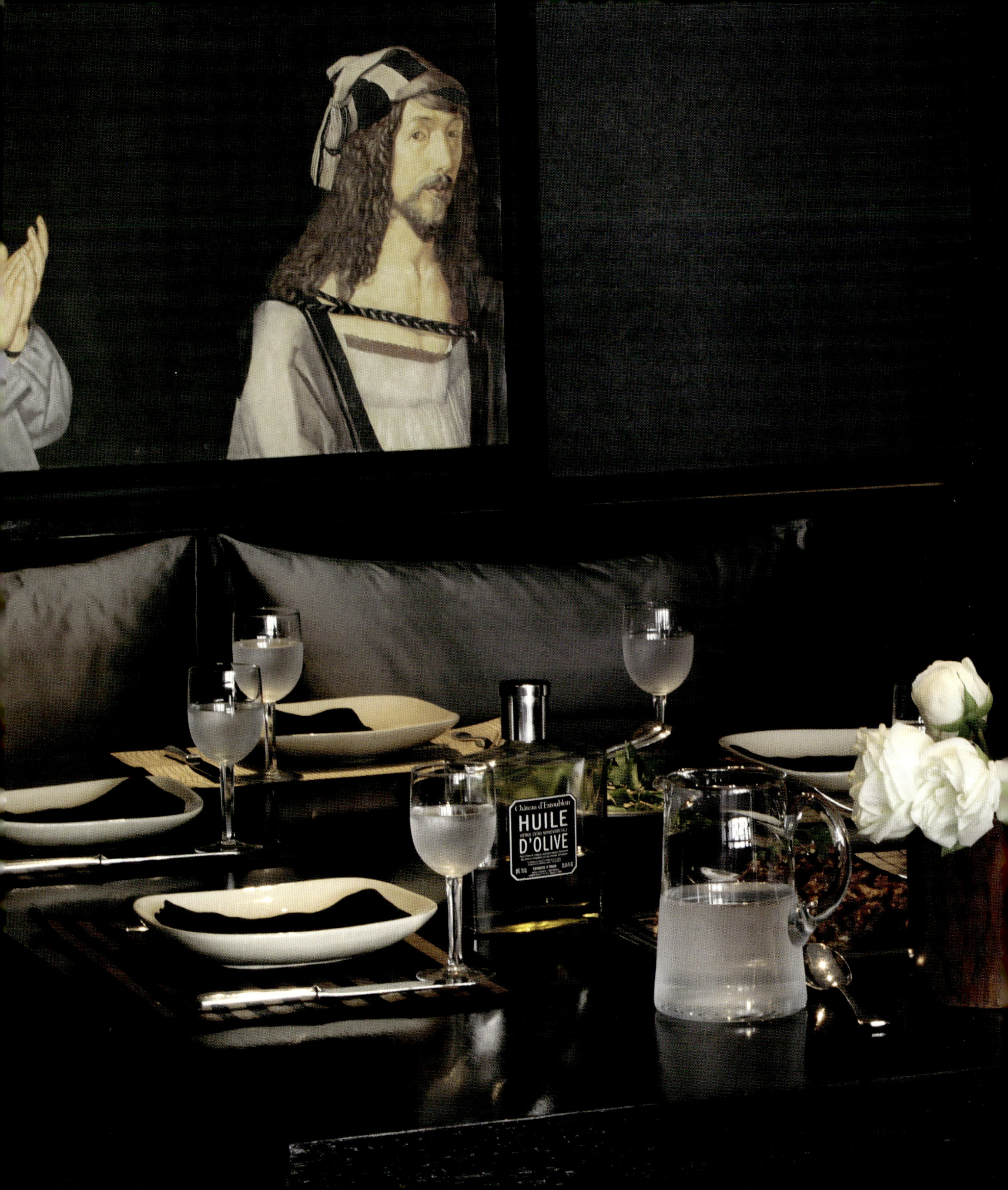
Château d'Estoublon
HUILE
D'OLIVE

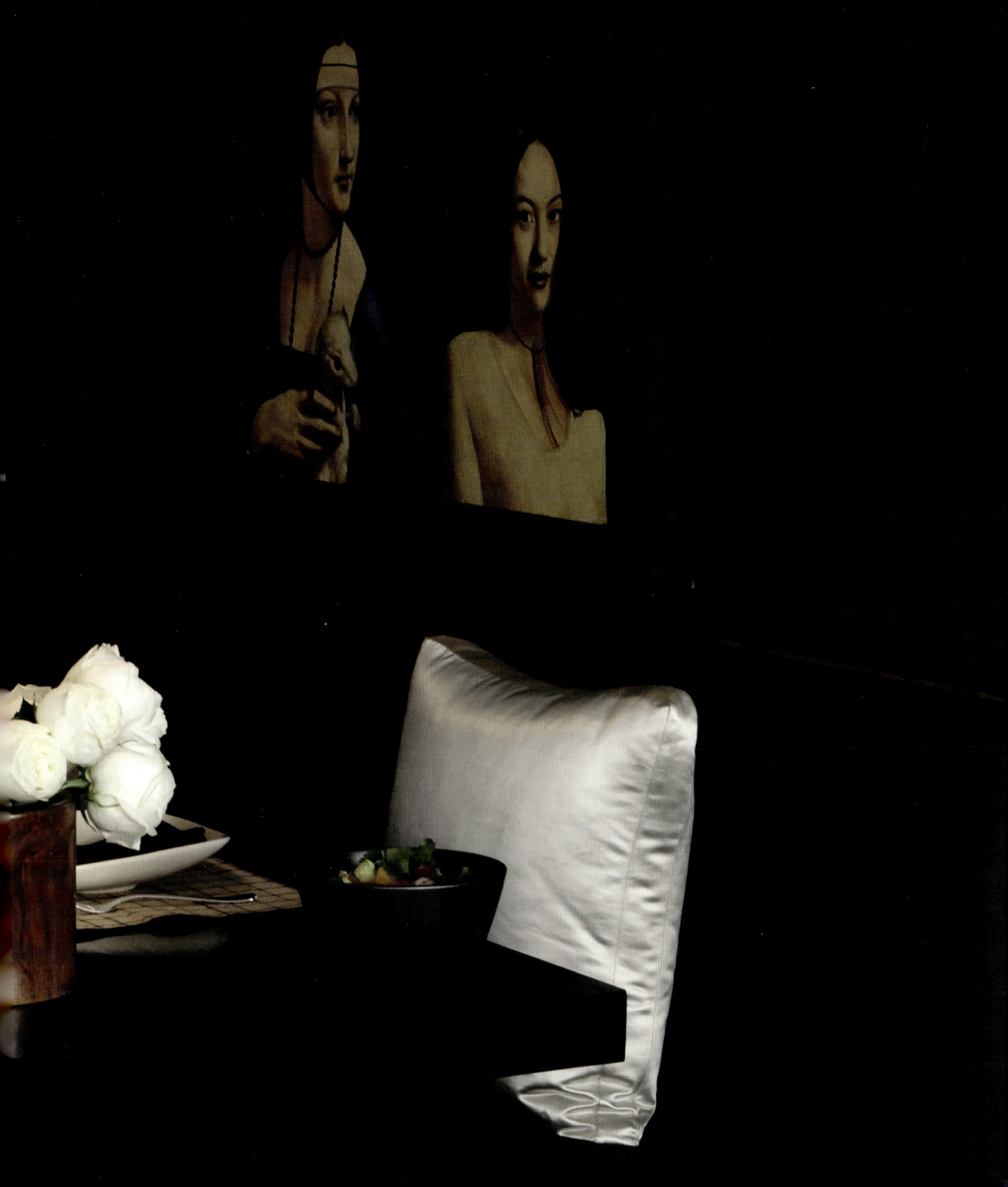

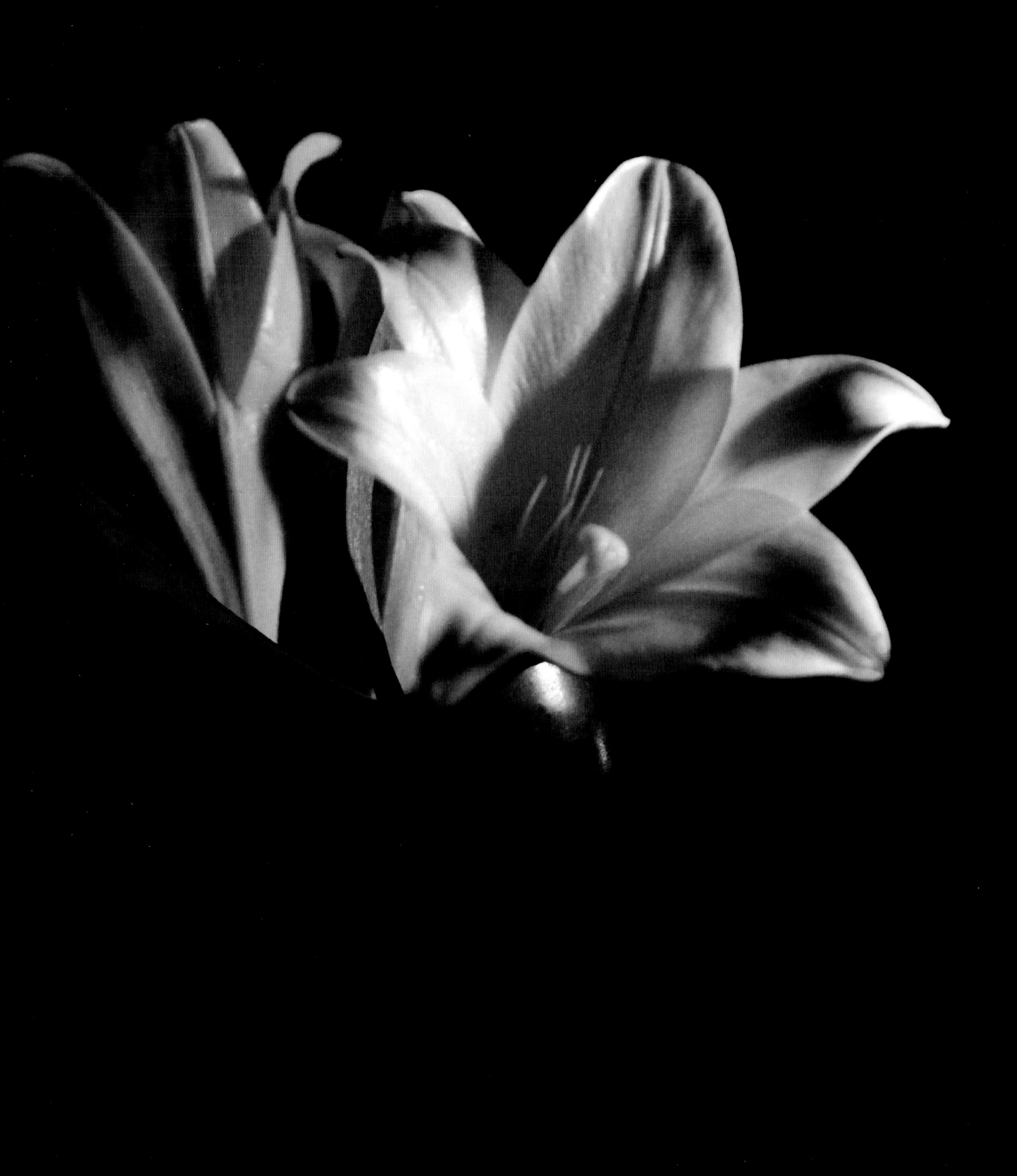

6

ESSENTIALS

1. (A SPLASH OF) COLOUR

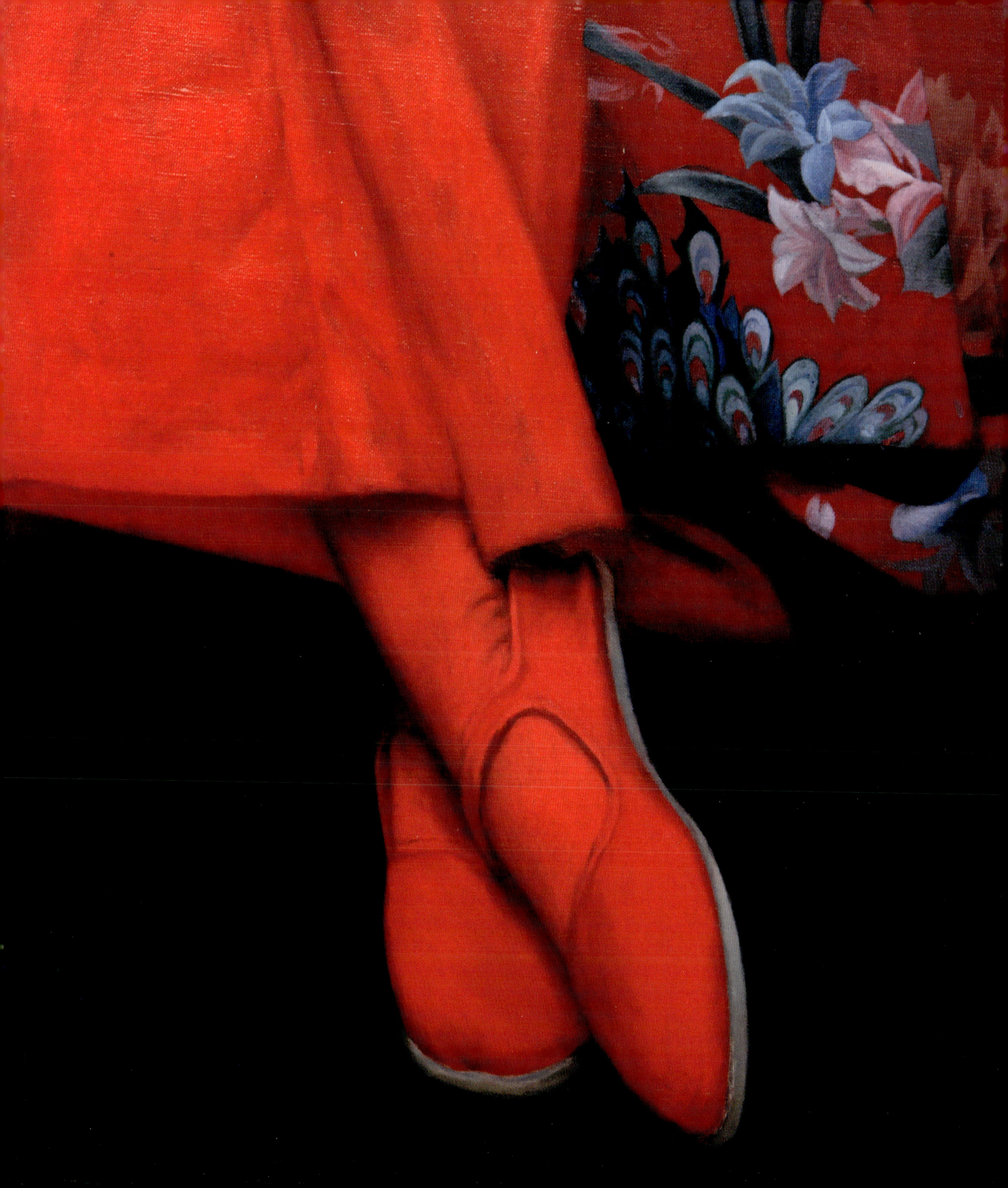

2. (SIMPLE) WHITE PLATES

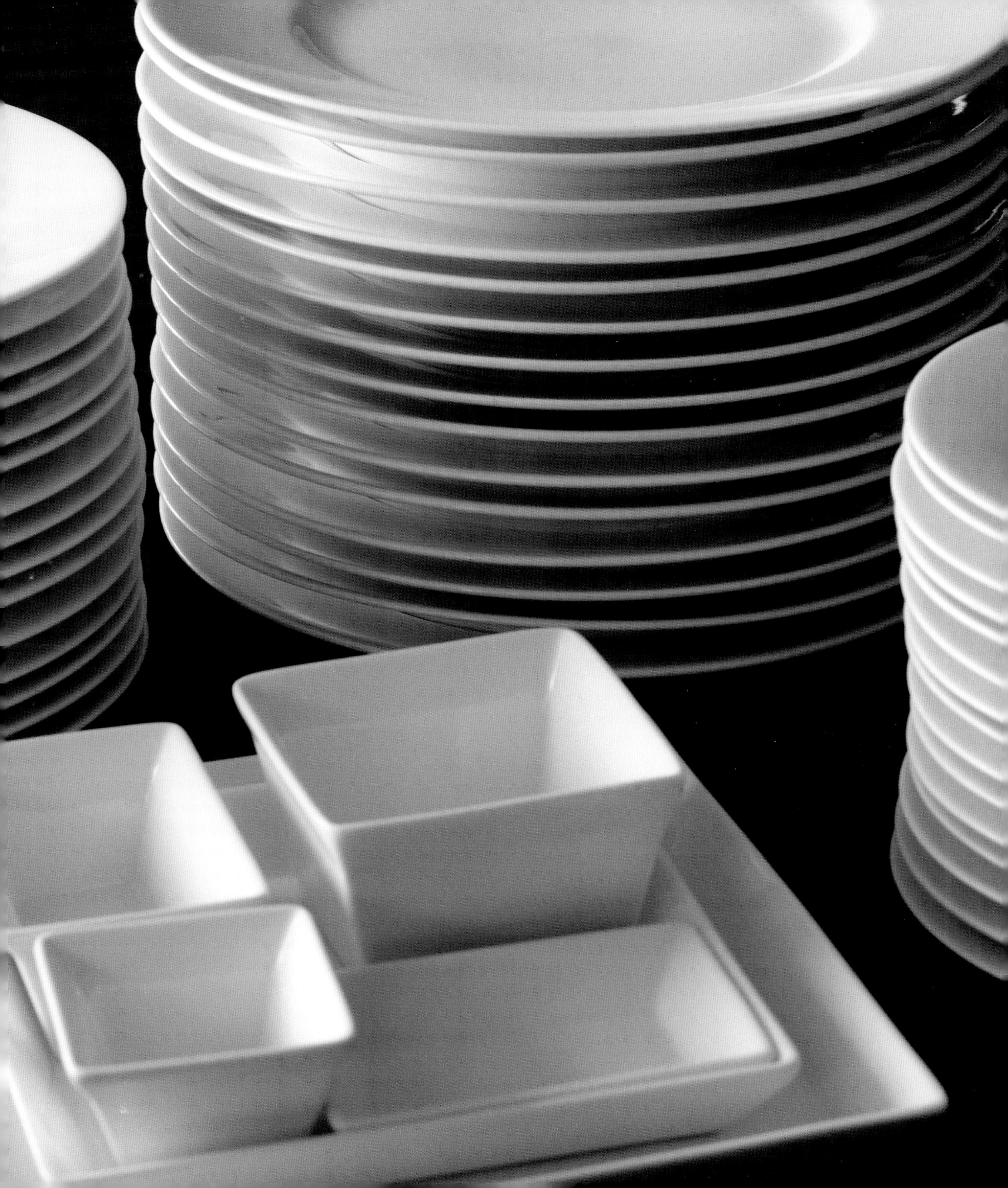

3. (PLAIN) FLOWERS

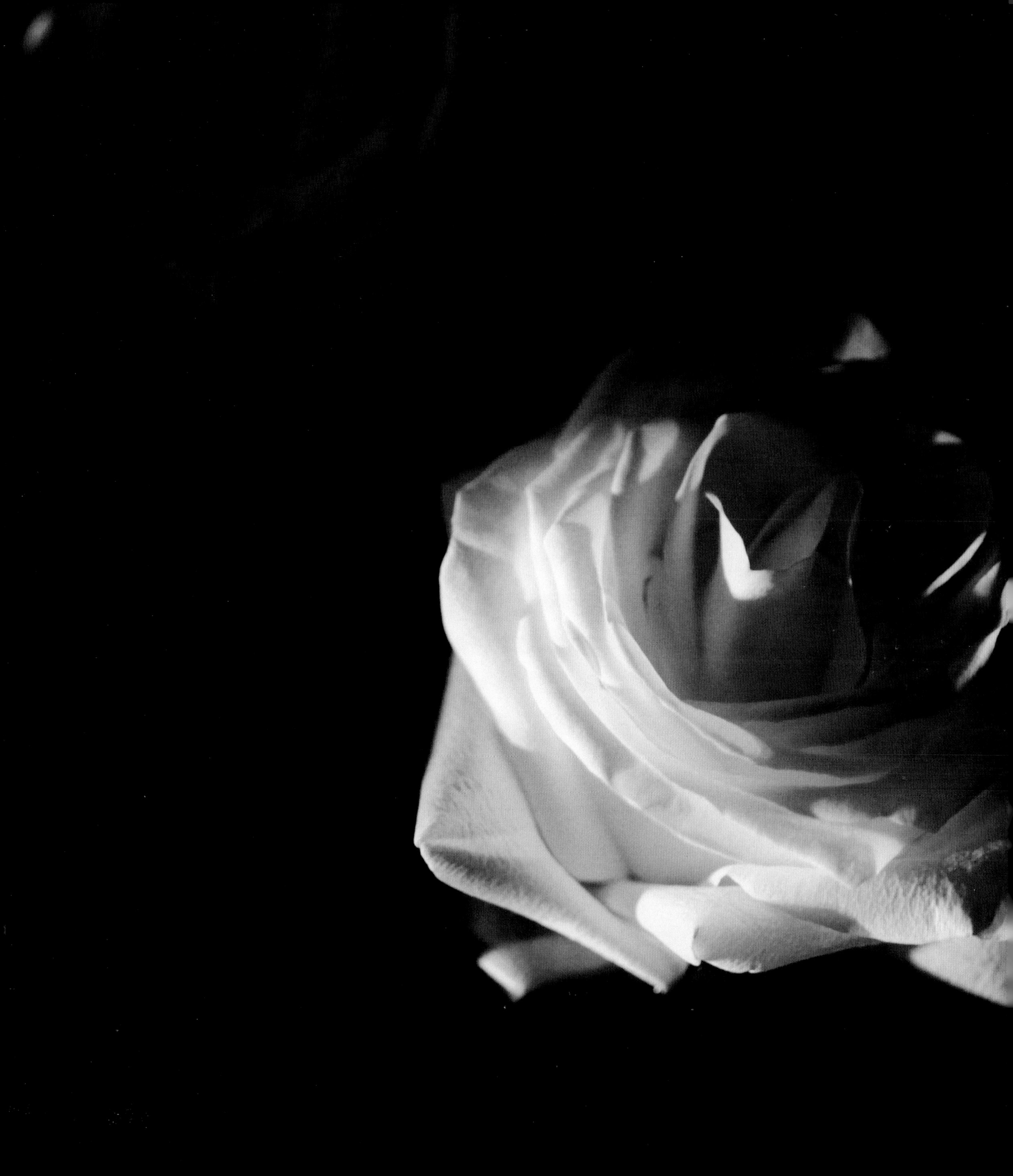

4. (AFFORDABLE) COLLECTABLES

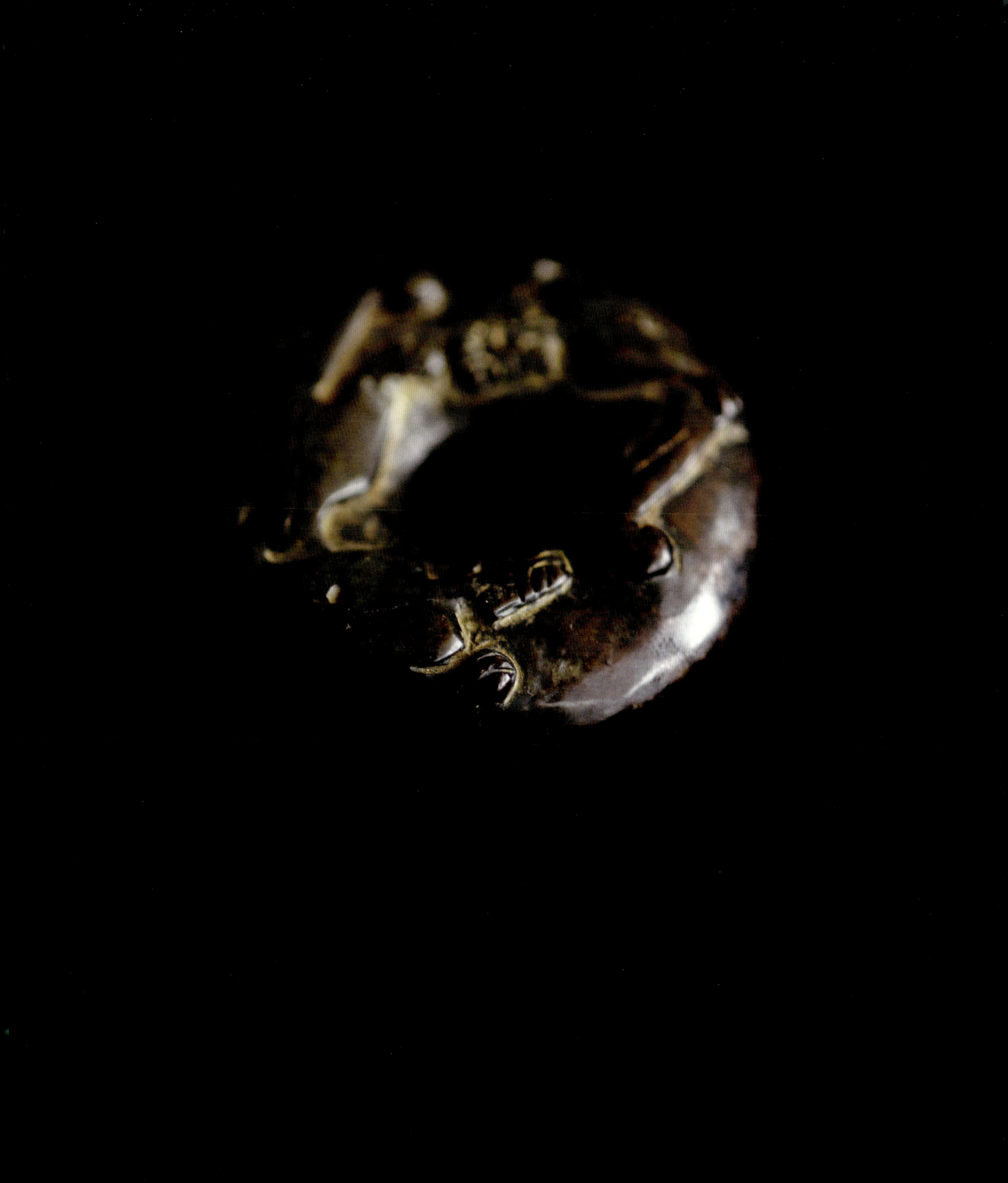

5. (TONS OF) TEA LIGHTS

6. (GENEROUS) WINE GLASSES

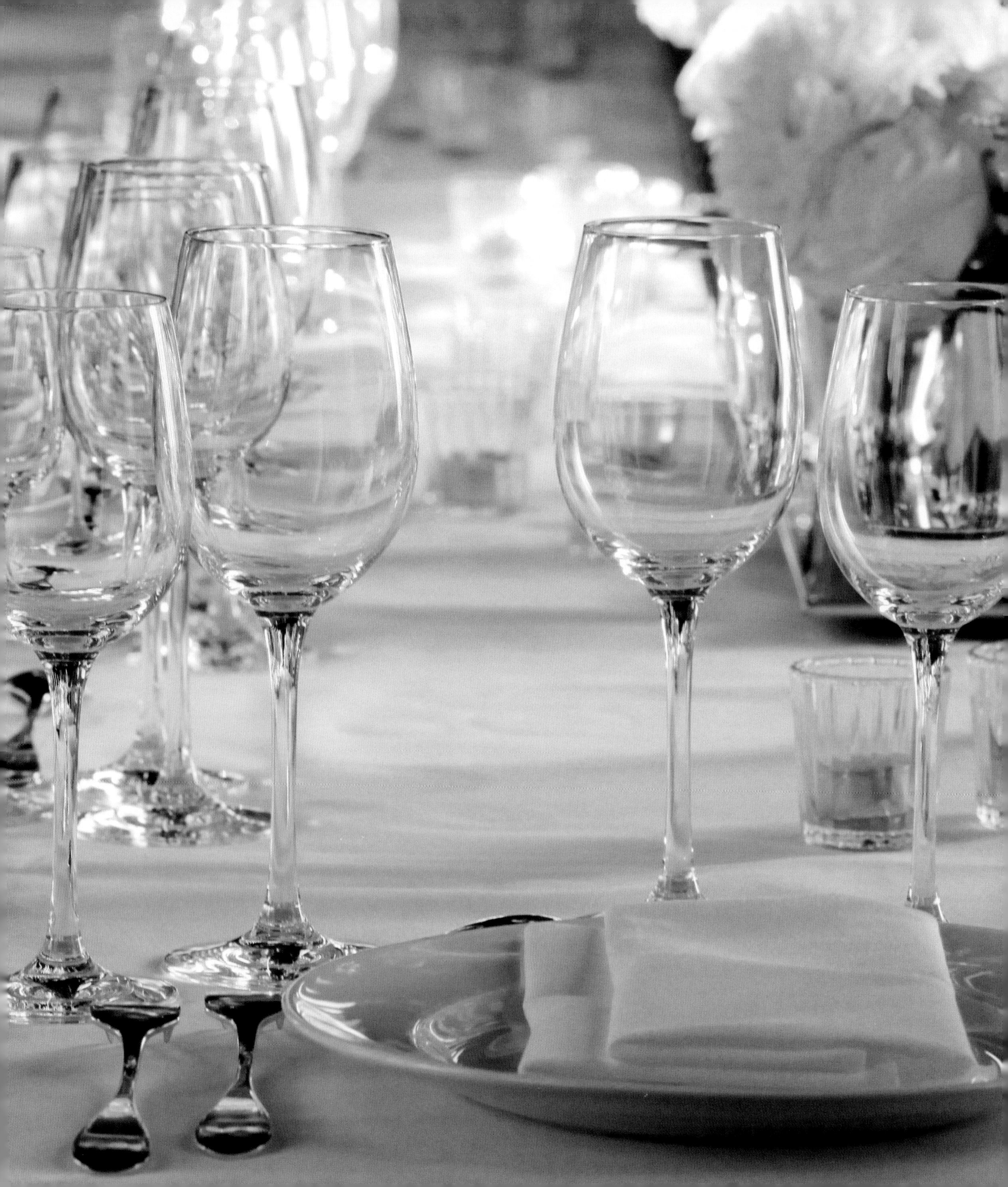

7. (BLACK OR WHITE) LINEN

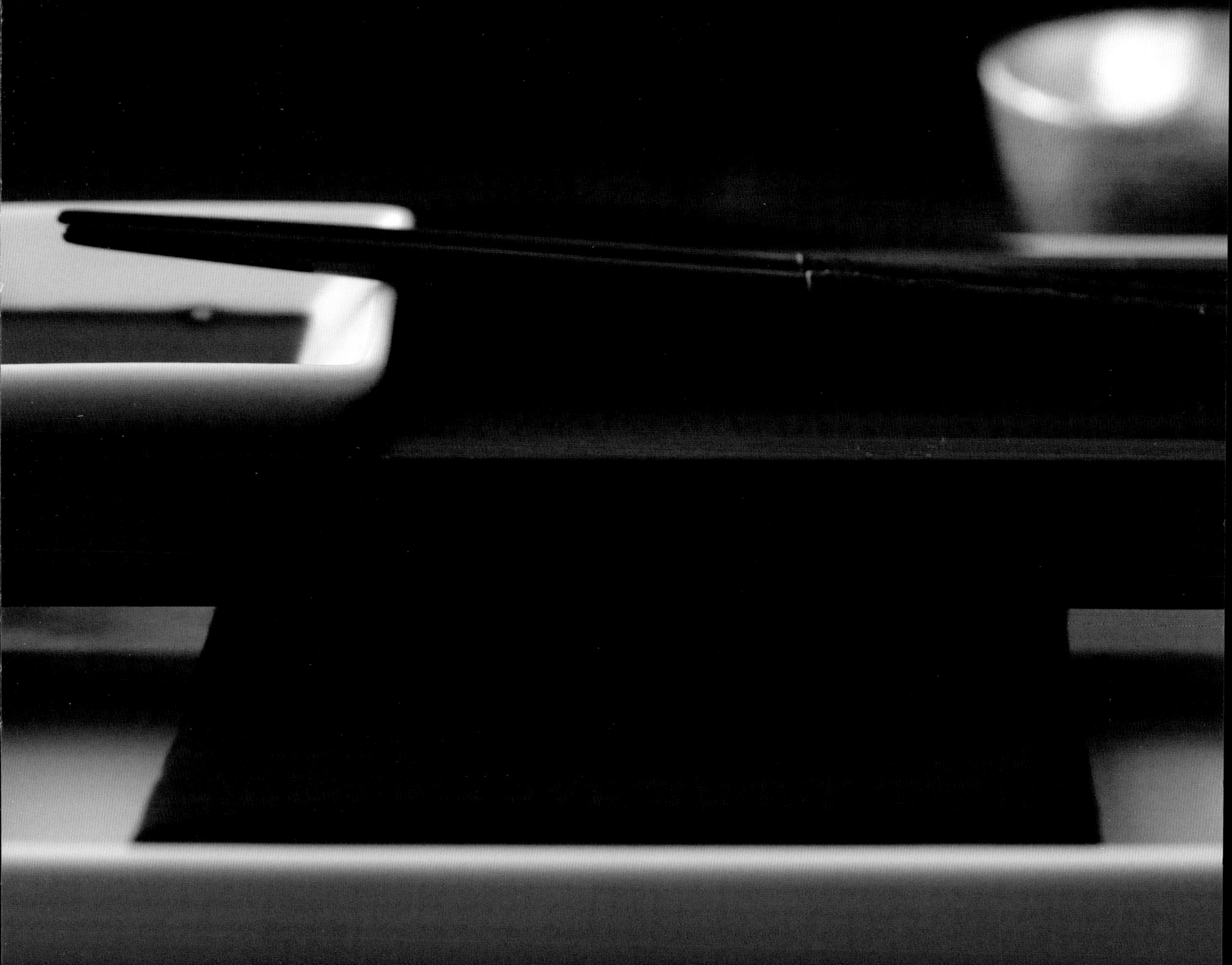

8. (INVENTED) VASES

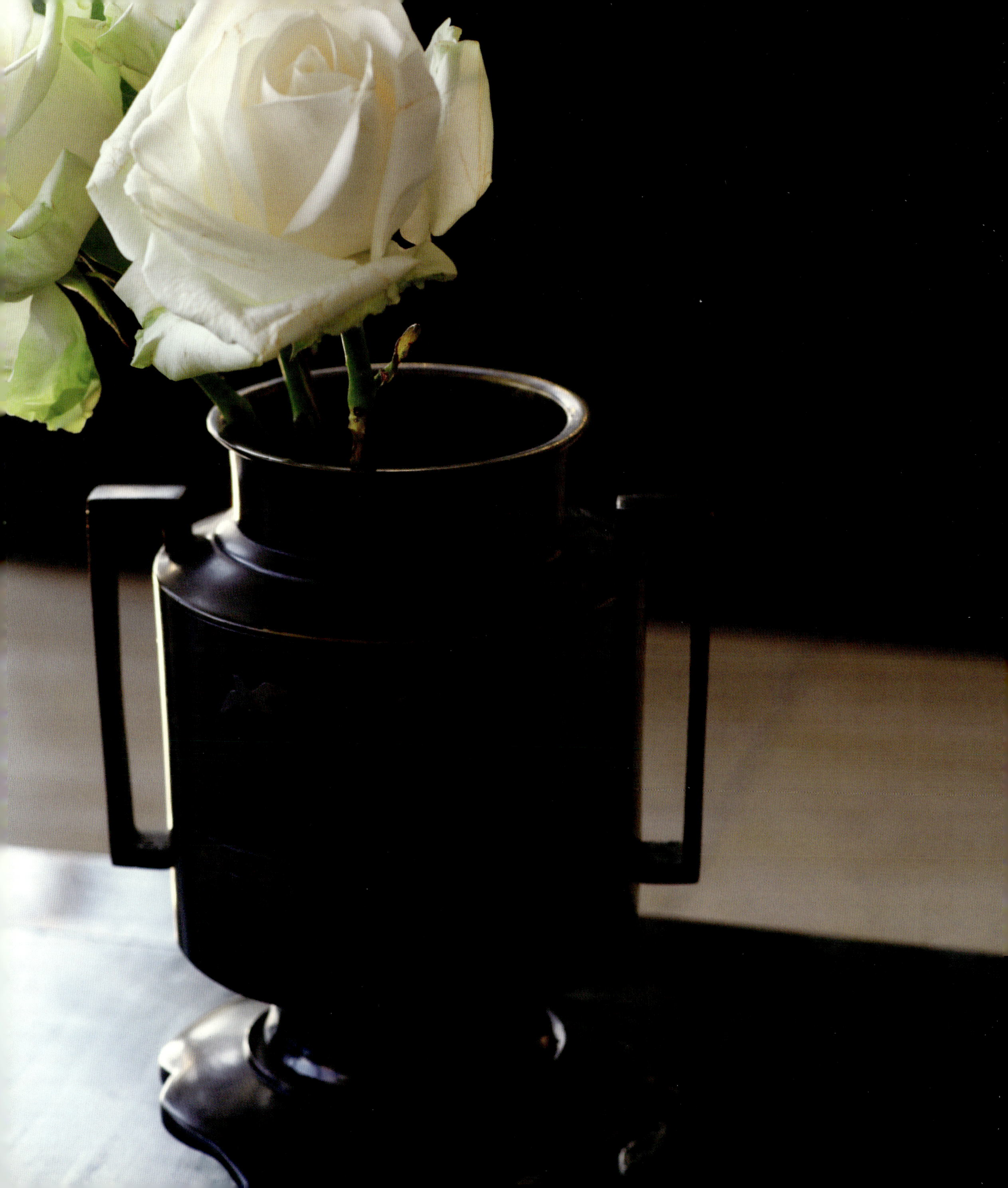

9. (UNCOMPLICATED) FOOD

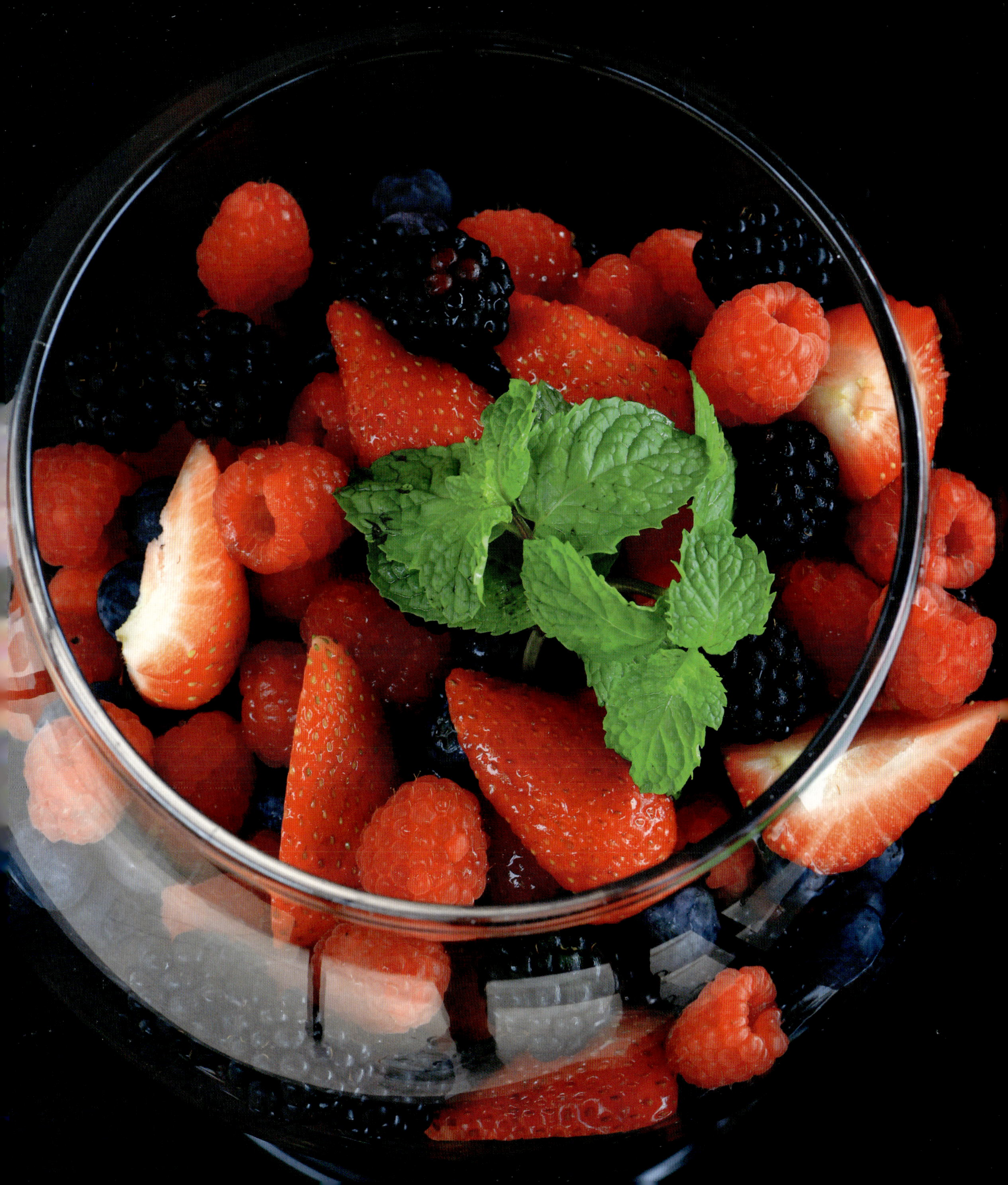

10. (DECENT) WINE

GRAND VIN

CHATEAU
LYNCH · BAGES

GRAND CRU CLASSÉ

PAUILLAC
APPELLATION PAUILLAC CONTROLEE
A CAZES Propriétaire à PAUILLAC (FRANCE)

2005

11. (ETHNIC) BASKETS

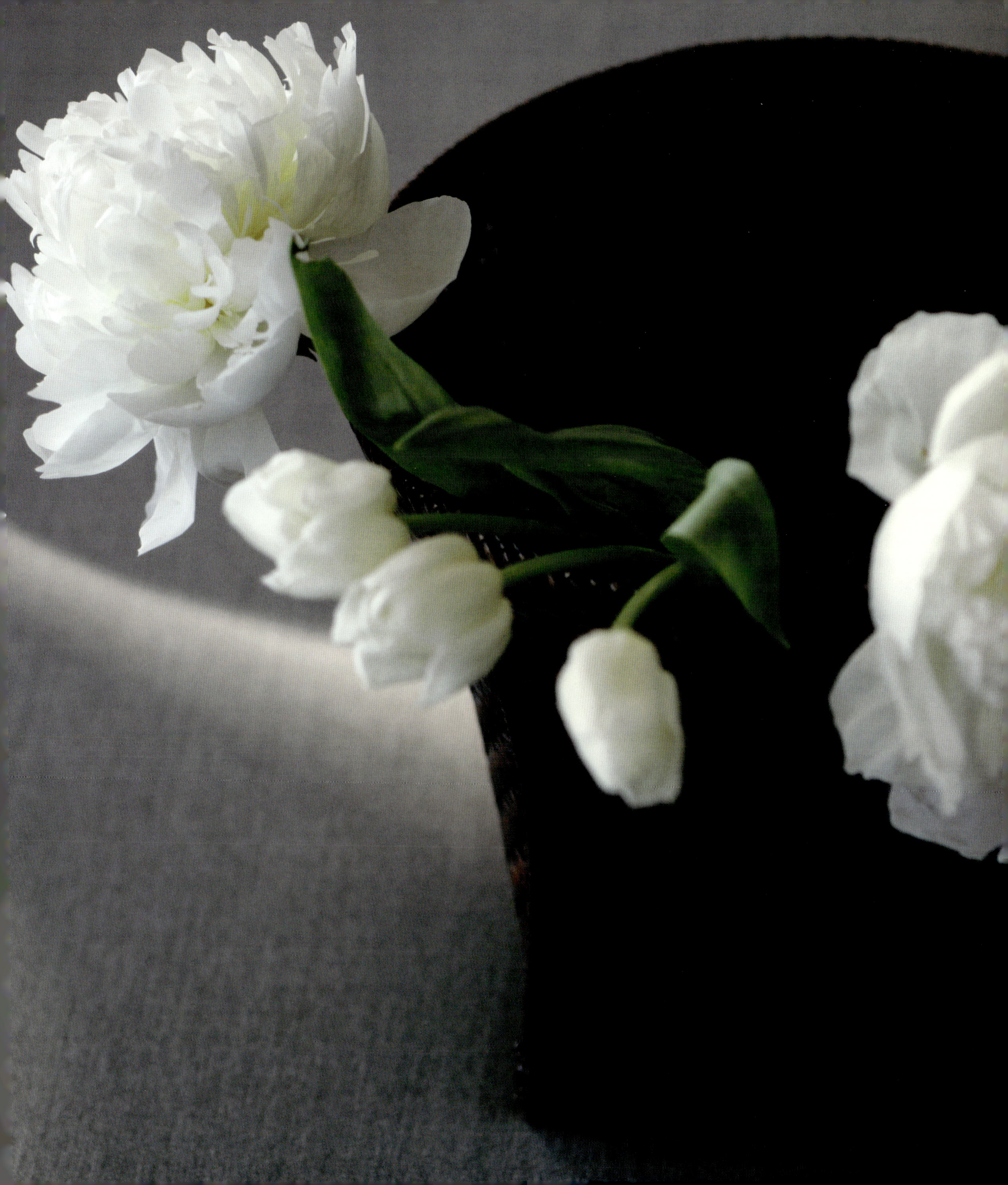

12. (FINE) ART

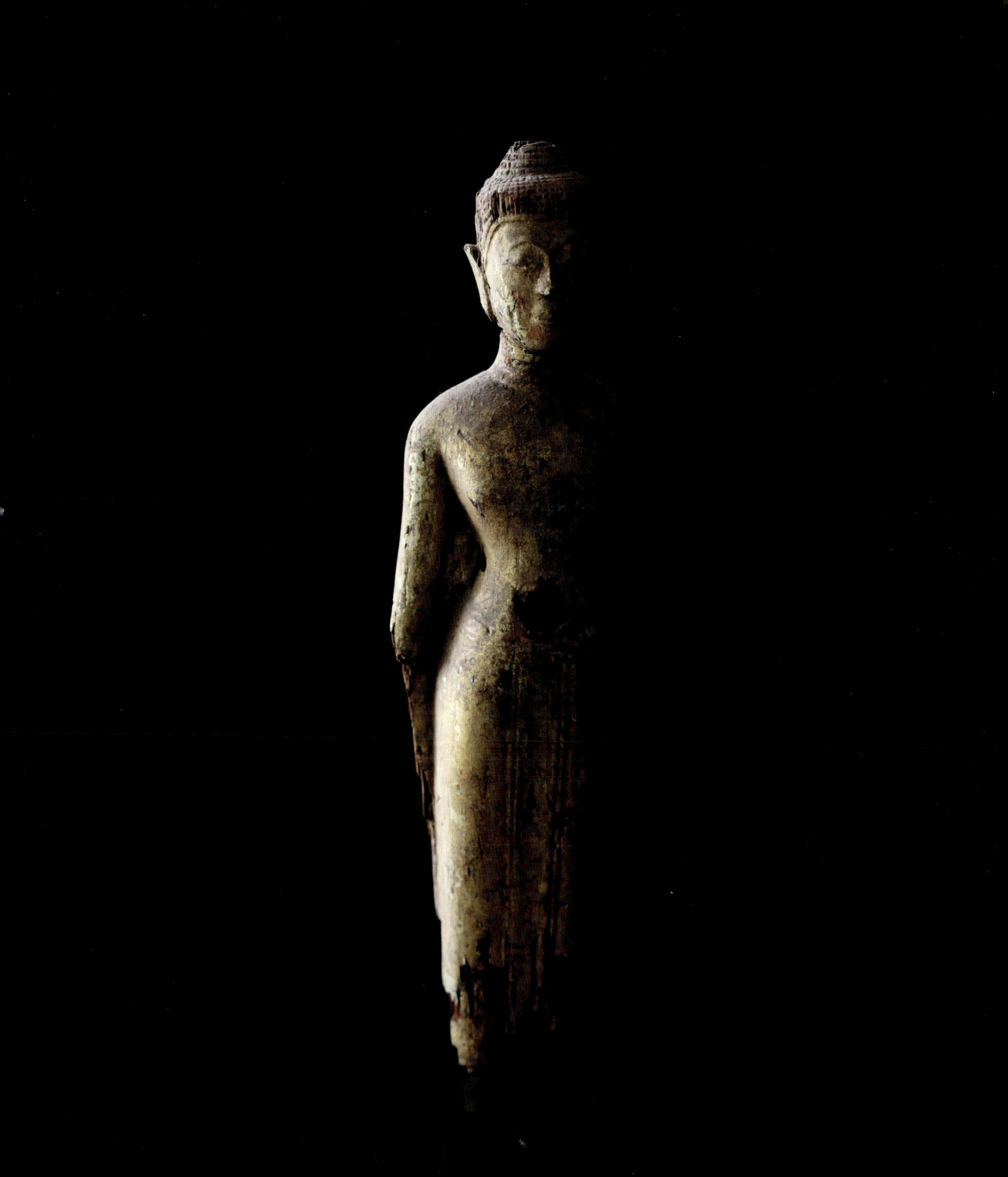

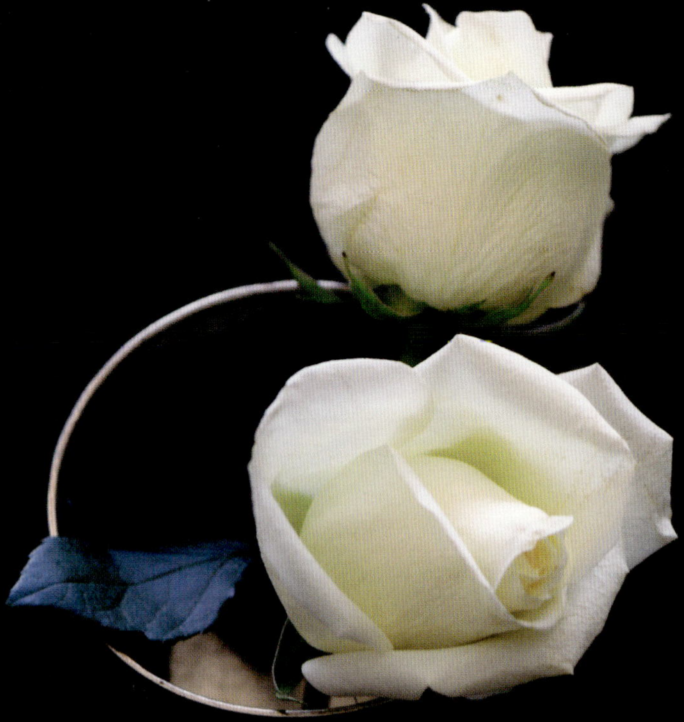
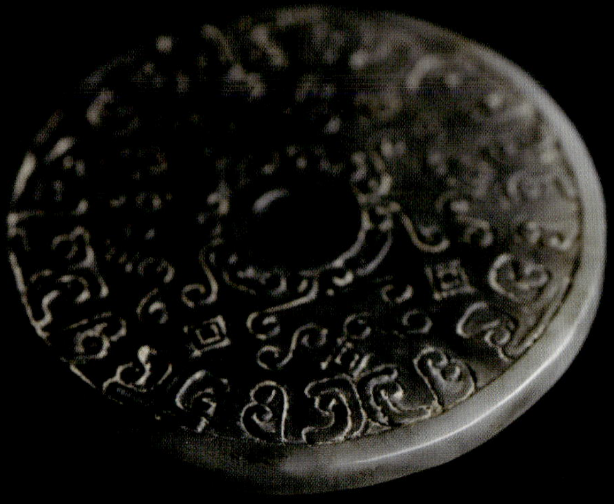
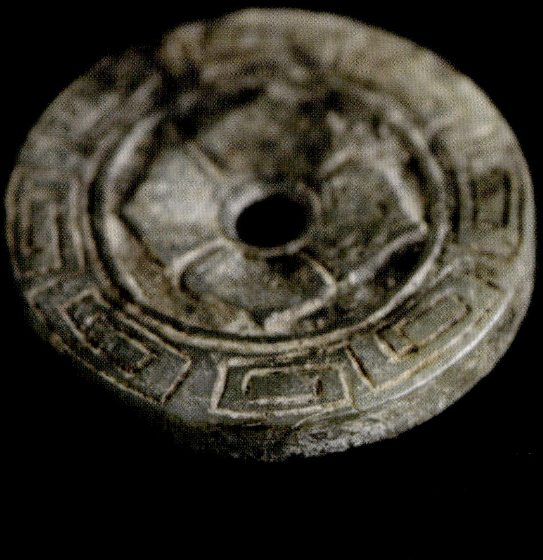
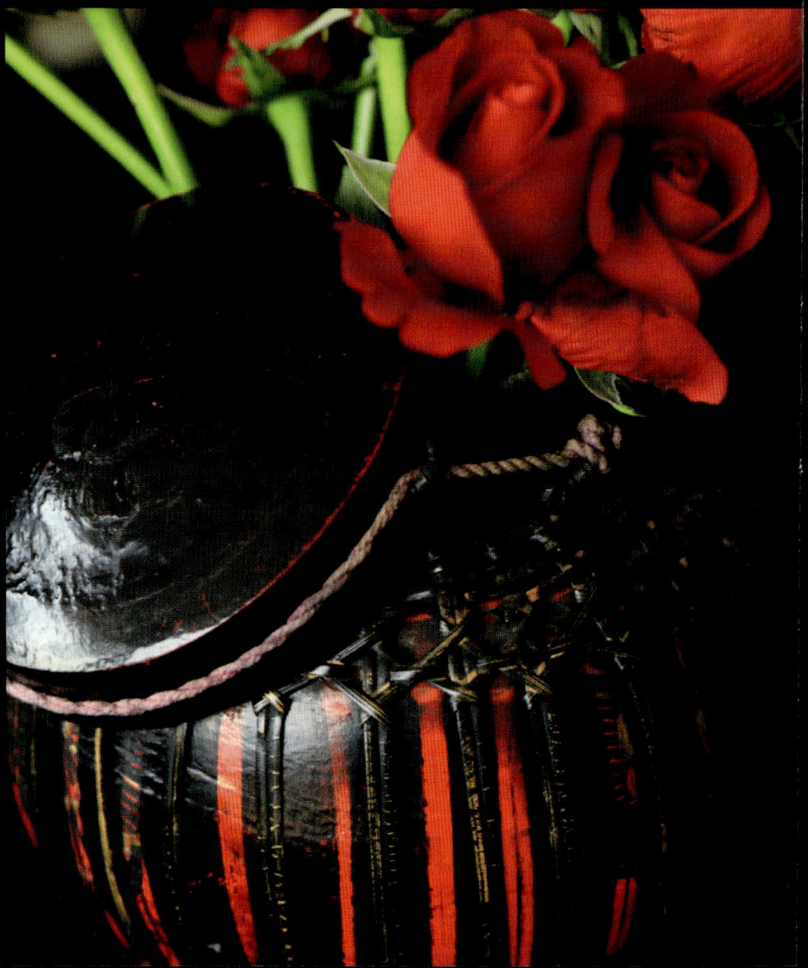

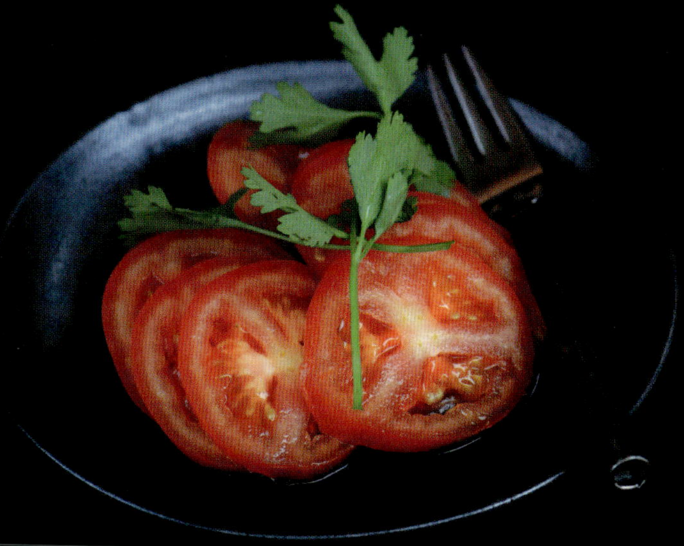

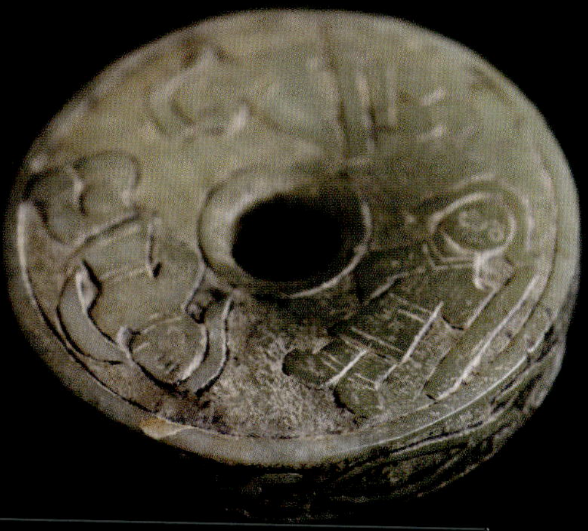

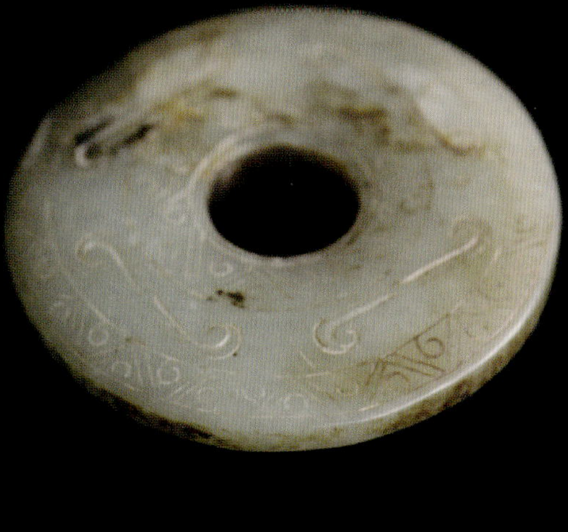

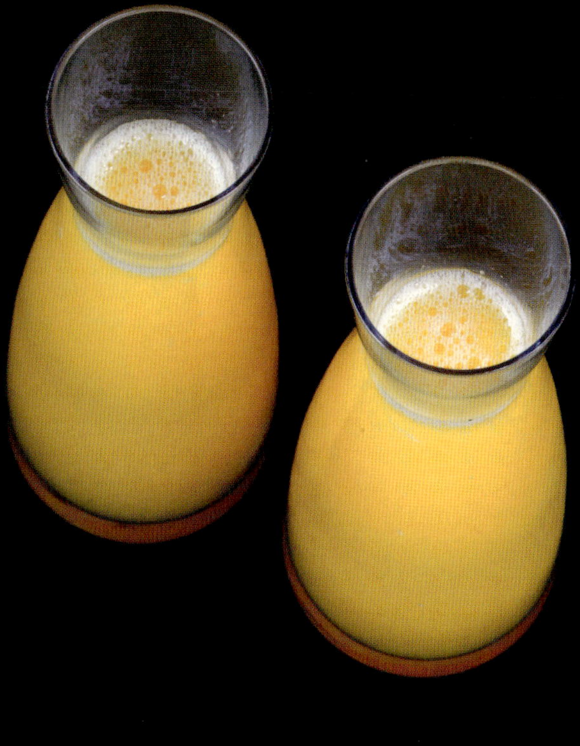

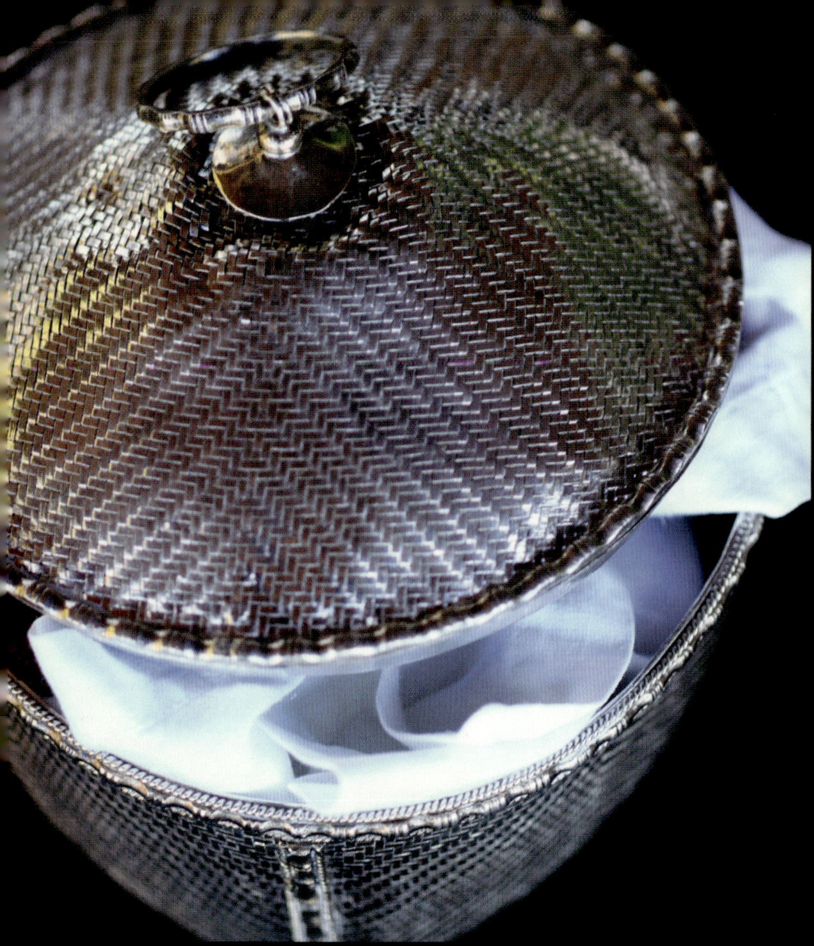
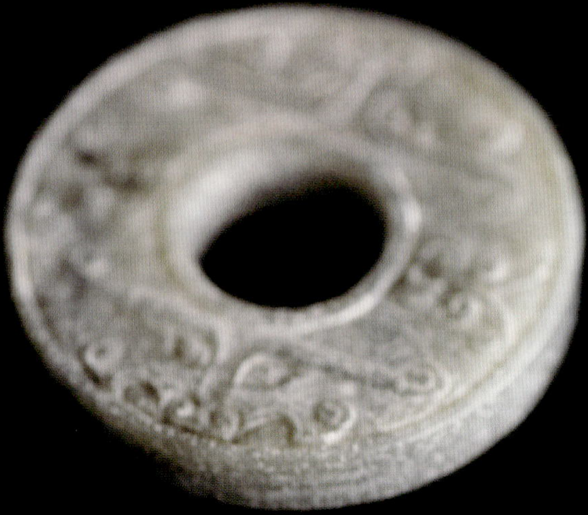
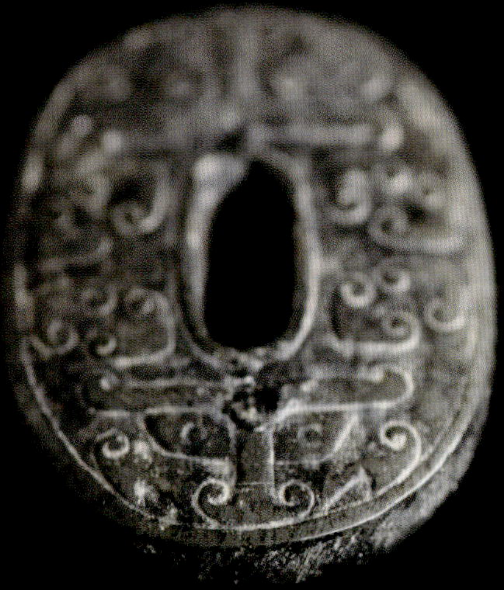
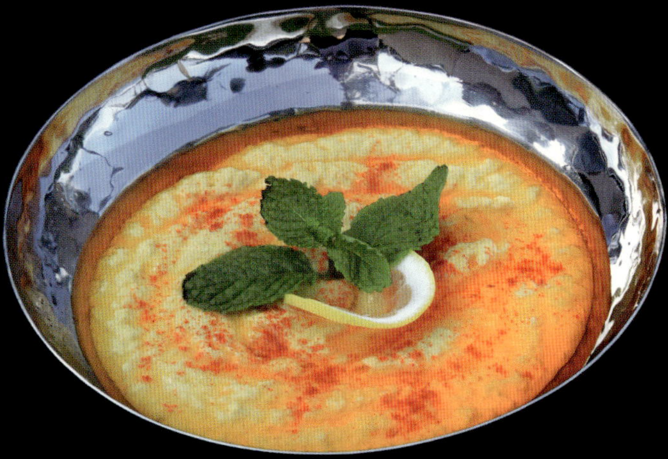

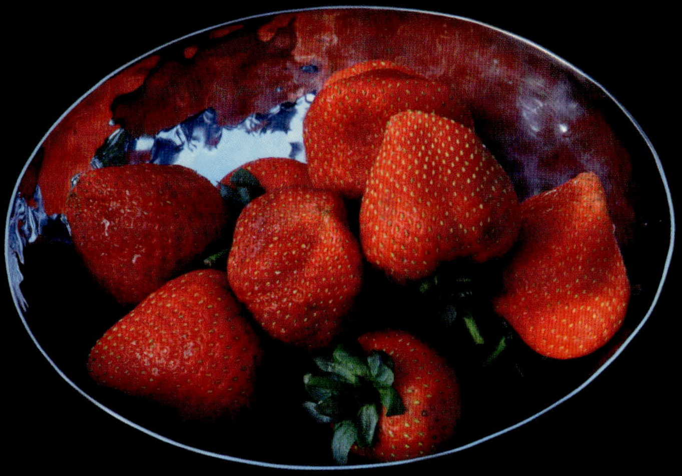

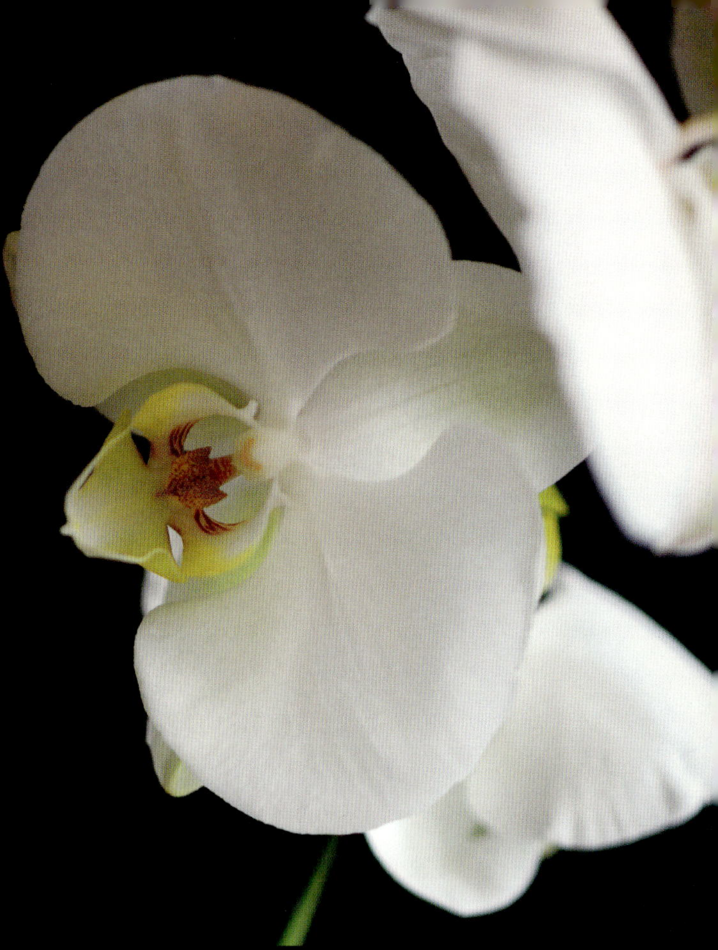

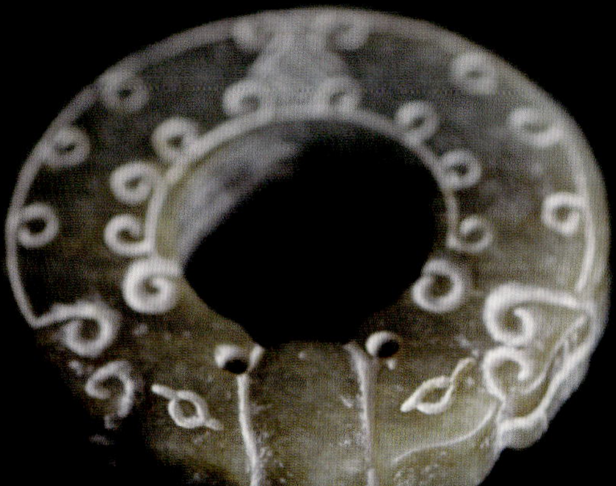

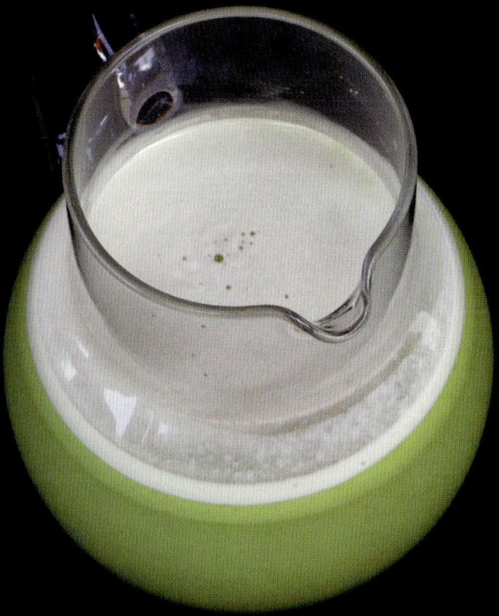

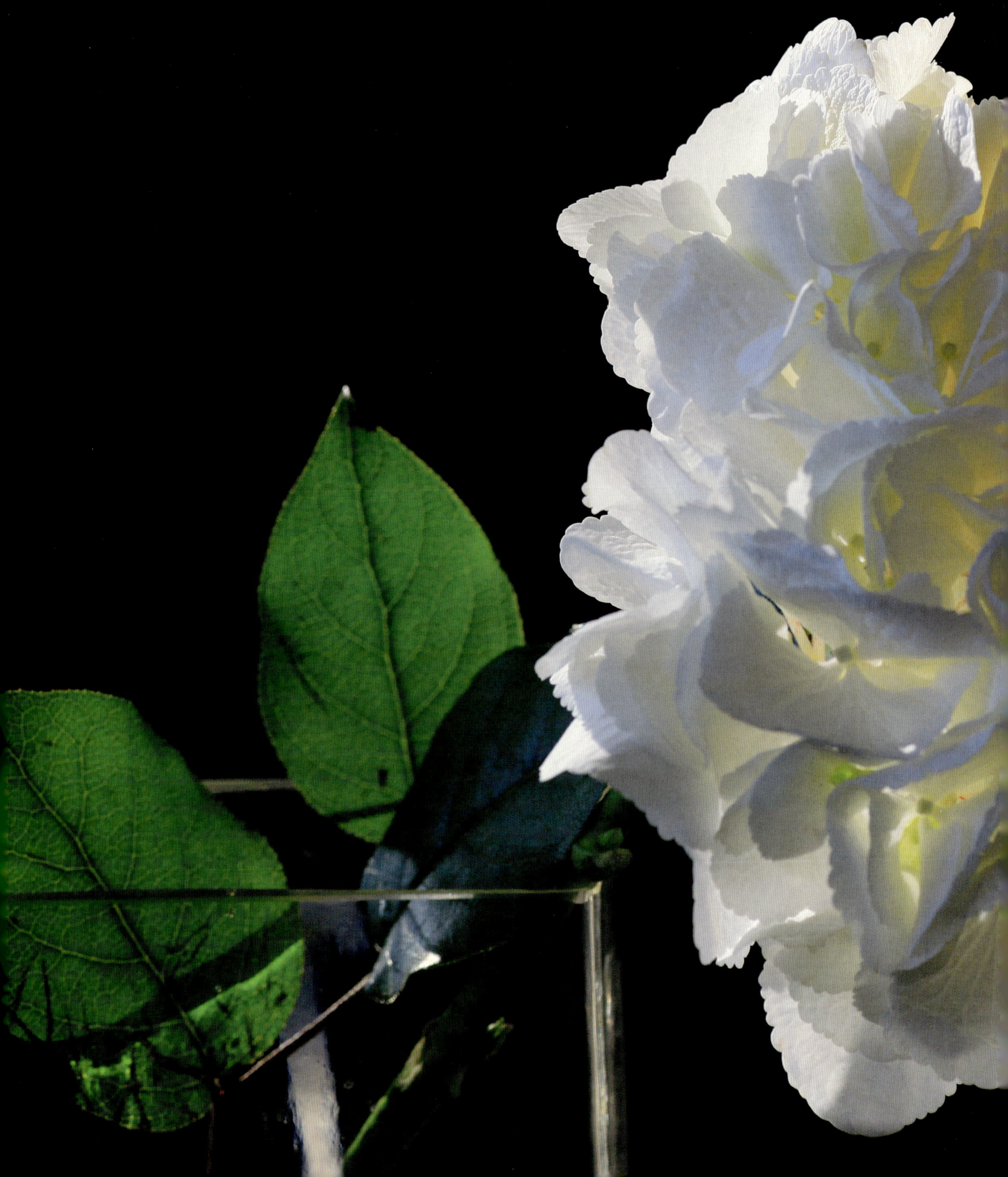

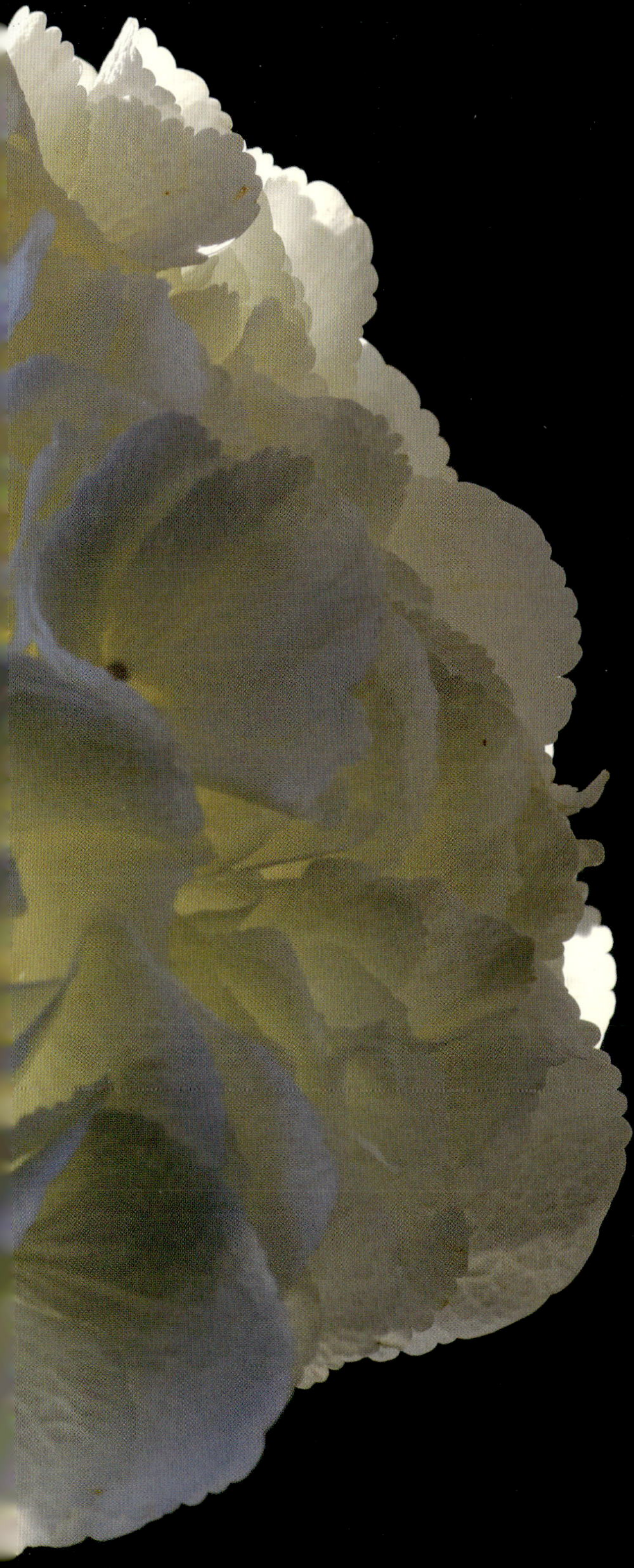

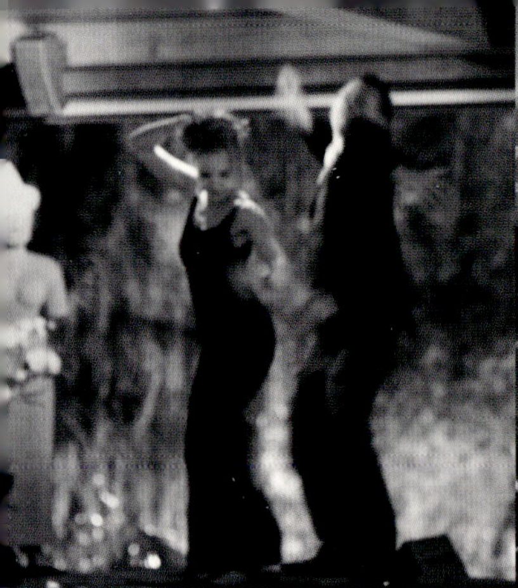
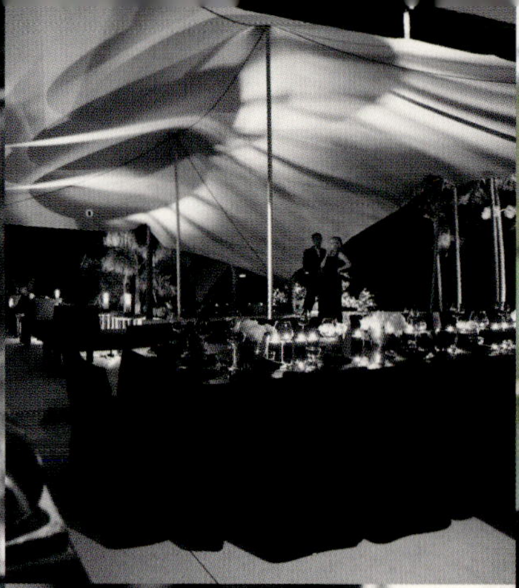
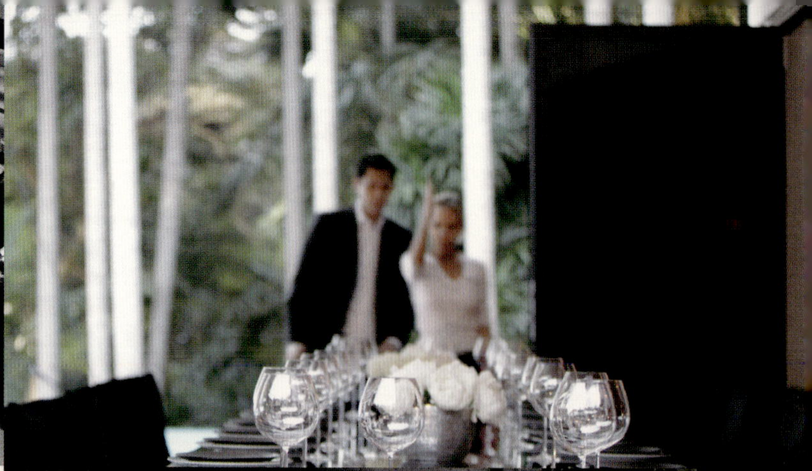
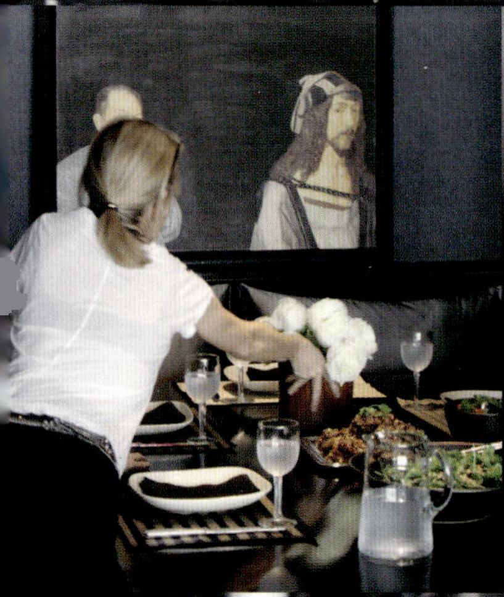
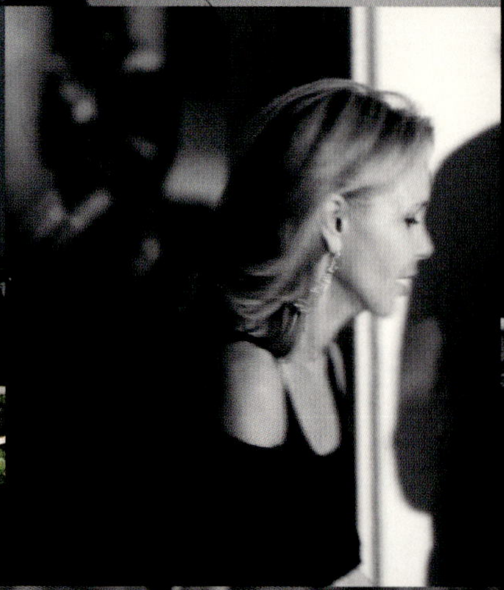
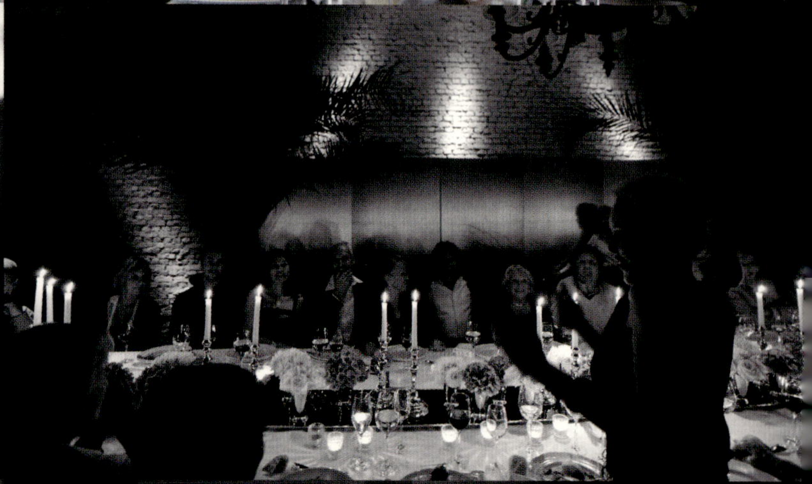
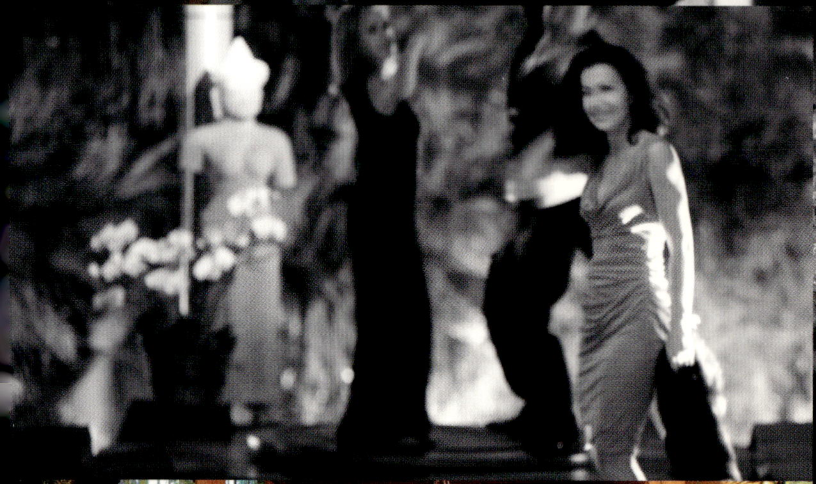
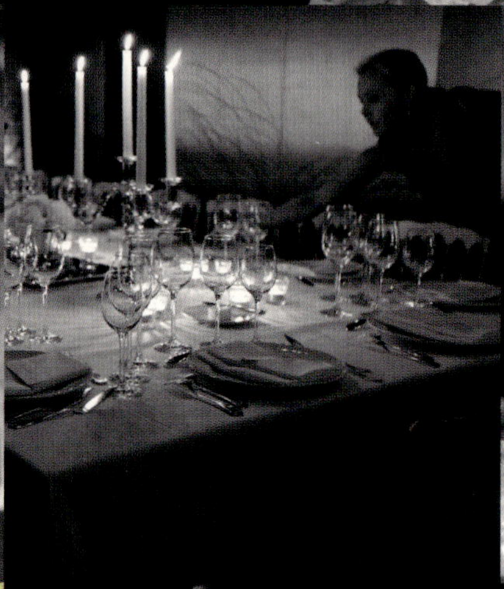
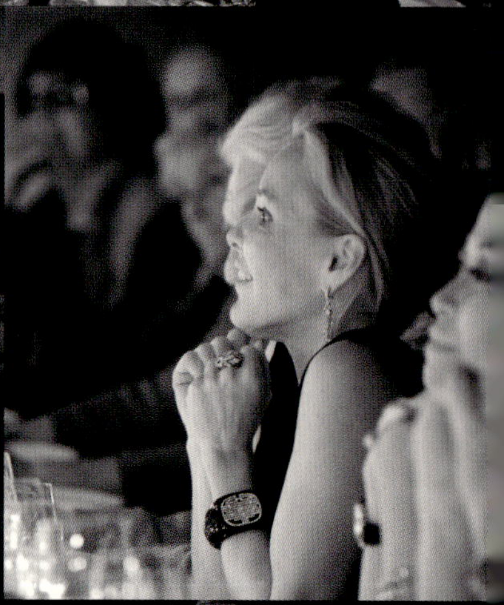
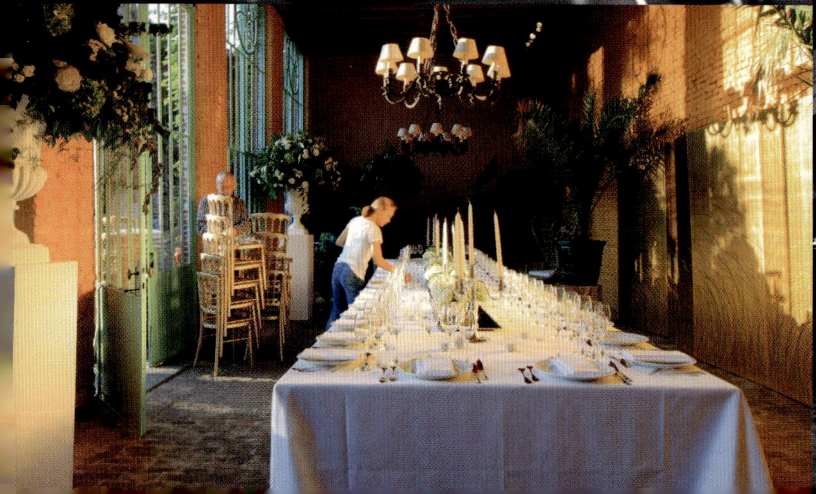
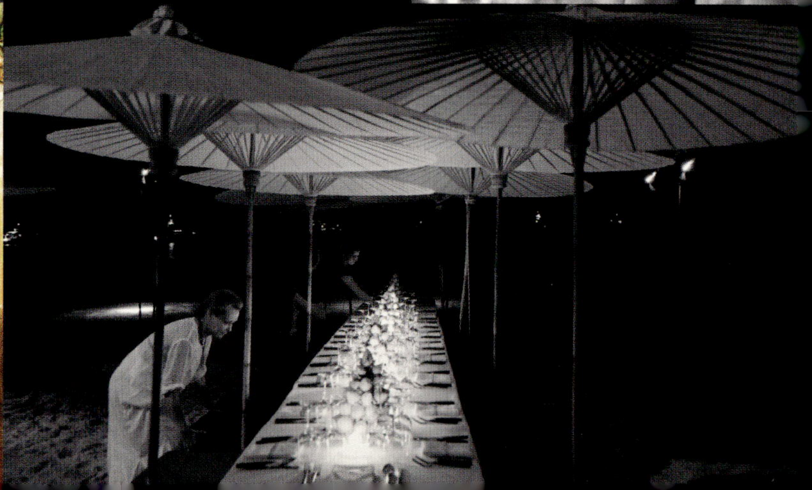

13. WORK BEFORE THE PARTY
(NOT DURING IT)

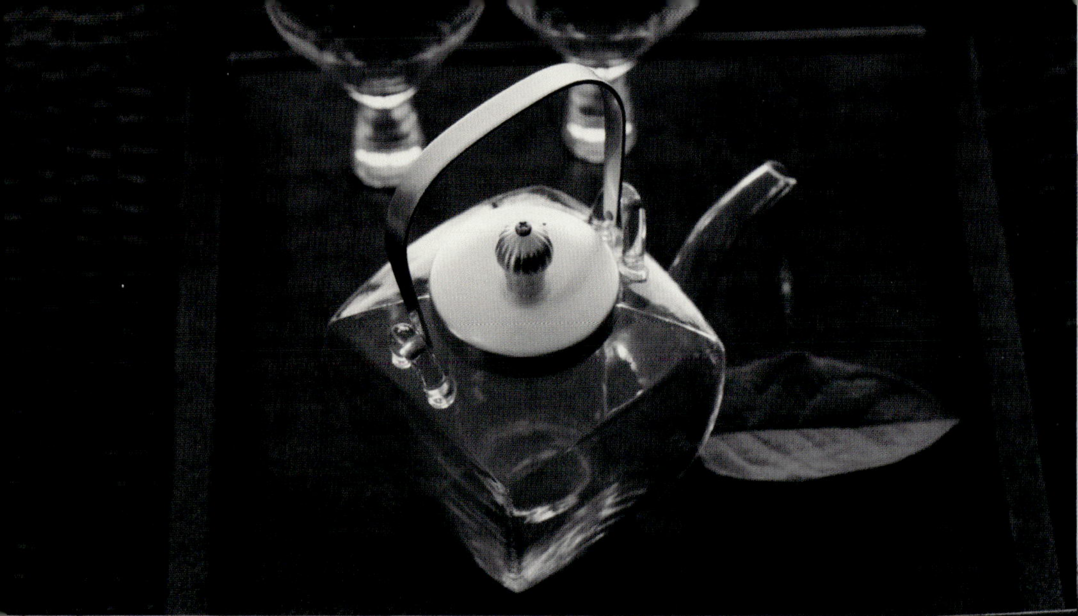
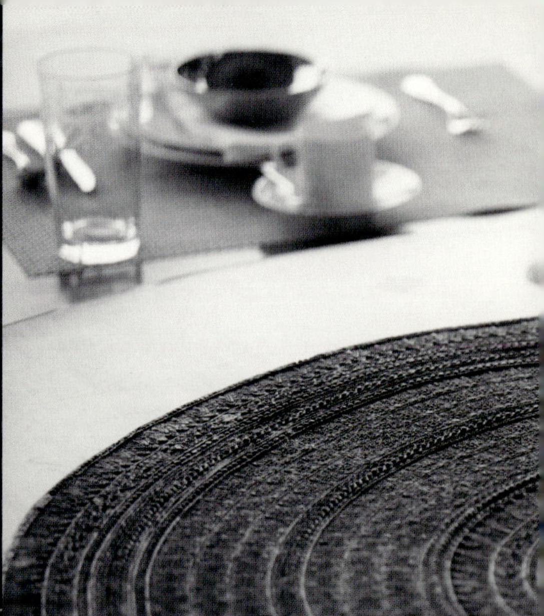
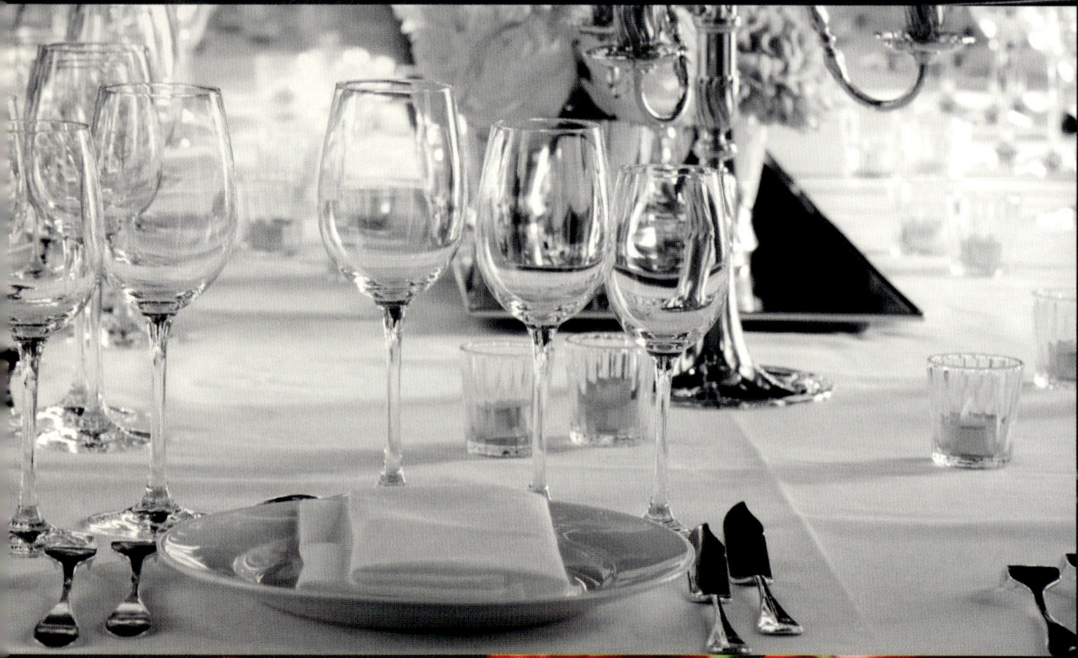
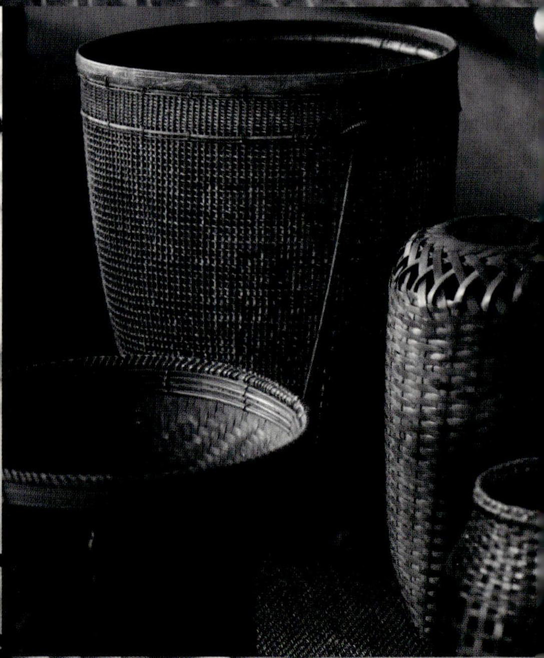
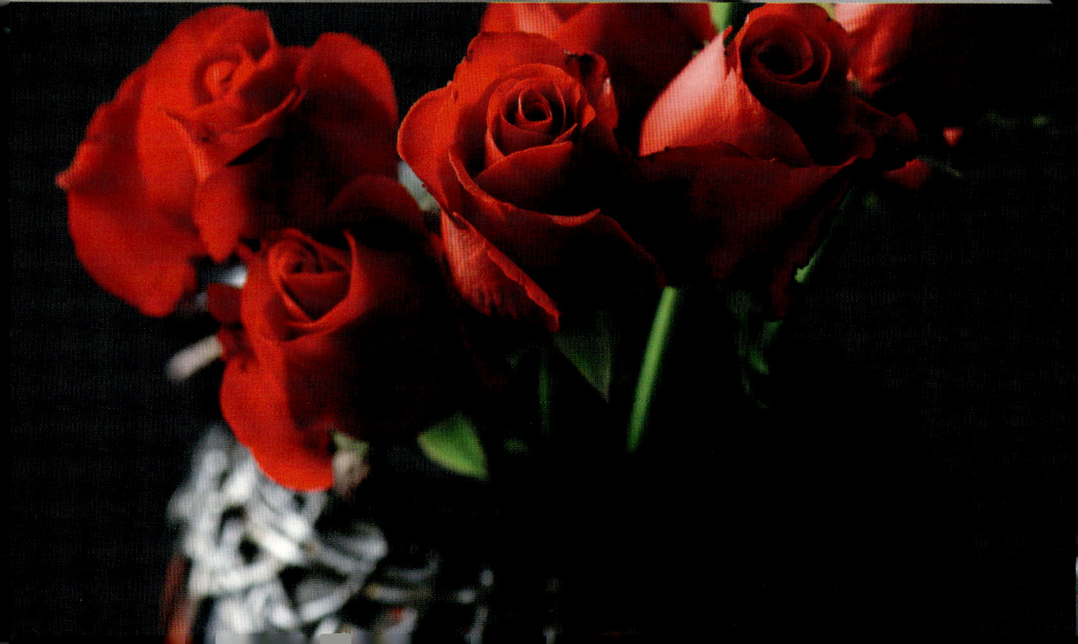
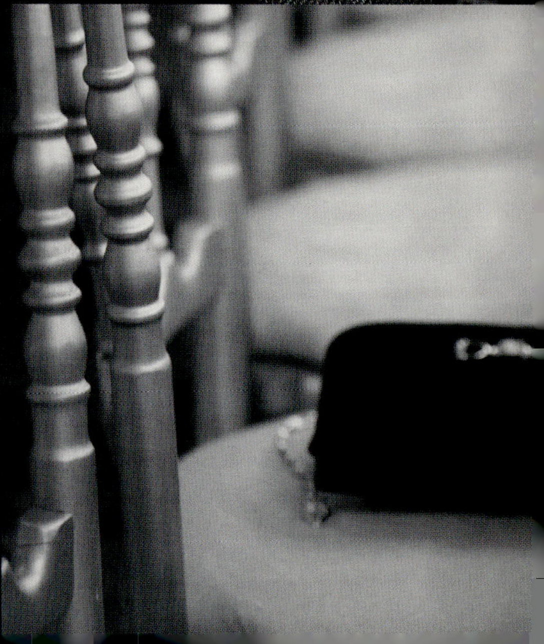

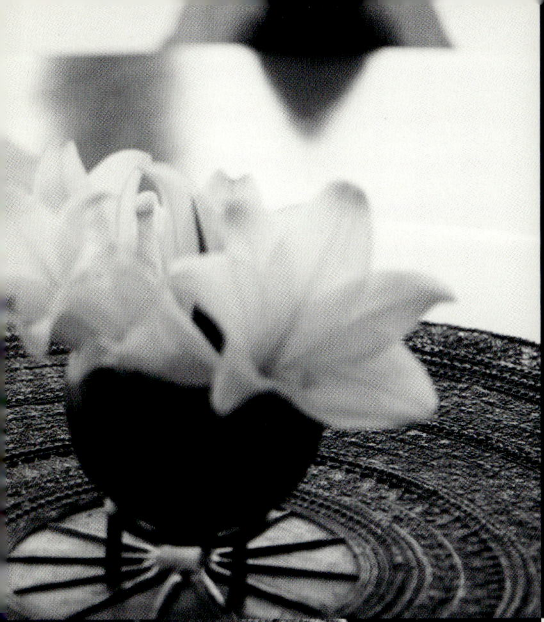
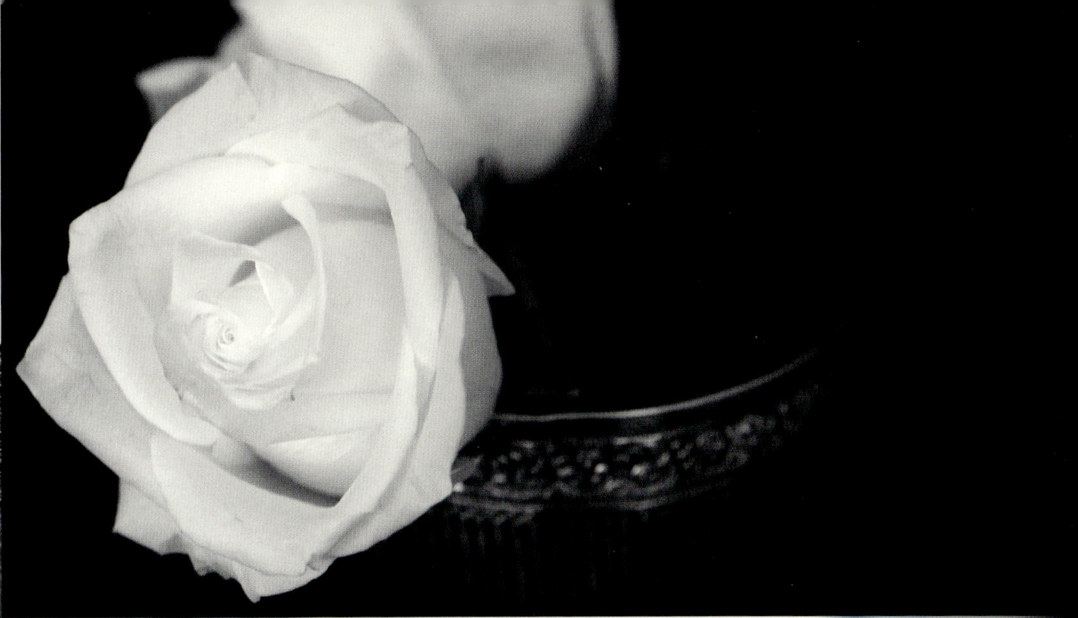
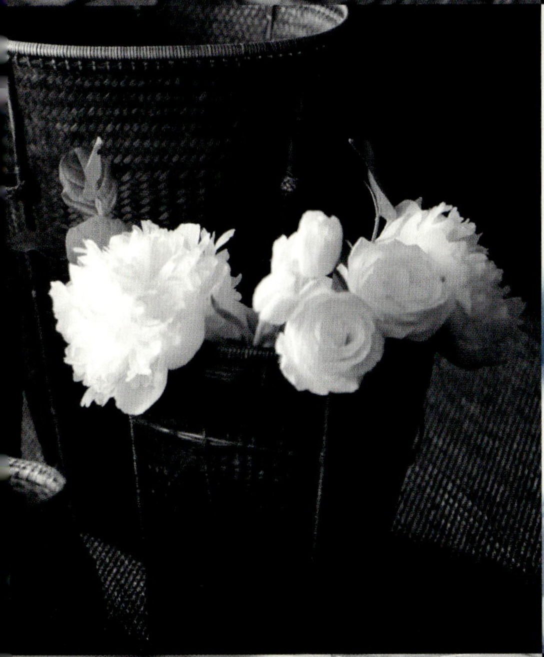
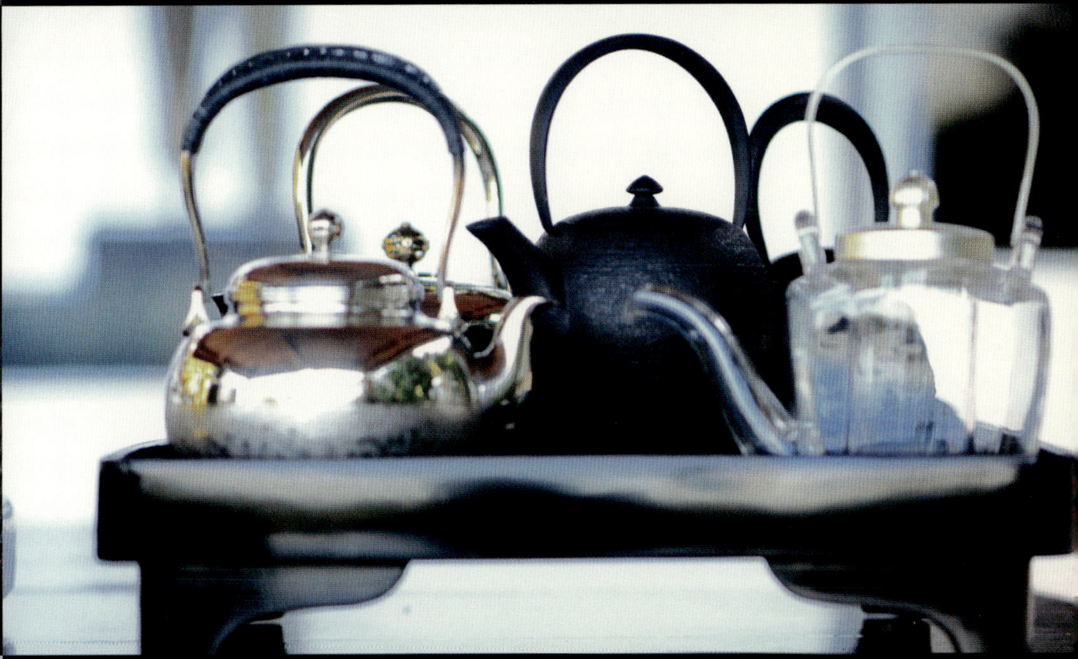
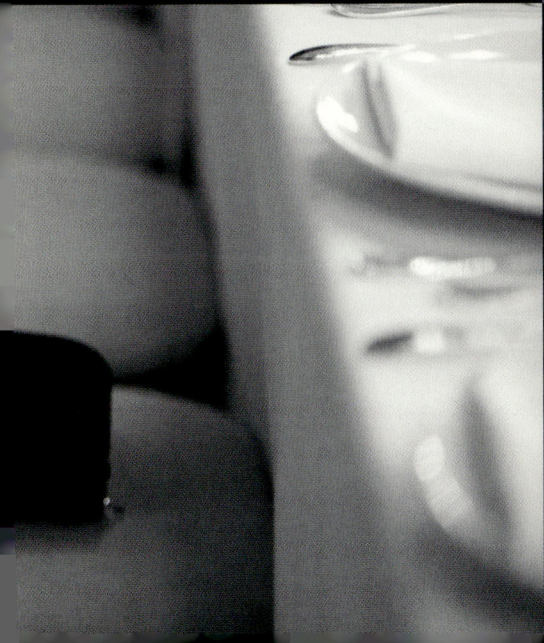
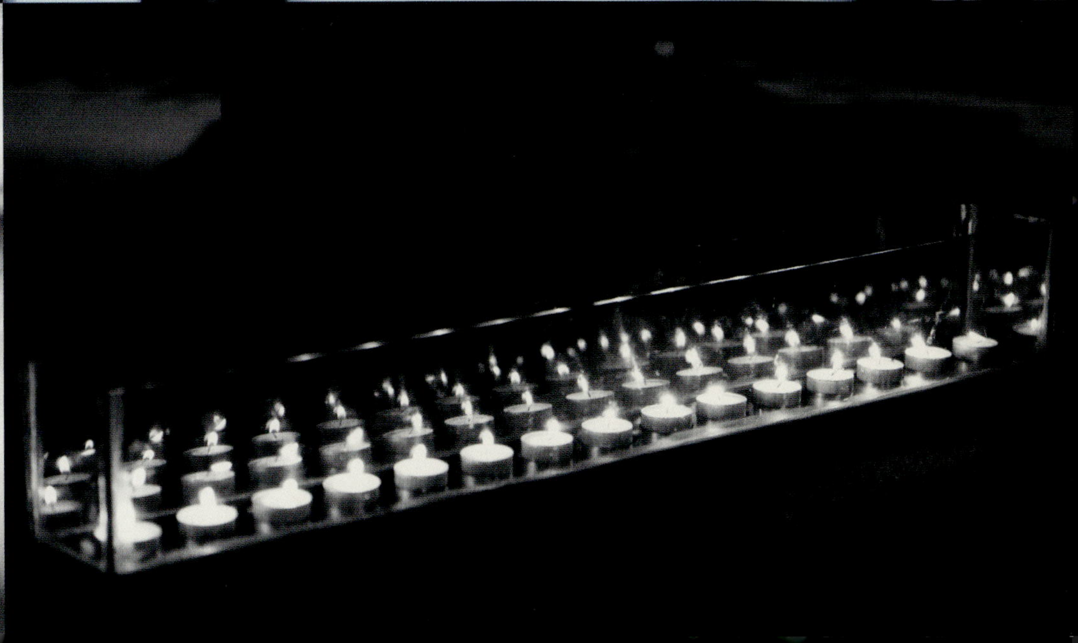

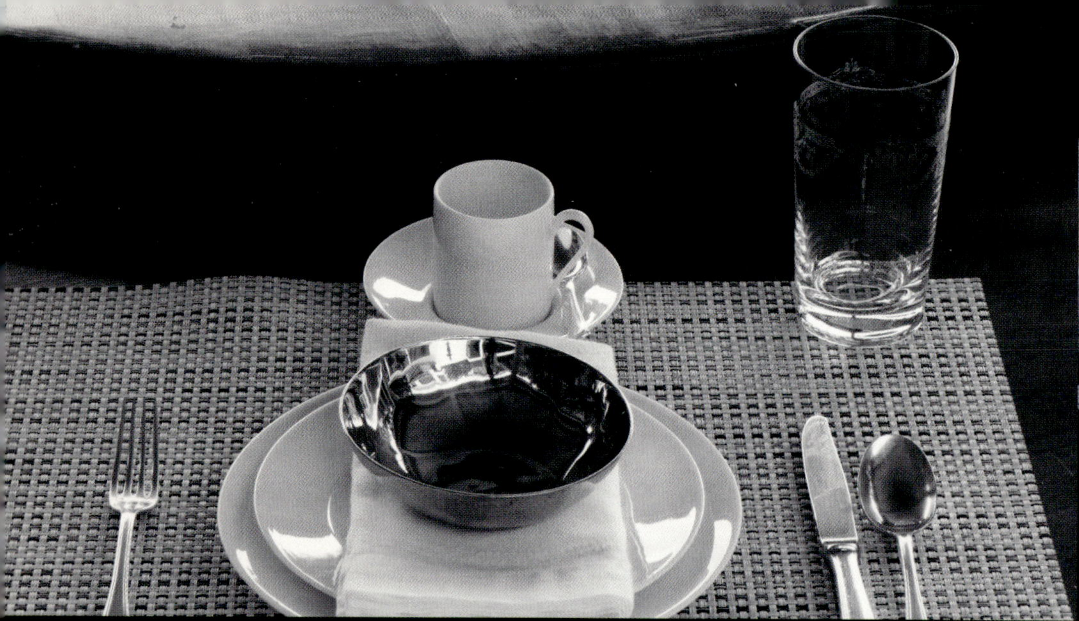
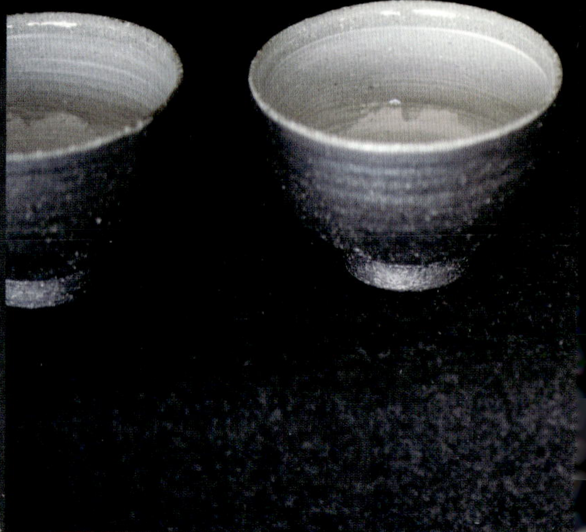
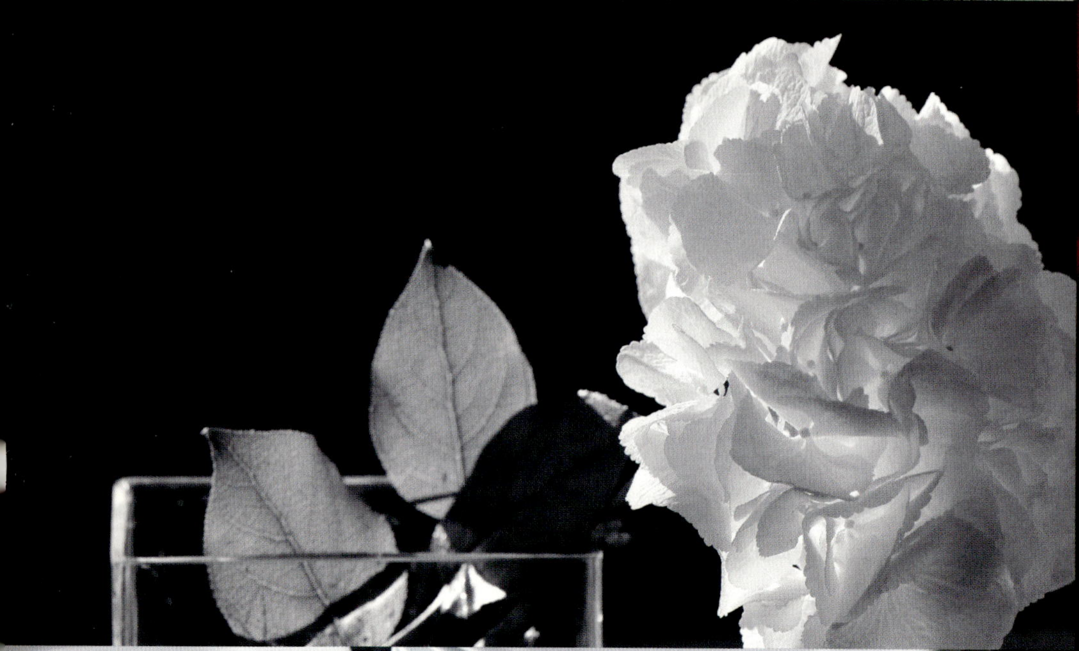
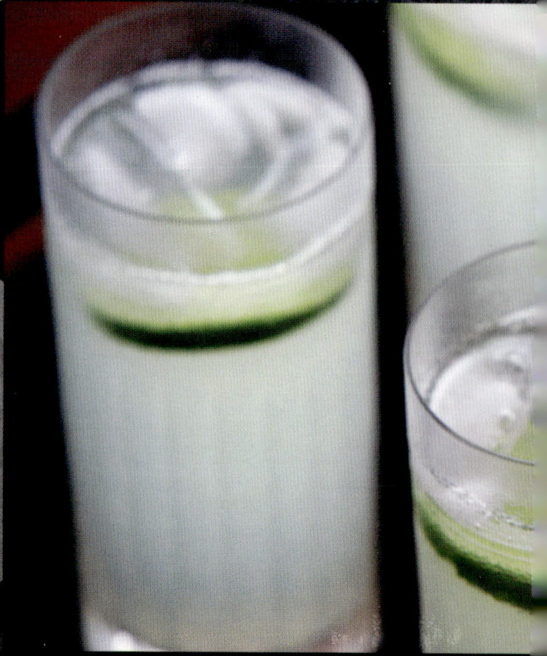
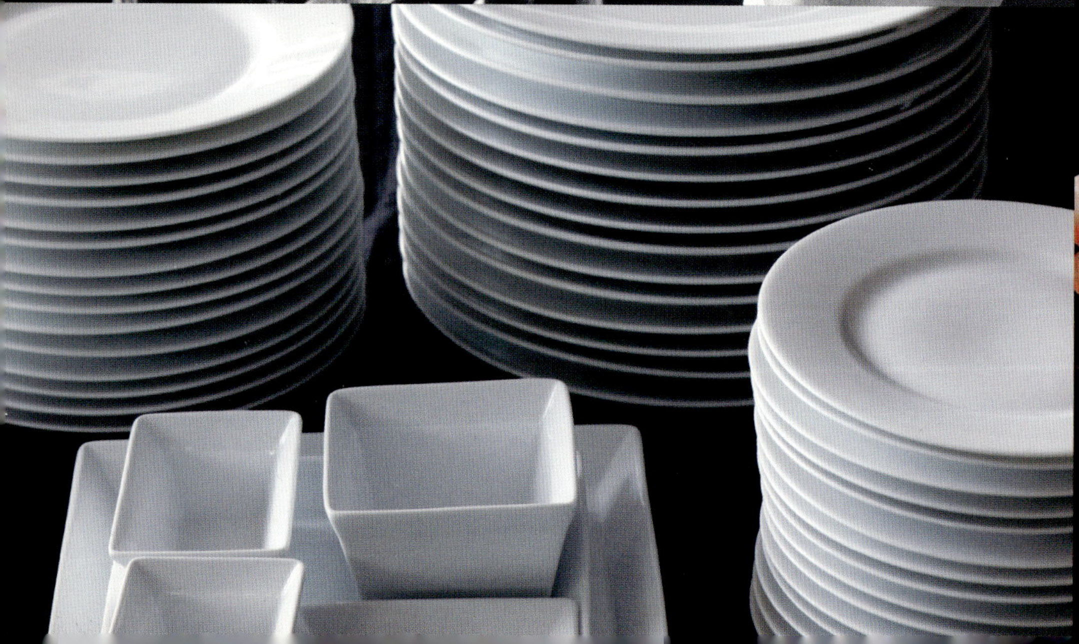
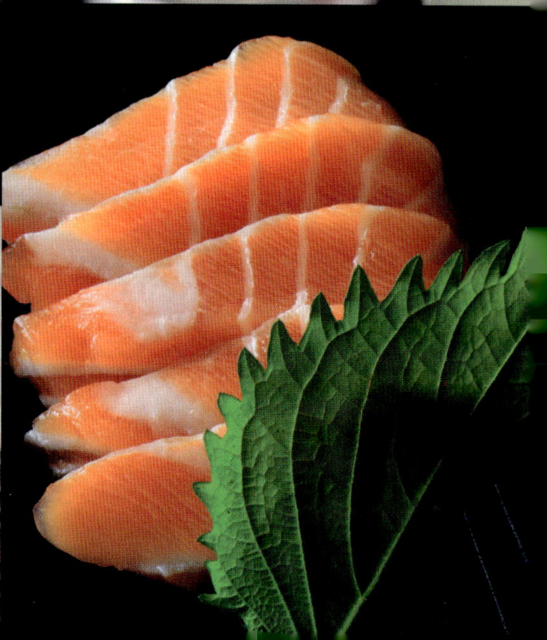

Acknowledgments

Li Shan, *Rouge Series No.1*: 52–53 (centre); Liu Fei, *Bold and Trendy*: 52 (bottom left), 173 (bottom left); Qi Zhi Long, *Untitled No. 2*: 129 (below right), 173 (centre); Wang Yi Dong, *A Quiet Moment*: 14, 50 (left centre); Wang Yi Dong, *Springtime*: 126 (below left), 128 (below right), 173 (top left, right centre); Wang Yi Dong (details): 173 (top right), 189; Wang Yi Guang, *Flying a Kite*: 168 (left); Zhu Yi Yong, *Memory of the Past (Cat's Cradle)*: 171; Zhu Yi Yong, *Shui Xiang Series 1-7*: 51 (left centre), 148 (below left, above right), 149 (below left, above right), 150 (below left, above right) 151 (below left).

First published in the United Kingdom in 2012
by Thames & Hudson Ltd, 181A High Holborn, London WC1V 7QX

Copyright © 2012 Herbert Ypma

Design by Maggi Smith

All Rights Reserved. No part of this publication may be reproduced or transmitted in any form or by any means, electronic or mechanical, including photocopy, recording or any other information storage and retrieval system, without prior permission in writing from the publisher.

British Library Cataloguing-in-Publication Data
A catalogue record for this book is available from the British Library

ISBN 978-0-500-51639-3

Printed and bound in China by Toppan Leefung Printing Limited

To find out about all our publications, please visit **www.thamesandhudson.com**.
There you can subscribe to our e-newsletter, browse or download our current catalogue, and buy any titles that are in print.